GREEK CLASSICS

NOTES

SUMMARIES AND CONCISE COMMENTARIES ABOUT THE
MAJOR WORKS OF CLASSIC GREEK WRITERS, INCLUDING

Homer • Hesiod • Aeschylus • Sophocles

Euripides • Aristophanes • Menander • Lysias

Demosthenes • Aesop • Sappho • Pindar

Herodotus • Thucydides • Plato • Aristotle

and others

Mary Ellen Snodgrass, M.A.
University of North Carolina

INCORPORATED

LINCOLN, NEBRASKA 68501

Editor

Gary Carey, M.A.
University of Colorado

Consulting Editor

James L. Roberts, Ph.D.
Department of English
University of Nebraska

ABOUT THE AUTHOR

Mary Ellen Snodgrass earned her B.A. in British
and classical literature from the University of North
Carolina at Greensboro, her M.A. in English from
Appalachian State University, and certification in gifted
education from Lenoir-Rhyne College. A member of the
American Classical League, Virgilian Society, Phi Beta
Kappa, AFT, NCTE, and IRA, she taught English and
Latin at Hickory High School for twenty years and has
served as chairman of the English department, coor-
dinator of language arts for the Hickory City Schools,
reader for the North Carolina Textbook Commission,
and writer, editor, and consultant for major textbook
publishers. Her published works include Cliffs *Teaching
Portfolios* as well as articles for *Islands* magazine, the
Presbyterian Center, ERIC, and other professional
groups. She was contributing editor of *The Short Story
and You* (National Textbook) and *The Great American
English Handbook* (Perma-Bound).

ISBN 0-8220-0566-2
© Copyright 1988
by
C. K. Hillegass
All Rights Reserved
Printed in U.S.A.

Cliffs Notes, Inc.   Lincoln, Nebraska

CONTENTS

GREEK TRAGEDY

GREEK COMEDY

GREEK PROSE WRITERS

GREEK LYRIC POETS

GREEK HISTORIANS

GREEK PHILOSOPHERS

Ω

GREEK
CLASSICS

Death Mask of Agamemnon
National Archeological Museum, Athens

Woven into the graceful folds of Greek literature are the classic concepts, motifs, and markings which Western civilization has adopted as its own. The Greeks knew a joy and facility with language, an admiration for clean lines and spare sentences. Their worship of the poet's gift approached religious fervor. To the ancient Athenian, attendance at a drama festival was more than entertainment; it was a purging of the soul, a union with goodness and truth. Likewise, to read Homer was to experience the best in human thought and behavior.

No other era has produced so notable an array of genius – the bold epics of Homer, Sappho's diaphanous images, Aristophanes' mirthful satires, and the poignant, gripping dramas of Sophocles, Euripides, and Aeschylus. To these must be added the all-encompassing philosophies of Plato and Aristotle, the keen histories and self-criticism of Herodotus and Thucydides, as well as Aesop's droll beast fables. Despite the passage of centuries, Greek literature retains its freshness and relevance, its ability to pierce to the heart of human situations in matters of love or war, government or social behavior. On most subjects, the Greeks said it first and said it well.

Our lives bear little likeness to Attica's Mediterranean existence, where tiny city-states experimented with systems of government and struggled to keep out a succession of aggressors. Why, then, does Greek thought permeate our every endeavor – from art, architecture, dance, and drama to philosophy, politics, science, and religion? Primarily because we often feel that we must escape twentieth-century complexity and self-doubt and reconnect our ties with the simple humanistic truths which formed the warp and woof of ancient thought.

The Greeks, adhering to the simple injunction, "Know thyself," were strong in self-awareness. Practical and perceptive, their early myths still challenge the modern mind, leading us to contemplate anew the spark of human fire which Prometheus stole from Olympian gods to brighten the dim prehistoric soul. The depiction of human ills escaping from Pandora's box, the pitiable cry of Icarus, tumbling to his death in the blue Aegean waters, and Phaethon's youthful body pierced by his father's thunderbolt bring into focus the ever-present human failing of pride.

There is much that separates the modern world from that earlier time. There are no firesides decked with skins where audiences lose themselves in the singer's recounting of the epic struggles of Jason and Theseus or the tearful plaints of Penelope and Hecuba. The magic, then, lies not in performance, but in the lines themselves, translated from an ancient tongue into myriad languages, still binding us to the wisdom and the humanity of a people long dead. The challenge of Greek literature remains a pinnacle which each generation climbs. From these heights come inner views, glimpses of human capability and foible. From these voices come a candor and a passion unequaled in modern times.

$$\Omega$$

GREEK EPIC POETRY

- **Homer**
- **Hesiod**

HOMER

- **Homer and the Epic**

- **The *Iliad***

- **The *Odyssey***

HOMER

There is no question that the writer of the *Iliad* and the *Odyssey* was one of the greatest poets in the history of Western Europe, but little else can be said with certainty about Homer, particularly concerning his personal life. Obviously, he made his living as a bard, or *rhapsode*, an itinerant singer of verses. Ancient Greek tradition, as well as a study of the language and style of the poems, indicates that he probably lived and wrote sometime in the ninth or eighth centuries B.C., but no more definite date can be determined.

In ancient times, seven different cities claimed the honor of having been Homer's birthplace. None of these assertions can be validated, but more than likely, he came from the island of Chios, on the western coast of Asia Minor, for in historical times, a family of the same name lived there, claimed him as an ancestor, and devoted themselves to the recitation of his works. Seemingly, Homer was a native and a resident of some section of Asia Minor, for the dialect in which he composed his works—a blend of Ionic and Aeolic—is that of the Asian Greeks.

Tradition has visualized Homer as blind, but there is no real evidence for this belief. It is based upon the portrayal of Demodocus, a blind minstrel in the *Odyssey*, who sings a poem about the fall of Troy. There is no reason, however, to believe that the poet was describing himself in this scene. Throughout the two epics, there is no consistent autobiographical information, and no other literature of the period survives which describes the poet.

The early Greeks unhesitatingly insisted that there had been a single individual named Homer, to whom they ascribed the *Iliad,* the *Odyssey,* and several minor works, including the *Homeric Hymns* (a series of poems addressed to various gods), *The Battle of the Frogs and Mice* (a poem of 303 hexameters), and *Margites,* a comic romance about the adventures of a simpleton. However, around the third century B.C., the so-called Homeric Question was first propounded. Several of the grammarians of the time asserted that the *Iliad* and the *Odyssey* were actually composed by two different writers. At various times, this view has been supported by later European critics. There has also been a school of thought, especially popular in the nineteenth century, which claims that Homer, whose name means *hostage,* never existed, and that the two epics are the collective works of groups of anonymous bards to whom the name Homer was later applied. These scholars suggest that the two poems were revised whenever they were recited and did not reach their present form until the sixth century B.C. when, in Athens, they were written down for the first time.

In general, contemporary scholars maintain that each of the two poems has a consistency of style and outlook that indicates that they are the work of one writer. The poet may have composed them completely, or he may have utilized parts of the work of some earlier bards, altering them to fit his own purposes and making them fully his own in the process. But since the people nearest to the composition of the poems believed them to have been the product of one hand, the modern critic has accepted this view and has attributed the differences between the *Iliad* and the *Odyssey* to their having been composed at different stages in the poet's life and to the differences in the themes of the works. Rather than take a defensive or apologetic position, the contemporary scholar insists that the burden of proof is on those who deny the existence of Homer. To date, this position has not been successfully challenged.

While little if anything is known of Homer's life, his works are an everlasting tribute to him. For thousands of years, the *Iliad* and the *Odyssey* have been the standards by which poets of all languages have measured themselves, and, for understanding human nature in all its aspects, for keen observation of the whole world in which men live, for essential sanity and good taste, and for superb control of all the technical devices of his medium, Homer has never been surpassed.

$$\Omega$$

HOMER AND THE EPIC

As a literary form, the epic began early in human history as an expression of belief in superhuman heroes who strove to achieve some worthy undertaking for the benefit of society. Examples exist in the literature of many emerging nations—*Gilgamesh* in Assyria, the oldest version of the epic in existence; the *Chanson de Roland* in France; *El Cid,* the Spanish epic; the Germanic *Nibelungenlied;* Finland's *Kalevala;* the East Indian *Mahabharata;* the Hindu *Ramayana; Beowulf,* the Old English epic; and the titles most familiar to the Western world, the Hebrew *Exodus,* Virgil's *Aeneid,* and Homer's *Iliad* and *Odyssey.* More recent versions of the epic include Dante's *Divine Comedy,* Milton's *Paradise Lost,* and Henry Wadsworth Longfellow's *Hiawatha.*

Epics fall into two distinct classifications—folk and art. Folk epics are long poems of obscure origin that have been patched together from oral folk tales of separate authorship, as is the case with the early examples listed above. Art, or literary, epics, on the other hand, are composed by a single author in imitation of earlier models, as exemplified by Virgil's imitation of Homer when he wrote the *Aeneid,* a piece of political propaganda commissioned by Augustus, Rome's first emperor, in the first century A.D.

Epics contain common traits that set them apart from other narrative poetry. Told with strict unity, grand simplicity, and a serious, moral tone, they focus on the exploits of a male character who is usually larger, stronger, more intelligent, or more resourceful than other men. The hero springs from noble or distinguished parentage and performs a dangerous feat that is crucial to national survival or tribal pride, such as the recovery of Queen Helen, who was abducted from Sparta by the Trojan prince Paris. In another example, the Hebrew hero Moses was born of ordinary Jewish parents, but was reared at the Egyptian royal court after Pharoah's sister adopted him. With the help of Yahweh, the Hebrew god, Moses leads the downtrodden Israelites out of slavery in Egypt to freedom in the Promised Land.

A unified retelling of the epic hero's adventures and accomplishments takes place against a vast setting, sometimes extending beyond national boundaries and even into the cosmos. Milton's *Paradise Lost,* for example, reaches beyond the Garden of Eden to heaven and hell; likewise, Aeneas travels to the Underworld to obtain advice from his father's spirit. The action of an epic encompasses valorous deeds against terrible odds, often in conflict with supernatural forces or the gods themselves, such as Odysseus' battle for survival against Poseidon, god of the sea. Epic language is sonorous and weighty, held together by a dignified meter. Homer and his imitators used dactylic hexameter, a long line composed of eighteen syllables divided into threes, the first syllable being accented and the last two unaccented (´⌣⌣|´⌣⌣|´⌣⌣|´⌣⌣|´⌣⌣|´⌣⌣).

Epic poets often invoke some supernatural power, seeking divine assistance in recalling and narrating the story, as when Milton calls on the Holy Spirit to help him explain the fall of human beings from God's grace. Other literary conventions that epic writers may employ include beginning at the most crucial point of the conflict (in Latin, this is called *in medias res*) and recounting at a later time the events which led to the situation. In addition, there may be long lists or catalogues of ships, warriors, or gods; an epic question as to the nature and cause of the conflict followed by a short, pithy response; lengthy descriptions, such as Homer's detailing of scenes pictured on Achilles' shield; eloquent speeches and great debates; and elongated, ornate similes.

In Western literature, Homer's epics occupy a central place. Because of their detailed genealogies, at one time they served as points of reference for the oldest and most respected families in the Mediterranean world. As literary masterpieces in ancient times, they were read and discussed by schoolboys, including Alexander the Great, who is said to have memorized all the passages that refer to his hero, Achilles. Homer's emphasis on humanistic values – honor, truth, compassion, loyalty, devotion to family and gods – gives his works religious and ethical significance as guidebooks to moral behavior. To historians and archeologists, Homer's works offer valuable information about life in the Bronze Age, such as burial customs, tribal organization, class distinctions, and warfare. As sources of enlightenment and entertainment, the *Iliad* and the *Odyssey* have influenced major writers, philosophers, sculptors, and painters since the eighth century B.C., including twentieth-century filmmakers.

Although the world has retained few facts about the great Greek singer of songs, Homer's influence reaches across time – from the eighth century B.C., through the Classical Age, into the Renaissance, and on into the modern era. The story of Achilles' great anger and Odysseus' ten-year trek about the Mediterranean are just as fresh and stirring as they must have been to listeners in ancient times who pushed their chairs away from the table and settled by the fireside to immerse themselves in the melodic tales of the bard. As his fingers strummed the familiar chords and his voice fell into cadence, his eyes may have looked beyond the audience to the distant plains of Troy, where two armies paid the terrible price of war.

$$\Omega$$

THE *ILIAD*

_____ BACKGROUND OF THE TROJAN WAR

The *Iliad* covers only a few months during the tenth year of the Trojan War. The ancient Greek audience, however, would have been familiar with all the events leading up to this tenth year, and during the course of the *Iliad,* Homer makes many references to various past events.

The legend begins ages ago, with the building of the city of Troy. It was a city under the protection of the sons of Zeus, king of the gods. Its king was Laomedon, and as the city prospered rapidly, the king decided to build a huge wall around it for protection. This, of course, is the wall that the Greeks have not been able to penetrate for nine years – the point at which the *Iliad* begins. To build such a magnificent wall, it was necessary to invoke divine aid. The god of the seas and the oceans, Poseidon, volunteered to help, but he said that he would have to be compensated for his efforts. However, after the wall was completed, the Trojans thought that it was so impenetrable that they refused to compensate Poseidon. He then withdrew his protection, and, thus, the unprotected city was vulnerable to attack.

At the time of the Trojan War, Troy was ruled by King Priam, who was married to Hecuba, who according to legend bore him forty-nine children, including the noble Hector, the prophetess Cassandra, the handsome Paris, and many more. When Hecuba was pregnant with Paris, she had a dream that Paris would be the cause of Troy's destruction. An oracle confirmed that this son would indeed be the cause of the total destruction of the noble city of Troy; therefore, for the sake of the city, Hecuba agreed to abandon her newborn infant to death by exposure on Mount Ida. But he was saved by shepherds and grew up as a shepherd, ignorant of his royal birth.

Just before the beginning of the Trojan War, Zeus arranged to have Thetis (a goddess) marry Peleus (a mortal); they became the mother and father of the noble Achilles. At the wedding, all the gods and goddesses were enjoying themselves when Eris, the goddess of discord, who, for obvious reasons, was not invited, threw a golden apple into their midst with the words "FOR THE FAIREST" inscribed on it.

Hera, Athena, and Aphrodite all claimed the apple and asked Zeus to serve as judge, but he wisely refused and, instead, appointed the shepherd Paris, who was tending his flocks close by, to decide the contest. The goddesses approached Paris, and each tried to bribe him by offering her specialty: Hera offered him a rich kingdom and power; Athena offered him wisdom and military successes; Aphrodite offered him love and the most beautiful woman in the world, the spectacular Helen. Paris therefore chose Aphrodite, thus making implacable enemies of Hera and Athena, both of whom vowed to destroy Paris and the city of Troy.

On learning that he would possess Helen, Paris first went to Troy and established himself as a true prince, the legitimate son of Priam and Hecuba. Then he sailed for Sparta to the court of King Menelaus, where he seduced and then abducted Helen and brought her to Troy.

When Menelaus returned to Sparta and found his wife gone, he summoned a number of Greek generals to go with him to conquer Troy and recover Helen. Long ago, each of these generals had courted Helen, and they had all entered into an agreement: to aid the winner of Helen's love and to avenge any dishonor that fell upon her future husband because of her. Thus, Paris precipitated the Trojan War, fulfilling the prophetic dream that his mother had given birth to a son who would cause the destruction of Troy.

Some of the Greek leaders were anxious to sack Troy, but two, Odysseus and Achilles, had been warned by oracles of their fate if they went. Odysseus was warned that he would be gone for twenty years. He feigned madness, but his ruse was quickly discovered, and he finally agreed to go. The Greeks knew that they could never capture Troy without the help of Achilles, who was the greatest warrior in the world. He was practically invulnerable as a fighter because at birth, his mother had dipped him in the River Styx, rendering him immortal everywhere except the heel, where she had held him; later, Paris shoots a poisoned arrow, and Apollo guides it into Achilles' heel — thus, we have the term "Achilles' heel," meaning one's vulnerability.

Achilles was warned that if he went to war, he would gain great glory, but that he would die young. To save her son from an early death, his mother disguised him in women's clothing, but the sly Odysseus discovered the trick, and Achilles finally consented to go.

Menelaus' brother, Agamemnon, was elected leader of the armies, and a thousand ships were assembled for the journey across the Aegean Sea to Troy. The winds died, and after consultations with a soothsayer, it was discovered that Agamemnon had killed a deer sacred to Artemis, the Goddess of the Hunt. Nothing could pacify her anger except the sacrifice of Agamemnon's daughter Iphigenia. After much anguish, Agamemnon sent for his daughter under the pretext that she was to marry Achilles. Once there, however, he had her sacrificed, and the winds immediately began to blow. The expedition was on its way.

After landing at the wrong place once, the Greeks (called "the Achaians" in the *Iliad*) finally reached Troy and surrounded the city, placing Achilles at one end and the famous Ajax at the other end. For nine years, they tried to penetrate the invulnerable wall of Troy. They assaulted and pillaged many smaller places, however, and at the end of the ninth year, they captured two beautiful women, Chryseis, who was awarded to Agamemnon, and Briseis, who was awarded to Achilles. Thus begins the *Iliad*, which will end with the burial of Hector.

LIST OF CHARACTERS

THE ACHAIANS (Greeks)

Achilles

The central character of the *Iliad* and the greatest warrior in the Achaian army. The most significant flaw in Achilles' temperament is his excessive pride. He is willing to subvert the good of the whole army and to endanger the lives of those who are closest to him in order to achieve emotional blackmail.

Agamemnon

The well-meaning but irresolute king of Mycenae; commander-in-chief of the expedition against Troy; he is a brother of Menelaus.

Ajax

Son of Telamon, he is often called Telamonian Ajax; his reputation is due primarily to brute strength and courage.

Ajax the Lesser

A distinguished warrior, but insolent and conceited.

Antilochus

The son of Nestor; a brave young warrior who takes an active part in the fighting and the funeral games.

Automedon

The squire and charioteer of Achilles.

Calchas

Soothsayer and prophet of the Achaians.

Diomedes

He ranks among the finest and bravest of the Achaian warriors; he is always wise and reasonable and is renowned for his courtesy and gallantry. He is, perhaps, Homer's vision of the perfect young nobleman.

Helen

The daughter of Zeus and Leda, a mortal, she was originally married to Menelaus, but she ran away to Troy with Paris and became his wife. Supposedly, she is the most beautiful woman in the world;

however, she is also self-centered. Although she constantly claims to regret the war that has resulted from her behavior, she seems to have little real sincerity or sensitivity.

Idomeneus

One of the most efficient of the Achaian leaders, he has the respect and liking of the whole Achaian army.

Menelaus

The brother of Agamemnon and the husband of Helen, who was abducted by Paris.

The Myrmidons

Soldiers of Achilles.

Nestor

He is the oldest Achaian warrior at Troy. Nestor has the wisdom and experience of age and is a valuable asset in the council. Although he can no longer fight, he remains at the front line at every battle, commanding his troops.

Odysseus

The shrewdest and most subtle of the Achaians and a brave warrior besides, as he demonstrates on many occasions.

Patroclus

Achilles' close friend and warrior-companion.

THE TROJANS AND THEIR ALLIES

Aeneas

The son of Aphrodite and Anchises; a Trojan nobleman. He is second in command of the Trojan army and a brave, skillful warrior.

Andromache

The wife of Hector; she seems to illustrate Homer's idea of the good wife and mother. She is loyal, lovingly concerned for her family, and willing to accept the decisions of her husband.

Antenor

A Trojan nobleman who unsuccessfully advocates the return of Helen to the Achaians.

Astyanax

The infant son of Hector and Andromache.

Cassandra

The daughter of Priam and Hecuba; Hector and Paris' sister. She is a prophetess who becomes Agamemnon's captive after the war.

Chryseis

The daughter of Chryses, the priest of Apollo. She is the "war prize" hostage of Agamemnon until Apollo demands that she be returned to her father.

Dolon

A Trojan nobleman, captured by Odysseus and Diomedes during their night expedition to the Trojan camp in Book 10.

Glaucus

A Trojan prince; a renowned warrior.

Hector

Prince of Troy and son of Priam and Hecuba. Hector is commander of all the Trojan and allied forces. The greatest of the Trojan warriors and one of the most noble persons in the *Iliad,* he is always conscious of his duty and his responsibilities to his people and will not let his personal interests interfere. He is a devoted and loving husband and father. His only serious weakness is a tendency to brag about his exploits and an over-concern for his reputation.

Hecuba

The wife of Priam and queen of Troy. Hector is the most prominent of her sons.

Helenus

A son of Priam and Hecuba; a prince of Troy and a seer.

Pandarus

A good archer, but a treacherous man; it is he who breaks the truce in Book 4.

Paris (Alexandrus)

A prince of Troy; a son of Priam and Hecuba; also husband of Helen. Hector frequently reprimands his younger brother for allowing the Trojans to fight in his place. His reputation is that of a "pretty boy." His smoothness and glibness are not admired by the warriors of either side, and they often accuse him of cowardice.

Priam

King of Troy. He is very old and no longer able to command his army in the field, but he demonstrates great courage when he travels to the Achaian camp one night to ransom Hector's body. A noble and generous man, he is one of the few Trojans besides Hector who treats Helen with respect and courtesy, despite her infidelity to her husband and the war caused by her actions.

THE GODS

Aphrodite

A daughter of Zeus; goddess of passionate love. She is Aeneas' mother and the patron of Paris, so she fights on the Trojan side (for an explanation of alliances, see "Background of the Trojan War"). She is married to Hephaestus, blacksmith of the gods, but she loves Ares, god of war.

Apollo

A son of Zeus; god of prophecy, light, poetry, and music. He fights on the Trojan side.

Ares

A son of Zeus and Hera, and god of war. The lover of Aphrodite, he fights on the Trojan side, despite an earlier promise to Hera and Athena that he would support the Achaians.

Artemis

A daughter of Zeus; sister of Apollo; goddess of chastity, hunting, and wild animals. She fights on the Trojan side, but with little effect.

Athena

A daughter of Zeus; goddess of wisdom and war. She plays a prominent role in the war, fighting on the Achaian side.

Hades

God of the dead and ruler of the underworld.

Hera

Both sister and wife of Zeus; goddess of married love. She is the most fanatical of all the Olympian supporters of the Achaians and goes to great lengths, including the deception of her husband, to achieve the defeat of Troy.

Hermes

Ambassador of the gods; conductor of dead souls to Hades and a patron of travelers. He sides with the Achaians, but he does little to aid them. He escorts Priam to Achilles' camp in Book 24.

Iris

Messenger of the gods.

Poseidon

A younger brother of Zeus; god of the sea. He is a strong supporter of the Achaian cause, having an old grudge against Troy. He built the Great Wall of Troy, but afterward, the Trojans refused to pay him. He is also somewhat resentful of Zeus' claim to authority over him.

Thetis

A sea nymph and the mother of Achilles. She is a staunch advocate of her son in his quarrel with Agamemnon and does all she can to help him, but she is not otherwise involved in the war.

Xanthus

A son of Zeus; god of one of the major rivers of Troy. He fights against Achilles in Book 21, but is defeated by Hephaestus' fire.

Zeus

The supreme god and king of Olympus. His duty is to carry out the will of Destiny, so he is officially neutral in the war, but he is sympathetic toward the Trojans, particularly Hector and Priam, and he supports Achilles against Agamemnon.

Ω

THE *ILIAD*

BOOK 1
ACHILLES AND AGAMEMNON QUARREL

The *Iliad* opens, as do all epic poems, with the poet's invocation to the Muse of Poetry. In this invocation, Homer states his theme, the wrath, or the anger, of Achilles and its effects, and he requests the aid of the Muse so that he can properly recount the story. The story begins in the middle, where the trouble originally arose.

During one of the Achaian (Greek) army's many raids on the towns located near Troy, they captured two beautiful enemy maidens, Chryseis and Briseis. These girls were awarded by the troops to Agamemnon, the commander-in-chief of the army, and to Achilles, the Achaians' greatest warrior.

Chryseis, the war prize of Agamemnon, is the daughter of Chryses, a priest of the god Apollo, and it is not long before Chryses comes to the Achaian camp hoping to ransom his daughter. But Agamemnon refuses and orders the old man to leave the camp. In despair, Chryses prays to Apollo for assistance. Apollo answers the priest's prayer by sending a deadly plague throughout the Achaian camp, killing hundreds of the troops.

On the tenth day of the plague, Achilles can wait no longer for King Agamemnon to end the plague. Usurping Agamemnon's authority, Achilles calls an assembly of the army, and he suggests that a soothsayer be called to determine the cause of Apollo's anger. Calchas, an Achaian soothsayer, volunteers to explain the cause of the pestilence, but only if he is guaranteed personal protection. Achilles agrees to this condition.

When the soothsayer reveals that the plague is the result of Agamemnon's refusal to return Chryseis to her father, Agamemnon is furious that he has been publicly named as the cause of the plague. He insists that if he is forced to surrender Chryseis, his rightful war prize, then he must be repaid with Achilles' war prize, Briseis. His demand infuriates Achilles, who considers stabbing Agamemnon. Achilles begins to draw his sword, but the goddess Athena restrains him. Finally, Nestor (the oldest and wisest of all the Achaian soldiers) rises to speak and has some effect in pacifying the two angry men.

However, Achilles, stunned by the public disgrace of having Agamemnon demand Briseis, refuses to accept the indignity which he feels that Agamemnon has made him undergo in full view of all the soldiers. Thus, he announces that he is withdrawing all of his troops from battle. Neither he nor any of his troops will fight any longer for the Achaians against the Trojans. He justifies this decision by saying that neither he nor any of his followers has any personal quarrel with the Trojans. He came along only to assist Agamemnon and Menelaus in retrieving Menelaus' wife, Helen, and it is grossly unjust that they take away his war prize, Briseis. Achilles is firm in his resolve to fight no more. Furthermore, he and his men plan to return to their own country as soon as possible.

Agamemnon decides to appease Apollo by returning Chryseis, Agamemnon's war prize. He installs her safely aboard a ship heading home, and then he sends his heralds to collect Briseis (Achilles' war prize) for him. Surprisingly, Achilles surrenders the girl without any difficulty.

Afterward, however, in deep sorrow, Achilles wanders alone along the seashore and weeps because he has been publicly shamed by King Agamemnon and treated like a slave. Soon, his mother, Thetis, a sea nymph, joins him. Confessing his problems to her, he asks her to use her influence with Zeus to ensure that the Trojan armies defeat his fellow Achaian soldiers. Achilles thinks that when the Achaians discover that they are losing the war because Achilles is not fighting with them, they will realize his true worth to them. As a result, they will make amends for Agamemnon's insult to him.

Thetis visits Zeus on Olympus, and the king of the gods agrees to aid the Trojans, although he expresses a fear that his wife, Hera, will be annoyed since she is jealous of Thetis and since she hates the Trojans and cannot bear to see them win the war. Hera does indeed hate the Trojans, but she fears Zeus' wrath even more, and so she quiets her protests. The first book ends with a banquet of the gods in Zeus' palace.

BOOK 2
THE PARADE OF THE TWO ARMIES

Zeus, fulfilling his promise to Thetis that he will help the Trojans, sends a fraudulent dream of hope to Agamemnon. Agamemnon is absolutely convinced by his dream that he can defeat the Trojans once and for all in battle the next morning. So, full of false hope, he and his council plan a mass assault on Troy.

But, to test the loyalty of his army before he begins this mass assault, Agamemnon announces to the soldiers that nine years of war is more than enough; they should return home. To his great surprise, his troops react to his suggestion with loud enthusiasm. Breaking ranks, they run to prepare their ships for the trip home. Odysseus, guided by Athena, halts their mad rush to the ships. Then he convinces the Achaians that it is far more honorable to remain and conquer Troy. Nestor adds his wisdom to that of Odysseus, and the army agrees to stay and fight.

Offering a sacrifice to Zeus, Agamemnon orders the army to prepare itself for the attack. He then holds a splendid review of the whole Achaian army, thus giving Homer an opportunity to enumerate all of the Achaian contingents and their heroes.

When the Trojans receive news of the Achaian maneuver, Hector orders his troops to prepare to meet the Achaians on the plain in front of Troy. Then, as the Trojan troops march through the city gates, Homer reviews the Trojan leaders and the cities which have sent military assistance to them.

BOOK 3
A TRUCE AND A DUEL

The two armies advance, and as they draw toward each other, Paris brashly steps forward and dares any of the Achaian warriors to meet him in personal combat. Menelaus accepts his challenge, but Paris is suddenly overcome by terror and hides within the Trojan ranks.

Hector, the Trojan commander, finds his brother Paris and gives him a stern tongue-lashing. Paris is so ashamed that he agrees to a duel with Menelaus. A truce is declared while Agamemnon and Hector determine the conditions of the duel, and it is arranged that Paris (Helen's lover) and Menelaus (Helen's husband) will engage in single combat. The victor will win Helen, and a treaty of peace will end the war, after which the Achaians will sail for home.

Meanwhile, back in Troy, King Priam and his council sit on the ramparts watching the battle. Helen accompanies them and identifies the Achaian commanders, telling a little about their deeds. Priam is called to the field to give his consent to the terms of the truce. When he arrives, he joins his arch-enemy, Agamemnon, in a sacrifice to the gods on behalf of both armies; then they solemnize the agreement.

Afterward, Priam returns to Troy while Paris and Menelaus prepare
to fight.

Dueling with javelin and sword in a large open area between the
two armies, Menelaus is the superior warrior, and he inflicts a slight
wound on Paris. The Trojan prince is taken captive, but while Menelaus is dragging him to the Achaian lines, Aphrodite intervenes and
rescues her favorite warrior. She conceals him in a mist and carries
him to his bedroom, where she brings Helen to join him.

Agamemnon steps to the front of his army, states that the duel
has unquestionably been won by Menelaus and demands the immediate restoration of Helen. The Achaians loudly applaud the decision
of their king and commander-in-chief.

BOOK 4
PANDARUS BREAKS THE TRUCE

The gods meet in conference on Olympus. Zeus proposes that
since Menelaus has obviously won the duel, the long, nine-year war
be brought to a close. Hera and Athena dislike this course of action,
and Hera, in particular, vehemently protests to Zeus. She wants the
complete destruction of Troy, a town she bitterly hates, and she rejects the idea of a truce. Zeus gives in and sends Athena to arrange
a resumption of the fighting.

At Troy, Athena seeks out Pandarus, one of the Trojan leaders,
and tempts him to kill Menelaus, thereby gaining great glory. Pandarus foolishly acts on her advice and draws his bow. He shoots an
arrow at Menelaus, but Athena makes sure that it only wounds Menelaus because she doesn't want him dead, but she does want the battle
to begin anew. Agamemnon and the Achaians are shocked by this
violation of the truce and by the seemingly serious injury to Menelaus.
Fortunately, the wound is not fatal, but while an army surgeon is
treating it, several of the Trojan regiments begin to advance in battle
order.

Agamemnon immediately orders his troops to prepare for fighting,
and he goes through the ranks of his army, praising the men. The
Achaians respond to their king's spirit by eagerly and cheerfully arm-
ing themselves and falling into line. The war begins again. The two
armies clash violently, and large numbers of men on both sides are
killed.

BOOK 5
DIOMEDES' GLORY AS A WARRIOR

The battle continues with great fury, and both armies perform many acts of valor. During this particular day's fighting, the outstanding warrior is Diomedes, whom the goddess Athena has inspired with exceptional courage and skill.

When Pandarus wounds Diomedes, the valiant Achaian soldier appeals to Athena for aid. She answers him by giving him additional courage, plus the privilege of being able to distinguish gods from men. She warns him, however, not to fight against any of the gods – with the exception of Aphrodite.

Diomedes returns to the front line and drives the Trojans back before him. He kills many Trojans, including Pandarus, and then he wounds Aeneas, the son of the goddess Aphrodite. Diomedes takes Aeneas' horses as a war prize and is about to finish off Aeneas himself when Aphrodite comes down to protect her son. Enraged at Aphrodite's interference, Diomedes pursues her and wounds her in the hand. With tears streaming down her face, Aphrodite flees in terror to Olympus and seeks solace from Dione, her mother. Zeus is angry at this turn of events and orders Aphrodite to stay off the battlefield in the future since warfare is not the same as love, her usual sphere of interest. Meanwhile, Apollo carries Aeneas off to safety.

Ares, the savage god of war, enters the Trojan ranks and helps Hector to rally his forces. With his aid, Hector and the Trojan army again attempt to advance. But the Achaians, led by Diomedes and other Achaian heroes, are able to hold their ground. As the bloody battle progresses, however, the strong and brutal influence of Ares is felt, and the Achaians gradually begin to withdraw toward their camp.

Hera and Athena then fly to the aid of the Achaians, after gaining permission from Zeus to bring Ares under control. On the plains before Troy, Hera gives fresh strength to the Achaians while Athena brings the now-wounded Diomedes back to the fray. She advises him to have no fear of Ares or any other god. Diomedes gallops into combat, encounters Ares, and drives a spear into his belly. With a bellow of pain and fury, Ares leaves the field and heads for Olympus.

Finding Zeus, Ares complains about the harsh treatment he has received, but the god of war gets no sympathy from Zeus. Zeus tells him that because of his quarrelsome and cruel nature, he has no love for him, but since Ares is a god, his wound will heal. Athena and Hera then return to the Olympian palace, and the battle between the Achaians and the Trojans continues to rage, but now there are no gods fighting on either side.

BOOK 6
HECTOR RETURNS TO TROY

The battle continues, and although the gods are no longer taking part, the Achaians drive back the Trojans. There is much slaughter, and in their ardor to defeat the Trojans, the Achaians do not even pause to collect loot.

The Trojan force is in full retreat when Helenus, a soothsayer, suggests that his brother Hector return to Troy and arrange for the queen and the other royal women to make an offering in the temple of Athena in hopes of placating the goddess. Hector agrees to the wisdom of this plan, and while he goes back to Troy, there is a short lull in the fighting.

During this interval, Diomedes and Glaucus step into the area between the two resting armies and challenge each other to personal combat. They discover, however, while explaining their individual pedigrees, that there were once ties of friendship between their grand-fathers; thus, according to the heroic code, they must maintain these same bonds of friendship. They promise to avoid fighting each other in the battles to come, and, as a token of their fellowship, they trade armor. Diomedes comes out ahead in this exchange because his bronze armor is worth only nine oxen, while the golden armor of Glaucus is worth one hundred oxen, but the two men part as comrades.

In Troy, Hector instructs his mother, Hecuba, about the rites to be held in Athena's temple and then goes to find Paris, who has been absent from the battlefield. He discovers his brother at home with Helen and her handmaidens, and he sternly rebukes him for his irre-sponsibility. Paris admits that he has been disgracing himself, and he prepares to join the fight.

Hector, meanwhile, goes to visit his own wife and baby son. He finds Andromache and the baby Astyanax on the walls overlooking the battlefield. Andromache pleads with Hector not to endanger himself any longer. Her father and brothers have all been killed by Achilles, and now Hector is her whole family. She begs him to have pity on her and their infant child.

Hector admits his concern for Andromache, but he says that he must consider his reputation and his duty. In his heart, he says, he knows that Troy *will* fall someday, but he is, above all, a soldier and a prince. He adds that he often worries about the fate of his wife and son after he is dead and his city has fallen, but that a mortal *cannot* change the will of the gods. Hector kisses Andromache and Astyanax and leaves. Paris joins him at the city gate, and they return to the battlefield together.

BOOKS 7 & 8
THE TROJANS REACH THE ACHAIAN WALL

Hector and Paris rejoin the Trojan forces, and the battle resumes. Athena and Apollo, after witnessing the continued slaughter, decide to end the day's combat by arranging a duel between Hector and one of the best Achaian warriors. The time consumed by this duel will result in a recess for both armies.

Helenus, the soothsayer, carries information about the duel to Hector. A truce is declared, and Hector offers a challenge to the Achaians. Because Hector is known as a fierce Trojan hero, however, at first none of the Achaians accepts it. Then Menelaus volunteers, but he is so ill-matched to Hector in fighting ability that Agamemnon will not permit the match. Finally, after a stirring oration by Nestor, nine Achaian champions, including Agamemnon, Diomedes, Ajax, the lesser Ajax, Odysseus, and Idomeneus, volunteer to fight Hector. They cast lots to select who will accept the challenge.

Ajax and Hector engage in a ferocious duel, but neither warrior is able to overcome the other. Finally, since it is growing dark, the two men are parted by heralds, and they exchange gifts as tokens of their respective valor.

That night, each of the armies holds a feast celebrating the safe return of its champion. In the Achaian camp, Nestor proposes a short truce so that funerals for the dead can be held; he also wants to use this time for his fellow Achaians to build a wall and a trench to defend their ships.

In Troy that same evening, one of the Trojan noblemen, Antenor, suggests that the Trojans return Helen to Menelaus. Paris refuses to give up his new wife, but he offers to restore all of Helen's property to Menelaus, plus some of his own as an indemnity. Priam sends a messenger to Agamemnon with this proposition, as well as a request for a truce during which the Trojans can bury their dead. The Achaians refuse Paris' offer but both sides agree on the truce.

The next morning, the two armies collect their dead and conduct the funeral rites. Great pyres are erected on which the slain are cremated, and then the bones and ashes are buried under hugh earth barrows. Following these ceremonies, the Achaians build the fortifications suggested by Nestor. The soldiers of both armies feast late into the night while Zeus' ominous thundering creates unrest.

At a council on Olympus, Zeus warns the gods that he is at last bringing the Trojan War to a finish and that any interference in favor of either side will be severely punished. However, when Athena asks to be allowed to advise the Achaians, Zeus consents.

In the morning, the Trojan forces come out of the city and the armies clash again. Zeus watches over the fighting from nearby Mt. Ida and decides to give the day's victory to Troy. A furious battle ensues, and soon the Achaians are routed. Most of the commanders flee also, and Diomedes rescues Nestor from Hector's spear.

Hera, who has always been a fanatical hater of the Trojans, tries to convince Poseidon to join her in helping the Achaians. The sea god, however, recognizes the superior power of his brother Zeus and refuses.

The Trojan spearmen and chariot warriors continue to pursue the Achaians. Hector is everywhere, fighting bravely and cheering on his men. The Achaian situation is critical. Hera and Athena prepare to intervene, but Zeus notices their approach. He repeats his earlier warning through his messenger, Iris, and the goddesses return to Olympus. Meanwhile, the Trojans drive their adversaries behind the fortifications protecting the Achaian ships.

Hector orders his army to camp on the plain for the night in order to prevent the Achaians from sailing off to safety in the darkness and to retain the advantage for the morning's assault. Supplies are brought from Troy, and the Trojan fires burn in front of the Achaian wall.

BOOK 9
AN OFFER OF RECONCILIATION

The routed Achaian army is completely demoralized. At an assembly of troops that night, even proud King Agamemnon bursts into tears. He insists that the war is lost and suggests sailing home. His dejected soldiers receive this speech in silence, but Diomedes leaps to his feet, reminding the king of his responsibilities and the troops of their heroic heritage. They can *all* return home, he says, but *he,* Diomedes, will remain alone, if necessary, in order to continue fighting, for it is fated that Troy *will eventually fall.* This brave declaration restores the confidence of the army and, on the recommendation of Nestor, guards are posted at the wall and the troops disperse to their tents for dinner and sleep.

At a meeting of the council, Nestor takes the floor and reminds Agamemnon that the absence of Achilles is causing the present distress of the army. The king admits that he was unwise to have insulted the great warrior. He decides for many valuable gifts, as well as the return of Briseis, if Achilles will rejoin the army. The king dispatches emissaries to the tent of the sulking hero with this message.

Achilles welcomes Ajax and Odysseus with great honor, but he refuses to accept Agamemnon's terms. He cannot be bought or sold, he says, and nothing, not even if it were all the wealth of Egypt, could erase Agamemnon's public insult. Therefore, he will *not* join in the battle, and in the morning, he and his men plan to sail for home.

Achilles' refusal of Agamemnon's offer is one of the major turning points in the story. Until now, it was possible to sympathize with Achilles because Agamemnon had clearly been in the wrong, but with Achilles' refusal to accept the honorable terms offered to him, he puts his *injured pride* above all other considerations. The moral balance begins to fall against him. Nothing will satisfy Achilles except the complete humbling of Agamemnon, a demand which is unreasonable and unwarranted. Achilles' desire for revenge has begun to overwhelm his better judgment, his loyalty to his friends, and the very code of chivalric honor which he claims to uphold.

Back in the Achaian camp, Agamemnon listens with great sorrow to the report of what happened in Achilles' tent. Finally, Diomedes rises and tells the assembled warriors that it was an error to try to appeal to someone as conceited and headstrong as Achilles. He advises them to make whatever preparations are possible to defend the ships against the Trojans the next morning. All agree, and after making libations to the gods, they retire to their quarters.

BOOK 10
SPYING AT NIGHT

Agamemnon is unable to sleep because of his concern for the fate of the Achaian army. After much tossing and turning, he rises and awakens all his senior commanders. They inspect the outposts, and, finding these in order, they hold a conference. Nestor advises that under cover of darkness, a scout enter the Trojan camp. With luck, this maneuver will enable the Greeks to learn the strengths, as well as the plans, of the enemy.

Diomedes volunteers to reconnoiter behind the Trojan lines and selects Odysseus to accompany him. The two men arm themselves and set out. In the area between the camps, they capture Dolon, a Trojan nobleman who was sent by Hector to conduct a reconnaissance of the Achaian camp. From Dolon, they learn the whereabouts of Hector and his staff, key information about the various units of the Trojan army, and the precautions which the Trojans have taken to guard the camp. Diomedes then kills the Trojan spy, and the two Achaians take his armor as a trophy for Athena.

The two Achaian heroes also learn that a new contingent of troops from Thrace lies asleep and unprotected on the Trojan flank, and that the Thracian king, Rhesus, has with him a team of magnificent chariot horses. Thus, they set out for the Thracian section of the camp, where they kill Rhesus and a dozen of his officers as they sleep and escape with the horses.

When the two heroes return to the Achaian camp with their valuable booty and describe their exploits, there is much rejoicing. Afterward, Diomedes and Odysseus sit down to a well-earned supper, which is followed by libations to Athena.

BOOK 11
ACHILLES WATCHES THE ACHAIAN DEFEAT

Agamemnon leads the Achaians into battle and, at first, they prevail, driving the Trojans back as far as the city gates. But then, in quick succession, Agamemnon and most of the other Achaian leaders are wounded and are forced to withdraw from the fighting. The Trojans soon regain the ground they lost and inflict many casualties on the Achaians.

Clearly, Achilles has continued to observe the progress of the battle. Although he is unable to voice the feeling, he is obviously troubled by the dangerous predicament of his Achaian comrades-at-arms and by his own *self-imposed inability* to help them. He senses with some relief that the time is drawing near when he will be able to get satisfaction for his wounded pride. Thus, he sends Patroclus to get information from Nestor because his own pride will not allow him to show any interest in the fate of the Achaians.

In the Achaian camp, Nestor gives Patroclus a long account of the day's events, with many reminiscences of past battles. Finally, coming to the point, he convinces Patroclus to try yet another time to persuade Achilles to return to battle against the Trojans. If Patroclus fails, Nestor says, perhaps Patroclus himself could put on the armor of Achilles and join in the fighting. Nestor says that if the Trojans recognize Achilles' armor, they would think that Achilles had settled his dispute with Agamemnon and that he had returned to the battle-front. This strategy alone might be sufficient to save the day. Patroclus, mulling over this advice, returns to Achilles' tent.

BOOKS 12–15
TROJAN SUCCESSES

The Achaians are forced to take refuge behind their wall while the Trojans continue their brutal assault. But the Trojans soon discover that they are unable to cross the Achaian trench in their chariots, so they attack on foot. There is much bloody combat.

Suddenly an eagle with a serpent in its talons flies over the Trojan army, which Poulydamas interprets as a bad omen. He asks Hector to fall back, but the commander refuses. The attack continues and after several attempts, the Trojans breach the Achaian wall. Forcing open one of the gates with a large stone, Hector and his men storm inside. The Achaians retreat in panic and take refuge among their ships.

Zeus has brought Hector and the Trojans as far as the Achaian ships, so now he relaxes and turns his attention to other matters. Poseidon takes advantage of Zeus' lapse of attention to come to the aid of the Achaians and, disguised as Calchas, he moves among the Achaian ranks, encouraging them to continue fighting.

While the violent battle continues, Nestor, in order to devise a plan of action, seeks Agamemnon, Diomedes, and Odysseus, all three of whom are wounded. Agamemnon is certain that heaven wills the defeat of the Achaian army, and he can think only of an escape by sea. Odysseus points out that his plan is not only dishonorable, but extremely dangerous. It would be difficult, he says, to launch and board their ships while under attack. To do this might make a Trojan victory even easier. The leaders then decide to go among the ranks and encourage their men.

From Olympus, Hera notices how Poseidon, the sea god, is trying to aid the Achaians. She makes plans to distract Zeus so that Poseidon will have even more opportunity to help the besieged Achaians. Dressing in her finest garments and borrowing the magic girdle of Aphrodite, Hera flies to Mt. Ida, where Zeus is sitting. She overwhelms him with her charms and easily seduces him. As was prearranged, the god of sleep casts a spell over Zeus.

BOOK 16
PATROCLUS FIGHTS AND IS KILLED

While the battle around the ships continues, Patroclus pleads with Achilles to be allowed to wear Achilles' armor and lead the Myrmidons, Achilles' troops, into battle. While Achilles is considering this request, flames rise from the ships, indicating Trojan success. Achilles consents, and Patroclus and the Myrmidons arm themselves with great enthusiasm. After Achilles has addressed them and offered a libation to Zeus, he warns Patroclus to *do no more than rescue the ships,* for if he attacks Troy, he may be killed.

The Trojans are panicked that Achilles will unleash his fury against them. In a short time, the addition of Achilles' fresh and well-equipped regiment of Myrmidons to the Achaian army destroys the Trojan advantage. Hector and his men flee toward Troy.

Patroclus pursues them to the walls of Troy, performing many heroic deeds on the way. However, Apollo decides to enter the fighting as an ally of Hector, and while Patroclus, almost godlike, slaughters nine Trojans in a single charge, Apollo slips up behind him and strikes him so fiercely on the back that Patroclus' visored helmet flies off. His spear is shattered, and his armor falls to the ground. Then, while Patroclus stands in a daze, a Trojan soldier pierces him midway between the shoulders with a javelin.

Patroclus tries to hide, but Hector sees him and rams a spear through the lower part of his belly. Patroclus falls with a thud, and the entire Achaian army is stunned. His voice failing, Patroclus declares that it was not Hector who conquered him, but the gods and "deadly Destiny."

BOOK 17
THE FIGHT FOR PATROCLUS' BODY

Menelaus attempts to protect the body of Patroclus from the enemy, but finally Hector drives him away. The Trojan commander strips Achilles' armor from the corpse and puts it on in place of his own. Almost immediately, a battle develops over Patroclus' naked corpse. The Trojans hope to take it to Troy in order to mutilate it as a warning to all the Achaians; the Achaians wish to give it a proper funeral ceremony. The leading warriors on both sides engage in this fight—and two gods, Apollo and Athena, also join in. During the fray, Hector attempts to capture Achilles' horses, but they escape to the Achaian camp. Finally, the body of Patroclus is rescued and safely carried back to the Achaian camp.

BOOK 18
ACHILLES' NEW ARMOR

When Achilles learns of Patroclus' death, he bursts into tears, tearing his hair and throwing himself on the ground. His mother, Thetis, hears his lament and comes to comfort him. She points out that if Achilles avenges Patroclus, he himself will be killed. Despite his mother's warning, however, Achilles chooses to undertake this risk, so great is his love for Patroclus. Thetis therefore promises to procure new armor for her son from the god Hephaestus to replace the armor that was captured by Hector.

Meanwhile, the Trojans pursue the Achaians who are bearing away the body of Patroclus. Achilles appears at the Achaian trench and shouts his ferocious and furious war cry. The sound strikes terror into the hearts of the Trojans, and they retreat in panic.

The sight of Patroclus' corpse intensifies Achilles' sorrow, and all of the Achaians join him in mourning. Achilles vows to kill Hector and to slaughter twelve Trojan warriors on Patroclus' funeral pyre. Meanwhile, Patroclus' corpse is washed and laid in state in Achilles' tent.

At a Trojan council of war that night, Poulydamas suggests that the Trojan army remain in the city and rebuff any Achaian assault from the battlements. Achilles' return to the Achaian force makes it too dangerous to fight in the open, he says. Hector refuses to heed this advice, however and insists that the Trojan army stay in the field. His opinion prevails.

On Olympus, Thetis calls upon Hephaestus, telling him all that has taken place on the battlefield that day and asking him to provide new armor for her son. Hephaestus assents and makes marvelous, beautiful armor for Achilles. The new shield alone is a masterpiece, being built up of five layers and having on it a representation of the signs of the zodiac and of two cities engaged in all the *peaceful* and *warlike* activities of humans. When the armor is finished, Thetis takes it in her arms, and, thanking Hephaestus, goes to find her son.

BOOK 19
ACHILLES REJOINS THE ACHAIANS

After receiving his new armor, Achilles calls for an assembly of the Achaian army. Then he announces that his quarrel with King Agamemnon is ended and that he is ready to return to war; the troops joyfully applaud his speech. Agamemnon rises and welcome Achilles back to the army. He says that at the time of their disagreement Zeus blinded him and robbed him of his wits. In compensation to Achilles, he vows to return Briseis to him, as well as many other presents.

Achilles accepts the offer, but clearly is more eager to attack the Trojans than to collect gifts. He demands that the army go into action at once. Odysseus sympathizes with Achilles' zeal, but points out that the troops are tired and hungry, needing time to renew themselves before fighting again. Achilles agrees to wait, but announces that the troops may eat if they wish, but he himself is going to fast until Patroclus is avenged.

When the Achaian troops are once more ready to fight, Achilles puts on his splendid new armor, and then, mounting his chariot, he prepares to lead the army. But first, he reproaches his horses for allowing Patroclus to be killed. One of the horses answers, saying that Patroclus' death was not *their* fault, but that of Apollo and Destiny. The horse then prophesies Achilles' death on the battlefield. Achilles answers that he *already knows* about his doom, but that *nothing* will prevent him from avenging Patroclus. Shouting his mighty war cry, Achilles gallops into battle.

BOOK 20
THE GODS GO TO WAR

While the Achaian and Trojan armies group for battle, Zeus calls for an assembly of the gods. When they gather, he gives them permission to openly assist *either* faction, for Achilles must be prevented from overstepping the bounds which fate has set on his achievements. At once, Hera, Athena, Poseidon, Hermes, and Hephaestus join the Achaians while Ares, Apollo, Artemis, and Aphrodite fly to the side of the Trojans.

The battle opens with great fury. Achilles is about to kill Aeneas when Poseidon rescues the Trojan prince because Aeneas is fated to be the sole survivor of the house of Priam. Undaunted by divine interference, Achilles continues fighting, slaughtering many of the Trojans and sweeping through the field unchecked.

BOOK 21
ACHILLES BATTLES THE RIVER

The Trojan troops flee in terror from Achilles. One portion of the army heads for the city while another group seeks refuge near the River Xanthus. Achilles cuts off the second group and kills many as they try to cross the stream. He also takes twelve captives, as he vowed he would. The slaughter continues, and soon the river is choked with bodies.

The bloodshed in his waters antagonizes the river god, who attacks Achilles with great waves and currents. Achilles begins to falter but Poseidon and Athena reassure him, while Hera and Hephaestus attack the river with fire. Seeing his water boil away in great, mysterious heat, Xanthus relents.

The gods, excited by human warfare, engage each other in combat. Athena defeats Ares and Aphrodite, while Hera drives Artemis from the field. Poseidon challenges Apollo, but the younger god will not accept his uncle's dare out of deference to his age.

Achilles continues to chase the Trojans. Agenor, Hector's half-brother, attempts to fight him in single combat, but Agenor is far inferior to Achilles and is finally rescued by Apollo. This diversion allows most of the retreating troops enough time to take refuge in the city.

BOOK 22
THE DEATH OF HECTOR

With the Trojans now secure in their city, Hector—their sole representative—stands outside the city gates and prepares to meet Achilles. His mother and father appeal to him to seek safety behind the city walls, but their pleas are in vain. While waiting, Hector considers the various courses of action open to him and decides that the only real possibility is to fight Achilles.

Yet, when Achilles arrives, Hector is overcome by fear and flees. Achilles pursues him around the city walls three times. As they run, Hector tries unsuccessfully to draw Achilles within range of the Trojan archers on the battlements.

Finally, Athena deludes Hector into believing that he will have assistance against Achilles. He turns and stands his ground. Before the two heroes fight, Hector attempts to make Achilles promise to treat his body with respect if he is killed, but Achilles, filled with fury, refuses.

The two warriors engage in a decisive duel. Achilles casts his spear first and misses the mark, but it is returned to him by Athena. Next, Hector throws his spear and hits the center of Achilles' shield, but the divine armor is impenetrable. The two men circle each other, slowly closing in. Hector carries only a sword, while Achilles still has his spear. After several feints, Achilles lunges and stabs Hector in the throat. As the Trojan dies, he begs that his body be returned to his family for a proper funeral. Achilles again refuses Hector's request.

All the Achaians run up to see the corpse of the almost mythic, now-dead Trojan leader. Many of them jest and stab Hector's corpse. Achilles strips off Hector's armor and fastens his naked body to his chariot by the heels. Then he gallops off, dragging the corpse behind him in disgrace.

When Priam and Hecuba, Hector's parents, witness the vicious treatment of their dead son, they wail and bemoan their fate, and all of the citizens of Troy join in piteous lamentations. Andromache hears their weeping, learns of her husband's death, and collapses.

BOOK 23
PATROCLUS' FUNERAL AND THE GAMES

After returning to the Achaian camp, Achilles and the Myrmidons drive their chariots in ritual procession around Patroclus' bier, and

Achilles leads his men in a dirge for the dead hero. That night, they hold a funeral feast. Afterward, while he sleeps, Achilles has a vision in which Patroclus' ghost asks that his funeral be held so that he can enter the realm of the dead in peace.

In the morning, the soldiers fetch wood and build a large funeral pyre. The army marches out in full military regalia, and Patroclus' corpse is placed on top of the pyre. Several horses and hunting dogs, as well as the twelve captive Trojan noblemen, are sacrificed on the lower part of the accumulation of wood. The whole pile is then set on fire. After the flames have burned for a while, the fire is extinguished with wine, and Patroclus' bones are placed in a jar for future burial alongside Achilles' body. A memorial barrow is erected over the remains of the funeral pyre.

Achilles now proclaims funeral games in honor of his friend. There are contests in chariot racing, boxing, wrestling, footracing, dueling, discus throwing, archery, and javelin throwing. Winners receive valuable prizes.

All during this time, Hector's body lies untended on the ground, but Apollo and Aphrodite protect it from the ravages of stray dogs and heat.

BOOK 24
PRIAM AND ACHILLES

Nine days pass after the funeral, and on each of these days, Achilles ties Hector's body to his chariot and drags it around Patroclus' barrow. The gods, however, continue to preserve the corpse so that it does not deteriorate.

Zeus then holds a meeting of the gods during which it is decided that Hector's body will be redeemed and given a suitable burial. In order to make this possible, the gods order Thetis to explain to her son, Achilles, that it is the will of Zeus that he restore Hector's body to Priam.

Escorted by the god Hermes, Priam and an old servant enter the Achaian camp that night, unseen. Priam appeals to Achilles as a suppliant, reminding Achilles of his own feelings for his dead father. Achilles is so moved by these reawakened memories of home and parents that he agrees to accept Priam's offer of ransom for Hector's body. The two men, Achilles and Priam, each suffering his own sorrow, weep together. Then Achilles has dinner prepared and provides

Priam with a bed for the night. He even oversees the preparations of Hector's body and grants the Trojans a twelve-day truce so that they will have sufficient time to conduct Hector's funeral.

All the people of Troy come out to mourn Hector. Andromache, Hecuba, and Helen lead the lamentations praising Hector and describing their individual reasons for regretting his death.

During the period of the truce, the Trojans gather wood in the mountains and burn Hector's body on a large funeral pyre. His bones are then placed in a golden chest, which is buried in a shallow grave. Over this, a barrow is erected. Afterward, a great funeral banquet is served in Priam's palace. At this point, the *Iliad* ends.

Ω

THE FALL OF TROY

After the burial of Hector, the Trojans called on outside forces for help, and the Greeks lost many good warriors. In one battle, Achilles encountered Paris, who shot an arrow which, guided by Apollo, struck Achilles in the right heel, the only place where he was vulnerable. Ajax and Odysseus were able, but only with great difficulty, to rescue Achilles' body, and immediately there arose a dispute over who should receive Achilles' splendid armor. When it was awarded to Odysseus, Ajax was so furious that he threatened to kill some of the Greek leaders. When he realized the error of his thinking, he committed suicide.

With the death of their two greatest and most valiant warriors, Ajax and Achilles, the Greeks despaired of taking Troy. After consulting various seers and oracles, they were instructed to secure the bow and arrows of Hercules, which were in the hands of Prince Philoctetes, a Greek who had been abandoned on an island because of a loathsome wound that would not heal. Odysseus and Diomedes convinced Philoctetes to return with the bow and arrows, and in his first encounter in battle, he was able to kill Paris. This death, however, did not affect the course of the war.

The Greeks were then given a series of things that would have to be accomplished to be victorious: (1) bring the bones of Pelops back to Greece from Asia, (2) bring Achilles' son, Neoptolemus, into the war, and (3) steal the sacred image of Athena from the Trojan sanctuary. These acts were accomplished, but none of them changed the course of the war. Then Odysseus conceived a plan whereby the Greeks could enter the walls of Troy: they constructed a great horse of wood with a hollow belly that would hold many warriors. In the dark of night, they dragged the horse to the Trojan plain, and some Greek warriors climbed into it. The rest of the Greeks burned their camp and sailed off to wait behind a nearby island, giving the impression that they were abandoning the war effort.

The next morning, the Trojans found the Greeks gone and the huge, mysterious horse sitting before Troy. They also discovered a Greek named Sinon, whom they took captive. Odysseus had primed Sinon with plausible stories about the Greek departure, the wooden horse, and his own presence there. Sinon told Priam and the others that Athena had deserted the Greeks because of the theft of her image from her temple. Without her help, they were lost and so they departed. But to get home safely, they had to have a human sacrifice. The Greeks chose Sinon, but he got away and hid. The horse was left to placate the angry goddess; the Greeks were hoping the Trojans would desecrate it, earning Athena's hatred. These lies convinced Priam and many other Trojans, and so they pulled the gigantic horse inside the gates to honor Athena.

That night, the soldiers crept down from the horse, killed the sentries, and opened the gates to let the Greek army in. The Greeks set fires throughout the city, began massacring the inhabitants, and looted the city. The Trojan resistance was ineffectual. King Priam was killed and by morning all but a few Trojans were dead. Only Aeneas with his father, his son, and a small band of Trojans escaped. Hector's young son was thrown from the walls of the city. The surviving women were divided among the Greek leaders as war prizes, as slaves or concubines. Troy was devastated. Hera and Athena had their revenge upon Paris and upon his city.

For a more comprehensive, in-depth analysis of this work, consult Cliffs Notes on the _Iliad_.

Ω

THE *ODYSSEY*

_____ LIST OF CHARACTERS

HUMAN BEINGS

Agamemnon

The king of Mycenae and leader of the Achaian expedition to Troy; the story of his murder by his wife and her lover on his return home is frequently referred to by Homer.

Alcinous

The king of the Phaeacians, husband of Arete and father of Nausicaa, he is a generous, kind, and good-humored ruler and father.

Antinous

The leader of the suitors and the first one slain by Odysseus. It is he who first mistreats Odysseus, who constantly harasses Telemachus and Penelope, and who plans Telemachus' murder.

Anticleia

The mother of Odysseus; she is encountered by him in Hades.

Arete

The queen of the Phaeacians, wife of Alcinous and mother of Nausicaa.

Demodocus

A blind bard who entertains at the banquets in the palace of Alcinous.

Elpenor

A young seaman in the crew of Odysseus who dies in an accident on Circe's island.

Eumaeus

The chief swineherd of Odysseus, who remains faithful to his master during his long absence and who plays an active part in assisting Odysseus to regain his position when he finally returns home.

Eupeithes

The father of Antinous. Like his son, he is rash.

Eurycleia

The faithful and devoted old nurse of Odysseus, who recognizes her beloved master on his return.

Eurylochus

One of Odysseus' officers; he is an unimaginative and sober person, who wisely avoids entering Circe's palace.

Eurymachus

The second most important suitor; he is as evil as Antinous, but far more soft and cowardly. His instincts are mainly pecuniary; he attempts to appease Odysseus.

Halisthernes

The soothsayer of Ithaca.

Helen

The wife of Menelaus, king of Sparta. She was the cause of the Trojan War in that the Achaians sailed to Troy to restore her to her husband.

Irus

A cowardly bully who is a beggar on Ithaca and a favorite of many of the suitors. He is severely beaten by Odysseus.

Laertes

The old father of Odysseus, who lives in isolation from the demands of public life, on a small farm in the back hills of Ithaca.

Medon

The herald of Ithaca. Although he is forced to serve the suitors, he remains loyal and is spared by Odysseus.

Melanthius

The chief goatherd of Odysseus. In his master's absence, he has ignored his duty and has ingratiated himself with the suitors by catering to their whims.

Menelaus

King of Sparta, husband of Helen and brother of Agamemnon.

Mentor

A faithful friend of Odysseus who was left behind in Ithaca as Telemachus' tutor; he is wise, sober, and loyal. Athena often disguises herself as Mentor when appearing among human beings.

Nausicaa

The daughter of Alcinous and Arete. She is a charming young maiden: her thoughts are occupied only by imaginings of her future husband and by various forms of girlish pleasures and games. She is evidently Homer's portrait of feminine innocence and virtue.

Nestor

King of Pylos, father of Peisistratus. A very wise and garrulous old man, one of the few survivors of the Trojan War.

Odysseus

(Latin: Ulysses) King of Ithaca, husband of Penelope, father of Telemachus, son of Laertes. He is the first of the Greek epic heroes to be renowned for brain as well as muscle; his courage and prowess are beyond criticism, but he is more like a modern hero than any of the other chieftains who fought at Troy, for he has a sharp and inquiring mind. His mental and physical attributes are of equal importance in helping him to achieve his ends, and he uses either, depending upon circumstances. Because he is able to reason and evaluate things, he often hesitates before taking action where other heroes would have rushed blindly into the fray. This must not, however, be interpreted as cowardice. Odysseus' main weakness is his pride, caused by the magnitude of his achievements, and it often involves him in trouble, as when he foolishly identifies himself to Polyphemus and so is subjected to the wrath of Poseidon. Nonetheless, his courage, wits, and stability enable him to endure all his difficulties and arrive home safely.

Peisistratus

The gallant young son of Nestor. He is the companion of Telemachus on his journey through the Peloponnesus.

Penelope

The wife of Odysseus. She is obviously meant to be a paragon of marital fidelity, having waited twenty years for her husband to return. She is serious and industrious, a perfect wife and mother, but is lacking in the fascination and zest for life that the other women of the *Odyssey* possess.

Philoetius

The chief cowherd of Odysseus; he is brave and loyal and, despite his great age, he stands beside his master during the battle with the suitors.

Telemachus

The son of Odysseus. He is just entering manhood and is very self-conscious about his duty, which he is still not fully capable of handling, and his father's reputation as a hero, which he feels he must live up to. His behavior wavers between rash antagonizing of the suitors and brow-beating of his mother, carefully conceived courses of action like his trip to Sparta and Pylos, complete indifference to goings on around him, and shamelessly pathetic appeals to others for aid. It is not until the close of the book that he shows great courage and steadiness; then, one begins to feel that he is, indeed, the son of Odysseus.

Teiresias

The most famous of all Greek seers. The legend was that in compensation for his blindness the gods gave him awesome visionary powers. His spirit is consulted by Odysseus in Hades, where he warns the hero of the dangers still awaiting him and predicts his ultimate success and happy life.

Argus

The old hunting dog of Odysseus who recognizes his master and dies.

GODS AND SUPERNATURAL BEINGS

Aeolus

A mortal whom Zeus has appointed keeper of the winds. He lives on a mysterious floating island in the western ocean with his wife and twelve sons and daughters.

Athena

(Latin: Minerva) Daughter of Zeus, goddess of wisdom and patroness of the arts and crafts, also known as Pallas. Odysseus is her favorite and protegé. Although a goddess, she, more than any other female characters in the *Odyssey,* is its heroine.

Calypso

The sea nymph who keeps Odysseus captive for nine years, hoping to make him her husband.

Circe

The enchantress who transforms the crew of Odysseus into swine and who, when she finds that she cannot conquer Odysseus himself, takes him as a lover and helps him with advice and supplies on his voyage home.

Hermes

(Latin: Mercury) Son of Zeus, ambassador of the gods, conductor of dead souls to Hades and patron of travelers, merchants, and thieves.

Hyperion

(Also known as Helios) The god of the sun. He travels through the skies each day in a fiery chariot and observes all that takes place on earth. On an island in the western ocean, he keeps several herds of sheep and cattle which are sacred to him; Odysseus and his men land on this island and are punished for the misdeeds they perpetrate there.

Polyphemus

A one-eyed giant (a Cyclops) who holds Odysseus and his men captive in his cave until he's made drunk and is blinded by Odysseus.

Poseidon

(Latin: Neptune) Younger brother of Zeus, god of the sea and of earthquakes, father of Polyphemus. Because Odysseus is a sailor and must travel home by ship, Poseidon is able to do him much harm. The god bears a grudge against him because of his rough treatment of Polyphemus; however, Poseidon is unable to hold out against the combined pressure of the other gods, of whom Odysseus is a favorite, and so he eventually relents.

Scylla

A sea monster with six heads whom Odysseus and his crew must pass during their voyage. Scholars have conjectured that this tale is the result of distorted reports by sailors of giant octopi or squids.

Zeus

(Latin: Jupiter) The supreme god and king of Olympus. He is officially neutral in human affairs; his duty is to carry out the will of Destiny, but he is often sympathetic toward humans. It is he who makes it possible for Odysseus to be aided by Athena, and he ends the civil war with one of his thunderbolts.

Ω

THE *ODYSSEY*

BOOK 1
ATHENA ADVISES TELEMACHUS

The *Odyssey* opens with Homer's invocation to the muse of poetry, in which he states the subject of the epic and asks for her guidance in telling his story properly. It is, he says, the tale of a lonely man who wandered the world for many years and suffered many hardships before returning home.

When the story proper begins, all the survivors of the Trojan War have safely reached their homes, with the exception of Odysseus. He is detained by the nymph Calypso, who hopes to make him her husband. While most of the gods are sympathetic to Odysseus, Poseidon, ruler of the sea, bears him a grudge and makes him undergo many torments.

In the absence of Poseidon, Zeus, king of the gods, calls a divine council on Mount Olympus. After his introductory speech about the punishment of Aegisthus, Agamemnon's murderer, Athena interrupts her father. She reminds him of poor Odysseus, separated from family and loved ones on the island of Ogygia, and demands that the gods resume their support of him. She points out that, while Poseidon is bitter because Odysseus has blinded one of his sons, the other gods can force him to submit. She suggests that Hermes hasten to Calypso and order her to free Odysseus. Meanwhile, Athena will disguise herself and visit Telemachus, Odysseus' son. Zeus and the other gods agree to her proposal.

Athena outfits herself as a warrior and goes at once to Ithaca, Odysseus' home. There she finds the hero's house overrun by a horde of petty princes and young noblemen who are ostensibly courting his wife, but who, at the same time, waste Odysseus' property in constant banquets and feasting.

Telemachus welcomes Athena, who is disguised as Mentes, a Taphian chieftain and an old friend of Odysseus. The two sit down to dinner, and the young man apologizes for the suitors' crude behavior. He requests news of his father. Athena reassures Telemachus that Odysseus is alive somewhere and that he will eventually return home to recognize his son and punish the suitors. Telemachus describes the problems caused by his father's absence and explains how Penelope, his mother, has refused to remarry. Athena recommends

that Telemachus call a meeting of the assembly at which he can give
the suitors notice to leave his house and at the same time announce
his intention of seeking news of Odysseus. Then, the goddess advises,
he should sail for Pylos and Sparta to learn what he can from Nestor
and Menelaus. Furthermore, Athena points out, if Odysseus is dead,
it is time for Telemachus to face his responsibilities by claiming his
inheritance, having his mother select a new husband, and evicting
the suitors. The goddess leaves, the two parting as friends.

Meanwhile, at the suitors' banquet, a bard sings of the Achaians'
adventures at Troy. Penelope appears and is upset at this reminder
of the long absent Odysseus, but Telemachus orders her to leave the
hall, where the entertainment is suited to hardy men, not sensitive
women. The suitors attempt to question the youth about his recent
guest. He announces that he will call an assembly the next morning.
In addition he discloses his planned voyage in quest of information
and his intended punishment of them all. They are surprised at his
sudden assertion of manliness, but continue with their wasteful feasting. Telemachus goes to bed and dreams of his impending journey.

BOOK 2
THE ASSEMBLY OF ITHACA MEETS

In the morning, Telemachus dresses, grooms himself carefully,
and orders the heralds to call the men of Ithaca to the assembly. At
the meeting, Aegyptius, one of the old chieftains, expresses his
pleasure that a meeting has been convened after such a long lapse,
for this is the first session of the assembly since Odysseus and the
army sailed for Troy nineteen years before.

Telemachus takes the speaker's staff and declares that he has
called the meeting not to proclaim any matter of civic danger or
necessity, but to denounce the scoundrels who are wasting his father's
wealth on the pretext of courting his mother. He points out that if
Odysseus were present he would oust them. In addition, Telemachus
declares that he would oust them himself if he were powerful enough.
The gathered assembly is silent in shame and pity for a few moments.
Antinous, one of the most insolent of the suitors, breaks the silence
to denounce Telemachus. Antinous arrogantly denies all guilt and
places the blame on Penelope, who, he asserts, has misled the suitors
while refusing to choose one of them, thus preventing them from
selecting other wives.

Telemachus repeats his threats against the suitors. Zeus causes two eagles to appear in the sky as signs of the god's approval. Halisthernes, the soothsayer, reminds the assembly that he predicted these events, including Odysseus' return within the coming year. He insists that his past prophecies have proved true and sternly warns them to take heed. Eurymachus, another suitor, accuses the old seer of accepting bribes from Telemachus and belittles his prophecies. He adds that the suitors will not leave until Penelope agrees to marry one of them. Telemachus then proposes that he be given a ship and crew so that he can seek news of Odysseus. He asserts that if his father is really dead, he will conduct a funeral ceremony; he guarantees that his mother will choose another husband. However, if his father is alive, Telemachus will submit to no more than one more year of the suitors' profligacy. An old friend of Odysseus, Mentor, praises the young man's wisdom, but the suitors harangue him and the assembly disperses without further action.

At the seashore, Telemachus prays to Athena for help. Disguised as Mentor she appears to him and together they plan to secure a ship despite the suitors' opposition. Telemachus returns home, where he argues with Antinous. The suitors mock Telemachus and his hopes. The youth tells his old nurse, Eurycleia, of his plans, and with her aid he secretly removes supplies for the trip from the storerooms. He orders her to keep knowledge of the journey from Penelope as long as possible so that she will not worry about him.

At the same time, Athena, disguised as Telemachus, roams the town, organizing a crew of twenty young men and procuring a ship. Again changing into Mentor's shape, the goddess joins Telemachus, and they, with the crew, load the ship. As night falls they set sail on the first leg of the voyage to Pylos.

BOOK 3
TELEMACHUS AND NESTOR

When Telemachus, accompanied by Athena in the guise of Mentor, reaches Pylos, he finds King Nestor with his sons and retainers on the beach, offering nine bulls in sacrifice to Poseidon. Nestor graciously receives the pair and invites them to partake of the ritual dinner.

After eating, the two identify themselves, and Telemachus explains the nature of his mission. Nestor, in his usual verbose fashion, describes the last days of the Trojan expedition. After the city fell, he says, a dispute arose between Agamemnon, the commander, and his brother, Menelaus. The army divided into two factions and sailed for home. Odysseus had put out from Troy with Nestor, along with Diomedes and others, but another quarrel took place at Tenedos, and Odysseus left this squadron to rejoin Agamemnon. This was the last time that Nestor saw Odysseus, although since then he had heard that he had not yet returned to Ithaca. The aged chieftain rambles on to tell of other heroes' homecomings, of Aegisthus' murder of Agamemnon, and of Orestes' vengence. He recounts the wanderings of Menelaus, whom a storm blew to Egypt, and who had only recently returned to his kingdom, after many adventures and with much newly acquired wealth. Nestor suggests that Telemachus consult Menelaus since he may have more recent information. Telemachus and Mentor agree that this is a wise suggestion. After further conversation, Nestor invites the young man to spend the night in his palace. Telemachus does so.

In the morning, they sacrifice to Athena. Then Nestor supplies Telemachus with a chariot so that he can travel to Sparta to speak with Menelaus. Accompanied by Peisistratus, Nestor's youngest son, Telemachus continues on his quest for news of his father.

BOOK 4
TELEMACHUS AND MENELAUS

When Telemachus and Peisistratus arrive at Menelaus' palace, they find a great feast in progress, celebrating the impending weddings of the king's son and daughter. Telemachus and Peisistratus receive a warm welcome, and after bathing and putting on fresh clothing, they take seats of honor in the banquet hall.

Proper etiquette does not permit a guest to be questioned before he has dined, so Menelaus does not yet know the identity of his visitors. In the course of conversation he refers several times to his old and dear friend Odysseus, and upon hearing this, Telemachus begins to weep. Queen Helen joins the group and immediately comments on the resemblance between the son and father. Peisistratus identifies his companion and himself, and explains their mission. Menelaus decides that it would not be appropriate to discuss Telemachus' business until the morning, since so many present at the feast have sad memories of the Trojan War. He and Helen recount a few of Odysseus' more brilliant exploits at the siege and then all retire.

The next day Menelaus and Telemachus have a private meeting. Telemachus explains the situation at Ithaca and his desire for knowledge of his father. Menelaus deplores the suitors' crudeness and greed. He tells Telemachus of his adventures in Egypt after the end of the war. During the course of his travels he encountered Proteus, the Old Man of the Sea, from whom he extracted information. After he had learned how he could return safely to Sparta, he inquired about his former comrades. Proteus told him the names of those who had safely reached home and those who had died; he also described Agamemnon's murder and mentioned that Odysseus was alive, but was detained on the distant island of the nymph Calypso. Telemachus thanks the king for his aid and prepares to leave, but before he goes, Menelaus gives him many valuable gifts.

Meanwhile, on Ithaca, the suitors discover that Telemachus has already sailed, despite their efforts to prevent the voyage. Led by Antinous and Eurymachus, they prepare a ship of their own and plot to ambush and kill the young prince in the straits leading to the island. Penelope also was ignorant of the expedition, and when Medon, her faithful herald, tells her of it, she is immediately overcome by grief and worry. Her servants attempt to comfort her, but with little success, and the queen remains locked in her room, crying and refusing to eat. That night Athena sends a dream in which Penelope's sister appears to her and reassures her that Telemachus is safe.

BOOK 5
ODYSSEUS DEPARTS FROM CALYPSO

At the divine assembly on Olympus, Athena once more raises the question of returning Odysseus to his home. Zeus finally agrees and dispatches Hermes, his messenger, to the far-off island of Ogygia where the nymph Calypso detains Odysseus, in the hope of making him her husband.

When he arrives, Hermes finds Odysseus sitting on a bench, yearning for his family and weeping. The god delivers his message to Calypso who, though bitter, consents to let Odysseus leave, because she knows she cannot defy Zeus. After Hermes goes back to Olympus, she tells Odysseus that she will help him return to Ithaca. The hero is understandably suspicious of the nymph's motives, but she eventually reassures him. With her aid, he builds himself a small boat and outfits it with all the necessary gear and provisions. When the work is completed, he eagerly sets sail for home.

Meanwhile, Poseidon, returning from Ethiopia, sees Odysseus sailing away. He raises his trident in anger and stirs up a savage storm. Amid the rain, wind, and waves of the tempest, Odysseus' small boat capsizes and breaks up, and Odysseus flounders in the raging sea, clinging to a bit of the wreckage, struggling to keep afloat. With the aid of Athena and a sea nymph, however, he manages, despite great danger and suffering, to reach land on the island of Scheria, the home of the Phaeacians. The exhausted hero staggers ashore and takes shelter among some olive bushes, where he immediately falls asleep.

BOOKS 6–8
ODYSSEUS AMONG THE PHAEACIANS

The next morning, while picnicking and doing the palace laundry near the river, Princess Nausicaa and her handmaidens discover the exhausted, ragged survivor where he washed ashore. They feed and clothe him and direct him to the city. Odysseus goes to the palace of King Alcinous and Queen Arete, where he is received with great kindness and generosity. The royal couple promise to help him make his way to Ithaca. A day or so later, at a banquet of the Phaeacian nobility, Odysseus reveals his true identity and tells the story of his adventures during the nine years after the fall of Troy.

The land of Phaeacia, where Odysseus now finds himself, is a utopian, fairy-tale place where life is easy and the people prosperous, wise, virtuous, and happy. Alcinous and Arete are portraits of the ideal rulers. Their kingdom is a human paradise.

The story of Odysseus' appearance in the king's palace as a helpless suppliant, his acceptance at the royal court, restoration to his true status and identity, and hints of Nausicaa's love for the unknown older man have many parallels in Celtic and Oriental folklore. The tale is similar to some of the stories in the *Arabian Nights* and to parts of old ballads from Ireland and Britain. Within the framework of the *Odyssey*, the visit to Phaeacia, the paradise where all human problems are solved and all needs are fulfilled, can be interpreted as an inspired vision, granted Odysseus after his purification and transformation.

Critics praise Homer's characterization of Nausicaa, one of his most popular and delightful creations. Samuel Butler, the Victorian author and translator of Homer, once attempted to prove that Nausicaa was the real writer of the *Odyssey*. From this idea Robert Graves developed an intriguing novel entitled *Homer's Daughter*.

BOOK 9
THE WANDERINGS OF ODYSSEUS – THE CICONES, THE LOTUS-EATERS, AND THE CYCLOPS

Odysseus identifies himself to the eager audience and begins his story. After leaving Troy, he and his men raided the land of the Cicones. Despite initial success, they were ultimately defeated and escaped after suffering numerous casualties. The ships sailed on, battling a severe storm, until they reached the country of the Lotus-Eaters. The inhabitants of this strange land were friendly, but the seamen who ate lotus, a local plant, forgot home and duty. Odysseus and the men who had not been exposed to the lotus were hard-pressed to rescue those affected by the narcotic.

Sailing farther westward, they eventually came to the island of the Cyclopes, a wild race of one-eyed giants. Leaving most of his men in a sheltered cove, Odysseus, with only one ship, landed on the island and went ashore with a party of twelve comrades.

The group wandered until they came across a huge cave, outfitted with a shepherd's equipment, and went inside to await the owner. After a while, a huge Cyclops named Polyphemus returned to the cave, driving his flocks before him. When he had secured the animals in their pens, he pushed a gigantic stone in front of the cave. Polyphemus discovered the Achaians in his den and immediately devoured two of them, sarcastically promising to eat the others later. Despite the men's appeal to Zeus' mercy, the savage giant defied the gods. In the morning, after gobbling two more men, he drove his flocks to the fields and locked the survivors in the cave by replacing the vast stone at the entrance.

Odysseus and his men realized that even if they were able to kill the giant as he slept, they would achieve nothing, since they would not be able to move the barrier at the cave mouth. However, the shrewd captain devised a plan to free them. First, they sharpened and hid a long olive pole. When Polyphemus returned that evening, Odysseus plied him with wine until the Cyclops fell into a drunken sleep. Before the giant passed out, he insisted upon knowing Odysseus' name. The wily Achaian answered, "Noman."

As Polyphemus slept, Odysseus and his men stabbed him in his only eye and blinded him. The giant screamed with rage and pain but could not locate his assailants. His cries attracted the other Cyclopes, but when he told them that "Noman" was responsible for his wound, they assumed that one of the gods was involved and chose not to interfere.

In the morning, the Cyclops reopened the cave to allow his sheep to graze. Although he tried to prevent anyone from escaping by feeling everything that passed through the entrance, Odysseus and his men got out by clinging to the bellies of the sheep.

Upon reaching their ship again, the Achaians set sail at once in great terror. Every member of the crew rowed furiously. While still near the island, Odysseus foolishly shouted to the Cyclops, bragging about his exploit. The giant frantically hurled great boulders in the direction of the sounds, but fortunately all missed the target. Carried away by pride, Odysseus unwisely announced his identity to the pain-stricken giant. As the ship passed out of range of his stones, Polyphemus called upon his father, Poseidon, to punish the man who had tricked him.

BOOK 10
THE WANDERINGS OF ODYSSEUS –
AEOLUS, THE LAESTRYGONIANS, AND CIRCE

After more days of sailing, Odysseus and his men landed on the island of Aeolus, the king of the winds, who greeted the seafarers warmly and entertained them in the royal palace. Upon their departure, Aeolus gave Odysseus a gift: a large leather bag containing all the adverse winds which could drive his ships off course. They set sail again and in ten days were within sight of Ithaca.

While Odysseus slept, his crew began muttering and dissension quickly spread through the ship. The jealous men assumed that the bag from Aeolus contained valuable treasures and were resentful that their captain had not shared with them. Finally, curiosity overwhelmed them and they ripped open the bag, setting all the winds free. A great gale arose and blew the ships far from Ithaca, back to Aeolia. Although Odysseus asked for forgiveness and help, Aeolus refused and, cursing him as a sinner and enemy of the gods, banished the hero from his island. The wanderers set sail again without the benefit of wind, so the crews had to strain at their oars. Several days later the ships landed on the island of the Laestrygonians. These vicious cannibals attacked the unsuspecting sailors, and all the ships, except that of Odysseus, were sunk. The survivors, mourning their dead comrades, sailed on until they reached the island of Aeaea, the home of the goddess Circe.

After camping on the beach for a few days, Odysseus sent half his men under the command of Eurylochus to explore this seemingly uninhabited island. Shortly afterward, Eurylochus returned alone, telling a strange tale. A strange and beautiful woman lured the men into a lavish villa in the center of the isle. After she fed and entertained them, she waved a wand and transformed them into swine. She and her servants locked them in a pen where they were now wallowing in the mud. Because of his suspicious nature, he alone stayed outside the palace and escaped.

This weird story terrified the remaining men, but Odysseus was resolute and set out alone to rescue the victims. On the way he encountered Hermes, in the guise of a young nobleman, who instructed him on how to circumvent the enchantress. He gave Odysseus a wondrous magic herb called Moly with which to protect himself.

On his arrival, Circe received Odysseus graciously and then attempted to bewitch him, but all her spells failed. He soon overcame her, and when he threatened her life, she returned his men to human form. Because of these events, Circe recognized Odysseus as someone whose eventual arrival had been predicted and whose acquaintance she eagerly anticipated. The two became lovers, and he and his crew stayed at her home for nearly a year.

The Achaians again began to yearn for Ithaca. Odysseus held Circe to an old promise to help him return home; she agreed. However, she pointed out to him that, in order to have a safe voyage, he must go to Hades, the land of the dead, to consult the spirit of the prophet Teiresias. She gave Odysseus directions for his journey to the end of the world and provided him with provisions and the necessary animals for sacrifice. And so Odysseus and his travel-worn men set sail once more.

BOOK 11
THE WANDERINGS OF ODYSSEUS –
THE DESCENT INTO HADES

Following Circe's instructions, Odysseus sailed to the very edge of the world. Here he and his men made libations to the dead out of milk, honey, wine, and water. Odysseus offered prayers and sacrificed a ram and a black ewe, pouring their blood into a trench. At once, hordes of dead souls, attracted by the odor of fresh blood, began to rush out of Hades. Odysseus held off the throng with his sword, awaiting Teiresias.

The blind seer finally arrived and after drinking some of the blood, advised Odysseus about his return home. He warned the hero of the various dangers that still awaited him on his journey and how he would finally arrive at Ithaca, unknown and friendless. After further difficulties, he would re-establish himself as master of his house, but his wanderings would not end until he was able to regain Poseidon's favor. Achieving this, Odysseus would live out a long and peaceful life.

When Teiresias had departed, Odysseus conversed with many other dead souls, who were eager for news of their friends and family who still lived. He spoke to Anticleia, his mother, who had died of grief after he left for Troy, Agamemnon, Achilles, and Elpenor, a member of his crew who had died on Circe's island. He also met Tantalus, Sisyphus, Hercules, Phaedra, Ariadne, Jocasta, and other great men and women of the past. Finally the sight of so many wraiths grew unbearable, and Odysseus fled to his ship. With sighs of relief, his men made for the open sea again.

BOOK 12
THE WANDERINGS OF ODYSSEUS –
THE SIRENS, SCYLLA AND CHARYBDIS,
AND THE CATTLE OF THE SUN

Odysseus and his men returned to Aeaea to bury Elpenor, in fulfillment of the poor sailor's last request. Circe again provided them with supplies for their journey and gave Odysseus further detailed instructions about the hazards of the next leg of the voyage. With its crew confident and in high spirits, the ship sets sail once more.

First they had to pass the island of the Sirens. These irresistible women attracted unwary mariners with their beautiful songs and lured them onto the reefs surrounding their island, where many ships had wrecked. Odysseus plugged the crew's ears with wax so that they were immune to the tantalizing music. Since he wished to hear the song, however, he had himself lashed to the mast. When the voices of the Sirens became audible he unsuccessfully strained to escape the bonds, but as he struggled, the ship passed the Sirens unharmed.

They then came upon the twofold horror of Scylla and Charybdis. Scylla was a ferocious monster with six heads who sat upon a cliff and devoured passing seamen. Across a narrow strait was Charybdis, a fierce whirlpool. To pass between both unscathed was impossible. They safely steered the ship around the whirlpool, but though Odysseus attempted to fight, Scylla grabbed six unlucky crewmen.

Shortly after this costly and perilous passage, the ship landed on the island where Hyperion, the sun god, kept his cattle and remained there for a month. Despite warnings of Teiresias and Circe, Odysseus was unable to control his men. Led by Eurylochus, they slaughtered some of the divine cattle for a meal, thereby incurring the gods' wrath. When they sailed from the island, a storm arose and one of Zeus' thunderbolts destroyed the ship, killing the entire crew. Odysseus was thrown overboard and narrowly escaped drowning in Charybdis as he was driven back through the strait. After nine days of aimless drifting in the raging sea, he washed ashore on Ogygia, the home of Calypso. Here Odysseus ends his story to the Phaeacians, since he has already told of his seven years stay with the nymph and his eventual escape.

BOOKS 13–16
ODYSSEUS RETURNS TO ITHACA

The generous Phaeacians give Odysseus many valuable gifts and transport him to Ithaca in one of their magic ships. Afterward, Poseidon punishes them for their kindness to his enemy. Meanwhile, Athena meets Odysseus on the beach. She disguises him as an aged beggar so he can wander freely on the island, reconnoiter the situation, and make his plans without being recognized.

After leaving Athena, Odysseus goes into the hills to the farm of Eumaeus the swineherd, one of his few loyal servants, where he receives welcome and courteous treatment, despite his disguise. Shortly afterward Telemachus returns to Ithaca from Sparta and also goes to the farm. While Eumaeus is away on an errand, Odysseus reveals his identity to his son, and they begin to lay their plans. They decide to keep Odysseus' return a secret, even from Penelope and Laertes. Telemachus will go back to the palace as if nothing had happened. Odysseus will follow, still in disguise. At the opportune moment, they will take vengeance on the suitors.

BOOK 17
ODYSSEUS GOES INTO THE TOWN

In the morning, Telemachus returns to town and visits his mother. Penelope is overjoyed that Telemachus has returned home safely. She listens eagerly to his report of his hospitable welcome by Nestor and Menelaus and of the rumor that Odysseus might still be alive on Calypso's island. Telemachus introduces his mother to the fugitive Theoclymenus, who claims to be a soothsayer and asserts that Odysseus, in disguise, is already somewhere on Ithaca and will soon avenge himself on the suitors. Penelope does not believe this tale, although she longs for proof that Odysseus is still alive.

Shortly afterward, Eumaeus and Odysseus also set out for the palace. On the way they encounter Melanthius, the chief goatherd. This wicked, disloyal servant of the royal house has betrayed his master by appeasing the suitors. When he sees the old beggar, he insults him cruelly and, without provocation, kicks him. Odysseus' hot temper is aroused, but he has a role to play and controls his anger. Eumaeus defends him from further harm.

At the palace gate, the two men discover an old, toothless dog lying uncared for in a pile of dung. Eumaeus explains that this is Argus, once Odysseus' favorite hound, who is now sick and near death. His master has been gone for nineteen years and everyone ignores the helpless animal. At the sight of Odysseus, the old dog lifts his head and whimpers, then dies. Unseen by Eumaeus, a tear trickles down Odysseus' cheek.

The two enter the palace, where the suitors are at their banquet tables. Telemachus provides Odysseus with a place to sit and some food, and gives him permission to beg from guests. Everyone contributes except Antinous, their leader, who reviles Odysseus and hits him with a footstool. Odysseus curses Antinous, and even some of the suitors are aroused by this needless savagery. Odysseus and Telemachus silently swear their revenge.

Penelope asks Eumaeus about the stranger and suggests that he be brought to her to tell his story and offer any news he may have of her husband. Odysseus agrees to see her that night.

BOOK 18
THE FIGHT BETWEEN ODYSSEUS AND IRUS;
THE SUITORS TORMENT ODYSSEUS

That afternoon, as the suitors exercise in the courtyard, Irus, a well-liked beggar, arrives at the palace. This vagabond is a big, portly man and quite a braggart. He immediately begins to bully Odysseus, to the amusement of the onlookers. He threatens to thrash the old man unless he leaves Ithaca at once, for Ithaca is Irus' private province for begging and he tolerates no competition. Odysseus retorts angrily, and the suitors, led by Antinous, arrange a boxing match between the two vagrants, with mock awards for the victor. Irus struts about, playing the hero and boasting about how he will win, but when the combatants undress, everyone is amazed at Odysseus' muscular body. The cowardly Irus avoids the fight, but Antinous forces him to face Odysseus. Though Odysseus tries to pull his punches, he breaks the bully's jaw. The suitors congratulate Odysseus, award him prizes, and return to the hall for dinner. Odysseus tries to warn Amphinomous, the kindest of them, of the impending danger to the suitors, but the young man pays him no heed.

Penelope appears before the suitors, her careful grooming and beauty enhanced by Athena. The lovely queen evokes the admiration of all who see her. She expresses her indignation at the fight between the beggars and chides the suitors for continuing to exhaust the resources of her husband's estate. She shames the noblemen, who send their servants to their homes and ships to bring gifts for the queen.

At dinner that evening Odysseus rebukes the disloyalty of Melantho, one of the palace maidservants, who has become the mistress of Eurymachus. His jibes drive her and the other serving girls from the hall. He and Eurymachus engage in an argument, and the young man throws a stool at Odysseus. Odysseus ducks; one of the stewards is hit. Everyone present grows excited, and in the uproar Telemachus suggests that they all go home for the night in order to calm down. Despite their surprise at Telemachus' audacity, the suitors do so.

BOOK 19
PENELOPE MEETS ODYSSEUS
DISGUISED AS A BEGGAR;
EURYCLEIA RECOGNIZES ODYSSEUS

After the suitors leave, Odysseus and Telemachus clear the hall and remove all the weapons that are stored there. They hide the arms in another part of the palace under lock and key. When they have completed this task, Odysseus sends Telemachus to bed. Penelope and her maids come down to the hall to clean it. Melantho and Odysseus again quarrel, and the queen severely scolds the insolent girl.

As the servants work, Penelope and Odysseus converse. She tells him about her husband's long absence and of the continued ordeal she faces in dealing with the suitors. The queen explains how she has tried to put the suitors off by every means at her disposal, including tricks, lies, and excuses about her son being too young for her to remarry. Now, however, Telemachus is a grown man and she will soon be forced to choose. Odysseus is deeply touched by this story and strives hard to remain silent. Penelope asks Odysseus about himself. The wily hero invents a tale, involving many hardships, in which he claims to have been acquainted with her husband. The authentic information about Odysseus which he provides moves the queen, as does the beggar's statement that Odysseus is still alive and on his way home. Penelope must supervise her servants at their work, but before she leaves, she asks one of her maids to bathe the old man's tired and worn feet.

Eurycleia, Odysseus' aged nurse, washes him; suddenly she spies an old scar on his leg and recognizes her master. She is about to tell the queen when Odysseus sternly warns her that his identity, for the time being, must be kept secret from everyone. The old woman agrees to remain silent.

Penelope returns to tell Odysseus that she has decided on a method to satisfy the suitors. There will be a contest in which they will be asked to duplicate one of her husband's most famous feats. Using Odysseus' bow, they will be required to shoot an arrow through a straight row of twelve axes. She will marry the winner. The beggar agrees that this is a good idea and predicts that Odysseus will return home before any of the suitors is able to string his bow, but Penelope does not understand the import of his remark. While Odysseus prepares a bed for himself on the floor of the deserted hall, Penelope

returns to her room. There she is overcome by the memory of her
lost husband and weeps into the night, until Athena helps her fall
asleep.

BOOK 20
ODYSSEUS LAYS HIS PLANS;
THE SUITORS IGNORE THEIR FINAL WARNING

During the night Odysseus tosses and turns, worrying about the
outcome of his encounter with the suitors. Athena appears to him,
however, and promises that he will have her aid in the struggle, a
guarantee of success. Penelope also is unable to sleep and prays to
Artemis, begging that she be rescued from marriage to another man,
even if it means her death.

In the morning Odysseus appeals to Zeus for a sign of his favor
and is answered by the ominous rumbling of thunder. Others notice
the omen, and a general mood of foreboding sets in. Odysseus continues to observe the behavior of his servants to identify the faithful.
Melanthius arrives with goats for the day's banquet and persists in
baiting Odysseus. Eumaeus comes to the palace, driving hogs for
slaughter, and again demonstrates his goodness; another loyal servant,
Philoetius, the chief cowherd, arrives from the mainland.

The suitors, again plotting to assassinate Telemachus, eventually
return to the palace. As they lunch, Ctesippus insults Odysseus and
hurls a bone at him. Telemachus is outraged and delivers a long tirade
to the suitors in which he enumerates their vices and misdeeds. His
unexpected boldness shocks the group, but their minds are befuddled
with drink and they merely laugh at his warnings. The soothsayer,
Theoclymenus, cautions them that a catastrophe is impending in
which they will suffer for their evil ways, but they are beyond re-
forming and mock the poor man until he leaves the palace in a rage.
The suitors continue to drink and carouse, but Telemachus stays alert,
waiting for his father's signal.

BOOK 21
THE CONTEST TO STRING THE BOW OF ODYSSEUS

Penelope brings Odysseus' great bow into the hall and announces
the contest to the suitors. The contestant who is able to string the
bow and shoot an arrow through the twelve axes will become her

husband. The suitors accept the challenge; Antinous derides the faithful swineherd and cowherd, who are visibly upset by the reminder that their master is dead. Telemachus digs a trench and aligns the twelve axes. He attempts four times to string the bow, eager to see if he is yet as strong as his father. He would probably succeed on the last attempt, but Odysseus prevents him from completing it. While the suitors prepare themselves, Odysseus takes Eumaeus and Philoetius aside and quietly identifies himself to them. The two are overcome by emotion and quickly agree to carry out their master's orders.

The suitors each have an opportunity, but however they strain and attempt to soften the wood by greasing and heating it, not one is man enough to bend the bow. Finally, Antinous suggests that they postpone further efforts until the next day. At this point, Odysseus, who has been sitting alone in a corner, asks for a chance to try the bow. The suitors are indignant at his request and refuse him. Penelope, however, agrees, although she assures the group that if he wins she would not marry him. Telemachus orders his mother and her women to leave the hall and then sends the bow to Odysseus. Meanwhile, unseen by the suitors, Eumaeus and Philoetius lock the gates of the palace and the doors of the hall.

Odysseus takes the bow, pretending not to hear the suitors' abuse. Effortlessly he strings the weapon and expertly fits a bronze-headed arrow to it. Slowly and effortlessly, he lets fly the arrow and it swiftly passes through the row of axes. As the suitors sit stupefied, Telemachus takes his sword and spear and steps to his father's side.

BOOK 22
ODYSSEUS KILLS THE SUITORS

With a shout, Odysseus leaps to the threshhold of the hall and kills Antinous with his next arrow. The suitors are outraged and horrified, thinking that the old beggar has gone berserk. As they mill about in confusion, Odysseus announces who he is. Eurymachus tries to place the blame for their misdeeds on the dead Antinous and offers to make restitution for the goods they have consumed. Odysseus, however, has vowed to exterminate these criminals, and with his next arrow he kills Eurymachus. The suitors attempt to defend themselves with their swords, using tables and stools as shields, but they are unable to get close enough to Odysseus to do him harm. Meanwhile he continues shooting into their midst; each arrow eliminates another enemy.

Telemachus produces armor and spears for his father and the two loyal servants. When the arrows are exhausted, these four stand side by side and continue the battle. Melanthius steals weapons from the storeroom and arms several suitors, but Eumaeus and Philoetius capture and bind him. As the fight continues, the four comrades fight bravely and eventually slaughter the suitors. Odysseus spares only Phemius, the bard, and Medon, the herald.

The king summons Eurycleia. When she sees the bodies, she prepares to sing a hymn of triumph, but Odysseus reminds her that it is impious to rejoice over the dead. He has her identify the disloyal maidservants. These twelve women are brought to the hall as prisoners. When they arrive, Odysseus forces them to remove the corpses, and scrub the entire area. Afterward, the women are taken outside and hanged. The treacherous Melanthius is also executed and his body horribly mutilated. Then the scene of the battle is fumigated with sulphur and the faithful servants welcome Odysseus. He remembers all of them, despite his long absence, and breaks into tears when they embrace him.

BOOK 23
ODYSSEUS AND PENELOPE ARE REUNITED

Eurycleia runs upstairs and awakens her mistress, whom Athena has put to sleep, to inform her of Odysseus' return and his bloody retribution. Penelope does not believe the story, but goes to the banquet hall to see for herself. Odysseus is there, still dressed in rags, so covered with blood and gore that Penelope does not recognize him. Telemachus chides his mother, but Odysseus sends him away so that the two may converse privately. When the prince is gone, Odysseus mentions certain secrets which only he and Penelope know. He convinces Penelope that he is the husband for whom she had waited twenty long years, and the two embrace each other tenderly.

Odysseus bathes and dresses in his royal garments. After arranging for servants to keep up a pretense of dancing and feasting to allay the suspicions of any passers-by, he and Penelope retire to their room. The newly united couple spend the first night after their long separation making love and telling each other of their adventures. In order to give them more time alone, Athena delays the sunrise.

In the morning, Odysseus arms himself and, accompanied by Telemachus, Eumaeus, and Philoetius, sets out for his father's farm.

BOOK 24
ODYSSEUS VISITS HIS FATHER;
THE CIVIL WAR ON ITHACA IS ENDED BY THE GODS

In Hades, the shades of Achilles, Patroclus, Antilochus, Ajax, and Agamemnon are speaking with each other when Hermes arrives, leading the souls of the dead suitors. The heroes are surprised by this sudden influx of more than one hundred young men. Agamemnon inquires about the circumstances of their deaths. Amphimedon relates the story of the slaughter in Ithaca's royal hall. Agamemnon is greatly impressed by Odysseus' prowess and Penelope's fidelity.

In Ithaca, Odysseus arrives at Laertes' house and identifies himself to his aged father. The joy with which the old man greets his son is touching. The Ithacans learn of the slaughter at the palace and claim the bodies. At a meeting of the assembly, though Medon and Halisthernes advocate peace, a number of the citizens, led by Eupeithes, Antinous' father, decided to avenge their sons' deaths. This group takes arms and sets off for Laertes' farm.

On Olympus, Athena consults Zeus. The king of the gods agrees that Odysseus' revenge is justified and that peace should be restored to Ithaca. He gives his daughter a free hand to settle the matter.

When the angry kinsmen of the suitors arrive at the farm, Odysseus leads out his small party to meet them. Laertes kills Eupeithes with a spear; Odysseus, Telemachus, and their supporters kill others in the group. The attackers are fleeing in panic when Athena intervenes and orders an end to the conflict. Zeus' thunderbolt reinforces the sanctity of this command and the battle ends. Later, Athena, disguised as Mentor, establishes peace between the factions, and Odysseus resumes his reign as king.

For a more comprehensive, in-depth analysis of this work, consult Cliffs Notes on the *Odyssey*.

Ω

HESIOD

- *Works and Days*

- *Theogony*

- **Minor Works**

HESIOD

A probable contemporary of Homer and certainly a student of the *Iliad* and the *Odyssey,* Hesiod lived in Boeotia, east of the central part of Greece and north of Athens. Unlike Homer, Hesiod's background is clearly documented. He lived around 800–700 B.C. His father, a ship owner, who is thought to have been named Dius, fled a poverty-stricken existence in Cyme on the coast of Asia Minor after his investment schemes went awry. He settled in Ascra, an unprosperous village near Thespiae, and bought a farm.

Hesiod and his brother, Perses, were probably natives of Cyme, but quickly adapted to the rural, agrarian attitudes and customs of southern Boeotia. After their father's death, Perses sued his brother for a greater share of the inheritance and won his suit by bribing the nobles who judged the case. Hesiod dedicated his poem *Works and Days* to his idle, scheming brother in order to foster in him a respect for hard work, an appreciation of righteousness and order, and an acceptance of the uneven lot that all people share.

An Iron Age homebody and hard-headed farmer, Hesiod despised and distrusted the sea, venturing forth only once on a sea journey to Euripus, and turned from his father's profession in order to till the hard land and raise sheep. His poetry shows no inclination toward romanticizing nature; yet, his account of the Muses' visitation on a hillside of Mt. Helicon suggests a less-than-realistic view of how he became a poet. According to lines 22–23 of the *Theogony,* the Muses interrupted Hesiod's sheep-tending to teach him a "glorious song," which became the *Works and Days.*

Inspired by the songs of the wandering *rhapsodes,* Hesiod developed his poetic gift, composing a hymn which won him a tripod at the poetry competition of the funeral games in honor of Amphidamas in Chalcis. He aspired to recapture the spirit of the Mycenaean age, a nobler era before humans were cursed by an unyielding soil and an unpitying sky. According to legend, Hesiod was murdered and buried at Oenoë, where nymphs washed his body and goat-herds sprinkled offerings to Zeus.

His major works, *Works and Days* and *Theogony,* contrast markedly with the heroic style of the *Iliad* and the *Odyssey.* Whereas Homer sings of the fortunes of wartime, Hesiod dedicates himself to the sober, workaday world – to toil and the toiler. His pessimism and bitterness appear to spring from his own hard scrabble to earn a living. Like the worn, scarred hands of the working man, Hesiod's austere verse employs no refinement, no embellishments.

Unlike Homer, he makes no glittering promises of lasting fame, honor among men, and a resting place with the gods. Rather, he is compared to writers of the Old Testament: to David, a poet who kept his father's sheep; to Ecclesiasticus, who warns of coaxing women, loose morals, and sluggardly habits; and to the Hebrew prophets, who decry the degeneracy of their day and denounce the excesses of the rich who sit in judgment over the humble.

Although Hesiod uses dactylic hexameter, the standard metric pattern of Homer, he prefers a didactic or instructive tone. His major theme – that mankind is sinking irretrievably as a result of the gods' jealousy and connivance – turns the reader toward earlier times, before corruption tainted human goodness. Hesiod's rhythms reflect the work year of the farmer, who sets his eyes upon the heavens as a trustworthy guide for his daily schedule. He avoids ornamentation, following his own advice to "get a house and a woman and an ox for the plough, and have your tools all ready in the house." Like Franklin's Poor Richard, Hesiod urges the seeker of fortune to organize himself and keep up day by day.

The material of Hesiod's poetry reflects the tastes of a born collector and organizer. Hesiod steeped himself in the folklore, wisdom, and commonalities of his day and of earlier times; his language reflects the Ionian influence of his father's homeland. Hesiod's verse is the distillation of his own musings and conclusions, heavily laced with the fatalistic philosophy which results from a life of hard knocks and unpredictable turns of fortune, and the sincere faith of a deeply religious man. There is evidence that Hesiod was superstitious, but his strength lies in a ready pragmatism, a belief in thrift and husbandry rather than luck.

Hesiod is best remembered as the dean of the didactic poets, a rebel against the glory-seeking fictional verse of the epic writers, and the composer of the "authorized version" of mythology, from which later poets adapted their ideas, ethics, and religious opinions. Therefore, Hesiod played a notable role in the establishment of later Greek literature and theology. The son of a pioneer, Hesiod notes the uneven struggle between peasants and nobles. From personal experience, he speaks for and of the laboring class. He calls for justice, which eventually followed in the laws set forth by Draco and Solon. Possibly the greatest testimony to Hesiod's place among Greek writers is the prominence of his work in the school curricula of ancient Greece.

$$\Omega$$

WORKS AND DAYS

Lines 1–275

The opening lines form an extensive prelude which introduces the theme of fate. Hesiod declares that no human being can know what fate to expect, for Zeus "humbles the proud and raises the obscure." An allegorical passage, dedicated to Hesiod's brother, Perses, describes two types of human strife: the first, a wholesome competitiveness, and the second, a petty, wasteful quarrelsomeness, which Perses invokes against his brother. Hesiod blames the gods for instigating trouble among men by planting "sorrow and mischief" and by hiding fire, which Prometheus steals from heaven and brings to men.

In retaliation against human beings, Zeus assigns Hephaestus the creation of a sweetly seductive female named Pandora as a tempting snare for Epimetheus, whose name means "hindsight." Although Prometheus (foresight) warns his brother not to accept gifts from Zeus, Epimetheus accepts the gift. Pandora, whose name refers to the gifts that all the gods give to mankind, removes the lid from the jar of gifts. The loss of the gods' blessings leads to constant sorrow, "for earth is full of evils and the sea is also full." Even though Hope clings inside the rim of the jar, human beings are forever subject to the will of Zeus.

A second illustrative tale explains how human beings have gradually degenerated from their original state. In the time of the Titans, the gods created a golden race of mortals, who lived like gods, never suffered evil or fatigue, and died during peaceful sleep. After the demise of the first generation, the Olympian gods made a second race of silver, which was foolish and corrupted by petty evil. Because the second generation refused to serve Zeus, he destroyed them.

In their place, Zeus created a bronze race of strong, hard-hearted mortals, who destroyed themselves, descended to Hades, and left no record behind. Zeus then replaced the bronze race with a god-like race called demi-gods. These are the great warriors of Homer's tales who fight for Helen and battle against the seven gates of Thebes. Their reward is a "grain-giving earth" that bears "honey-sweet fruit." Cronus, released from captivity by his son, rules over this honorable and glorious generation.

The poet laments being a part of Zeus' fifth generation, the "race of iron," who never rest from their toils and who suffer constant earthly troubles. Hesiod predicts that Zeus will destroy this evil genera- tion when they begin to be born with gray hair. Their final days will be marked by disrespect between parent and child, sacrilege, lying, deceit, and violence. "Envy, foul-mouthed, delighting in evil, with scowling face, will go along with wretched men one and all." In their last hours, Aidôs (shame) and Nemesis (righteous indignation) will desert them and they will live out their days in anguish.

After a short fable about the nightingale that is held fast in the talons of the pitless hawk, Hesiod returns to Perses, dissuading him from violence and "crooked judgments." He warns that sinful people "perish away, and their women do not bear children, and their houses become few, through the contriving of Olympian Zeus." Hesiod adds a personal note to corrupt princes that judgment is at hand for peo- ple who take bribes and plot evil.

Lines 276–828

The second section contains a loosely organized list of suggestions for improving human life. Hesiod recommends a righteous life, gener- osity toward friends, and an avoidance of bad neighbors, enemies, and coaxing women. For the accumulation of wealth, he proposes a farm calendar based on the movements of constellations, and an avoidance of sea journeys, particularly during fall and early winter.

In a note to unmarried men he advises, "Let your wife have been grown up four years, and marry her in the fifth, . . . For a man wins nothing better than a good wife, and, again, nothing worse than a bad one, a greedy soul who roasts her man without fire, strong though he may be, and brings him to a raw old age."

The remaining passages include a series of injunctions against a variety of evils, such as undependable friends, a taunting tongue, improper worship procedures, and gossip. Hesiod concludes with a careful listing of lucky and unlucky days.

Ω

THEOGONY

Lines 1–452

After a miraculous meeting with the Muses on Mount Helicon, Hesiod, formerly a humble shepherd, accepts their challenge to tell the truth about the gods. With the assistance of a magic laurel branch, he sings of the union between Zeus and Mnemosyne (memory), which produces nine daughters: Clio, Euterpe, Thalia, Melpomene, Terpsichore, Erato, Urania, Polyhymnia, and Calliope, queen of epic poetry and the chief muse.

Beginning with a chronological listing of the gods, Hesiod describes how Chaos produces Erebus, Night, and Day; Earth, who lies with Heaven, brings forth the Hills, Pontus, Oceanus, Hyperion, Iapetus, Rhea, Phoebe, and finally, Cronus, the "wily, youngest and most terrible of her children." Earth urges her children to punish Heaven for his sinful acts. Only Cronus accepts her challenge. After he dismembers his father and throws his parts into the sea, Aphrodite is born from the foam.

Lines 453–1022

Cronus, too, begins to produce children with Rhea, including Hestia, Demeter, Hera, Hades, and Zeus. Because Cronus swallows each of his newborn children, Rhea plots to save the last child and gives Cronus a stone wrapped in baby clothes. Zeus is taken to a secret cave in Crete and reared by Earth, his grandfather. Cronus is later "beguiled by the deep suggestions of Earth" to disgorge the children he swallowed. Afterward Zeus frees his siblings from their treacherous father and is rewarded by his uncles with thunder and lightning, by which he "rules over mortals and immortals."

The genealogy continues with the story of Iapetus' family, famous for two strong sons, Atlas and Prometheus. The cataloguing of the immortals ends with Zeus' clash with the Titans, whom he drives from heaven. After a cosmic struggle, Zeus blesses the Olympian gods by awarding powers to each. Fearful of another threat to his throne, Zeus swallows Metis and gives birth from his own head to Pallas Athena, "arrayed in arms of war." Hesiod concludes with a farewell to the Olympian gods, whom the muses have assisted him in praising.

Ω

MINOR WORKS

Hesiod indicates his authorship of additional lines, including the *Divinition by Birds* at the end of the *Works and Days* and a possible third section entitled *Astronomy*, or *Astrology*. The *Theogony*, too, is followed by the *Catalogues of Women*, a series of genealogies of the Hellenic race from a single patriarch. Other poems attributed to Hesiod include the *Epithalamium of Peleus and Thetis*, the *Descent of Theseus into Hades*, the *Circuit of the Earth*, and some interpolated episodes, notably the *Shield of Heracles*, the *Suitors of Helen*, the *Daughters of Leucippus*, *Eoiae*, *Aegimius*, *Melampodia*, and the *Marriage of Ceyx*.

Ω

GREEK DRAMA

- **Origins**
- **The Theater**
- **Costumes**
- **Acting**
- **The Chorus**
- **Plot**
- **Structure**

GREEK DRAMA

_____ORIGINS

Greek drama has its roots in the Athenian seasonal festivals honoring Dionysus; the date usually assigned to this era is around 700 B.C. Dionysus was the god of wine, as well as the god of fertility, and not surprisingly, these festivals were filled with drunkenness and sexuality. Some scholars believe that the Greeks patterned their celebrations after traditional Egyptian pageants in honor of Osiris, whose death and resurrection resembles the life-cycle of the grapevine, the wine god's symbol, which is severely pruned at the end of the season, lies dormant, but sprouts into new life each spring.

Usually these four festivals were performed during the first weeks of seasonal changes, the times associated with planting, tending the vine, harvesting, and wine-making: the Festival of Vintage (Rural Dionysia) in late December, the Festival of the Winepress (Lenaea) in early February, the Festival of Tasting (Anthesteria) in early March, and the Great Festival of Celebration (City Dionysia) in early April. These were natural times of festivity when people felt like singing, praying for good crops, giving thanks, and making sacrifices for bountiful harvests.

The core element in these early festivals seems to have been revelry. Drunken men often dressed up in rough goat skins (goats being noted for their sexual potency), donned fake phalluses, symbols of fertility, and sang and cavorted in choruses to imitate the capering of goats. A company of revelers welcomed Dionysus, whose entrance on an ornate float decked with vines commemorated the god's arrival from the sea. The goatlike frolicking of the local participants set the tone for the remainder of the festival. (The word "tragedy" literally means "goat song," from the Greek *tragos* and *ode.*)

As "goats," these Pan-like creatures, dressed like Dionysus' companions, would boast and bray about their potency, singing hymns to the glory of Dionysus. Fertility was important for good crops and the perpetuation of small city-states. To add to the atmosphere of abundance, tradesmen sold honey and almond cakes, flat bread, chestnuts, chickpeas, and broadbeans from roadside stands. Wine, the focus of the festival, flowed freely. Filmmakers have relished in depicting these colorful and lusty, wine-soaked orgies, but from all evidence, their films are pale imitations of the original excesses.

Despite the fact that there was much drinking and an abundance of raucous horseplay, however, there was also a serious and sacred dimension to these early, mystical, sacrificial dramas. The early choruses of fifty men, dancing in a circle, which was at first an earthen threshing floor and later a permanent alter of Dionysus, sang not only of fertility, but of the sorrow that comes with winter, the pruning of the grapevine, and death. They also sang of spring, the appearance of green shoots on the vine, and rebirth. Worshipping Dionysus, similar to the Christian observance of Lent and Easter, served as a kind of wish for immortality through the continuous cycles of birth and death and rebirth, the triumph of life over death.

The songs, which commemorated events in which Dionysus played a major role, were hymns – choral hymns, which took the form of chants, songs, paeans, and poems; they are usually referred to as dithyrambs. They began as extemporaneous devisings, but were replaced by traditional lines suited to the occasion. Eventually, a choral leader evolved; he recited lines alone and awaited an answer from the chorus. This theatrical development was the first dialogue. Later, an actor – separate from the chorus and the leader of the chorus – was added.

Around 534 B.C., ten years or so before Aeschylus' birth, Thespis, an Athenian from the borough of Icaria, traveled from village to village and organized local celebrations throughout Attica. He is usually credited with the introduction of the first actor, although some scholars insist that his successor, Phrynichus, deserves the credit. A character in the modern sense, the actor conversed with the chorus leader and with the chorus itself. In fact, he could take on several roles at different times during the intervals of choral singing. These early "dramas" soon became the first tragedies – for they focused on human matters; they were not merely songs or hymns to Dionysus.

According to Plutarch, the aging Solon disapproved of Thespis' diversions, which he considered "lies." However, his successor, Pisistratus, tyrant of Athens, declared a new festival, featuring "tragedies," elevating them in importance to the status of athletic contests. He assigned the festival a permanent home, on a steep slope south of the Street of Tripods, where the Theater of Dionysus was consecrated. There is some reason to believe that it was Aeschylus who first wrote tragedy in the sense that the word is used today, with emphasis on content rather than on lyric or stylistic matters. The production of tragedy reached a great height of literary artistry under Aeschylus' successors, Euripides and Sophocles, giving Greece its "Golden Age."

It was during the fifth century B.C. that tragedy matured. Its technique was improved with the addition of more actors and a greater complexity of plot and theme until it evolved into the sophisticated literary form seen in the plays of Sophocles, near the end of the fifth century B.C. Thus, five hundred years before Christ, people congregated in amphitheaters to see dramas which were specifically written to be performed. The drunken spontaneity was gone, relegated to short, bawdy "satyr" plays, which were largely comic relief from the heavier tragedies. Almost always at these drama festivals, one could expect the tragedies to focus on vengeance, severe punishment, exile, or death. Early Greek myths, particularly those in which Athens was mentioned, usually served as the basis for the plots of the dramas.

The most prestigious of the drama festivals held in Athens was the City Dionysia, held over a six-day period. Throngs of visitors, dignitaries, and rural citizens crowded the city to see the spectacle, which represented a major aspect of religious worship. There were two processions, from Dionysus' temple to his sacred grove and back again, and public sacrifices were performed at his altar. A few days before the main performance, in a spot near the theater, the playwright offered a *proagon*, a preview of coming attractions to build enthusiasm.

On three successive mornings, three dramatists who had been selected competitively by the archon, or mayor, earlier that same year, each presented a tetralogy, consisting of three tragedies and a satyr play. The play began at sunrise and ended around noon. Audiences brought the essential ingredient – a willing suspension of disbelief – and sometimes ran from their seats in fright at the appearance of menacing figures, such as the Erinyes, or Furies. Yet, drawn into the illusion of dramatization, the playgoers followed the argument of each character and gravely weighed the evidence which the playwright presented in defense of his thesis. Attending the theater in fifth century Athens was serious business.

The state, which considered theater a form of public edification, paid each actor's salary from public funds. The *choregos,* or patron, usually a wealthy Athenian, considered it an honor to underwrite other production costs, including food for the cast. The actors provided their own costumes and masks, which often passed through generations of the same family and were repainted for each performance. At the close of the festival, ten judges, who had been chosen by lot, determined the winners and awarded prizes.

In contrast to tragedy, comedy developed from another aspect of the Dionysiac festival. Derived from *komos,* the Greek work for *revel,* comedies evolved from the mummery that accompanied processionals. The townspeople along the parade route exchanged ribald witticisms with the young men who took part in the pageant, indulging coarse jest, mockery of notables, gossip, insults, and other forms of merrymaking. After Epicharmos formalized comedy for stage presentation in Megara during the second half of the sixth century B.C., comic plays came to resemble tragedies in format and structure. The audience, deeply involved in the satire, expressed their approval or dislike by shouting, booing, inserting asides with the dialogue, and even pelting the players with olives, fruit pits, nuts, and small stones.

Each performance of the City Dionysia ended with a comedy, rather like dessert after a full meal, but it was the Lanaea that showcased comedy as the entree around 442 B.C. Humor was heavily localized, lampooning local officials for their imperfections and commenting on embarrassing public situations and scandals. Because the drollery often got out of hand, officials eventually barred women from attending the Lanaea.

Officials, usually one in every wedge of seats, oversaw the behavior of the outspoken, often unruly audience. To assure order and guarantee a good performance, committees censored material that appeared on stage, excising both violence and licentious or profane language. It would seem that playwrights risked extreme criticism for small reward – usually a skin of wine and a basket of figs for the best comedy and a goat for the best tragedy. In actuality, however, the playwright commanded a respect in Athens unequaled by authors in more recent times, including Shakespeare.

Besides writing the plays and composing the accompanying music, of which we have no remnants, the poet-dramatist was responsible for directing the production, auditioning performers, and supervising rehearsals. Choreography, set to the music of flutes and stringed instruments, was intricate, sometimes involving antiphonal choruses. Often, the dramatist acted the role of the protagonist, or central character, but this tradition seems to have stopped by Sophocles' time.

Because attendance was a civic and a religious obligation as well as a source of entertainment, admission to the theater was originally free. When it eventually became necessary to charge for tickets, the state provided reimbursement for all citizens who could not afford the price. The seasonal festivals were so important to Greek life that everyone was encouraged to participate, including women, children, slaves, and prisoners, and all public and private business was suspended for the occasion. Although only thirty-three tragedies, eleven comedies, and one satyr play remain of the outpouring of creative talent, this representative sampling gives us enough of a glimpse to appreciate the birth of drama in the Western world.

Ω

THE THEATER

The Greek theater was built in the open air and was generally quite large; the Theater of Dionysus at Athens, for example, begun by Pericles about 435 B.C. and finished during the reign of Lycurgus in 360 B.C., had more than 17,000 seats. The theaters were usually built in hollowed-out hillsides, and despite their size, they had excellent acoustics, so that words spoken by the performers could easily be heard in all sections. The Theater of Dionysus served as a model for theaters all over the Mediterranean world.

The *theatron,* or "seeing place," was the area in which the audience sat. It was shaped like a horseshoe and had rows of stone bleachers rising upward and backward in tiers. In the first row were seats of honor for the city officials, the choragus, and the priest of Dionysus. Behind them sat male citizens and a special section of *ephebi,* eighteen-year-old boys enrolled in military training. In the two sections above were women and, at the top, slaves. Some of the seats were designated by number, which matched the number on the circular token or ticket held by the theatergoer. Non-citizens had to negotiate a place to sit by bribery or more violent methods.

The circular area at ground level, which was enclosed on three sides by the U-shaped *theatron*, was known as the *orchestra*, or dancing place of the chorus—a simple dirt floor, later paved in stone, which offered good sightlines to all seats. In its center was the *thymele*, an altar to Dionysus on which sacrifices were made and which served as a stage prop, becoming, by a stretch of imagination, a monument, rock, ship, or other tangible object. The chorus assembled in the orchestra after marching in through the right or left *parodos*, or entrance passage, and remained there during the rest of the performance. The flute player and occasional harpist who provided musical accompaniment for the tragedies generally sat in a corner of the orchestra.

On the side of the *orchestra* which formed the open end of the *theatron* stood a wooden structure, the *skene*, or scene building. This was a dressing room for the actors, but its facade was usually made to resemble a palace or temple. It served as a backdrop for the action of the play. The three doors of the *skene* were used for entrances and exits. Extending from the central door was a massive, T-shaped platform, on which scenery was erected.

The *proscenium* was the level area in front of the *skene* on which most of the play's action took place, although at times the actors might move to the orchestra or even to the roof of the *skene*. There was no stage, but the *proscenium* may have been raised one step higher than the orchestra. There was no curtain or artificial lighting. Ramps leading up to the acting area provided entrance points for the chorus.

A few items of technical equipment were available for special effects. These included devices for imitating lightning and the sound of thunder; other brass noisemakers; *pinakes*, or painted scenery; three-sided prisms or *periaktoi* set in holes on the stage floor; the *eccyclema*, a wheeled platform which was rolled out of the *skene* to reveal a tableau of action that had taken place indoors (for example, at the end of *Agamemnon*, when the doors of the palace are opened to show the bodies of the dead king and Cassandra, and also at the end of the *Choephore*); and the *mechane*, or "machine," some kind of derrick consisting of pulleys and ropes that could be mounted on the roof of the *skene* and used to bring about the miraculous appearances of gods. The theatrical term *deus ex machina*, or "god from the machine" refers to the intervention of a supernatural being, such as a god, devil, or angel, to resolve a dramatic dilemma.

Ω

_____ COSTUMES

At the high point of theatrical development, the actors, who in earlier times smeared their faces with wine dregs to hide their identities, performed in elaborate costumes, wigs, and makeup. To emphasize the dominant traits of the characters they were impersonating, they wore masks. In early dramas, costumes were long, flowing robes and hightopped leggings. Eventually, tragic actors evolved an ornate costume with long sleeves and an eye-catching belt worn above the waist, to increase the illusion of stature. Colors symbolized various aspects of the drama—green for mourning, red for procurers, and white bordered with purple for royalty. Travelers indicated their role by wearing hats. Ornamentation became extensive, including mantles, tunics, sashes, and heavy jewelry. The tragic hero was set apart by gloves, body padding, and high-heeled buskins, known as *cothurnus* boots, all of which added height and significance to the figure.

The masks, which have come to symbolize the concept of drama itself, served two purposes. Viewed from the outside, their exaggerated expressions amplified the emotion which the character portrayed. On the inside, a small megaphone amplified the actor's words, easily projecting the voice beyond the device to the back row. (From this use of sound amplification comes our word "person" from the Latin *persona*.) The frame of the mask, made of cork or wood, fit over the actor's whole head and was covered with painted linen or leather. The hero's mask was extended by a domed top, or *onkos*. Since only three actors appeared on stage at a time, multiple masks made possible the doubling of roles.

Costuming for comedy varied from the more dignified tragic attire. Comic actors wore shorter tunics, tights, excess padding for the sake of caricature, and a red leather phallus. Comedic masks were more grotesque, suggestive of modern cartoon characters. In addition to human costumes, some plays called for fantastic characters, such as bees, birds, and monsters. Satyrs wore a standard uniform – hip fur, tail, and phallus. Because of their abbreviated dress, comic actors could cavort about the stage in quick, sometimes obscene movements, in contrast to the more sustained movement of tragedians.

Ω

ACTING

All members of the cast – including the *hypocrites*, or actors, and the *choreuti*, or chorus members – were male. Acting ranked in importance with athletics as a means of competition. Actors, therefore, had to be sturdy, well-trained performers, because the costumes and masks were cumbersome and slowed the actors' movements. They also had to be competent singers as well because many of their lyrical lines were chanted to music. The role of the *protagonist* was assigned to a tenor; the *deuteragonist*, or second in importance, to a baritone; and the *tritagonist*, or least important, to a bass. The mode of acting seems to have been conventional and stylized rather than naturalistic, but it could not have been too artificial, since many scenes call for lively, realistic action.

On the whole, tragic performances must have been very stately and colorful spectacles, in which a pageant-like quality was derived from the brilliant costumes and organized movements of large numbers of players and extras. This blending of drama, poetry, music, and dance created a solemn yet entertaining act of devotion to the gods. The participants took on a godlike status because they often acted the parts of deities. Actors joined an actors guild, called the artists of Dionysus, and were exempt from military service on the basis of their importance in the worship of Dionysus. They were highly thought of, often representing their country on official state business. Stars of the Greek stage were idolized and demanded outrageous salaries.

Ω

THE CHORUS

The chorus, the key to understanding the meaning and purpose of theater, was the nucleus from which tragedy evolved, and it continued to have a central place in the drama throughout classical times. The use of the chorus varied, depending on the method of the playwright and on the needs of the play being performed, but most often it acted as the "ideal spectator," the conservative spokesman of the community, as in *Oedipus Rex*, wherein it clarifies the experiences and feelings of the characters in everyday terms and expresses the conventional attitude toward developments in the story.

In some plays, like Aeschylus' *Suppliants*, the chorus was itself a central figure in the tragedy rather than a group of interested bystanders, a fact which had a direct effect on the size and nature of its role, but usually the chorus was not so closely involved in the action of the drama. In general, the tragedians used the chorus to create a psychological and emotional background to the action through its odes; it introduced and questioned new characters, chastised and admonished wayward characters, sympathized with victims, elucidated events as they occurred, established facts and affirmed the outlook of society, covered the passage of time between events, and separated *episodes*.

The trend in tragedy resulted in a decline in the importance of the chorus, caused mainly by the introduction of additional actors and increasing sophistication in their dramatic use, and also because of the more personal and complex nature of the stories selected for dramatization. With the passage of time, the proportion of choral lines to individual lines decreased significantly, and the dramatic functions of the chorus, aside from the continued use of choral odes between *episodes*, were greatly reduced.

At a typical performance of tragedy in the fifth century, the chorus, which often danced barefoot, marched into the *orchestra* chanting the *parodos* and remained there in formation until the end of the play. At various points, it divided into semi-choruses and moved around the *orchestra* to suit the requirements of the play. Its most important moments came when it changed the choral odes to music, accompanied by stylized gestures and by a series of intricate group dances. At times, the chorus also engaged in a lyrical dialogue with one of the characters and made brief comments or inquiries during the course of an *episode*.

Ω

PLOT

The stories used in tragedy were taken almost exclusively from the great cycles of mythology, although occasionally, as in Aeschylus' *Persians*, a poet might draw upon a contemporary theme. These ancient myths and heroic legends were like a bible to the Greeks, for they recorded what was thought to be the collective social, political, and religious history of the people; they included many profound and searching tales about the problems of human life and the nature of the gods. The custom requiring the use of these mythological stories in tragedy satisfied an essential requirement of the religious function of drama, for it enabled the poets to deal with subjects of great moral dignity and emotional significance.

From a dramatic point of view, the use of plots and characters already familiar to the audience gave the poet many opportunities for incorporating irony and subtle allusions that are not available to the modern playwright. Suspense as it is known in the present-day theater could not easily be evoked, but the audience's attention was held by the poet's freedom to change or interpret the myths as he thought necessary. The spectators, already aware of the outlines of the story, learned from tragedy what personal motives and outside forces had driven the characters to act as they did. It is thought that the dramatist's reinterpretation and explanation of the ancient myths was one of the most important factors considered by the Greeks in evaluating his work.

The solemn and exalted quality of Greek tragedy, and the purposeful examination of the meaning of life in which its characters engage, are even today able to make a deep impression on readers, and are direct results of the use of stories based on mythological themes. Then, as now, the audience learned from the experience of seeing a play; they learned about the origins of Athenian culture, about morality, and about their identity as human beings. In the natural order of things, the era produced the first great drama critic, Aristotle, whose *Poetics* provides the world with a history and rationale for dramatic productions. The *tour de force* of Greek theater ranks among the great intellectual achievements of the fifth century B.C.—democracy, history, philosophy, and rhetoric.

Ω

_____ STRUCTURE

Classical tragedies were composed within a definite structural framework, although there are occasional minor variations in some plays. It should be remembered that these structural divisions are merely a convenience for the discussion of the drama, since Greek tragedy was performed without intermissions or breaks. The following are the main structural elements of a typical tragedy:

- *Prologue*—the opening scene; here, the background of the story is established, usually by a single actor or in a dialogue between two actors.

- *Parodos*—the entrance of the chorus, usually chanting a lyric which bears some relation to the main theme of the play.

- *Episode*—the counterpart of the modern act or scene, in which the plot is developed through action and dialogue between the actors, with the chorus sometimes playing a minor role.

- *Stasimon*—the choral ode. A *stasimon* comes at the end of each *episode* so that the tragedy is a measured alternation between these two elements.

- *Exodos*—the final action after the last *stasimon*, ended by the ceremonial exit of all the players.

Ω

GREEK TRAGEDY

- Aeschylus
- Sophocles
- Euripides

AESCHYLUS

- *Agamemnon*

- *The Choephore*

- *The Eumenides*

- *Prometheus Bound*

- *The Persians*

- *The Seven Against Thebes*

- *The Suppliants*

AESCHYLUS

LIFE AND BACKGROUND

Aeschylus (524?–456 B.C.), the first of Athens' three great trage-dians and a contemporary of Pindar, was born of an aristocratic, land-rich family at Eleusis, to the northwest of Athens, at the height of the city's greatness. Neglecting the more winsome themes of love and passion, he attuned his thinking to somber theology and devoted his genius to serious contemplations of humanistic questions, such as the nature of justice. He credits much of his poetic success to the epic, labeling his plays the "scraps from Homer's banquet." His main con-tribution to the development of drama was an intensification of the dramatic element over narrative, lyric, or elegaic poetry, by which he aroused the audience to heights of anguish, pity, and terror.

His innovations began thirty years after Thespis introduced his one-man tragedies. To the monotonic beginning of serious plays, Aeschylus added a second actor, whose presence provided a flexibility and a dramatic dimension unknown in the Western world. Late in his career, he imitated the neophyte Sophocles by including a third actor. In addition he is credited with the invention of spectacle, derived from massive, painted scenery and complex machinery capable of interjecting ghosts and gods from above. A musician of some renown, he included flute solos and dancing, although no musical or choreo-graphical details have survived. To increase the stature and impor-tance of the actors he added long-sleeved garments and high-heeled *cothurnus* boots.

A latecomer to literary fame, Aeschylus launched his maiden voyage in 499 B.C. at the annual festival in honor of Dionysus; his competition, Choerilus and Pratinas, were the leading dramatists of his day. It was not until 484 B.C., fifteen years later, that Aseschylus won the highest prize, an acknowledgement of his brilliant achieve-ments. Interposed among his literary successes, he served as an infan-tryman during the Persian Wars and distinguished himself at two decisive battles, Marathon (490 B.C.), where his brother, Cynegeirus, died heroically, and Salamis (480 B.C.). In 472 B.C. he won a second-place award for *Persae* (*The Persians*), his only historical play, which honors the Battle of Salamis. To lead the chorus in *Persae*, Aeschylus chose twenty-year-old Pericles.

Although he lost to Sophocles in 468 B.C., he tasted sweet victory another time in 471 B.C. with his Theban tetralogy and again in 462 B.C., at the age of sixty-two, with the *Oresteia*, winning a total of thirteen prizes during his career. Of the ninety plays with which he is credited, some seventy-odd of which are identified by title, six tragedies remain as examples of his artistry, plus some fragments of satyr plays. Despite the prominence of *Prometheus Bound*, which has traditionally held an important place in the canon, recent discussions of its authenticity leave it in question.

Because of his earnest pursuit of humanistic themes, Aeschylus considered himself a moralist and teacher. Ironically, his reputation was marred by a trial for impiety. Although he was acquitted of the charge, his name is forever linked with the publication of the secret rites of Demeter, a serious matter in his day. He appears not to have joined the initiates of the Eleusian mysteries, preferring instead the worship of Pythian Apollo. Although Aeschylus was known for piety, he was a private man, keeping his faith to himself and spurning public demonstrations of religiosity.

On several occasions he traveled to Sicily as a guest of Hieron I, the tyrant of Syracuse, where he enjoyed the company of Simonides, Bacchylides, and Pindar. Aeschylus retired in Sicily and died at Gela. The epitaph which he chose for himself omits his literary triumphs:

> Beneath this stone lies Aeschylus the Athenian, son of
>   Euphorion,
> Buried in the fertile soil of Gela;
> Well-known for his prowess in battle,
> As the wood of Marathon and the Medes bear witness.

A decent, pious man, Aeschylus dedicated his life to old-fashioned virtues and obviously derived much satisfaction from his military service during Athens' great war with the Persians. Yet his tomb became a shrine for poets on pilgrimage. Also to his honor, both his sons, Euaeon and Euphorion, as well as his nephew Philocles, became tragedians and sired a line of great literary men.

Scholars attach great importance to his prize-winning trilogy of 458 B.C., *Agamemnon, The Choephore (The Libation Bearers),* and *The Eumenides,* which comprise the only remaining trilogy from ancient times. The depth of theme and complexity of mythic detail represent a remarkable achievement. For the first time in recorded literature, an author weighs the meaning of suffering and questions whether God can exist in multiple form. As he examines the legends surrounding Agamemnon's family, Aeschylus ponders the nature of justice and God's influence in human affairs.

Honored by Aristophanes fifty years after his death as a worthy moralist, Aeschylus became a legend, a symbol of lofty, ethical thought. His statue graced the Theater of Dionysus. The Romans honored his plays by translating them into Latin. Later poets, thinkers, and playwrights, including Percy Bysshe Shelley, Karl Marx, and Eugene O'Neill, used his works as touchstones for their own creativity.

$$\Omega$$

_____ *AGAMEMNON* _____

The first play of Aeschylus' trilogy, the *Oresteia,* the play *Agamemnon* deals with the Greek commander-in-chief's return from a ten-year siege at Troy on the western coast of Asia Minor. The play opens at Argos before Agamemnon's palace, where a watchman speaks the prologue. The king has arranged a series of beacons stretching from Mount Ida in Troy to Argos, so that Queen Clytemnestra will know when the war is ended. The watchman, weary with his lonely task, comments on Clytemnestra's "male strength of heart." Suddenly, he discerns a blaze in the distance, evidence that his nightly vigil is finished.

The chorus, a gathering of old Argive men, enters, chanting the story of Menelaus and his brother, Agamemnon, "twin-throned, twin-sceptered, in twofold power of kings from God." When Clytemnestra approaches, they continue their verses, concluding each set with the somber refrain, "Sing sorrow, sorrow." They call upon Zeus when they reach the pitiful episode in which Agamemnon sacrifices his daughter (Iphigenia) in order to wage war for Helen, his sister-in-law.

The chorus leader asks for news; Clytemnestra replies that Troy is taken. Far from overjoyed at the revelation, the old men intone a mournful hymn describing the violence and grief that accompanies bloodshed. A herald interrupts and announces, "He comes, Lord Agamemnon, bearing light in gloom to you . . ." Amid the chorus' exultations, the messenger continues his speech, proclaiming that Agamemnon performed the grisly work of war skillfully and honorably. Before the chorus can pass along the news to Clytemnestra, she asks, "Why should you tell me then the whole long tale at large when from my lord himself I shall hear all the story?" She sends a reply that Agamemnon may expect to find a faithful wife waiting for him at his palace.

While the chorus reflects on the fate of Menelaus (Agamemnon's brother), King Agamemnon himself and his captured war-prize, Cassandra, enter in a chariot. The chorus admits in their greeting that they doubted him when he dragged Argos into the war, but now they gladly greet him on his victorious return. Agamemnon turns at once to two important tasks: to thank the gods for their help in quelling the Trojans and to cleanse the city of corruption.

Clytemnestra approaches the chorus and reminds them that women suffer loneliness and fear when their husbands fight in foreign wars. She has often attempted suicide, but now, "with griefless heart I hail this man, the watchdog of the fold and hall . . ." She sets her handmaidens to spreading tapestries at Agamemnon's feet. He hesitates to accept such divine treatment, but he yields when the queen assures him that "for the mighty even to give way is grace." He removes his sandals, lest he spoil the carpet, and entrusts Cassandra to his wife, urging her to be kind. On their way over the exalted path, Clytemnestra prays that Zeus will answer her prayers.

The chorus, beset with nagging fear, wonders why they cannot relax and enjoy their king's return. Clytemnestra returns to address Cassandra, who waits in the chariot, and to try to persuade her to join them in the palace. Although the chorus and the queen make repeated gestures of welcome, the girl makes no reply. Clytemnestra returns to the house. Alone with the chorus, Cassandra cries out her anguish to Apollo. She spews a twisted tale of sins committed by Agamemnon's father, intermingling prophecies of "this new and huge stroke of atrocity." The chorus realizes that Cassandra possesses the gift of prophecy, but they are unable to fathom her meaning.

Step by step, Cassandra describes a crime: the husband is bathed in water, hands grope menacingly, a net enshrouds him, a "black horn strikes," and he collapses in the bath. Cassandra asks if Apollo has brought her to Argos to die with the victim. When the trance passes, she speaks plainly to the chorus and acknowledges that she was once seduced by Apollo. Because she broke her word that she would bear Apollo's children, he placed a curse on her: although she would remain his prophetess, no one would believe her prophecies.

Cassandra again sinks into a trance and envisions "this accursed bitch, who licks his hand, who fawns on him with lifted ears, who like a secret death shall strike the coward's stroke . . ." The chorus interprets correctly Cassandra's references to Thyestes, Agamemnon's uncle who was tricked into eating his own children, yet they fail to grasp her prediction that Clytemnestra will murder the king. Once more, Apollo's powers sweep the priestess' brain, filling her with pain. She rambles on about the woman who lies with the wolf "when her proud lion ranges far away." Facing her own last moments, Cassandra asks that the hand which kills her "be true, and that with no convulsion, with a rush of blood in painless death, I may close up these eyes, and rest."

The chorus marvels that Cassandra can foresee her own destruction and still walk calmly toward it. At the door, Cassandra suddenly shies away, like an animal that smells fresh-spilled blood. The chorus assures her that the odor is only sacrificial blood. The chorus murmurs words of pity as Cassandra resumes her slow steps toward the palace. Her last request is for the king's avengers to strike a mortal blow in her memory.

Two cries from within prove Cassandra's prophecy – Agamemnon has been foully ambushed. Stricken by terror and indecision, the chorus wanders distractedly. Before they can adopt a plan of action, the doors open revealing Clytemnestra standing over the corpses of Agamemnon and Cassandra. Drunk with the success of her scheme, the queen gloats that she netted her husband like a fish, stabbed him, and received the king's spattered blood like gardens in the "showers of God in glory at the birthtime of the buds." The chorus demands an explanation of her blatant treachery.

Clytemnestra defies the old men of Argos to blame her for avenging her daughter's murder. They chastise her proud tongue, but she refuses to be chastened. Defiant and determined, the queen proclaims, "He lies there; and she who swanlike cried aloud her lyric mortal lamentation out is laid against his fond heart, and to me has given a delicate excitement to my bed's delight." The chorus blames Helen for starting the conflict. Clytemnestra, Helen's twin, rejects their simplistic conclusion. Still, the chorus refuses to be squelched and persists in their lamentation for Agamemnon.

Clytemnestra continues to maintain her obligation to avenge Iphigenia's death. Confronting the tearful assembly with haughty demeanor, she speaks a queen's reply: "Through us he fell, by us he died; we shall bury." Aegisthus, her accomplice, enters with an armed bodyguard and joins his lover in her rejoicing. He justifies his part in the crime as rightful vengeance for Atreus' wrongs against Thyestes, Aegisthus' father.

The chorus refuses to exonerate him. Instead, they find him guilty of pride and impiety in killing a king. They accuse him of "shaming the master's bed with lust" as well as plotting a treacherous death, which he lacked the manhood to execute, relying instead on the hand of a woman. Already swollen with regal self-importance, Aegisthus reminds them that some day they may repent of their harsh condemnation. The chorus clings to their only hope, that Orestes will return from exile to avenge his father's murder.

For a more comprehensive, in-depth analysis of this work, consult Cliffs Notes on *Agamemnon, The Choephore,* **and** *The Eumenides.*

Ω

—————————— THE CHOEPHORE ——————————

Set a decade after *Agamemnon, The Choephore* (or *The Libation Bearers*), the second tragedy of Aeschylus' trilogy, opens in Argos at Agamemnon's tomb. Orestes and his companion, Pylades, enter, dressed as travelers. Prince Orestes, who was living in Phocis when Clytemnestra murdered the king, honors his father's grave with a ceremonial lock of hair. At a distance he sees a chorus of veiled women accompanying his sister, Electra, who still mourns her father's death. Moved by sight of her grief-bowed form, Orestes pledges vengeance against the murderers.

The women lament their sufferings in Argos, where an age of woes has plagued the house of Atreus. Electra's first words indicate that she finds herself in a difficult situation: she loathes her mother for murdering Agamemnon. The chorus assures her that she may number among her friends all those who despise Aegisthus, the man who helped Clytemnestra lay a fatal trap for her husband. Still hesitant to commit impiety against the gods, Electra prays for someone to kill the queen and her lover, Aegisthus.

Electra spies footprints similar to her own. Orestes moves out where Electra can see him and reveals his identity, which he proves by their identical footprints and hair color and a familiar piece of figured cloth. Seething with rage over his lost patrimony, Orestes mourns for the brave Argives, heroes of the Trojan War, who returned in victory to be governed by "this brace of women; since his [Aegisthus'] heart is female . . ." In despair at the king's ignominious death, Orestes wishes that his father had met with a noble death on the battlefield.

A trio made up of the chorus, Electra, and Orestes bewails the savagery of Agamemnon's death, his hands trussed under his armpits. Electra grieves that she, a princess of the royal house of Argos, has been cast aside, "a dishonored, nothing worth, in the dark corner, as you would kennel a vicious dog . . ." She asks why Clytemnestra has sent libations for the king's tomb, and she learns that the queen is beset by bad dreams in which she gives birth to a serpent, and swaddles and suckles it. Orestes recognizes the symbolism: he is the monster which will wound the breast of its mother.

To succeed in his plan, Orestes explains the parts each must play. Electra must return to the palace and keep his arrival a secret while he arranges a plot similar to the net in which the king was snared. Orestes and Pylades, speaking in a Parnassian dialect, will seek entrance to the palace. As soon as Aegisthus appears, Orestes promises to "plunge my sword with lightning speed, and drop him dead." They separate, leaving the chorus to ponder the dangers of life on earth.

Meanwhile, Orestes and Pylades hail the palace guards, and a servant summons the queen to speak with the two strangers. Clytemnestra is hospitable to her guests, but she leaves state business to Aegisthus. Orestes explains that he comes to deliver a message: Strophius sends word from Phocis that Orestes is dead. Clytemnestra, who mourns her son's passing, invites the guests to stay the night and hastens to deliver the sad news to Aegisthus.

The chorus, left alone outside the gates, sees Cilissa, Orestes' old nurse, exit the palace, her eyes streaming with tears. As she departs to fetch Aegisthus, she reveals a savvy awareness of Clytemnestra's duplicity: "She put a sad face on before the servants, to hide the smile inside her eyes . . ." She predicts that Aegisthus, too, will be pleased that another obstacle to his power has been removed. The chorus urges Cilissa to tell Aegisthus to come without guards, so that he can arrive more quickly. They imply that Cilissa may be mourning too soon for her favorite charge. The old woman, delighted by the hint, hurries on her way. The chorus invokes Zeus in a prayer for the success of their undertaking.

Aegisthus arrives, seemingly saddened by the news of Orestes' death and eager to find an eyewitness to corroborate the story. The chorus waits outside as Aegisthus enters the palace. A cry issues from inside. One of Aegisthus' followers, grieved by his lord's sudden death, warns Clytemnestra to take care, as "her neck is on the razor's edge and ripe for lopping, as she did to others before." Clytemnestra bustles past, muttering that the man speaks in riddles, and she calls for an ax to slay the murdering stranger.

Orestes and Pylades, armed with swords, confront Clytemnestra, who mourns her lover's death. Orestes vows to send her to "lie in the same grave with him . . ." Clytemnestra, mindful that her son has murder in his eye, appeals to him that she once suckled him at her breast. Pylades strengthens Orestes, recalling that Apollo has prophesied this day and that Orestes has sworn to carry out the deed. As Orestes summons his mother to her death, she tries a second ploy, warning him that he will be cursed for matricide.

Orestes and Clytemnestra engage in a hot exchange of words and rehash family animosities. The queen realizes that her nightmare is coming to life. Orestes and Pylades escort her into the palace as the chorus reviews the history of the house of Atreus. Orestes returns with the corpses of his two victims and the robe which the queen used to ensnare Agamemnon before stabbing him in his bath. Orestes defiles his mother's name for her treachery, pledging to remain wifeless and childless rather than suffer so vile a mate.

The chorus, perceiving Orestes' plight, pities him. He, too, realizes that the cycle of vengeance will not end with these two deaths. Comparing himself to a charioteer, Orestes foresees a totured road ahead, "for I am beaten, my rebellious senses bolt with me headlong and the fear against my heart is ready for the singing and dance of wrath." Bayed about by the invisible dogs of blood guilt, he struggles on his way. The chorus questions, "Where shall the fury of fate be stilled to sleep, be done with?"

For a more comprehensive, in-depth analysis of this work, consult Cliffs Notes on *Agamemnon*, *The Choephore*, and *The Eumenides*.

Ω

_____ *THE EUMENIDES* _____

The Eumenides, the third tragedy in Aeschylus' trilogy, the *Oresteia* (458 B.C.), completes the cycle of vengeful family murders that began with Agamemnon's father, Atreus, and passed down to Agamemnon's son, Orestes. Set before Pythia's shrine at the temple of Apollo in Delphi, the play opens with Pythia's sonorous tribute to the god. She enters the temple and quickly returns to the stage, weakened with terror from a vision. Her prophetic powers warn her of the presence of Orestes, surrounded by the Furies, foul monsters, "black and utterly repulsive."

The doors of the temple swing open to reveal Orestes, Apollo, Hermes, and the sleeping Furies. Apollo pledges to support Orestes, yet he cannot hinder the stalking monsters, who will never halt in their pursuit and torture of Orestes until he reaches Athena's citadel. To cheer Orestes on his dismal way, the god sends his brother, Hermes, to "shepherd him with fortunate escort on his journeys among men."

After the trio make their exit, the ghost of Clytemnestra appears and goads the Furies into action. The Furies stir, whimper, and moan in their sleep before rousing to chant in unison: "Get him, get him, get him, get him. Make sure." Climaxing their speech with desultory words for Zeus' son, who robs the Furies of their prey, they rededicate themselves to torment Clytemnestra's son/killer. Apollo returns to his temple of healing and castigates the defilers: "This house is no right place for such as you to cling upon; but where, by judgment given, heads are lopped and eyes gouged out, throats cut, and by the spoil of sex the glory of young boys is defeated, where mutilation lives, and stoning, and the long moan of tortured men spiked underneath the spine and stuck on pales."

Before quitting their refuge, the Furies exchange hostilities with Apollo, who encouraged Orestes to commit matricide. Apollo contends that Agamemnon's death called for revenge. Quick with retort, the Furies condemn him for sheltering Orestes from his rightful punishers. Apollo refuses to be overruled and calls for a final verdict from Pallas Athena. They exit separately to take their power struggle before the goddess, who resides on the Acropolis in Athens.

When the second scene begins, Orestes has just arrived, wearied by his long exile. The Furies converge on him with chilling incantation: "You must give back for her blood from the living man red blood of your body to suck, and from your own I could feed, with bitter-swallowed drench, turn your strength limp while yet you live and drag you down where you must pay for the pain of the murdered mother . . . Hades is great, Hades calls men to reckoning there under the ground, sees all, and cuts it deep in his recording mind."

Orestes, near the end of his strength, calls on Athena, despite the Furies' claim that neither she nor Apollo shall save him "from going down forgotten, without knowing where joy lies anywhere inside your heart, blood drained, chewed dry by the powers of death, a wraith, a shell." At the conclusion of their frenzy, Athena appears in full armor and demands that both sides present their case in orderly fashion.

The Furies speak first, revealing the single fact that Orestes has killed his mother. Athena, not to be taken in by half an argument, insists that Orestes tell his side of the crime. The chorus declares that Orestes will not swear an oath, but Athena refuses to relent on a technicality. The Furies agree to yield their authority to the higher court. Athena turns to Orestes for more information.

Humbly, but manfully, Orestes explains his origin and the family entanglements that led to Agamemnon's death and Clytemnestra's murder, for which Apollo must be held accountable. After Orestes' brief statement, he concludes, "This is my case. Decide if it be right or wrong. I am in your hands. Where my fate falls, I shall accept." Athena realizes the gravity of the case and goes to find jurors to help her settle a complex matter.

In her absence, the Furies continue their harangue against matricide. Thundering doom and damnation, they compare Orestes to a sailor whose tempest-tossed ship loses sail and founders on the "reef of Right." Athena returns with twelve citizens to judge Orestes' case. Others crowd in to view the drama. Athena orders the herald to blow a blast on the trumpet; the court begins formal proceedings.

Apollo appears to testify to his part in the killing. The chorus objects to his presence, which is outside his jurisdiction. Athena cuts short their protests and demands an opening statement against Orestes. Question by question, the chorus elicits the facts: Orestes, guided by Apollo, killed his mother by slitting her throat with his sword. His motive was to avenge her murder of Agamemnon. He interposes a legal point: why did the Furies not punish Clytemnestra? Their answer makes sense: they punish only crimes between blood kin.

Apollo intervenes, claiming that Zeus himself condoned the murder. The chorus counters that Zeus shackled and killed Cronus in similar fashion to Clytemnestra's murder of Agamemnon. Apollo settles a major side issue by explaining that a mother is not a parent but merely the vessel which holds the developing fetus, which is engendered by the father alone. As evidence he points to Athena, motherless offspring of Zeus. His parting shot is a promise of greatness for Athens and its people, for whom Orestes shall fight.

Athena charges the jury to defend their city's reputation for justice. The chorus adds a veiled threat: "We can be a weight to crush your land." Apollo's dire retort fails to deter their petulance. Both parties face off for another round of venom. Athena ends their exchange by casting the deciding vote–in favor of Orestes. In gratitude, Orestes swears that "never man who holds the helm of my state shall come against your country in the ordered strength of spears, but though I lie then in my grave, I still shall wreak helpless bad luck and misadventure upon all . . ." With a blessing on Athena and her city, he and Apollo exit.

The remainder of the play concerns the anger of the Furies, who spew their righteous indignation at the goddess. To quell their spite, she makes gracious reply: "In complete honesty I promise you a place of your own, deep hidden underground that is yours by right where you shall sit on shining chairs beside the hearth to accept devotions offered by your citizens." Not to give in too quickly, the Furies pout that their power has been weakened, leaving them open to mockery and dishonor. Athena reminds them that they are goddesses and welcomes them to her shrine to share her worship. Gradually, the Furies release their hatred and replace it with kindness. Now, as the Eumenides, the "kind ones," they bestow a gracious blessing on all Athens.

For a more comprehensive, in-depth analysis of this work, consult Cliffs Notes on *Agamemnon*, *The Choephore*, and *The Eumenides*.

Ω

_____ *PROMETHEUS BOUND* _____

Aeschylus' *Prometheus Bound*, which is undoubtedly the first of a trilogy, cannot be dated with certainty. Its sequel, *Prometheus Unbound*, exists only in fragments, and the concluding tragedy, *Prometheus the Firebearer*, is completely lost. On a barren peak in the Caucasus, a mountain range that lies between the Black and Caspian Seas, two demonic servants of Zeus, Might and Violence, supervise Hephaestus, muscular blacksmith of Olympus. Might orders Hephaestus to chain Prometheus, son of Themis, the Earth goddess, to a desolate rock in punishment for his theft of fire, which he gave to humanity. The purpose of the penalty is to force Prometheus to "change his too-favorable attitude toward human beings."

Hephaestus admits that he is caught between his sympathy for a kinsman and his fear of Zeus. He chooses obedience, pronouncing Prometheus' doom: "I shall nail you in bonds of indissoluble bronze on this crag far from men. Here, you shall hear no voice of any mortal; here, you shall see no form of mortal. . . . For you, a God, feared not the anger of the Gods, but gave honors to mortals beyond what was just. Wherefore you shall mount guard on this unlovely rock, upright, sleepless, not bending the knee." The blacksmith concludes that Zeus is a hard deity because of the newness of his power over gods and men.

The cruel bonds lock the prisoner's arms and legs into tortured, immovable positions. Before withdrawing, Might sneers at Prometheus' name: ". . . you yourself *need* Forethought to extricate yourself from this contrivance."

Alone in his agony at the end of the earth, Prometheus calls on the winds and waters, the sea, earth, and sun to witness his suffering, which he must endure for ten thousand years. He admits that he "hunted out the secret spring of fire" in order to teach human beings the crafts which sustain and lighten their lives. He pauses as the rustle of wings announces the approach of the chorus, the daughters of Ocean.

Like ministering angels, the girls hurry to Prometheus' side and now, tearful and trembling, wring their hands at his predicament. Like Hephaestus, they are wary of the new regime on Olympus and fearful of Zeus' tyranny. Prometheus regrets that he was not executed and sent to Hades; this punishment, which makes him "plaything of the winds," forces him to endure the scoffing of his enemies. Prometheus and the chorus anticipate a time when Zeus will rue his hardness of heart, a day when he will need Prometheus on his side to save his throne.

The women urge Prometheus to tell the story of his capture. At the beginning of the struggle between the Titans and the Olympians, Prometheus and his mother supported the Titans, who, in their conceit, ignored Prometheus' warnings of the Olympians' trickery. Prometheus and Themis therefore altered their allegiance. Through Prometheus' strategy, Cronus and his allies were incarcerated in the black pit of Tartarus. For his pains, Prometheus finds himself chained to a rock, bitter at the "sickness rooted and inherent in the nature of a tyranny."

The reason for Prometheus' penalty is that he defied the new ruler and saved the human race from extinction. His gift of fire, which offers humanity a "blind hope," has cost him his freedom. He blames no one for leading him astray. Prometheus knew from the outset the consequences of his noble action. Despite his dire condition, he doubts that he shall have to live out the sentence alone.

True to his prediction, Ocean, riding on a hippocamp, or sea monster, visits the crag to comfort his friend. Prometheus, wallowing in self-pity, urges his friend to "gape in wonder at this great display, my torture." Ocean gives him a word to the wise: Prometheus must mend his ways and bridle his proud tongue before he destroys all hope for redemption. Before Ocean leaves to plead Prometheus' case with Zeus, Prometheus warns him that words will not move the stony-hearted god and that Ocean, too, may run afoul of the Almighty through association with a criminal. He reminds Ocean that Prometheus' two brothers, Atlas and Typho, also groan in torment, one wedged against the pillars that support heaven and earth, the other a "sprawling mass" brought low by Zeus' thunderbolt, "pressed down beneath the roots of Aetna."

Lulled by the antiphonal choirs of Ocean's daughters, Prometheus rehashes his crime. He salves his wounded ego by congratulating himself for his goodwill offering to humanity—a means to build houses, plant crops, study the stars and the seasons, combine letters into words, harness beasts into service, and sail wind-driven ships. "Such were the contrivances that I discovered for men—alas for me," he wails, aware that no contrivance will alleviate his pain. He continues his catalog of kindnesses to humanity—the invention of medicines, divination of dreams and omens, interpretation of sacrifices, and discovery and use of metals.

Prometheus reveals one hopeful tidbit—that Zeus, like all beings, must bow to the Fates and the Furies. The chorus demands more information, but he hesitates to tell all he knows. Io, a demented girl decked in bovine horns, struggles up the mountainside, bitten at every step by Argus' gadfly. Prometheus recognizes her as one of Zeus' conquests who now suffers the torments of his green-eyed wife, Hera.

Io presses Prometheus for a glimpse of her future, but agrees to explain first to the chorus the reason for her distress. After night voices plagued her sleep, luring her to a tryst with Zeus, Io told her father of the messages. He consulted Apollo's oracle, but was unable to unravel the cryptic reply. At last he yielded to the god's wishes—he cast out his innocent daughter to wander the earth. Her girlish shape was distorted into the bulky form of a heifer. A nagging gadfly stung and bit, goading her into frenzy. Hundred-eyed Argus followed her tracks. Her tortured path led her to Prometheus.

The chorus shudders at her miserable fate. Prometheus compounds the dismal story with prophecy, for Io must wander farther into the mountains, pass through the land of the Amazons, and into Asia by way of the Bosporus, which shall be named Cow's-ford in her honor. Woeful that her end shall be so full of trouble, Io demands to know whether Zeus shall ever get his comeuppance. Yes, Prometheus assures her, he shall bear the brunt of his conniving and be challenged by his own son.

Zeus' only reprieve shall come from Prometheus, once he is freed from bondage. Prometheus shall be rescued by Io's descendant from the thirteenth generation. Io is saddened to learn how far in time the event will occur. The chorus, eager to hear Io's fate, seconds her request for more information. Promethus accedes to his audience with the end of her wanderings: the cow-maiden must continue through desert and sea, past gorgons and the monsters that guard Hades, until she arrives in the land of black people. After crossing Ethiopia, she will settle at last in the Nile delta and found a colony.

Restored to sound mind, Io shall bear Zeus' child, Epaphus, "dark of skin, his name recalling Zeus' touch and his begetting." The end of the prophecy links Prometheus' fate to Io's, for one of her descendant daughters shall rebel against the gods and give birth to a race of kings, among them a great archer, who shall set Prometheus free. Io, overcome by the whirling frenzy that drives her onward, goes her way, the chorus pitying any female fated to share the bed of Zeus.

Prometheus gloats over his one trump card, the knowledge that Zeus shall sow the seeds of his own destruction. "Nothing," Prometheus spits out through clenched teeth, "shall all of this avail against a fall intolerable, a dishonored end." The chorus marvels at his temerity in scoffing at the Almighty, but Prometheus persists in blasphemy: "Worship him, pray; flatter whatever king is king today; but I care less than nothing for Zeus."

At the end of Prometheus' bold words, Hermes, Zeus' footman, arrives and demands to know the meaning of Prometheus' gleeful prediction. Prometheus shoos him away as though he were a tiresome toddler. Hermes declares him mad and charges that "No one could bear you in success." Prometheus replies in a word, "Alas," to which Hermes counters, "Zeus does not know that word." Hermes warns

Prometheus to leave off his boasting and seek more "prudent counsel." His words only fan the flames of Prometheus' spite. His reply is meant to gall: ". . . there is no disease I spit on more than treachery." Prometheus looks out on the universe, awhirl with manifold terrors, and prays to mother Earth for comfort.

Ω

THE PERSIANS

The Persians is part of a tetralogy that was first performed at the dramatic festival of 472 B.C. and won first prize; the *choregos,* or benefactor, for this production was the famous Athenian statesman Pericles. The names of the other plays in the tetralogy are known, but they seem to bear no relation to the theme of *The Persians,* indicating that the dramatic trilogy was beginning to lose its organic quality even in the time of Aeschylus. *The Persians* is the only existing Greek tragedy on a contemporary subject, for it is an exaltation of the great Athenian naval victory over the Persians at Salamis in 480 B.C. The story is told from the Persian point of view, all the characters are non-Greek and the setting is the exotic and remote royal court of Persia.

Some time ago, a group of elders was selected by Xerxes to look after Persia while he added to Persia's accomplishments by conquering Greece. Xerxes, however, took all of the country's healthy young men with him, and now the elders are fearful, since they have heard nothing about the Persian army's fate.

The queen of Persia, widow of Darius and mother of Xerxes, arrives to discuss her dreams with the elders; she has had frequent dreams since her son departed for Greece, and it is time to find out what they mean. The previous night, in fact, she had her most disturbing dream. In it, she saw two beautiful women – one in Persian garb and the other in Greek robes. When the women cast lots for their fathers' lands, one received Greece and the other Asia. The women began to argue and Xerxes arrived to soothe them. Instead, he yoked them to a chariot – and while one submitted, the other resisted and snapped the chariot's yoke in two. Xerxes fell to the ground and his father appeared at his side, pitying him. When the queen woke up, she went to give a sacrifice, and she saw a falcon plucking away at the head of an eagle. The queen does not believe that Xerxes should be held responsible if Persia loses the war.

The elders urge the queen to make sacrifices to the gods and to beg Darius to send blessings from the underworld. The queen wonders how far away Athens is; she cannot imagine why her son would go so far merely to conquer another country. She is surprised to hear that the Greeks are free people and strong enough to have withstood Darius' attack years earlier.

A herald arrives with news that the Persians have been defeated. The herald and elders mourn Persia's loss, but the queen interrupts them to ask of Xerxes' fate. Her son is alive, the herald says, but many men have died—despite the fact that there were more than 1,200 Persian ships and only 310 Greek vessels.

The herald then explains the details of the battle in answer to the queen's questions. It seems that a Greek soldier told Xerxes that the Greeks were planning to escape in their ships after dark. Thus, Xerxes ordered his captains to surround all entrances to the bay in order to prevent the Greeks' escape; the penalty to anyone failing to enforce these commands was the loss of his head. After dark, the Persians maneuvered into place, but heard nothing until daylight, when the Greeks began to charge the Persian ships. Since the Persian ships were moored closely together, the Persians were unable to move with ease. The result was that they were encircled by the Greek vessels. Xerxes had stationed some men on shore in order to catch any Greeks who might have tried to escape. Instead, the Persian soldiers were trapped by the victorious Greeks and quickly slaughtered. Xerxes saw the massacre and immediately tore his robes, causing the rest of his soldiers to try to escape.

The queen leaves to give prayers for all the men who died in the service of their country; she hopes that Persia will soon know a brighter future, and she asks the elders to escort her son home if he returns before she has finished with her prayers and sacrifices.

The elders also mourn Persia's defeat. The queen returns with libations for her dead husband's grave. She asks the elders to recall the ghost of Darius for help, so the elders summon the gods, requesting that Darius be sent to help them.

The ghost of Darius arrives, aware that there is a problem when he sees the extensive sacrifices and great mourning. Darius urges the elders to be quick in their explanation because the trip from Hades was difficult and he was allowed to come only because of his exalted position. The queen reveals to him that Persia has been destroyed. Darius is shocked that his son would attempt to conquer the Helles-pont since such a feat means "conquering the sea." The queen tries to defend Xerxes' actions by explaining that advisers had made fun of him for staying at home and not increasing Persia's wealth or power. Darius argues that he never put Persia in such a dangerous position or lost so many men.

When the elders question Darius about their future strategies, he orders that no more expeditions be led against Greece, and he predicts that many of the Persians left in Greece will be unable to return.

Darius orders the queen to go to the palace and get robes for her son. She must comfort Xerxes upon his return since he will listen only to her. Before Darius leaves, he urges the elders to give themselves some pleasure since mourning will no longer benefit the dead.

The queen leaves to get the robes, sorry that her son has been dishonored. The elders then recall a time when Persia was both pros-perous and successful at battle – during the rule of Darius. Suddenly, Xerxes arrives and reveals the names of the men lost at sea and in battle. He sings a dirge with the elders and blames himself for the defeat. He ends the drama by acknowledging the power of the Greeks.

Ω

THE SEVEN AGAINST THEBES

The Seven Against Thebes is part of a tetralogy based on the Theban cycle of legends that was first performed at the dramatic festival of 467 B.C. and won first prize. The other tragedies in the tetralogy were entitled *Laius* and *Oedipus;* the satyr play was *The Sphinx. The Seven Against Thebes* tells the story of the civil war between Eteocles and Polyneices, the sons of Oedipus, after their father's death. This same story is told in *The Phoenician Women* of Euripides. Three plays by Sophocles, *Oedipus Rex, Oedipus at Colonus,* and *Antigone,* as well as other plays by Euripides, are based on incidents in the same cycle of legends, for it was one of the most popular in ancient times.

Eteocles, ruler of Thebes, announces that all men, young and old, must stand ready to defend the city in battle. A prophecy has declared that the Achaians are planning a night assault on the city. Having heard the prophecy, Eteocles sent a messenger to the enemy camp to learn about their battle plans.

The messenger arrives with news that he saw seven commanders take an oath with bulls' blood, swearing that they would sack and destroy Thebes, or else die. The messenger urges Eteocles to place his strongest commander at each gate since, when he left, the Achaians were casting lots to decide who would attack each gate. Eteocles begs Zeus not to destroy the city or to send the people into slavery. But almost immediately, the chorus of women hears shouting and sees the enemy approach. The women beg the gods to protect the city.

Eteocles condemns the women for their fearful behavior and orders that any man or woman who disobeys him will be executed. The women persist with their fears of losing the city and becoming slaves. Eteocles silences them and approaches the altar with his prayers, vowing to offer sacrifices and to dedicate trophies if the Thebans are allowed to be victorious. The chorus, however, does not feel comfort from Eteocles' prayers. They fear the worst.

The messenger returns with a list of the Achaian commanders who have been stationed at each gate. To oppose Tydeus at the Proteid gate, Eteocles appoints the son of Astacus. Polyphontes will be stationed at Electra's gates to attack the Achaian Capaneus. Eteocles will fight Megareus at the gates of Neis. Hyperbius will protect the gates of Onea Athena against Hippomedon. Eteocles orders Actor to defend the Northern gate against Parthenopaeus of Arcadia. The Achaian Amphiaraus will fight Lasthenes at the Homoloian gate. When Eteocles learns that Polyneices will attack the seventh gate, he decides to confront Polyneices himself.

Although the chorus tries to convince Eteocles not to shed his brother's blood, he leaves nonetheless for battle. The chorus fears that if the brothers die at each other's hands, there may be no one to give them a proper burial. The chorus blames Laius, grandfather of Eteocles and Polyneices, for disobeying the gods' order to produce no children.

Instead, Laius produced Oedipus, who was abandoned as an infant, was raised by a shepherd, and eventually killed his father unknowingly and fathered children by his mother. Because of the way in which Oedipus' children treated him, Oedipus cursed them, vowing that they would have to divide his possessions by force. Now Thebes is suffering from that curse.

The messenger arrives with word that the city is safe and that all is well at six of the gates. At the seventh gate, however, Laius' disobedience to the gods has been punished with the deaths of both Polyneices and Eteocles. The chorus is not sure if they should rejoice or lament for the city. Ismene and Antigone, sisters of the slaughtered princes, arrive with the bodies.

A herald announces the decisions of the city counselors. Because of his loyalty, Eteocles is to be given the proper rights of burial. Polyneices' body, though, is to be left unburied because of his desire to destroy the city. Antigone vows to bury Polyneices because she is not ashamed of his actions. The herald tries to discourage her action, and the chorus is divided: half of them support the idea of burying Polyneices, since his death is a grief to the family, and the rest go off to bury Eteocles, who saved the city from "foreign" invaders.

$$\Omega$$

THE SUPPLIANTS

The Suppliants is probably the earliest surviving tragedy by Aeschylus and is thus the earliest extant drama in Western literature; it probably dates from around 490 B.C., although there is some evidence to indicate that it may actually have been written as late as 468 B.C. The Suppliants is the first play of a tetralogy which also included The Egyptians, The Daughters of Danaus, and the satyr play Amymone. It was based on the legends about the fifty daughters of Danaus, who were descendants of Zeus and Io, a mortal woman, and the establishment of the family of Danaus as the royal house of Argos. The Suppliants is of particular interest to literary historians because it seems to represent a stage of development halfway between the choral dithyramb and conventional tragedy – the chorus of fifty maidens is the central character of the tragedy; about half the play consists of choral lyrics, and much of the remaining dialogue is spoken by the chorus. The story has little action and the characterization and use of the actors is very limited.

The fifty daughters of Danaus have fled from Egypt into exile in Argos in order to escape being forced to marry the sons of Egyptus. They ask Zeus to have the men drowned at sea in a storm, hoping to find someone to protect them even though they are exiles. They invoke both Artemis and Zeus to protect them and their virginity.

Danaus, who has accompanied his daughters, sees people approaching. Not knowing whether they are friends or foes, he urges his daughters to make white suppliant wreaths and stand before the altar. They must tell the story of their exile – and they must do so with respect, not as though forced by the possibility of murder. The maidens invoke Apollo (since he was once an exile), Poseidon (for delivering them safely to Argos), and Hermes, the messenger of the gods. Danaus reminds his daughters that the lustful always pay for their crimes.

A group of men enter and are surprised to see people in clothing that is neither Argive nor Greek. One of the men speaks, and the maidens request to know who he is. He reveals that he is King Pelasgus, whose ancestors claimed the island. Pelasgus is astounded that the women claim to be Argive by birth; he thinks they look more like Amazons. The maidens reveal that their mother, Io, was, at one time, changed into a cow by Hera and that Zeus, as a bull, bred Io. Furious at Zeus' cunning, Hera sent a stinging fly to punish Io, driving her from Argos. Io then had a son by Zeus and she named him Epaphus; his daughter, Libya, had a son named Belus, who fathered two sons – Danaus and Egyptus. And this brings the maidens to their explanation of their Argive lineage, which Pelasgus now understands.

Pelasgus questions them about their sudden departure. The maidens reply that they refused to be forcibly wed to Egyptus' fifty sons – whereupon they beg Pelasgus to protect them. Although he wants to help, Pelasgus fears this act might bring war to his country. The maidens assure him that justice will be on his side, but Pelasgus maintains that he must ask the citizens of Argos if they will agree to accept the consequences for protecting the women. When the maidens retort that he is an absolute ruler and can make his own decisions, Pelasgus explains that although he sympathizes with their problems, he alone cannot make the final decision; he must consult his citizens. The maidens warn him that Zeus' wrath is fearful if those who ask for help are not assisted.

Pelasgus wonders whether it is correct to oppose any laws stating that the maidens must be married to their cousins. The women argue that they do not want heartless marriages. Pelasgus still refuses to take a stand until he has talked with his citizens; he does not wish to be blamed for his city's destruction, if that were to occur. Even when the maidens remind him of Zeus' anger, he refuses to make a decision. The maidens then warn Pelasgus that they will hang themselves if he abandons them.

Pelasgus suggests that Danaus gather the altar wreaths and take them to the city's altars to encourage piety from the citizens – along with hatred for Egyptus' sons and their arrogance. Danaus requests that a guard be sent with him since he is a stranger to the town and could be killed. Pelasgus complies with his wishes and tells the guard that Danaus is a sailor who is being escorted to the altar.

When the suppliants ask what they should do, Pelasgus suggests that they go into a nearby cove. But the maidens are alarmed that they will be unprotected while away from the altar. Pelasgus assures them that they will not be alone for long; he intends to gather some people together and coach Danaus on what to say. He urges the suppliants to ask the gods for help.

The women beg Zeus to remember their ancestry and to protect them. Danaus soon returns with news that the Argives have voted unanimously that the suppliants can remain and that they will be protected by the city. Anyone refusing aid to them will be banished. The women offer prayers to Zeus to protect the Argives from any dangers that may befall them.

Danaus sees an Egyptian ship arriving and reassures his frightened daughters that the Argives will fight for them. Before he leaves to get help, he reminds the maidens that it will take time for the ship to be anchored and that they will be safe until his return.

The suppliants are terrified and would rather die than submit to Egyptus' sons. A herald enters from the ship and threatens them if they do not go immediately to the ship. The maidens try to escape, but the herald begins dragging them toward the vessel.

Pelasgus enters and orders the herald to stop. When the herald questions Pelasgus' authority, Pelasgus refuses to reveal who he is. He warns the herald that if Egyptus' sons try to take the maidens by force, they will encounter men prepared to fight. After the herald leaves, Pelasgus tells the maidens to go into the city for protection; there, they may live with others or alone. The suppliant women wish good tidings upon the Argives.

Danaus urges his daughters to give sacrifices and prayers for the Argives. He begs them to value their modesty more than their lives so that no shame will fall on the family.

The suppliants praise Artemis for helping them escape from the forced marriages. Then they invoke Aphrodite to help them secure marriages in which they will be happy.

Ω

SOPHOCLES

- *Oedipus Rex*

- *Oedipus at Colonus*

- *Antigone*

- *Ajax*

- *Electra*

- *The Trachiniae*

- *Philoctetes*

SOPHOCLES

Sophocles, Attica's most distinguished tragedian, lived and wrote during Athens' most memorable age. The major source of information about his life, an anonymous biography, was discovered in Paris in the thirteenth century. A native of Colonus, a mile northwest of Athens, he was probably born in 496 B.C., lived to be ninety, and was buried in the family plot at Decelea, a mile and a half outside the city walls. To adorn the theater at Athens, Lycurgus commissioned a bronze portrait bust which may be the original from which extant models were made. In his honor, Athenians proclaimed Sophocles "the Entertainer" and made annual sacrifices at his shrine.

His father, Sophillus, was a wealthy armorer who managed a sizable gang of slave-craftsmen and maintained a middle-of-the road political stance in order to preserve precious military contracts. His young son, reared in comfort and cultivation, grew to be a model of the Athenian notion of beauty, grace, intelligence, and sociability. Sophocles studied music with Lamprus, the best music teacher of his day and a champion of the old school, which scorned the excesses of contemporary music in preference to the dignity and conservatism of the classical era.

At the time of the Battle of Salamis, sixteen-year-old Sophocles was chosen to lead a chorus of young male singers in the traditional hymn of victory and to accompany their performance on the harp. Already known for his physical perfection and vocal talent, he won a considerable public following for his stage appearances, especially in his roles as the lyric bard Thamyris and as Nausicaa, ball-tossing princess and savior of Odysseus.

He began writing poems and hymns of his own and, at an early age, he selected the writing of tragedies as his life's work, producing his first effort in 468 B.C. When his voice grew weak, Sophocles left the stage, thereby breaking a tradition of the playwright's participation in his own dramas. At age twenty-eight, he defeated Aeschylus, the reigning champion of tragedians, for first place and continued to outstrip both Aeschylus and Euripides in subsequent contests, never falling below second place in any competition. He is thought to have written at least a hundred and twenty-three plays, as well as many prose works, poems, and hymns which were lost in antiquity. The *Lexicon* of Suidas credits him with a total of twenty-four drama victories—eighteen at the Dionysian festival and six at the Lenaean.

A devoted, worthy citizen, Sophocles followed his father's conservative political thinking. He avoided the political spotlight, but he accepted appointments on several occasions to several embassies and also accepted a position of importance among the treasurers of the Delian League. Twice he rose to the rank of general, serving with Pericles in the Samian War at the age of fifty-four and later with Nicias. His selection appears to have been based on his reputation as a solid citizen and patriot rather than on overt military prowess.

Except for these journeys necessitated by civic duty, he rejected invitations to foreign courts and is not known to have ventured from Athens in his lifetime. When the cult of Asclepius, the god of healing, was established in 420 B.C., Sophocles assumed a major role in housing the sacred statue and composing appropriate liturgy, which survived into the third century B.C. After Athens suffered a major setback at Syracuse in 413 B.C., Sophocles, by then an octogenarian, was appointed to the board of ten commissioners and served his city until a more substantial government could be arranged.

He is known to have valued physical beauty and was upbraided by Pericles for admiring a young cupbearer. Since religion and morality were two separate spheres in Greek philosophy, his predilection for boys did not conflict with his reputation as a reverent, god-fearing man. He had an Athenian wife, Nicostrata, and four legitimate sons—Leosthenes, Stephanos, Meneclides, and Iophon—the last of whom followed his father's profession and competed with him for prizes in tragic poetry.

Late in his life, Sophocles took a foreign lover, Theoris of Sicyon, and he sired an illegitimate son, Ariston. Sophocles' favoritism toward Ariston's son, Sophocles the Younger, a noted poet and tragedian and winner of seven victories, is reputed to have caused an unfortunate court battle in which Iophon accused the aging playwright of senility. Sophocles reportedly demonstrated his mental competence by reading a portion of his last play, *Oedipus at Colonus,* aloud to the jury.

Another legal battle is said to have occurred because a courtesan, Archippe, induced Sophocles to will his property to her. This scenario is most likely legend, because Athenian law did not allow parents to disinherit their legitimate offspring. Other tall tales, including varying descriptions of Sophocles' death by strangling on an unripe grape, overexertion during a public reading of *Antigone,* and excessive elation over a literary victory, illustrate the extent to which the public desired to lift their hero from the common sphere in order to immortalize him.

A close friend of Herodotus and a devotee of the arts before all else, Sophocles founded a philosophical organization, the first of its kind. He was admired by his contemporaries for his charm, modesty, and wit. Nicknamed "the Attic Bee," he lived up to the sobriquet by busying himself at extracting honey from the blossoms of his verse. According to the critic Edith Hamilton, Sophocles was the "quintessence of the Greek," a summation of the spirit of fifth-century Athens.

Sophocles' tragedies achieve a height in Western literature that goes unchallenged by later playwrights. His plays are crafted to near-perfection, modifying the Greek drama with the addition of a third actor and thereby affording a flexibility unknown in earlier classical drama. He is credited with three other innovations—the painting of scenery, enlargement of the chorus from twelve to fifteen, and the separation of tetralogies, which had traditionally featured a single theme.

Sophocles once wrote: "The world is full of wonders but nothing is more wonderful than man." His desire to "paint men as they ought to be" led him to choose some of the most poignant dramatic situations in literature, particularly those from the Oedipus cycle. Extracting his characters from the familiar fables and myths of his culture, Sophocles scrutinizes their humanity, interweaving human foible with the workings of fate.

His themes, rising above political muck-raking during the collapse of Athens' empire, concentrate on the individual's confrontation with and acceptance of suffering. Although he himself was a serene, contented man who enjoyed the fruits of a well-tempered life, Sophocles' characters epitomize the depths of sorrow, the extremes of folly, and the bitter pangs of regret.

Ω

OEDIPUS REX

Set in Thebes near the altar outside the royal palace of King Oedipus, the story opens with a meeting between the king and a priest of Zeus, who speaks for a delegation of citizens seeking relief from a terrible pestilence. Oedipus acknowledges their sufferings and promises that his emissary, the queen's brother, Creon, has gone to Delphi to consult with Pythia, priestess of Apollo, the god of prophecy and healing.

Creon arrives while the king and priest confer and publicly announces the oracle's words: a defiler, the murderer of their former king, Laius, is being harbored within the city and must be removed before Thebes can return to health. Oedipus, curious about the details of the murder, listens as Creon describes how a single survivor returned to Thebes to tell of the robbers' attack. The citizens, vexed at that time by the "riddling Sphinx," failed to take action in the matter. Oedipus vows "to leave nought untried; for our health (with the gods' help) shall be made certain—or our ruin."

The chorus, injecting an ominous note, chants a prayer for Thebes' recovery from the plague, yet it fears that further investigation into the past will uncover dreadful truths. With an elaborate declaration that he shall search for Laius' killer as though he sought to avenge his own father, Oedipus launches an investigation. Teiresias, the blind prophet, at first refuses to testify, then grudgingly accuses Oedipus of being an "unwitting foe to thine own kin." Oedipus, fierce with rage, accuses Teiresias of conspiring with Creon to oust Oedipus from the throne.

Teiresias escalates his dark prophecy, concluding that "no one among men shall ever be crushed more miserably than thou." Before he is led away, Teiresias envisions Oedipus' future sufferings: "A blind man, he who now hath sight, a beggar, who now is rich, he shall make his way to a strange land, feeling the ground before him with his staff. And he shall be found at once brother and father of the children with whom he consorts; son and husband of the woman who bore him; heir to his father's bed, shedder of his father's blood."

The elders keep faith with Oedipus, whom they consider both wise and innocent of all wrongdoing. Creon, indignant that Oedipus has made false accusations against him, quarrels with his brother-in-law. Jocasta separates them and lingers to reassure her husband. She relates the prophecy that caused Laius to abandon his infant son, who was destined to kill his father. Her account of Laius' subsequent death in Phocis, where the road to Delphi intersects the road to Daulia, disturbs Oedipus, bringing to mind a man whom he killed at that same crossroad. He urges Jocasta to summon the surviving witness, a herdsman, who can answer their questions about the killing and put their minds to rest.

Memories of his own childhood in Corinth and the oracle which warned him that he would one day slay his father, King Polybus, and defile the bed of his mother, Merope, cause Oedipus to pour out his life story to his wife. While the royal couple retire to the palace, the chorus intones their dismay at human pride and irreverence, particularly in regard to doubters of oracles. Jocasta returns to lay a wreath on the altar and beg Phoebus Apollo to rid Thebes of its uncleanness. She rejoices when a messenger arrives to announce Polybus' death and the accession of his son to the throne of Corinth.

As Oedipus and Jocasta ponder Oedipus' second fear, that he will defile his mother's bed, the messenger interrupts with comforting news – Oedipus was a foundling, who relieved Polybus and Merope's childlessness. Therefore, Merope was not Oedipus's real mother; he need not fear her. Jocasta, realizing that the terrible prophecy has come true, tries to dissuade her husband from probing further into the past. In contrast to her disquietude, the chorus sings a happy song of Mount Cithaeron, where Oedipus was found.

The herdsman arrives and is greeted by the messenger, who remembers a time when they herded sheep together. Avoiding the subject of the abandoned child, the herdsman is at last forced to confess that he disobeyed orders to abandon Laius and Jocasta's infant son. Oedipus suddenly comes to full knowledge of his past: "All brought to pass – all true! Thou light, may I now look my last on thee – I who have been found accursed in birth, accursed in wedlock, accursed in the shedding of blood!" The chorus notes the vicissitudes of human life and the cruel fate that has befallen him.

A second messenger brings news of Jocasta's suicide and describes how Oedipus, in a frenzy at the disclosure of his sin and the sight of his wife's/mother's corpse, swinging in the noose, tore out his eyes with Jocasta's golden brooches, the gore gushing out and staining his beard.

Oedipus is then led forth by attendants, and he chants a sorrowful duet with the chorus, pleading for a hiding place on land or sea "where ye shall never behold me more!" The chorus concurs, noting that Oedipus is "better dead than living and blind."

Creon, who replaces Oedipus on the throne of Thebes, consoles Oedipus and sends for Oedipus' two young daughters, Antigone and Ismene. Clutching his children to him, Oedipus begs for banishment and the company of his daughters, but Creon reminds the former king that he may no longer decide the fate of others. The chorus ends the play with a warning: life is full of woe and no man, while he lives, can count himself fortunate.

Oedipus Rex, which was written at the height of Sophocles' career, and, ironically, which received only a second place in the annual competition, holds an honored position in world literature. It has become a touchstone – a standard by which all subsequent tragedies are measured and evaluated. Aristotle, in his dissection of the tragedy in the fourth century B.C., repeatedly refers to the play as the most perfect example of tragic drama.

Longinus, a Greek literary scholar of the third century A.D., poses the rhetorical question, "Would anyone in his senses regard all the compositions of Ion put together as an equivalent for the single play of the *Oedipus?*" Other critics have labeled the play an unsurpassed masterpiece of success gone to ruin; a profound statement of the human condition, of the ultimate sacrifice for self-knowledge.

For a more comprehensive, in-depth analysis of this work, consult Cliffs Notes on *Oedipus the King, Oedipus at Colonus,* and *Antigone.*

$$\Omega$$

OEDIPUS AT COLONUS

In the township of Colonus, a mile or so northwest of the Acropolis, Oedipus, bearing the marks of his self-mutilation twenty years earlier, wanders onstage. Old, blind, frail, and dependent upon his daughter Antigone to guide him, he trespasses in the rocky grove sacred to the Furies, or Eumenides, where, according to Apollo's prophecy, Oedipus will die.

A courteous, but insistent stranger warns him to avoid holy ground. Oedipus, realizing that he has reached his destination, declares that he will never leave and requests a conference with Theseus, king of Athens. The stranger, mindful of Oedipus' high-born station, exits to inform the people of Colonus that Oedipus has violated holy ground.

Alone with his daughter, Oedipus prays to the "ladies whose eyes are terrible." Recognizing that the Eumenides have brought him to Colonus, he implores them to "pity a man's poor carcass and his ghost" and to grant him a resting place and an end to his bitter life. The chorus, curious about the identity of the "impious, blasphemous, shameless" stranger, but cautious lest they contaminate themselves, question Oedipus; they vow that he will be safe in the grove.

Bit by bit, Oedipus reveals his identity. Horrified to behold the accursed son of Laius, the chorus changes its opinion and orders the stranger to leave. Antigone intercedes on her father's behalf, and the chorus speaks kindly to her, but remains adamant concerning Oedipus' immediate departure from Colonus. Oedipus describes his tragic past and begs for justice. The chorus is moved and decides to refer the matter to higher authorities.

Ismene, Antigone's sister, arrives on horseback with news of her brother Eteocles' *coup d'etat* and Polyneices' banishment. She shares the latest oracle, which predicts that the Thebans will clamor for Oedipus before his death and that his burial place shall prove auspicious. She warns that Creon is on his way to detain Oedipus so that his grave will bring luck to Thebes. Oedipus grieves that his sons are locked in mortal struggle for a doomed throne. The chorus, pitying Oedipus' trials, meticulously describes how he must propitiate the Eumenides with holy libations and prayers. Ismene, taking the place of her enfeebled father, hurries to obey.

The chorus encourages Oedipus to speak of his troubled past. Sighing with emotion, he recounts how fate caused him to kill his father and marry his mother and, unaware of his incest, produce children. Oedipus justifies his unholy acts, declaring before God that he is innocent.

Theseus arrives with his soldiers. He recognizes Oedipus from stories he has heard. He consoles the old man, noting that he himself has wandered strange lands and confronted danger and death; he commiserates with fellow wanderers. Oedipus is gratified at Theseus' courtesy and nobility.

Oedipus' mysterious promise to bring grace to Athens intrigues Theseus, but Oedipus declines to elaborate. He asks only for burial. Theseus listens intently to Oedipus' account of Polyneices' treachery, declares Oedipus a citizen, and offers to take him into his own house. Oedipus, however, prefers to remain in the grove. Theseus promises to protect the old man from Creon. The chorus concludes the scene with an ode in praise of Colonus, "where leaves and berries throng, and wine-dark ivy climbs the bough, and the sweet, sojourning nightingale murmurs all day long."

Antigone announces Creon's arrival. Creon prefaces his business with honeyed words to soothe the citizens' fears. He urges "poor Oedipus" to come home to Thebes where the citizens demand his return. He appeals to Oedipus' love for Antigone, who leads the life of a beggar and has no hope of marriage. Oedipus, still quick of wit, castigates his brother-in-law for verbal trickery and accuses him of trying to subvert the vengeance of the prophecy.

Creon brags that he has seized Ismene and plans to take Antigone as well. The chorus cries out in rage at the injustice. Creon threatens war if Colonus' citizens harm him. Theseus arrives and rouses his people to action. He shames Creon for his heavy-handedness, calling his strategy a disgrace on Thebes. Creon attempts to justify his villainy by disparaging Oedipus, whom he calls an "unholy man, a parricide, a man with whom his mother had been found." Again, Oedipus speaks of his past, blaming the fates for entrapping him in such an unspeakable marriage. Theseus takes Creon into custody and marches him away.

The chorus, imagining Athenian soldiers in pursuit of the Theban kidnappers, sings a hymn of victory. Theseus returns with Ismene and Antigone, and Oedipus rejoices, apologizing for talking so long with the daughters whom he feared were lost forever. Theseus interrupts their homecoming with news of a stranger from Argos who claims to be Oedipus' relative and who is praying at Poseidon's altar. Oedipus immediately guesses the stranger's identity – Polyneices. Although Oedipus rejects his son, Antigone pleads that Oedipus speak to him. The chorus, decrying the trials of old age, rounds out the scene with a sympathetic ode.

While Oedipus remains aloof, Polyneices bemoans his father and sisters' degraded lifestyle. He narrates his own miserable fate and his plans to "lead the fearless troops of Argos against Thebes" and to reestablish his family in Thebes. Oedipus, in reply to the chorus, brands Polyneices a scoundrel, predicts the failure of Polyneices' venture, and reinvokes his curse upon his son. Despite Antigone's advice that her brother abandon his foolish scheme, Polyneices sets out, pledging that "You will not ever look in my eyes again."

The chorus surmises that new sufferings lie in store for Oedipus' family. A sudden peal of thunder galvanizes Oedipus into action. He summons Theseus and prepares for death. Ismene, Antigone, and Theseus obediently follow the blind man, who seems rejuvenated by the gods' power. The chorus prays for Oedipus' soul. A messenger returns to announce Oedipus' miraculous death: after the girls cleansed Oedipus' body with holy water, the thunder again sounded. Oedipus' daughters clung to him, and he comforted them with loving words. A god-like voice chided Oedipus for his delay. Oedipus commended Ismene and Antigone into Theseus' care and vanished to his eternal rest.

Antigone, confused and dismayed, longs to return to Thebes. She and Ismene beg to be taken to Oedipus' tomb, but Theseus keeps his oath of secrecy. Antigone turns her attention toward stopping the civil war that is about to break out in Thebes.

For a more comprehensive, in-depth analysis of this work, consult Cliffs Notes on *Oedipus the King, Oedipus at Colonus,* and *Antigone.*

Ω

ANTIGONE

The action begins a day or so after Eteocles and Polyneices, Oedipus' sons, kill each other in a civil war over possession of the throne of Thebes. Creon, Oedipus' brother-in-law (who assumes the throne after Eteocles' death) accords high honors and a state funeral to Eteocles, but decrees that Polyneices' corpse must rot in the open air and be picked by predatory animals and birds in retribution for his treachery in attacking his own city. Yet, Polyneices was supposed to reign jointly with his brother, but Eteocles betrayed Polyneices and had him exiled. Thus, later, Antigone is protecting a wronged brother.

Before the royal palace, Antigone and Ismene, sisters of the deceased, hold a private conference about the disposition of Polyneices' corpse. Antigone insists that it is her sacred duty to perform sacrificial rites over Polyneices so that his soul can find rest. Ismene, eager to ward off further misfortune from their family, advises Antigone to forego disobedience to the will of Creon. Antigone counters that, in a choice between sacred law and human law, obedience to the gods deserves first place. Accepting the consequences of the act and shaming Ismene for taking the easy way out of their dilemma, Antigone pledges to bury their brother.

After the chorus comments on the recent victory of the Theban army over the Argive invaders, Creon enters and justifies his decision to dishonor the treacherous Polyneices by refusing him burial. A nervous guard interrupts, announcing that an unidentified person has disobeyed Creon's edict and buried the corpse while sentries, temporarily blinded by a sandstorm, stood their watch. Creon threatens the guard with torture and an ignoble death if he does not produce the criminal.

The chorus appears a second time to proclaim the wonders of human achievement and to warn the audience that "no city hath he who, for his rashness, dwells with sin." The appearance of Antigone, in the custody of the guard, exemplifies the chorus' horror of wrongdoing. She is accused of pouring a libation to the gods and scattering dust on her brother's body. Antigone boldly acknowledges her act. Creon castigates both his audacious niece and her sister. Although Antigone defends her sister's innocence, and Ismene reminds Creon that Antigone is soon to marry his son, Haemon, Creon shows no pity to either girl and vows to imprison both of them.

The chorus returns to bemoan the evil fate of Labdacus' hapless descendents—Laius, Oedipus, and Oedipus' children. Haemon, in contrast to his obdurate father, urges clemency for the two girls. Caught between respect for his parent and love for his future wife, he warns his father of negative public opinion: "For the dread of thy frown forbids the citizen to speak such words as would offend thine ear; but I can hear these murmurs in the dark . . ."

In anger at his son's interference, Creon calls him a "woman's slave" and rejects his "wheedling speech." Creon vows to kill Antigone "before his eyes—at her bridegroom's side!" He rescinds the charge against Ismene, but vows to the leader of the chorus that Antigone shall die in the customary manner—sealed alive in a cave with only enough food "as piety ascribes." The chorus murmurs a hymn to Aphrodite, blaming excessive love for Haemon's madness. As Antigone emerges from the palace and joins the singers in a melancholy duet, the chorus cannot hide their tears.

Teiresias, the blind seer, is led onstage, and he denounces Creon for his heavy-handedness, warning him of dire consequences to the city if he persists in the plan to execute Antigone. Creon, rejecting Teiresias' advice, sneers at the "prophet-tribe," whose fraud and greed he condemns. Before Teiresias is led away, he brings the heat of his anger closer to home by predicting that the "wailing of men and of women" will soon come to Creon's house. Creon admits that he is troubled by the prophecy.

On the advice of the chorus leader, Creon overturns the death decree and hurries to free Antigone from her rocky tomb. As the chorus rejoices, a messenger arrives to announce that, upon the discovery that Antigone hanged herself, Haemon tried to murder his father, and when his attack failed, Haemon turned his sword on himself. Haemon's mother, Eurydice, hears the news of her son's fate and withdraws to the palace.

Creon returns, bewailing his bitter lesson, and learns that Eurydice, in grief for Haemon, stabbed herself in the heart. Creon implores the fates to end his life and thereby end his suffering. The chorus leader closes the play with a reminder that "great words of prideful men are ever punished with great blows, and in old age, teach the chastened to be wise."

(Note: In 1944, Jean Anouilh presented an updated version of *Antigone* to audiences in Paris. His setting of the classic story brought to mind the sufferings of French citizens during the Nazi occupation and the difficult decisions that faced a loyal, disenfranchised people who risked death to express their outrage.)

For a more comprehensive, in-depth analysis of this work, con-

sult Cliffs Notes on *Oedipus the King, Oedipus at Colonus,* and *Antigone.*

Ω

AJAX

The play, probably Sophocles' earliest extant work, opens before Ajax's tent in the Greek camp near Troy. It is the day after the most despicable event in Ajax's life: having failed to receive the armaments of his fallen hero, Achilles, Ajax sets out to murder Menelaus and Agamemnon, leaders of the Greek army, in their sleep because they have favored Odysseus' claim over his. Athena, however, punishes Ajax's excess of pride by sending a frenzy into his brain. Deluded that he is wreaking his vengeance, Ajax tortures and slaughters bulls, sheep, and herd dogs.

As the play opens, Athena meets Odysseus, who has tracked down the errant Ajax to his tent. Athena summons Ajax, and Ajax enters, still in the power of the goddess' spell. Content that he has slain the Greeks who wanted to belittle his warlike prowess and battlefield heroics, Ajax explains that he spared Odysseus, whom he thinks he holds captive. Athena urges Ajax to kill his prisoner. Athena comments to Odysseus that the "gods love the wise of heart; the forward they abhor." The chorus ends the scene with a recounting of Ajax's grievous folly.

Tecmessa, Ajax's concubine, laments her lover's insanity and joins the chorus in a woeful duet. She details his hideous crime and his pitiable state after his reason returned. She realizes that his motionless posture forebodes some terrible retribution, and she begs the chorus leader's aid. Ajax calls out for the two people he cherishes – his son, Eurysaces, and his brother, Teucer. Opening the door of the tent, Tecmessa reveals Ajax, who sits amid the carnage of the previous night and begs his shipmates to execute him.

Tecmessa attempts to assuage his grief and shame, but Ajax, still yearning for revenge, brushes her aside and wallows in his torment.

He dreads facing Telamon, his father, with news of his disgrace. Despairing of a solution, he concludes, "Nobly to live, or else nobly to die befits proud birth. There is no more to say." Tecmessa, who has known an equal measure of strife in her lifetime, begs him to consider her plight. He asks for his son, whom Tecmessa has hidden from his crazed hand, and praises her foresight in protecting the boy.

In hope that Eurysaces will excel in warlike strength, Ajax asks the attendant to lift the child so he can view the slaughtered animals. Ajax entrusts Eurysaces to Teucer and wills the boy his "firm-stitched thong, this sevenfold spear-proof shield." As Ajax returns to his solitary brooding, the chorus, fearful of Ajax's meaning, sings an apprehensive ode.

Ajax reappears carrying his sword and departs in search of a private place. The chorus calls on Io, Pan, Apollo, and Zeus to stop the terrible act that Ajax intends. A messenger announces the arrival of Teucer, whom the Greeks are taunting as the brother of a maniac. Calchas, mindful of Ajax's destiny, detains Teucer. The leader of the chorus becomes concerned with Ajax's long absence and summons Tecmessa to his aid.

On a lonely stretch of beach, Ajax contemplates his suicide. He begs for Hermes to guide him to the underworld and for the Erinyes (the Furies) to punish Menelaus and Agamemnon for causing his death. Before the chorus can intervene, Ajax falls on his sword and lies motionless in the undergrowth.

A semi-chorus of sailors enters in search of Ajax. Tecmessa's piercing cry stops them in their tracks. Before anyone can view her lover's body, she shrouds him in her mantle and mourns aloud, "Hapless Ajax, who was once so great." The chorus blames fate for working out a "dark doom of ineffable miseries." Teucer gazes at the torn body and, like the chorus, blames the gods, who "plan these things and all things ever for mankind."

In the final episode, Menelaus declares that Ajax shall remain unburied as punishment for treachery. The chorus leader admonishes Menelaus' "outrage to the dead," and Teucer upbraids the Greek commander for his haughty pride. As Teucer and Menelaus engage in heated discussion, Tecmessa returns with her son. Teucer exits to dig Ajax's grave. The chorus chants a mournful song filled with rhetorical questions concerning the luckless Ajax.

Agamemnon, scornful of Ajax's brother, pretends that he cannot understand Teucer's words and tells him to find a more civilized spokesman. Odysseus intervenes, entreating Agamemnon to allow him to "speak out the truth, yet still as ever ply his oar in stroke with thine." With Agamemnon's blessing, Odysseus settles the matter, declaring that although Ajax was his own bitter foe, he would not dishonor so great a Greek warrior. Agamemnon softens his callous spirit and allows the burial. The leader is impressed with Odysseus' wisdom. Odysseus generously offers to help Teucer inter the body; Teucer acknowledges the gesture, but begs to complete the rites alone.

Ω

ELECTRA

Electra is the twin sister of Orestes and the daughter of Aga-memnon and Clytemnestra. Clytemnestra, with the help of her lover, Aegisthus, schemed to assassinate Agamemnon upon his return from the Trojan War. As the play opens, Orestes has returned from Phocis after learning from the Pythian oracle that, alone and unarmed, he must avenge his father's death.

Employing Pylades, his pedagogue, as a spy, Orestes awaits infor-mation about the situation in Mycenae and retreats to his father's tomb to leave a libation and the traditional lock of hair. Orestes optimisti-cally notes, "O my fatherland, and ye gods of the land, receive me with good fortune in this journey, – and ye also, halls of my fathers, for I come with a divine mandate to cleanse you righteously; send me not dishonored from the land, but grant that I may rule over my possessions, and restore my house!"

After their departure, Electra, dressed in servant's garb, enters and chants a duet with the chorus, lamenting her sad state. Without her brother's help, she cannot avenge herself on her father's murderers, the same two people who now force her to serve at their table and who waste her father's fortune in wanton luxuries. Electra is aware of a nagging compunction that fills her with sadness and prevents her from marrying and leading a normal life. She is peeved with her brother, whom she once saved, for delaying to come to her rescue and end this awful vow of bloody revenge.

Chrysothemis, their compliant sister, also grieves for the family's plight, but she lacks the strength to combat Clytemnestra and Aegisthus. In contrast, Electra has no patience with her sister; she denounces her weakness. Chrysothemis retaliates with the ominous news that Electra will be entombed in a distant dungeon if she does not leave off her perpetual mourning.

Chrysothemis offers unintentional encouragement by announcing a vision which has caused Clytemnestra to send her with a libation for Agamemnon's tomb. In their mother's dream, Agamemnon plants his scepter in the earth, and it grows into a tree that overshadows the land. Electra takes this omen as a sign that her prayers have been answered. She urges Chrysothemis to cast aside Clytemnestra's unholy gifts and to offer locks of their hair and Electra's girdle instead. The chorus then sings a hopeful song that the "portent will not fail to bring woe upon the partners in crime."

Clytemnestra berates Electra for displaying herself outside the gates in defiance of Aegisthus' command. She also taunts Electra for siding with Agamemnon, whom Clytemnestra blames for sacrificing their daughter (Iphigenia) to the gods. Content with her bloody retaliation for Agamemnon's crime, Clytemnestra encourages Electra to speak freely of her discontent.

Electra's side of the story exonerates Agamemnon. She views the killing of Iphigenia as a hunting accident, one which was committed innocently at the will of the goddess Artemis. Clytemnestra warns her that Aegisthus will punish his stepdaughter's effrontery. Clytemnestra then prays to Phoebus to accept her offering, to overcome those who plot against her, and to extend her rule over the House of Atreus in the company of those children who support her.

The pedagogue announces a fabricated story about Orestes' death. Clytemnestra shushes Electra's cries and asks for particulars of Orestes' demise. Pylades describes in great detail a disastrous chariot accident at the Delphian games, where Orestes' body was so mangled that his corpse was cremated and his ashes sent to Mycenae. Clytemnestra teeters on the brink of joy and looks forward to relief from the second source of her uneasiness, Electra. Electra, in despair of her one hope, evokes Nemesis. Clytemnestra treats the bringer of good news to hospitality, leaving Electra outside to mourn Orestes.

As Electra and the chorus chant an antiphony of woe, Chrysothemis brings joyful tidings – the remnants of recent libations and a
lock of Orestes' hair. Electra refutes the evidence, declaring the lock
to be a remembrance brought from her brother's corpse. Pledging
herself to action, Electra declares herself "ripe" and exhorts her sister
to join in a plot of vengeance. Chrysothemis thinks Electra is men-
tally unbalanced. As Chrysothemis takes her leave, the chorus laments
the seriousness and danger of Electra's dire task.

Orestes conceals his identity and greets his sister with the funeral
urn, which she tearfully clutches. At length, he reveals his father's
signet ring and embraces his sister, who proclaims her brother's existence to the chorus leader. Preparing a hoax to conceal their deadly
plot, Orestes and Electra meet Pylades on his way out of the palace.
He, too, realizes the danger of their situation and urges them to make
quick work of killing their mother.

Orestes enters the palace in search of Clytemnestra, whose cries
can be heard within, as Electra stands watch outside lest Aegisthus
intervene. Orestes returns, his hands red with his mother's blood,
which Electra terms an offering to Ares. Aegisthus approaches with
questions about the visitors from Phocis. Electra explains that "they
have found a way to the heart of their hostess." Aegisthus, cheerfully
anticipating his view of Orestes' corpse, opens the doors of the palace
and pulls back the shroud. He is alarmed to find his paramour murdered and instantly realizes his own situation. Orestes and Pylades
force him into the palace to his doom.

$$\Omega$$

_____ THE TRACHINIAE _____

As a prologue, Queen Deianeira reminisces about her rescue from
Achelous, the river god, while she still lived at Pleuron in the home
of her father, Oeneus. Hercules, mighty son of Zeus and Alcmena,
having saved her from marriage with a bestial deity, made her his
bride, but her married life has been filled with anxiety. Hercules now

lives an itinerate life during a year's enforced service and rarely sees
Deianeira and her children. The family, exiled after Hercules murdered Iphitus, lives in Trachis in northeast Greece and receives little
news of Hercules.

The nurse pities the queen's distress and urges her to send Hyllus,
Deianeira's son, for news of his father. Hyllus reports a rumor that
his father is free of his obligation to Omphale, barbarian queen of
Lydia, and is involved in a war with King Eurytus of Euboea as a
means of avenging himself on his oppressor. As Hyllus sets out on
his quest, the Trachiniae (unmarried women who serve as Deianeira's
confidantes) arrive and sing a sympathetic ode to her, whom they
picture as a "bird lorn of its mate."

Deianeira verbalizes her apprehension at Hercules' latest departure. Usually he is in a warlike mood, but in his last farewell he left
an ancient tablet containing cryptic writings, and he outlined his will,
making provisions for his wife and sons should he not return. Citing
a prophecy from the ancient oak at Dodona, Hercules predicted that
the next fifteen months would prove whether he would die or whether
he would survive and live an untroubled life.

An elderly messenger brings news from Lichas, a herald, that
Hercules is returning to Trachis, but has been delayed by the Malians,
who press him for news. Lichas precedes Hercules and brings the
women whom Hercules captured as war prizes. He reveals Hercules'
rationale for killing Iphitus, son of King Eurytus: Eurytus humiliated
Hercules by ejecting him from his home, and Hercules retaliated by
hurling the innocent Iphitus from a cliff. Zeus punished Hercules for
his savagery by enslaving him for a year. At the end of his servitude,
Hercules avenged himself by attacking Oechalia, killing Eurytus, and
capturing his daughter, Iole. After hearing these dire details, Deianeira
takes pity on Iole, who remains silent.

Lichas then leads the captives into the house; then when Lichas
is absent, the messenger contradicts Lichas' story. He tells Deianeira
that Hercules' motive was lust – not vengeance – and that Hercules
invented the slight as justification for a war on the city of Oechalia
so that he might capture Iole. When Lichas returns, the messenger
upbraids him for concealing the truth from his queen. At first, Lichas
refuses to acknowledge Hercules' passion for Iole, but after Deianeira
asks for the truth, Lichas admits Hercules' infatuation. The gracious

queen rewards him for his honesty, and the chorus sings an ode describing the violence that accompanied the queen's courtship.

Deianeira readily concedes Iole's youth and beauty. To save Hercules from her rival, Deianeira locates a vial of blood which she has saved in a bronze urn to assure herself of Hercules' love. She uses it now to anoint a handwoven robe in order to endow it with the magic of Nessus, the centaur whom Hercules shot with a poisoned arrow for touching Deianeira "with wanton hands." As he lay dying, Nessus promised Deianeira that his blood would protect her from any rival. Lichas departs, carrying the garment to his master. The chorus then sings a hopeful song that the charm will reunite the queen and her husband.

When a wisp of wool consumes itself when it comes in contact with sunlight, Deianeira is seized with misgivings – this time concerning the virulent arrow poison which permeated the centaur's blood and caused his death. She fears that it will also kill Hercules. Hyllus returns from his mission to announce that her fears were well-founded. Hercules, wearing the gift robe while making his thanksgiving offering to Zeus, was seized with an agony "that racked his bones."

Hercules accused Lichas of treachery and, despite Lichas' explanation of Deianeira's part in the gift, dashed out his brains on the sea-cliffs. Cursing the day of his marriage, Hercules begged his son to bring him home to Trachis. Without a word of explanation, Deianeira turns toward the house as Hyllus reviles her and the chorus leader urges her to justify her actions. The chorus bemoans the ancient prophecy and blames the gods for Deianeira's sufferings.

The nurse appears and announces that Deianeira, lying on her husband's bed, bared her left side and stabbed herself in the heart with his sword. Hyllus blames himself for his harsh treatment of his mother and grieves for both his parents.

Hercules is borne in on a litter and begs to be freed from his misery. Hyllus, who is unable to kill his father, reveals Deianeira's death. When Hercules exults that she has suffered for her wrongdoing, Hyllus explains Deianeira's innocence of evil intent and describes the love-charm that Nessus gave her to save her marriage.

Hercules realizes that the prophecy – that a creature already in Hades would cause his death – has been fulfilled. He persuades Hyllus to swear a sacred filial oath to carry out his command. On pain of a perpetual curse, Hyllus must cut oak and olive branches and build a funeral pyre for his father. Hyllus is dismayed at such a responsibility and promises to provide the wood but not to light the fire. In addition, Hercules requires Hyllus to marry Iole. The boy is torn by indecision but agrees to obey. As the attendants carry Hercules away, Hyllus chants to the gods, begging forgiveness and blaming Zeus for "sorrows manifold and strange."

Ω

PHILOCTETES

By order of Agamemnon and Menelaus, joint commanders of the Greek invaders, Odysseus and Neoptolemus, Achilles' son, leave the battlefields of Troy and search the lonely island of Lemnos for Philoctetes. Odysseus is cautious, mindful that Philoctetes bears a grudge against him; he convinces Neoptolemus that they must use deception against Philoctetes if Neoptolemus is to gain his share of wartime glory. Odysseus then departs so that he will not be recognized.

The chorus, composed of the men's companions, discusses Philoctetes' dismal fate – abandoned by the Greeks on Lemnos after fate caused him to be bitten by a serpent. His perpetual misery from a malodorous wound, coupled with his meager life in a cave subsisting on wild game, makes him an object of pity. Dressed in rags, Philoctetes approaches. He is eager for friendship to relieve his loneliness, and he begs for news of the war. Neoptolemus introduces himself and listens to Philoctetes' lengthy complaint about his ten years' exile and his mistreatment at the hands of his fellow Greeks.

Neoptolemus pretends to hate Agamemnon, Menelaus, and Odysseus, Philoctetes' sworn enemies. He tells Philoctetes which Greeks have died in the war – Achilles, Ajax, Patroclus – and the events that brought Neoptolemus into the war. Bidding farewell, Neoptolemus makes a show of setting sail to Scyros, his home and refuge from the hated war. Philoctetes begs Neoptolemus to take him away from

Lemnos and warns that destruction often falls on people who are blessed by fortune. The chorus agrees.

A spy, dressed as a merchant, brings news that a band of Greeks, led by Phoinix, is pursuing Neoptolemus to bring him back to Troy. After assuring himself of Philoctetes' loyalty to Neoptolemus, the spy offers information about Odysseus, who has set out to retrieve Philoctetes in response to Helenus' prophecy that Troy will be secure until Philoctetes arrives on the scene. Philoctetes urges Neoptolemus to hurry and set sail so that they may avoid confrontation with Odysseus.

Philoctetes requires little packing: he needs herbs for his wound and his bow and arrows. They enter the cave together; the chorus decries Philoctetes' lamentable state and rejoices that he will soon be delivered from undeserved exile. Returning from the cave, Philoctetes is seized with a spasm in his injured foot and begs to be put out of his misery. He entrusts his bow and arrows to Neoptolemus, who pledges loyalty to his friend. In anguish, Philoctetes sinks down and falls asleep. The chorus prays to the "patron of mankind, great physician of the mind," to grant him relief.

Philoctetes awakens, refreshed and grateful for Neoptolemus' faithfulness. Neoptolemus' conscience gnaws at him for his duplicity. He admits that he plans to take Philoctetes to Troy. At first, Philoctetes is furious with Neoptolemus for his betrayal, but he realizes that Neoptolemus is being manipulated and pities him. Odysseus suddenly appears and boldly admits his deception, crediting the will of Zeus for Philoctetes' wretched fate. Philoctetes vows to commit suicide; Odysseus orders him bound.

Odysseus decides to take Philoctetes' weapons and leave the wounded man behind. As Odysseus departs toward the shore, brandishing the weapons and exulting in his victory, Philoctetes labels him "so vile, so base, so impious." The chorus, however, declares Odysseus a patriot and urges Philoctetes to agree to accompany him to Troy. Philoctetes, longing to die, retires to the cave.

Neoptolemus returns to expiate his crime against Philoctetes, and Odysseus follows at his elbow, arguing the need to fulfill their duty to Greece. They reach for their weapons; Odysseus realizes that Neoptolemus is committed to an honorable act – the return of Philoctetes' weapons.

Odysseus departs, and Neoptolemus makes amends to Philoctetes for stealing his weapons. Just as he returns them, however, Odysseus again appears. Philoctetes takes aim at Odysseus, but Neoptolemus prevents him from loosing the arrow. Philoctetes denounces the Greek warriors as "loud pretending boasters, brave but in tongue, and cowards in the field." Neoptolemus pleads with him that sailing to Troy is the right choice to make, both as a source of medical care for his wound and as a response to Helenus' prophecy. Philoctetes, however, pleads with Neoptolemus to desert the war effort and take him home.

Miraculously, Hercules appears from above with a decree from Zeus that Philoctetes must obey the will of the gods. He urges both Philoctetes and Neoptolemus to "go then, and, like two lions in the field roaming for prey, guard ye each other well." Philoctetes agrees and bids farewell to his lowly cave and to Lemnos. The chorus prays that the ocean nymphs grant a safe voyage.

Ω

EURIPIDES

- *Electra*

- *Medea*

- *Hippolytus*

- *Andromache*

- *The Trojan Women*

- *Alcestis*

- *The Heracleidae*

- *Hecuba*

- *The Suppliants*

- *Heracles*

- *Ion*

- *Iphigenia in Tauris*

- *Helena*

- *The Phoenician Women*

- *Orestes*

- *The Bacchae*

- *Iphigenia in Aulis*

- *The Cyclops*

EURIPIDES

In sharp contrast to the winsome personality of his contemporary, Sophocles, Euripides was a loner and a reputed woman-hater—a contemplative, controversial man who often found himself at odds with the sophists, whose elaborate style of logic was in vogue at the time. At times ridiculed and rejected by his peers, Euripides ignored the political and social gossip and intrigue in which cosmopolitan Athenians delighted and sought refuge in reading and thought. He is described as gray-haired with a long beard and prominent moles on his face. Differing opinions show him as either sensitive and introspective or gloomy, sad-eyed, and unapproachable, depending upon the attitude of the observer. Whichever the case, however, the fruit of his inner turmoil has ennobled theater beyond measure.

Euripides was born on the island of Salamis around 484 B.C. One legend declares that he was born on the day that Athens overcame the Persians at the battle of Salamis, although this conjunction is unlikely. The son of Mnesarchus, a retailer in a village near Athens who eventually went bankrupt, and Cleito, whom comic writers ridiculed for selling vegetables, Euripides served as both dancer and torchbearer at the rites of Apollo Zosterius. He probably enjoyed prosperity in his early youth, as indicated by his liberal education and relative leisure.

Euripides' father is said to have believed an oracle predicting "crowns of victory" in his son's future and to have insisted that he train for a career in athletics. Probably, however, Euripides completed his military obligation in 466 B.C. before studying athletics, painting, and then philosophy under Prodicus and Anaxagoras. He took up drama at the age of twenty-five, but won no first prizes until 441 B.C.

Despite his reputation for distrusting women and for enduring at least two disastrous marriages to unfaithful wives, first Melite and then Choerine, mother of his three sons, Euripides achieved fame for his sensitive studies of female characters, especially Medea and Phaedra. He has been accused of misogyny, but he appears to have been asocial rather than hostile to women. He preferred solitude to the lionized life of a writer in Athens, and so he made his home in a cave on Salamis, where he built an impressive library and pursued daily communion with the sea and sky. In fifty years of writing, he earned only five first prizes for his ninety-two plays, the last a posthumous award; he often attained last place at the Dionysian Festival.

Late in his life, around 408 B.C., Euripides journeyed to Thessaly and Macedon and lived among Athenian notables, including Timotheus and Agathon, at the rustic court of King Archelaus. He died in 406 B.C. and is thought to have been buried in Pella. A cenotaph near Piraeus was supposedly struck by lightning, which some construe as an omen befitting an atheist, and which some consider a mark of Zeus' favor. The youngest of his three sons followed his father's profession.

Euripides was the least successful in his lifetime of the three great tragedians of fifth-century Athens, yet his plays enjoyed a greater demand in the ensuing centuries than those of either Aeschylus or Sophocles. He left a larger body of extant plays – eighteen or nineteen, compared to seven each for his rivals – among them *The Cyclops,* the only satyr play to survive from antiquity. He enlivened the ancient myths which formed the basis of his plays by altering their plots and adding more credible dimensions. As Aristotle notes, Euripides made aggressive appeals to his audiences, exciting them to both pity and fear.

Despite his reliance on wooden prologues and convenient *deus ex machina* conclusions, Euripides earned the reputation for being the most tragic of the tragic dramatists, appealing more to human emotions than to religious sentiment. He faulted sexual passion for causing great human sorrow. His characters make drawn-out speeches which rely upon intricate turns of phrase, allusion, and sophistry. Yet, his keen insight into human motivation indicates a sympathy which even Sophocles applauded.

Euripides, however, poses a problem for the critic. Some have labeled him a kind of new-wave romantic; some have expounded upon his realism in portraying human frailties, such as cowardice and jealously; others have accused him of fervent pacifism, probably the most loathsome pill for Athenians to swallow. Whatever "-ism" appears most applicable, though, ancient audiences patronized his productions, even if the playwright denigrated their chauvinism and forced them to experience moments of terror and illumination.

Scenes from Euripides' greatest triumphs – *Medea* and *Hippolytus* – still have the power to grip an audience. The shock of Medea's decision to slaughter her own children and Phaedra's intense wrestling with lust for her stepson put the audience in touch with their own nameless demons. Euripides, the humanist, identifies with the victims of oppression, particularly women and slaves. He rejects simple answers. His belief in the dignity of the individual proved prophetic, for the next generation of Athenians came to acknowledge the failure of its traditional militarism. Euripides' epitaph, ironically, proved true: "All Greece hath Euripides won."

Ω

ELECTRA

Euripides' dramatic version of the Electra legend – the story of the ill-fated children of Agamemnon, whose wife plotted with her lover to murder her husband upon his return from the Trojan Wars – was performed about 413 B.C. and varies somewhat in plot and theme from Sophocles' *Electra*. The story opens after Electra's marriage to a peasant, who speaks the prologue, explaining how Aegisthus, Clytemnestra's lover and Agamemnon's killer, decided to kill Electra to rid himself of a possible obstacle to his evil ambitions. Although Clytemnestra actively took part in her husband's murder, she intervened and rescued her daughter. Aegisthus enacted a second plan whereby he betrothed Electra to the peasant so that her sons would be humbly born and pose no threat to his hold on Argos' throne. The peasant, a gentle and noble man, out of respect for Electra's high station, maintains a platonic relationship with her.

Electra appears, dressed in rags and bearing a water jar on her head, and she explains why she toils at such menial labors – to dem-

onstrate to the gods the untenable situation in which Aegisthus has
thrust her. Then she and the peasant depart to do more chores.

Orestes, Electra's brother, arrives, accompanied by his companion,
Pylades. Orestes divulges the reason for his journey—he has made
a pilgrimage to Apollo's shrine to pledge himself to avenge his father's
murder. After leaving the customary lock of hair and a blood sacrifice
at his father's tomb, Orestes skirts the town walls in order to learn
from the locals some crucial information about his sister, who he has
learned is now married. Electra returns with her load of water and
recounts the misfortunes of her life.

A chorus of Argive peasant women sings responsively with Electra
about a festival in honor of Hera which will take place in three days.
Electra declines to participate and resigns herself to a life of woe. The
chorus leader blames Clytemnestra's sister, Helen, for initiating the
dire chain of events that led to the Trojan War. Electra spies the two
strangers and fears they are brigands lying in ambush. Orestes, who
chooses to conceal his identity, assures Electra that his mission is
peaceful—he brings news of Electra's brother.

Electra answers the stranger's questions, explaining her domestic
arrangement with her husband and rallying to the stranger's question about her commitment to avenge Agamemnon's death. Electra
regrets that her brother was taken away at an early age; she says that
she would no longer recognize him, but that her father's old servant,
the man who took Orestes to a safe home, is the only friend who could
identify him. Orestes asks for more information, and the chorus, ignorant of city gossip, is also eager to hear more details. Electra elaborates
on the despicable state of her father's home—his blood still stains a
wall in the palace, while his widow enjoys the luxury of his Trojan
captives, and Aegisthus desecrates the bare monument over Agamemnon's grave and ridicules the absent Orestes.

As the group pursues their conversation outside the peasant's gate,
Electra's husband arrives and chides her for her immodesty. When
he learns the nature of the strangers' visit, however, he apologizes
for his hasty criticism and extends his hospitality to them. Orestes
praises the peasant's good manners and worthy outlook and accepts
lodging for the night. Electra speaks in private with her husband,
lamenting their meager home; she urges the peasant to send for her
father's old servant to provide entertainment for the noble visitors.

The chorus then sings an ode celebrating Achilles' war deeds and denouncing Clytemnestra's treachery.

The old servant, bringing a lamb, cheese, wine, and garlands, arrives at the hut. He sheds a tear, which Electra construes as a mark of his sympathy for either herself or her exiled brother. The old servant says that on his way from the fields, he stopped at Agamemnon's tomb to do honor to his former master and discovered the sacrifice of a black ram and a ritual lock of hair, which matches the color and texture of Electra's hair. Electra doubts that her hair or even her footprint could serve as proof of relationship to the doer of the deed; she also doubts the existence of a home-loomed garment that Orestes would still be wearing after so long a time.

When the old servant sees Orestes, he examines him at close range, amazed that the stranger is really the boy whom he once spirited out of Argos. The scar above Orestes' eye convinces Electra, and the two share a joyous reunion, accompanied by paeans from the chorus. Orestes pursues the business of his journey and learns from the old servant that he has no friends who will assist him in righting the wrongs done to Agamemnon. The old man suggests a possible approach: he says that he passed Aegisthus near the stables, unaccompanied by soldiers and in the act of sacrificing oxen to the nymphs. Orestes immediately sees a way of gaining audience with Aegisthus. He must move accordingly.

Electra relieves Orestes' concern for Clytemnestra by promising to kill her mother. She sends the old man with news that she has borne a son. Orestes offers a prayer to Zeus and Hera for their success. They part, and the chorus sings of bloody Aegisthus' alliance with Clytemnestra. The leader summons Electra to hear the sounds of fighting. Orestes' servant bears the message that confirms their hopes: Aegisthus has been slain. He describes how Aegisthus offered Orestes the knife so that he might take part in the sacrifice. Orestes dismembered the calf, revealing irregularities in the entrails, an inauspicious omen. As Aegisthus studied the signs, Orestes hacked through the villain's spine with a cleaver. The servants, assured by an old man's positive identification of the rightful heir to the Argive throne, allied themselves with Orestes and Pylades.

The chorus rejoices, and Aegisthus' body is carried in. At first, Electra flaunts their success, but she soon ceases her celebration in fear that she will offend the gods. She speaks chastising words to the corpse and punctuates her disgust with a shove of her foot. The attendants hide the body, and everyone awaits Clytemnestra's arrival. Orestes, in fear of the outcome, suddenly weakens in his resolve to murder his mother.

Clytemnestra makes an impressive entrance in a chariot adorned by the Trojan maidens that Agamemnon brought to Argos as the spoils of war. She considers them her rightful property in exchange for the child that Agamemnon sacrificed years ago. She elaborates on Agamemnon's offense against their marriage when he carried off Cassandra as a war prize and installed her in their home as his mistress.

Clytemnestra brazenly admits her part in her husband's murder and urges Electra to prove her wrong. Electra speaks at length about her mother's vanity, about her deliberate attempt to lure a lover after Agamemnon left Argos to return Helen to her rightful home. Electra's ominous summary identifies Aegisthus' error in judgment: "Who so fixes his gaze on wealth or noble birth and weds a wicked woman, is a fool; better is a humble partner in his home, if she be virtuous, than a proud one."

Clytemnestra clucks a motherly admission of Electra's devotion to her father; she admits that her own bloody deed was shameful. She attempts to justify their miserable family arrangement in which her son remains an exile, her present husband tyrannizes his stepdaughter, and her daughter lives the tattered, ignoble life of a peasant. Electra begs advice on offering the usual sacrifice on the tenth day after giving birth; Clytemnestra, complaining about the lack of neighborly assistance, agrees to help.

After they enter the hut, the chorus chants a song of vengeance. From within, Clytemnestra can be heard pleading for mercy. The chorus remains adamant in its condemnation of Clytemnestra's multiple sins. Overcome with their deed, Orestes and Electra return, dripping with gore and wide-eyed with the horror of their bold deed. Orestes describes his mother's piteous gestures of baring her breast and laying her hand on his chin just before execution.

The chorus interrupts their woeful retelling and points out the miraculous appearance of the Dioscuri, Castor and Polydeuces, above the house. The holy pair blame Apollo for instigating the butchery and chart a path for Electra and Orestes' redemption. First, Electra must marry Pylades, and Orestes must again leave home to avoid the madness of the Furies. He must seek Athena's temple in Athens and have his case tried at the Areopagus. If the votes are even, Orestes will be exonerated, and Loxias will take the blame for the advice given by his oracle.

In addition, the Argives must bury Aegisthus; then Menelaus, newly arrived from Troy, shall join Helen in burying Clytemnestra. The Furies shall sink into the earth, Orestes will make a new home for himself near the river Alpheus, and the peasant-husband shall be rewarded for his dignified treatment of Electra. In the future, Orestes shall live a trouble-free life.

The chorus begs a word with the Dioscuri and questions their unwillingness to spare the children this dread task of avenging their father. The Dioscuri blame the fates and Apollo for placing a fatal curse on the house of Atreus. Orestes and Electra, after their brief reunion, weep because they must be parted once more. The Dioscuri utter a parting benediction: "Yet as we fly through heaven's expanse we help not the wicked; but whoso in his life loves piety and justice, all such we free from troublous toils and save. Wherefore let no man be minded to act unjustly . . . such the warning I, a god, to mortals give."

For a more comprehensive, in-depth analysis of this work, consult Cliffs Notes on *Euripides' Electra & Medea.*

Ω

_____ *MEDEA* _____

First produced in 431 B.C., the play opens at a point well into the intense romantic involvement of Jason and Medea. In the events that precede, Jason, at the command of Pelias, his uncle, led a band of heroes and demigods on an expedition aboard the *Argo* to Colchis, the land between the Black Sea and the Caspian Sea, where King Aeetes guarded the fabled Golden Fleece. Medea, Aeetes' daughter, spurred by her passion for Jason, employed sorcery, tricked Aeetes, and murdered her brother in order to assure Jason's success in stealing the Golden Fleece.

After their return to Pelias' kingdom, Medea committed another atrocity – against Pelias this time – but the couple, along with their two sons, was unable to grasp the throne, and so they fled to Corinth. The first scene, set near Creon's palace, reveals a nurse, whose lament characterizes the powerful theme that undergirds the drama – love turned to bitter, unbridled hatred. Jason has jilted Medea, forsaken his sons, and married Creon's daughter. The nurse fears that Medea's explosive passion will lead her to some unthinkable bloodbath.

The children's attendant passes along a tidbit he overheard – that Creon plans to drive Medea and her children out of Corinth. The nurse, fearful of Medea's wrath, chants antiphonally with the chorus and Medea, who remains inside the house – the nurse lamenting the dissolution of the family, Medea longing for vengeance and relief from guilt, and the chorus of Corinthian women concerned about the state of affairs in general. Medea then joins the chorus onstage and bemoans the injustice of a woman's life.

Without mincing words, Creon exiles Medea and her children, confessing his fear of Medea's supernatural machinations. Medea denies her reputation for witchcraft, but Creon is unconvinced. Still, she gains a single day's respite from him, upon pain of death if she remains longer than sunrise of the next day. After Creon's departure, Medea weighs several possibilities for vengeance, including fire in the couple's house, a sword through their hearts, and poison. The chorus, echoing Medea's fiendish mouthings, lends moral support.

Jason enters, mocking Medea's anger. Medea calls him a "craven villain" and enumerates the ways in which she assisted his expedition. Jason scolds Medea for expecting too much. He delivers a formal justification for his choice of a bride – he needs a political alliance with Creon to assure his safety. He degrades womankind with an arrogant generalization: "You women have such strange ideas; you think all is well so long as your married life runs smooth. But if some mischance occurs to ruffle your love – all that was good and lovely before, you reckon as enemies now."

Medea parries with a swift condemnation of his "villain's heart." Jason counters by blaming Medea for cursing Creon. Her rejoinder is not unexpected – she extends the curse to Jason's house as well. At the conclusion of this vitriolic exchange, the chorus begins an ode about the excesses of love, blaming Aphrodite for causing the trouble.

Aegeus, king of Athens, passes through and offers Medea a home in exile in exchange for her promise to relieve his childless state. His only stipulation is that she must exit from Creon's jurisdiction on her own. They strike a bargain.

At the chorus' return, Medea speaks and chills their blood with her plot to murder Jason's bride with a poisoned robe and chaplet and then to slay her own children. She brushes aside their warnings and immerses herself in vengeance. Jason arrives in answer to her summons and succumbs to her trickery and to the calculated tears that she lets fall "for her children's sake." Jason agrees to have their banishment rescinded and to persuade his bride to take them in. Medea offers the robe and chaplet as tokens of gratitude and bids her sons deliver them with their own hands.

In dread, the chorus awaits the outcome of Medea's plotting. The children return, and their attendant announces that they are freed from exile and that the bride has accepted Medea's gifts. Medea mourns the destruction that is to follow. The attendant, thinking that she fears for her sons, misconstrues her emotion. Left alone with the children, Medea wavers between strength of will and compassion for her offspring. Then she kisses them and sends them into the house. The chorus contemplates the pathos of parents whose children die in childhood.

A messenger enters and tells Medea that Creon and his daughter have died. Astounded at Medea's delight, the messenger doubts her sanity. She asks for particulars of the deaths and learns that Jason's new wife turned away from her future stepchildren but willingly accepted the robe and chaplet. He recounts how the royal household was thrown into a fury when the princess suffered twofold torments — flames on her head and about her body from the double treachery. The servants shied away from her unrecognizable corpse, but Creon, unaware of the danger, embraced her lifeless form and died the same tortured death.

Again, Medea spurns the warnings of the chorus and sets about the second prong of her revenge. Inside the house, the boys raise their cries in vain as Medea strikes them with her sword. The chorus, amazed at Medea's coldbloodedness, doubts that any deed can rival a mother's slaughter of her innocent children. They disclose the deed to Jason, who prepares to strike Medea down in retaliation.

Medea suddenly appears over the house in a chariot drawn by dragons. She bears the children's corpses with her, and she calls to

Jason, taunting him that he cannot harm her now. He regrets his marriage to a woman who could kill her own brother and compares her
to Scylla and a she-lion. She exults at having "wrung [his] heart," refuses
to allow him to embrace or bury the two boys, and predicts an ignoble
death for their father beneath the "shattered relic of Argo." Jason yells
out a curse and regrets having given life to his ill-fated sons. The
chorus chants a reminder that, in the affairs of human beings, the
gods often work in strange fashion.

**For a more comprehensive, in-depth analysis of this work, con-
sult Cliffs Notes on _Euripides' Electra & Medea._**

Ω

_____ _HIPPOLYTUS_ _____

One of Euripides' most successful plays, _Hippolytus,_ performed in
428 B.C., was his second attempt to write about this tragedy of love.
His first version, which failed to please the audience, has unfortunately not survived to illustrate what changes he made to improve
it. The story deals with a complex _menage à trois_ – Hippolytus, illegitimate son of King Theseus of Athens by the amazon Antiope; Hippolytus' father; and Hippolytus' stepmother, Phaedra.

The play opens before the royal palace at Troezen, where statues
of Aphrodite and Artemis adorn the facade. Aphrodite speaks the prologue. She boasts her power "to ruin all who vaunt themselves at me,"
singling out Hippolytus, a faithful follower of Artemis. To Aphrodite,
Hippolytus is a source of rancor because of his disdain of love and
marriage. The goddess vows to destroy him that very day. Aphrodite
further explains how she has already involved Phaedra, filling her
heart with illicit passions for her stepson, and how she intends to cause
Theseus, Hippolytus' father, to kill Hippolytus.

Hippolytus returns home with his hunting companions and adorns
the statue of Artemis, remarking about the goddess' delight in human
self-control. The leader of Hippolytus' retinue reminds Hippolytus that

other people scorn an excess of reserve; he urges Hippolytus to give
equal devotion to the goddess of passion. Hippolytus rejects the advice
and flaunts his faithfulness to celibacy. He requests a rubdown for
his horses so that he can exercise them after dinner and exits the stage,
leaving the leader in prayer before Aphrodite's monument.

A chorus of local women enters, pondering the unexplained frenzy
that is consuming Phaedra. A nurse comes in and leads Phaedra to
a couch. The nurse, fearful that Phaedra is dying, laments her inability
to conquer the wasting disease that causes Phaedra's unease. She
advises her patient that "mortal men should pledge themselves to
moderate friendships only, not to such as reach the very heart's core."
The chorus leader admits that she too is perplexed by Phaedra's dis-
tracted meanderings and weakened state.

When the nurse reminds Phaedra that her death will deny her
children an inheritance and that Hippolytus will assume his father's
throne, Phaedra snaps to attention. The nurse siezes the opportunity
to wrench Phaedra from her malaise, but Phaedra is too ashamed to
admit her fatal attraction for Hippolytus. The nurse probes deeper
and learns the truth. She is shocked and dismayed that Phaedra has
become a victim of Aphrodite's whims. The chorus, too, abandons
hope that Phaedra can be saved from Aphrodite's schemes.

Phaedra elaborates on her plan to counter her illicit passion – she
will remain silent and endure the pain without giving in to a sordid
relationship that would sully her reputation. The nurse has second
thoughts in the matter. She urges Phaedra to admit her passion and
avoid an excess of chastity lest she become a victim of pride. Her solution is simple – they will look for a charm to soothe Phaedra's suffering. The chorus leader, in opposition to the nurse's simplistic solution,
maintains her preference for chastity.

The nurse proposes that they tell Hippolytus of Phaedra's desire
for him. Phaedra is revolted by the idea. Then the nurse suggests a
second plan: secure a token to be used in the charm. Even though
Phaedra fears the nurse's plan will lead to disaster, the nurse squelches
all argument and departs to make her preparations. The chorus sings
a song about love, filling it with dire examples of passion gone awry,
including the woeful tale of Deianeira's marriage to Hercules.

An uproar within indicates that Hippolytus is aware of Phaedra's
infatuation and of the nurse's meddling. He blames Zeus for creating
women as a snare for men, and he vows to leave home until Theseus'

return. As Hippolytus stalks off, the chorus and Phaedra chant a duet of despair that the nurse's plan failed. Phaedra heaps blame on the nurse, who declares that love for Phaedra was her only motive. The nurse again searches for a solution to Phaedra's quandary, but Phaedra dismisses her and searches for a means to commit suicide. After her departure, the chorus bemoans Phaedra's innocence and evil fate.

Suddenly, the nurse runs screaming from the palace in consternation that Phaedra has hanged herself. Theseus arrives in the midst of their panic and grieves over the loss of his noble wife. The chorus chants antiphonally with him a dirge for the dead queen. Theseus spies a letter in Phaedra's hand, and the chorus anticipates more tragedy to come. Theseus is aghast: he believes Hippolytus guilty of dishonoring Phaedra and vows to Poseidon to take immediate revenge. The chorus leader advises him to reconsider, and Theseus says that Hippolytus will meet one of two fates – either death at the will of Poseidon or exile.

Hippolytus returns, is astonished to see Phaedra's corpse, and questions his father about her death. When Theseus mutters an incomprehensible reply about wisdom, Hippolytus fears his father is deranged. Theseus denounces his son, who registers both amazement and alarm at his father's callous reply. Theseus accuses Hippolytus of duplicity, charging that Hippolytus bragged of celibacy while concealing lust for his father's wife. He sends Hippolytus into exile.

Hippolytus coolly responds to his outraged father that the charge is groundless and that he is still chaste. Yet, when he puts himself in his father's place, he wonders why Theseus has not condemned him to death. Theseus declares that death is the easy way out, that exile will be a more wretched punishment. Hippolytus cries out against the injustice, but Theseus is not moved to pity; he returns to the palace. Hippolytus summons his comrades and departs. The chorus mourns his going.

A messenger hurries in to announce a fatal accident – Hippolytus, praying to Zeus to strike him dead if he has sinned, set out on the road to Argos and Epidaurus. An abnormally large wave rose up and a great bull menaced from the sea. Hippolytus tied the reins to his body and attempted to manage the startled horses, but was dragged out of the chariot onto the rocks. A shred of life remained in his battered body as the horses and the bull galloped out of sight. The speaker, though only a slave in the royal household, professes his belief in Hippolytus' innocence.

Theseus can feel neither sorrow nor joy at the news, but he orders his son's body to be carried back. The chorus laments the stubborn hearts of gods and men, blaming Aphrodite in particular for the tragedy. Artemis appears above and chastises Theseus for condemning his son without waiting for proof of his guilt. She champions Hippolytus' purity as well as Phaedra's honor and blames unbridled passion for causing Phaedra to write the false letter. Theseus moans a reply, but Artemis pursues her condemnation of a father who would pray to Poseidon to kill his son. Then she offers her sympathy, "for when the righteous die, there is no joy in heaven, albeit we try to destroy the wicked, house and home."

The chorus, announcing the arrival of the dying Hippolytus, sings a dismal song. Hippolytus implores the gods to end his suffering. Artemis, although pitying Hippolytus, reminds him of his own sin of pride. With some coaching from his patron goddess, Hippolytus is able now to pity his father, who is also a victim of Aphrodite. Artemis promises to bless the city of Troezen, and then she withdraws so that Theseus may spend a few last moments with his dying son. Hippolytus forgives his father and urges him to sire only legitimate children in the future. Theseus mourns a "splendid hero" and blames Aphrodite for causing him such woe.

$$\Omega$$

ANDROMACHE

Owing to structural faults, Euripides' *Andromache* is not one of his more memorable plays. It was not presented in Athens, but in a rural festival. The date is uncertain. The familiar story details the trials of Hector's widow after she was given to Neoptolemus at the end of the Trojan War. The inordinate number of surprise entrances destroys the play's focus, causing the audience to lose sight of the central character, Andromache.

Euripides has the title character speak the prologue in Thessaly before the temple of the sea nymph Thetis. Dressed as a suppliant, Andromache recounts her betrothal to Hector, the loss of both her husband and her child during the war years, and her new role as Neoptolemus' concubine. She now lives with her son on the edge of Phthia, where Achilles' old father, Peleus, rules Pharsalia. The latest torment in her life, Neoptolemus' Spartan bride, Hermione, has brought added hardship, because Hermione charges Andromache with casting an evil spell over her, making her childless and distasteful to Neoptolemus. Andromache swears before Zeus that she does not intentionally try to be Hermione's rival.

At Thetis' shrine, Andromache takes refuge from Menelaus, who has come to rid Hermione of her rival. In addition, Andromache has hidden her son at a neighbor's house because Neoptolemus is at Delphi, seeking the god's forgiveness for his war crimes, and therefore cannot protect them. Andromache's maid warns that Menelaus has gone to fetch the child to slay him. Andromache has sent messengers to beg Peleus' aid, but the messengers pay no attention to her commands. She dispatches the maid on the errand.

Andromache and a chorus of Phthian women recount the woes that have befallen her. At this point, Hermione, dressed in regal embroidered robes which her father brought from Sparta, makes a dramatic entrance. She forces Andromache to crouch before her, and she accuses her of springing from barbaric ancestry. Hermione castigates her rival for bedding with her own husband's killer. The leader of the chorus comments on women's jealous nature, which leads to hatred among rivals.

Andromache counters with a series of rhetorical questions, each denying that she has any power to harm Hermione. Instead, Andromache blames Hermione herself for lacking the qualities that make a good wife. Andromache accuses Hermione of setting great store by Menelaus, exalting him above Achilles, and thereby alienating Neoptolemus. Citing her own exemplary behavior toward Hector's bastards, Andromache advises Hermione to abandon her jealousy and to avoid the lustful ways of her mother, Helen.

Hermione and Andromache squabble, each making hateful claims about the other's background and motives. Andromache refuses to abandon her sanctuary; Hermione threatens to set fire to the temple. Andromache reminds her that the deity will punish her impiety. Hermione chooses a new route to lure Andromache out of her hiding place before Neoptolemus' arrival, but she keeps the plan a secret. The chorus then sings a melancholy lament about Paris' part in the destruction of Troy.

Menelaus enters with young Molossus and threatens to kill the boy if Andromache refuses to leave Thetis' protection. She tries to reason with him, but finally concludes that Menelaus has earlier shown intemperance in destroying Troy for the sake of a woman. Menelaus rephrases his offer – either death for the child, or for his mother. Andromache gives up her safety to save Molossus.

The chorus leader urges Menelaus to reconcile the two women and spare Andromache further sorrow. Menelaus orders his slaves to seize Andromache and leaves the fate of Molossus to Hermione. Andromache decries his treachery and vilifies the Spartan race for their trickery and savagery. Andromache is led out. The chorus counsels against a marriage which pits rival wives against each other. Their song ends with pity for Andromache and her ill-fated son.

Andromache, her hands bound and her son clinging to her, bewails her final moments. Menelaus, "hard as the rock and deaf as the wave," refuses to relent. Then, suddenly, the chorus announces the arrival of Peleus, tottering toward them. The old man denounces Menelaus for his evil intentions toward the two innocents. Andromache falls on her face before her benefactor, begging for rescue. Peleus and Menelaus challenge each other. With jeering reminders of Helen's unfaithfulness, Peleus denigrates Menelaus and his daughter and declares, "Far better is it for mortals to have a poor honest man either as married kin or friend than a wealthy knave; but as for thee, thou art a thing of naught."

Menelaus alters his stance, calling on Peleus to consider the plight of his childless daughter and the possibility of Phthia falling into the hands of Molossus, a half-Trojan. He exonerates Helen of all blame, accusing the gods of causing the Trojan War. The chorus leader, in vain, encourages both men to curb their tongues.

Menelaus and Peleus continue their verbal battle. Peleus frees Andromache from bondage, and Menelaus withdraws, giving as an excuse a war he must fight in a nearby town. He makes a parting gibe: "Thy voice is all thou hast, and thou art powerless to do aught but talk." Peleus, Andromache, and Molossus exit, Andromache fearing an ambush at every turn. The chorus sings an appropriate song in praise of Peleus' victory.

Hermione's nurse approaches the chorus, warning that her mistress, in anguish at her failure to kill Andromache, seeks to hang herself. Hermione escapes her servants' watchfulness and, carrying a sword, runs toward the nurse. The nurse disarms her. Hermione laments her attempts to kill her husband's illegitimate son and concubine. She rants on, considering either death by fire, or drowning, or escape from Phthia on the first outgoing ship. The nurse attempts to ease her fears that Neoptolemus will reject her or Menelaus desert her.

As the nurse departs, Orestes enters on his way to the oracle of Zeus at Dodona. He inquires about Hermione, his cousin. She describes her thwarted attempt to rid herself of her rival; Orestes quickly grasps the situation. Hermione blames advice by evil women for leading her into the abortive plot against Andromache. The chorus leader reminds Hermione that she has overstepped the boundaries of sisterhood by blaming women too heavily for their faults. Orestes takes pity on Hermione and offers to take her back to Menelaus. Hermione agrees to go, but she fears Peleus may intervene. Orestes, who considers Hermione his rightful bride, insists that Apollo will guarantee their safety. The chorus then chants an ominous ode about Orestes' bloody revenge against his mother, Clytemnestra.

Peleus returns and demands information about the rumor that Hermione has deserted Phthia. The leader acknowledges the news, adding that Orestes intends to kill Neoptolemus. Before Peleus can organize a party of rescuers, a messenger arrives with news that Neoptolemus has been killed by the "stranger from Mycenae" and the men of Delphi. Peleus staggers from the blow.

The messenger imparts the details: Orestes spread rumors that Neoptolemus wanted to steal the temple treasure of Apollo. Armed men interrupted Neoptolemus at his prayers for forgiveness and stabbed him in the back. Rising to his former military stature, he shielded himself, warded off the blows of darts, javelins, and stones, and leaped upon his attackers, scattering them like doves. A voice from the inner sanctum rallied the crowd to new fervor. Neoptolemus was at last overcome by a sword wound, and his servants gathered his remains and brought them home for burial.

The chorus mourns their fallen prince, and Peleus regrets that his children are all dead. He also blames Neoptolemus' ill-advised marriage to Hermione. In despair, he casts his scepter on the ground. At this moment, Thetis descends with a message of hope and reassurance. She reminds Peleus that she, too, lost a son when Achilles died. She instructs Peleus to bury Neoptolemus at the Pythian altar in Delphi as a reproach to his killers.

Thetis then makes provision for Andromache, who must marry the Trojan prophet Helenus, and she predicts a prosperous line of kings from Molossus. With tender regard for her former husband, Thetis promises to release him from his human form and make him a deity. After his metamorphosis, he will be rejoined with Achilles. Her parting words summarize the human situation: "This is the lot which heaven assigns to all, and all must pay their debt to death." Peleus yields to her wisdom, ending the play with a reminder to all prospective husbands that worthless women make bad wives, even if they bring great riches as their dowry.

Ω

THE TROJAN WOMEN

A vivid, moving anti-war statement, Euripides' *Trojan Women* was first presented in spring of 415 B.C., while most of the Greek world was embroiled in the Peloponnesian War between Athens and Sparta. The tetralogy of which the play is a part won second prize. The drama questions one of the most pathetic situations of any war—the fate of noncombatants who, through no fault of their own, must suffer bitter hardships and endure the loss of home, family, pride, and country. Euripides was no doubt deeply disillusioned by Athens' ill-advised capture of the island of Melos and the resultant massacre of its men and the enslavement of its women.

The play opens on a battlefield near the walls of Troy a few days after the final battle. Just before sunrise, Poseidon appears and speaks the prologue. He claims to have built Troy with the aid of Apollo and now surveys the devastation wrought by Greek forces. After the

Trojans fell prey to the great wooden horse, carnage covered field and altar alike with corpses.

Poseidon bows to Hera and Athena, whose alliance caused the fall of Troy. He turns toward Hecuba, Priam's gray-haired queen who lies sleeping outside the rude huts that house the women who will become war prizes for the Greek leaders. Her sons are slaughtered; Cassandra, her virgin daughter and priestess of Apollo, will go to Agamemnon's bed.

Athena appears and joins forces with Poseidon. He is puzzled by her shift in allegiance until she explains her anger: she will punish the Greeks with a bitter homecoming because of Ajax's brutality toward Cassandra, a priestess. Poseidon agrees to join Athena in wreaking vengeance on the Greeks, and he ends their conference with a soliloquy that serves as a warning to all conquerors: "How are ye blind, ye treaders down of cities, ye that cast temples to desolation, and lay waste tombs, the untrodden sanctuaries where lie the ancient dead; yourselves so soon to die!"

As dawn illuminates Troy, Hecuba awakens to the horror of her city in ruins. She mourns her children, her husband, and her nation, as well as the women who have fallen from high station to humiliation and servitude. Several women approach from the huts. They dread the departure which will take them far from Troy in the very ships which brought the hated Greeks to their shores. Hecuba requests that they let Cassandra sleep to spare Hecuba at least one of her many trials. Eventually, fifteen women join to form the chorus, lamenting whatever fate holds in store in strange houses where they will soon serve harsh masters, the most despicable being Menelaus, Helen's husband.

Suddenly, the chorus leader spies Talthybius, a herald, exiting the Greek ships. The Greeks have drawn lots for the Trojan women. Hecuba asks first about Cassandra's lot. She is dismayed to learn that Agamemnon has won Cassandra. According to Talthybius, Polyxena, Hecuba's other daughter, shall watch over Achilles' tomb. Hecuba asks next about her daughter-in-law, Andromache, wife of Hector. He answers that Neoptolemus, Achilles' son, has won her. Hecuba's last question is about her own fate. Talthybius reports that Odysseus will be her master. Hecuba grieves that she must serve a lying, pitiless lord.

The leader of the chorus asks her fate, but Talthybius busies himself with his most pressing business—fetching Cassandra so that she can take her place with Agamemnon, the Greek commander-in-chief. He interrupts his orders to the men after spotting a fire among the huts. Hecuba recognizes the rays as manifestations of one of Cassandra's religious frenzies. Cassandra appears, dressed in her priestly robes and bearing a torch. Oblivious to the scene outside her door in her devotion to Apollo, she sings to herself a marriage hymn. The leader halts Cassandra in her dreamlike wandering, and Hecuba takes the torch.

Cassandra predicts death for Agamemnon and doom for the house of Atreus. She enumerates the woes of the Greeks – separation from families, death and burial on foreign soil, lonely wives and parents. The Trojans, in contrast, fought at home, protected their own, and died near families, who washed the bodies of their loved ones and entombed them in their homeland. Cassandra rejoices that Hector received great glory from his military victories and even that Paris knew the love of a "child of heaven" rather than the embraces of an ordinary wife.

Talthybius, mindful of Apollo's part in her mental state, interrupts Cassandra's wandering litany. Fearful of her connection with a powerful god, he escorts Cassandra to her new master. Before departing, he offers a heartening comment to Hecuba, assuring her that her welcome in Ithaca will be gracious and that Odysseus' wife is both wise and gentle.

Cassandra comes to her senses and utters a prophecy concerning Odysseus' twenty years of wandering. She resigns herself to her fate as Agamemnon's bride and tears the wreaths from her head, blaming the house of Atreus for the bitter fate of Troy. Hecuba falls to the ground, overcome by her loss of sons, daughters, and husband, whom she saw murdered at the altar. She foresees a slave's life for herself and longs for relief in death. The chorus chants a song of suffering and grief.

A chariot approaches piled high with the spoils of war, among them a woman clutching a child. The chorus leader recognizes Andromache and Astyanax. Hecuba and Andromache lament together. Andromache reveals Polyxena's fate: she lies dead across Achilles' grave. Hecuba reinterprets Talthybius' earlier statement and realizes the true meaning of his words. Andromache declares Polyxena's death sweeter by far than the destiny of the living. Her memories of love for Hector are so moving that the leader of the chorus takes heart from her example.

Talthybius hesitates at his next task. Finally, he announces that Odysseus has convinced the Greeks that Astyanax must be thrown from the battlements. Andromache wishes the same fate on Odysseus' sons. She consoles her frightened son with the comfort of a quick death. She pleads, "Quick! take him: drag him and cast him from the wall, if cast ye will! Tear him, ye beasts, be swift! God hath undone me, and I cannot lift one hand, one hand, to save my child from death." Talthybius, wishing for more steel in his backbone, regrets that he must perform so grim a task.

Following the chorus' lament for Troy's sad history, Menelaus enters in full regalia and searches for his wife, whom he can scarcely bring himself to call by name. He halts outside her hut, momentarily arrested by Hecuba's strange prayer. She offers him her blessing if he will murder Helen, bringer of ill luck to Troy. Helen appears, calm, composed, and well-groomed, and asks what is to be her fate. Overcome with emotion, Menelaus replies that no Greek wants her. Her fate rests in his hands alone.

Hecuba insists that Helen have her say. Menelaus agrees. Helen describes how Paris escaped Priam's death sentence, judged the three goddesses, and came to Menelaus' hall to claim his prize. Helen blames Aphrodite for misguiding her, and she assures Menelaus that, once Paris lay dead, she tried many times to flee to the Greek ships by lowering herself on a rope over the battlements. The chorus leader begs Hecuba to break the spell of Helen's words.

Hecuba refutes Helen's side of the story, claiming that the goddesses had no need of Paris' judgment of their beauty and that, furthermore, Helen left Menelaus' hall of her own will. She cites as evidence the testimony of Castor and his brother, neither of whom heard Helen cry out for rescue. In Hecuba's eyes, Helen is an opportunist who "watched Fortune's eyes, to follow hot where she led first."

Hecuba scoffs at Helen's account of her attempts to escape over the wall. A "true wife," Hecuba says, would have found a way to commit suicide and spare herself shame. She testifies that often she offered to help Helen run away from Paris, but that Helen gloried in her role as a princess among the Easterners. In disgust at Helen's vain appearance and lying mouth, she urges Menelaus to kill his wife. The chorus leader echoes her sentiments.

Menelaus savagely turns on Helen, thrusting her toward an ignoble death by stoning. Helen kneels and grasps his knees in supplication. Despite Hecuba's urging, Menelaus chooses to send Helen to the Greek ships and to take her home. The chorus sings a questioning song of the gods' rejection, while individual voices cry out for a violent death on the seas, a death which will devour Helen along with them.

Talthybius returns with the body of Astyanax, which he has cleansed and readied for burial. He lays it in Hecuba's arms and shares the news that Neoptolemus has set sail for Greece, taking Andromache as his concubine. With sympathy for the old woman's hardships, Talthybius sets out to dig the boy's grave. Hecuba leans over Astyanax, noting how much he resembles his father. She recalls a tender moment at dawn when Astyanax slipped into her bed, calling her by sweet names and promising to honor her at the time of her death. Hecuba mourns the irony of her grandson's death at so young an age. The chorus brings garlands and what garments they can find for suitable burial robes. Together, Hecuba and her Trojan sisters arrange Astyanax's small body on Hector's shield.

Suddenly, Hecuba sees a vision that promises that all is well. The women bear the child to his resting place, and Talthybius returns to the walls and orders the captains to burn what remains. He herds the women toward Odysseus' soldiers. Hecuba attempts to throw herself into the flames but is stopped. Talthybius warns them to guard her well because she is Odysseus' war prize. As the towers crash to the ground, Hecuba and the others harden themselves to face the days ahead. The trumpet sounds, and the Trojan women go forth in darkness.

$$\Omega$$

ALCESTIS

First produced at the dramatic festival of 438 B.C., Euripides' *Alcestis* exemplifies the playwright's early, less polished work. The play was defeated by Sophocles' entry and won second place. It is based on the legend depicting Apollo's banishment from Olympus to serve Admetus, king of Thessaly; Alcestis' voluntary death; and Hercules' rescue of Queen Alcestis from Death, all of which is foretold in the prologue.

The play opens at Pherae outside Admetus' palace on the day when Alcestis is to die. Apollo makes a majestic entrance and explains how Zeus, angered when Apollo killed the Cyclopes in retaliation for Zeus' murder of Asclepius, forced Apollo to labor as slave for a mortal. Apollo tricked the three Fates and saved Admetus, his earthly master, from death. After neither friend nor parent would volunteer, Alcestis offered herself in Admetus' place and lies within, near the end of her life.

Although Apollo makes a hasty departure in order to avoid contaminating himself with Death's contagion, Death, with sword drawn, confronts him outside the palace. Apollo wrangles with Death and tries to delay Alcestis' going, but Death is adamant about claiming his young victim. Apollo, demonstrating his powers of divination, predicts the arrival of Hercules, who serves Eurystheus of Mycenae. Although Apollo cannot stop Death from taking Alcestis, Hercules will triumph over Death and bring the woman back from the Underworld.

A chorus of elders anticipates sounds of woe from the palace, but hears no cries and sees no burial procession. One of the queen's personal servants exits the women's quarters in tears and informs the chorus of Alcestis' condition. Knowing that she will soon die, Alcestis bathed herself and put on royal robes. She prayed for the welfare of her children, soon to be motherless. Then she busied herself with the sacrificial duties, matter-of-factly decking the altar with myrtle boughs while holding back her tears. At last, flinging herself on her bridal bed, she wept at the thought of leaving her husband. Children and servants said their farewells to the dying queen. Admetus embraced her failing body, lamenting the imminence of death.

Admetus escorts Alcestis outside while the chorus sings a tearful song. Husband and wife join in a sad duet as Alcestis begins to envision her departure with Charon, the ferryman of Hades. Surprisingly, Alcestis recovers her strength and makes a final request that Admetus take good care of the children and not marry again, so that the children will avoid the misery of having a stepmother. Admetus promises not to remarry as a gesture of honor to so noble a first wife. He promises to wear mourning for the rest of his days and to give up his lyre, as well as singing, feasting, and drinking.

When Alcestis has said her last word, Eumelus, her son, who is to be "left like a lonely ship," grieves for his mother. Alcestis swoons and dies, and Admetus orders the chorus to cut their hair and dress themselves in black. He commands the servants to shear the horses' manes. As Alcestis' body is borne back to the palace, the king and his two children follow, hand in hand. The chorus chants a funeral hymn, noting how Admetus' aged parents refused to take his place in death.

Hercules arrives from Tiryns and explains his business: Eurystheus has commanded him to yoke the four-horsed chariot of Diomedes. Hercules intends to succeed at the task. The chorus leader announces the approach of Admetus, who wears no royal robes and bears the traditional mark of mourning—a shaved head. To avoid imposing sorrow on his guest, Admetus evades the truth, but finally admits that an unnamed woman, a visitor to his household, has died.

Hercules regrets having intruded on his grief, but Admetus insists that Hercules stay. Admetus sends his guest to quarters that are distant from the sound and sight of funeral preparations. The leader is dismayed that Admetus would contemplate hosting a visitor at such an awkward time. The chorus praises Admetus and predicts that "the devout man shall have joy."

After the matter of Hercules' visit is settled, the funeral cortege arrives. Alcestis' body lies in state on a bier, followed by a train of servants carrying funeral offerings. Admetus bids the citizens of Pherae to pay their respects. Pheres, Admetus' father, arrives with a gift of garments and eulogizes Alcestis for her unselfishness. Admetus, angry that Pheres refused to die in his place, scorns his father's gifts. The chorus leader upbraids the king for disrespect to his old father. Pheres chides his son for insolence, remarking, "And you call me a coward, you, the worst of cowards, surpassed by a woman who died for you, pretty boy? . . . Learn that if you love your life, so do others."

The chorus leader tries, in vain, to separate the quarrelers. Pheres leaves in a fit of pique, predicting that Acastus, Alcestis' brother, will avenge his sister. Admetus compounds his sin by cursing both his parents. The funeral procession continues.

A servant enters the empty stage and remonstrates over Hercules, who not only inflicted himself on a grieving household, but also deliberately got drunk and howled "discordant songs." Hercules, obviously in his cups, totters up to the outraged servant and demands an explanation of his gloom. The servant hesitates and then blurts out the truth – the queen is dead. Hercules sobers up on hearing of Admetus' loss. Embarrassed by his gaucherie at such a painful time, he vows to wrestle Death in order to return Alcestis to the living. He hurries toward Hades.

Admetus returns from the grave site. He is unable to relax, and so he sings an emotional duet with the chorus, who stopped him from leaping into the grave with Alcestis. Admetus realizes how dismal his life as a widower will be. He regrets having alienated his father by requesting his voluntary death. The chorus then chants a reminder of the Fates' inexorable hold on human life.

Hercules appears, leading a silent, veiled woman. He humbles himself for abusing a guest's rightful privileges, and he offers the woman as a gift to his host until Hercules returns from completing his task and killing the king of the Bistones. Admetus, still eager to fulfill his role as host, rejects the sight of a woman so soon after Alcestis' death, yet he notices that her body bears a resemblance to Alcestis' own lovely body. Hercules and Admetus debate the situation. Hercules insists that Admetus receive the woman as a gift, and the chorus concurs that all gifts from God must be accepted.

Hercules removes the woman's veil. Admetus is amazed that Alcestis has returned from the dead. He fears that she is a shade. After Hercules reassures him that the silent woman is indeed Queen Alcestis, Admetus embraces her. Hercules explains that Alcestis may not speak until she has been purified, after the passage of three days, and then he departs. Admetus calls out, "Good fortune to you, and come back!" The chorus acknowledges that "God makes a way for the unexpected."

Ω

THE HERACLEIDAE

Motivated by intense nationalistic feelings during the early years of the war between Athens and Sparta, Euripides wrote _The Heracleidae,_ or _Children of Hercules,_ probably around 427 B.C., glorifying the virtues of Athens. The playwright intentionally sets the drama at Marathon because of its significance as the site of a great military victory, and he emphasizes Athens' dedication to piety, democracy, charity, and nobility. These elements, however, in addition to faults and omissions within the text, weaken the artistic purpose of the drama by destroying its unity. The play, which lacks focus, direction, and force, is one of the weakest among the canon.

The play opens before the altar and temple of Zeus at Marathon; the prologue is spoken by Iolaus, an old man and kinsman of Hercules. Iolaus explains that he, along with Hercules' mother, Alcmena, guards Hercules' orphaned children. In order to escape the vengeance of King Eurystheus, they wandered as exiles from Argos. Then, arriving at Marathon, they now sit as suppliants near the altar of Zeus in hopes that Theseus' sons, their kinsmen, will aid them.

Eurystheus' messenger, Copreus, interrupts their rest and, snatching up the children, orders Iolaus to return to Argos in order to face a just penalty—death by stoning. A chorus of aged Athenians halts Copreus from committing so impious an act in the god's presence. Demophon, Theseus' son, accompanied by his brother Acamas, approaches and upbraids Copreus for his behavior. Copreus explains that Iolaus and the children are runaways from Argive law and warns that Athens will either win or lose Argive sympathies depending upon the decision concerning the fugitives. Demophon refuses to be intimidated and asks Iolaus to explain his side of the disagreement.

Iolaus makes gracious reference to the ruling family of Athens, who share kinship with Alcmena, Hercules' mother. Making reference to a blood kin, Iolaus begs Demophon to rescue them from certain death. The leader of the chorus concurs. Demophon, moved by their plight, cites three reasons for siding with Hercules' children: they are suppliants of Zeus, they are his cousins, and for the sake of Athens' reputation as a bastion of freedom, the refugees deserve honorable treatment. Despite Copreus' mutterings and threats, Demophon prevails. Iolaus encourages the children to be grateful to Athens.

Demophon sets out to prepare the citizens for possible hostile action from Argive forces. Before going, however, he invites Iolaus and the children to take refuge in his house. Iolaus prefers to stay at the altar, praying for Athens' success in the coming struggle. Demophon returns, his brow furrowed with concern over Eurystheus' rapid response to the challenge and over the oracle's instructions — Demophon must sacrifice to Demeter a maiden of noble parentage.

Iolaus, distressed at the news, offers himself as a willing victim of Eurystheus' spiteful laws. Demophon rejects Iolaus' offer and continues to ponder the oracle's demands. Macaria, one of Hercules' daughters, learns of Demophon's dilemma and offers herself as a sacrifice to save Athens from harm. The chorus leader commends her bravery and nobility. Iolaus, too, is impressed with Macaria's generosity, but in fairness to her, he insists that all of Hercules' daughters should draw lots to decide who should die. Macaria remains adamant and is led away to her death. Iolaus withdraws to mourn her going.

The servant of Hercules' son Hyllus enters and asks the reason for Iolaus' sadness. Iolaus, overjoyed that the servant brings news of the approach of Hyllus' army, summons Alcmena. Alcmena, too, is gladdened by her grandson's nearness. Over the objections of the servant, Iolaus sends him into the temple to fetch armor so that Iolaus may join the assault on Eurystheus. Alcmena and the chorus try to dissuade the old man from his folly, but he refuses to yield and exits in high spirits, reminiscing over the days when he helped Hercules sack Sparta. The chorus sings a hymn to Zeus and Athena.

The servant returns with a message of victory; he further delights Alcmena by describing Iolaus' prowess. The battle was stalled by Hyllus' offer to fight a duel with Eurystheus. The cowardly Eurystheus, however, declined to face Hercules' son, and the battle began. At first favorable to the Argives, the battle turned in the Athenians' favor when Hercules and Hebe transformed Iolaus once more into a youth so that he could overtake Eurystheus' chariot and capture the enemy leader.

Alcmena rejoices with proof of her son's deification and exhorts her grandchildren to express their gratitude to the ancestral gods. She questions the wisdom of allowing Eurystheus to live. The servant explains that Iolaus wanted Alcmena to enjoy seeing her enemy chafing at his bonds. The chorus bursts forth in song of victory to Cronus, Athens, and Hymen. A messenger escorts Eurystheus to Alcmena, who berates him for his evil schemes against her family and anticipates the joy of seeing him die.

The messenger reminds Alcmena that the rulers of Athens disapprove of his execution. Alcmena offers to do the deed that Iolaus and Hyllus have neglected to do. Eurystheus acknowledges his plight and, foregoing any plea for mercy, he explains why he pursued Hercules' children, who are his kinsmen: he perpetuated the feud to ward off future conflicts when the "lion's angry whelps" grew up. He reminds her that, should she choose to slay him, by Greek law, she will suffer a curse. The chorus leader urges Alcmena to let Eurystheus go. Alcmena proposes that she kill him and then give up the body to the Argives. Eurystheus staunchly faces his doom, promising that Athens shall receive double gain by his death. Alcmena agrees with his point of view and sends him to his death, ordering that his carcass is to be thrown to the dogs.

Ω

_____ *HECUBA* _____

Presented around 425 B.C., Euripides' *Hecuba,* the first of his antiwar dramas, depicts the plight of the Trojan queen after her homeland has fallen to the Greeks and she is made a prisoner of Agamemnon, leader of the enemy forces. The play opens before Agamemnon's tent on the shores of Thrace, with an appearance by the ghost of Polydorus, the youngest son of King Priam and Hecuba. The ghost explains that Priam, fearing danger to his kingdom, sent Polydorus in secret to Thrace to King Polymestor with enough gold to assure the welfare of Priam's surviving children, should Ilium (Troy) fall to the invaders. After the death of Hector, Troy's champion warrior, Polymestor murdered Polydorus for the gold and threw his corpse into the sea.

Polydorus' spirit hovers over Hecuba for three days while the Greeks delay their return home after Achilles' spirit appeared above his grave demanding that Polyxena, Hecuba's daughter, be sacrificed over the tomb as his just reward. Polydorus' ghost laments that Hecuba will suffer two losses in one day, for his corpse will appear in the waves so that his remains can be buried. He mourns for his mother's suffering at the hands of a jealous god.

Other Trojan captives support Hecuba as she departs from Agamemnon's tent. She chants a dismal account of her trials and her vision of Polyxena's and Polydorus' deaths. Despairing for Helenus and Cassandra, her two prophetic children, Hecuba fears the dream which pictured a wolf snatching a hind from her lap. The chorus of captive women bemoans the sad truth: despite Agamemnon's argument with Theseus' two sons, Odysseus' wisdom prevailed. Polyxena must die to satisfy the ghost of Achilles.

Hecuba wails piteously and summons her doomed daughter. The girl is horrified at her fate, but she grieves for her mother's sufferings more than her own. Odysseus comes to fetch Polyxena. Hecuba reminds him that she once saved him when he was dressed as a beggar in order to spy on Troy. Although Helen recognized him, Hecuba spared his life. Hecuba urges Odysseus to sacrifice Helen over Achilles' tomb and to spare Polyxena, Hecuba's one comfort. The stony-hearted Greek, reminding Hecuba that Greek wives and parents have also suffered, rejects her plea with his customary logic.

Hecuba, her own request denied, directs Polyxena to throw herself at Odysseus' feet, but the noble princess refuses to humble herself and plead for mercy. The chorus leader commends her nobility. Undaunted in her hopes to save Polyxena, Hecuba offers her own life in exchange, reasoning that she is more deserving of punishment because she is Paris' mother. Odysseus, however, obeys the command of Achilles' ghost and insists upon the girl's death, rejecting a second death as unnecessary.

Polyxena serves as mediator between Hecuba and Odysseus and encourages her mother to acquiesce to the Greek decision. They bid tender and piteous farewells, Polyxena promising to take her mother's message to Hector in the underworld and reminding her mother that Polydorus, her one remaining son, still lives. Hecuba swoons to the ground, disparaging Helen for bringing destruction to Troy. The chorus sings a tender lament.

Agamemnon's messenger, Talthybius, searches for Hecuba and extends both courtesy and sympathy to the aged queen before expressing his master's wishes: Hecuba must return to bury Polyxena's body. Eager for a command that will end her own life, Hecuba bows under this new grief and listens to his description of Polyxena's last moments.

According to Talthybius, Neoptolemus made the sacrificial wine offering and ordered that the girl was to hold steady for his blade. Polyxena cried out that she willed herself to be killed and begged to be free of restraint. Then she ripped open her robe, bared her breast to the sword, and sank to her knees, ready for death.

After Neoptolemus made the fatal stroke, the Greeks readied a pyre of pine logs and leaves. Neoptolemus chastised the warriors for bringing no robe or ornament to honor Polyxena's courage. Hecuba takes some comfort from Talthybius' narration and orders the Greeks away from her daughter's corpse. She sends her handmaid for a pitcher of sea water and sets about collecting ornaments from any captive Trojan who has managed to hide a treasure. The chorus intones a mournful ode on the evils of war.

The handmaid returns, leading bearers of a draped corpse. She unveils the body of Polydorus; Hecuba says that after this last tragedy, her life is over. The maid realizes that Hecuba already knows of Polydorus' death. Hecuba and the chorus leader chant antiphonally questions and answers about Hecuba's vision. Agamemnon arrives to learn why Hecuba delays in her duties to Polyxena's corpse, and then he stops short at the sight of the dead Trojan youth. Hecuba considers keeping her son's identity a secret, but decides to tell him the truth in order to avenge her children. Agamemnon openly displays his pity and regard for Hecuba.

Hecuba uses this opportunity to plead to Agamemnon to wreak vengeance on Polymestor for murdering her one remaining son and denying his body a decent burial. Agamemnon hesitates to champion the cause of the Trojan queen lest his comrades reproach him. Hecuba promises to take the task on herself with the aid of her fellow captives. She sends a servant to summon Polymestor and his two small children; Agamemnon allows her to go on her errand. Because the gods withhold a favorable breeze, Agamemnon allows Hecuba to execute her plan for vengeance. Again, the chorus intones a lament for the wartime plight of women.

Polymestor and his children arrive, and he puts on a display of courtesy. Hecuba, pleading modesty, invites Polymestor and his children into the tent so that she can explain a private matter. She asks after Polydorus, and Polymestor assures her the boy and the gold are safe. Hecuba informs him that more gold is hidden under the shrine of Athena and is marked by a projecting black rock. She reveals that she herself has hidden treasure within her tent. After assuring himself that all is safe, Polymestor and his children enter. The chorus chants a song of justice as sounds of slaughter are heard within the tent.

Polymestor, blood streaming from his sightless eyes, rushes out, lamenting his plight. He and the chorus chant antiphonally the fate which he has suffered. At the sound of Hecuba's voice, Polymestor shrieks with anger, but Agamemnon prevents him from harming her. Polymestor attempts to justify his slaughter of Polydorus by telling Agamemnon that a remaining Trojan might have raised a force and carried a new offensive to Greece.

Polymestor complains of Hecuba and the Trojan women's deception: they used concealed daggers to slaughter his innocent children and they used brooches to stab his eyes. He appeals to Agamemnon, whom he claims to have spared the enmity of Polydorus. Hecuba refutes his logic, vowing that his barbaric race could never ally itself with Greece. She notes that, while Troy still stood, Polymestor did not see fit to execute Polydorus. She adds further proof of Polymestor's greed and calumny: he hoarded the gold to himself rather than share it with Greece when it was most needed. Agamemnon agrees with Hecuba and judges Polymestor to be a worthy victim of Trojan vengeance.

Humiliated by a "woman and a slave," Polymestor mourns his blindness and the fate of his small children. He quotes Dionysus, a Thracian prophet, predicting that Hecuba shall hurl herself from the mast during the journey to Greece. Her tomb shall be called the "hapless hound's grave" and shall serve as a landmark for mariners. According to the prophecy, Cassandra, too, shall die. Hecuba spurns the predictions, but Polymestor continues the prophecy, presaging that Clytemnestra shall kill both her husband and his Trojan concubine with an ax. Agamemnon has Polymestor's mouth stopped and orders him cast onto a desert island. He sends Hecuba on her way to dress the two bodies for burial, and he sends the Trojan women back to their masters' tents. He welcomes a favorable breeze that will carry them all toward Greece.

Ω

THE SUPPLIANTS

Euripides' *Suppliants*, which was first presented around 420 B.C., depicts an unusual segment of the Theban legend – the burial of the seven warriors who joined forces to make an assault against Thebes to reclaim Polyneices' rightful throne from King Creon. Under the prevailing influence of the Peloponnesian War, the playwright chose a war theme which would cast a positive light on Athens by emphasizing the city's religiosity, fair play, and generosity toward the underdog.

The play begins at Eleusis, to the northwest of Athens, before Demeter's temple. Aethra, Theseus' mother and widow of Aegeus, sits with a chorus of Greek mothers, all of whom are dressed as suppliants and carry ceremonial boughs. Before the altar lies Adrastus, the defeated king of Argos, prostrate in grief. Aethra calls on Demeter, patron of Eleusis, to grant contentment to her family, to Athens, and to her native land. She prays on behalf of the assembled mothers whose seven sons died and lie still unburied outside the gates of Cadmus. Adrastus, leader of the warriors, begs Aethra to persuade Theseus, king of Athens, to inveigh against Theban law so that the men may have a traditional burial. Holding boughs before the twin altars of Demeter and Persephone, Aethra awaits Theseus. The suppliant mothers and the temple attendants speak a duet in lament for the fallen.

Fearful for his aged mother's welfare, Theseus approaches and demands the reason for the assembly. Aethra presents the women to Theseus and identifies Adrastus and the children of the fallen warriors. Adrastus then explains what he hopes to gain from Theseus: an intermediary who can convince the Thebans to release the bodies for burial. Theseus asks significant questions, including the reason for Adrastus' ambitious war against Thebes. Adrastus explains that he hoped to aid his sons-in-law, Polyneices and Tydeus, both of whom were outcasts, the former marked by the curse of his father, Oedipus, and the latter, the murderer of a kinsman. Theseus questions the wisdom of Adrastus' choosing foreigners for his daughters to marry. Adrastus justifies his choices as an interpretation of Apollo's oracle that his daughters should marry a wild boar and a lion. After a few more probing questions, Theseus elicits a confession from Adrastus that his actions were unwise.

Adrastus humbles himself and pleads for Theseus' intervention. The chorus echoes his sentiments. Theseus declares that human beings are more good than bad, but he upbraids Adrastus for his folly in joining just men with the unjust. Finally, he declines to represent Adrastus' case before his fellow citizens, men who prize reason above all. Adrastus indicates that he came for help, not judgment, yet he acquiesces to Theseus' decision. The suppliant women rush toward Theseus and make a dramatic plea for help.

Meanwhile, Theseus is moved by Aethra's display of emotion. Aethra speaks boldly for the customs of Hellas, which include the appropriate burial of the dead, and she encourages her son to avoid being too careful of danger and to exhibit the openhandedness that has made Athens great. Theseus acknowledges her words and pledges to present her request for a vote and to carry the deed to its conclusion by asking Creon to give up the bodies of the fallen warriors. He rounds out his message with a gracious gesture toward his mother, whom he honors by escorting her home. The chorus supports his decision.

Theseus phrases a verbal message for Creon, begging the favor that his mother has pressed him to ask. As he speaks, a Theban herald arrives and seeks the "ruling despot." Theseus informs him that Athens, a free city, has no despot. The messenger makes derogatory comparisons between Thebes and Athens, favoring Thebes because it is not ruled "by the mob." Theseus takes the implied challenge and champions the democratic state as the best environment for all; he demands to know what message the foreigner brings.

Creon sends word that Athens must drive Adrastus away and take no part in the suppliants' cry for humane burial. The message boldly threatens war if Athens sides with the suppliants. Adrastus hurls an epithet, and Theseus answers the audacious words of Creon's messenger. He denies Creon power over Athenian decisions, and he notes that death ends the act of war and that burial of dead combatants lies beyond the pale of vengeance. Denial of decent interment is so barbaric an act that it harms all Greece by rejecting values that Greeks have traditionally honored.

Theseus bases his wisdom on his understanding that human life is fraught with misery and that adherence to common decency comes before political differences. He underscores his words by promising to bury the corpses – by force, if need be. The messenger and Theseus trade hostilities, and Theseus orders the fellow out of Athens. Then Theseus organizes a party to set out for Thebes, bidding Adrastus to stay behind. A divided chorus ponders the dangers involved in Theseus' bold undertaking.

A messenger, a servant to Capaneus, one of the fallen seven, arrives with good news – Theseus' army is victorious. Arriving in three divisions, the Athenians advanced from the heights near the river Ismenus. With a ringing cry, Theseus announced his intentions to uphold Greek traditions of honorable burial. Creon maintained silence. The battle was hard fought, with a great loss of life on both sides. Then Creon and Theseus met in combat, shield to shield. Theseus demonstrated his great prowess, but he stopped his forces at the city gates lest their task degenerate into a more bloodthirsty endeavor.

The suppliants breathe a contented sigh that the enemy paid a just penalty for their hardheartedness. Adrastus then interposes a personal comment on the fruitlessness of combat.

The messenger continues his narration, explaining how he himself escaped during the fracas and how Theseus is returning the bodies of the seven fallen leaders after burying the recent dead in the shadow of Mount Cithaeron. The messenger clarifies the fact that slaves were not employed for the task of gathering the dead chiefs. [At this point, a speech belonging to Adrastus has been lost.] The messenger also describes Theseus' tender ministrations to the seven. Adrastus regrets that he has survived the men he led to war. The suppliants chant a dirge for their sons.

Theseus and his troops enter, carrying the seven corpses, and Adrastus and the chorus chant a duet of woe mingled with bitter regrets. Theseus asks about the young men's bravery. Adrastus undertakes a fitting eulogy, naming the individual strengths of Capaneus, who was killed by Zeus' thunderbolt; Eteocles, a young man of character; Hippomedon, a hardy hunter; Parthenopaeus, Atalanta's handsome son; and Tydeus, skilled in military science. Theseus identifies the last two – Oecleus, whom the gods themselves snatched from earth; and finally, Polyneices, Oedipus' son. He proposes a joint funeral pyre for all but Capaneus, whom Zeus singled out for special treatment.

Adrastus urges the mothers forward to their sons' corpses, but Theseus discourages such action, noting the piteous state of their neglected flesh. Adrastus agrees and promises the mothers their sons' bones. The corpses are carried offstage to the pyre; the children follow, and those on stage watch the proceedings from a distance. The women sing songs of remorse. Dressed in her best robes, Evadne (Capaneus' wife and Eteocles' sister) appears on a rock overhanging the pyre and longs to join her husband in death. Iphis, Evadne's father, searches for his grief-deranged daughter. He tries to dissuade her from any rash action, but she leaps to her death onto Capaneus' funeral pyre. Iphis mourns the loss of his two children and departs.

The children of the dead warriors return to the stage bearing the ashes of their dead in funeral urns. The chorus joins them in a threnody. Theseus makes a formal gift of the consecrated bodies to Adrastus and the suppliants. He reminds the children to honor Athens for her kindness to them, and he calls Zeus to witness the noble deed. Adrastus pledges everlasting gratitude. Athena appears from above and urges Adrastus to swear an oath on the bones of the seven: he must swear never to raise an army against Athens; if he does, Argos will be destroyed. The oath is to be sealed with the sacrifice of three sheep at the shrine of Pythia and the knife buried. The land itself, at the meeting of three roads on the isthmus, is to be hallowed. Athena urges two warriors' sons—Aegialeus and Diomedes—to avenge themselves on Thebes as soon as they attain manhood. For their deed, the sons shall be known as the "Afterborn" and will earn the bard's praise. Theseus accedes to Athena's request.

$$\Omega$$

——————————— *HERACLES* ———————————

Euripides' adaptation of the Heracles, or Hercules, myth strays from the usual version by interposing an act of friendship as a means of restoring Hercules' will to live after a fit of madness leads him to murder his wife, Megara, and their three sons. Various critics have dated the manuscript about 420 B.C. to link it with Euripides' pro-Athens period, but other evidence suggests that his sympathy with the problems of aging indicates that the play was written late in his life, possibly around the time that he wrote *The Trojan Women*.

In the presence of Megara (Hercules' wife) and her sons, Amphitryon (Hercules' father) speaks the prologue before the altar of Zeus at Hercules' palace in Thebes. Amphitryon outlines the notable lineage of both sides of the family, detailing Megara's link to Creon, king of Thebes, and Alcmena's liaison with Zeus, which produced the mighty Hercules. He explains how Hercules left his wife and his home to live in Argolis, where he hoped to lift his father's burdensome exile for the slaying of Electryon, Hercules' grandfather, by performing mighty deeds for Eurystheus and, by his strength and guile, freeing the world from monsters. The story begins as Hercules completes his twelfth labor – removing Cerberus, the three-headed dog of Hades, to the upper regions.

In Hercules' absence, the wily and deceitful Lycus has killed Creon and usurped the throne of Thebes. Lycus' consuming passion – to annihilate Hercules' entire family – has forced the aged Amphitryon into extreme poverty and oppression as he hovers near Zeus' altar and guards his grandchildren. Megara, who is torn with anxiety for her husband and concern for her children's welfare, echoes his alarm. Amphitryon comforts his daughter-in-law with the hope that Hercules will soon return to defend them from harm. A chorus of old men of Thebes chants a compassionate verse.

Lycus, the unlawful king of Thebes, enters, taunting Amphitryon for claiming that Zeus sired Hercules. He sneers at Megara's pride in her magnificent husband. He questions the gallantry of a warrior who puts his trust in the bow rather than face his enemy at close quarters with the spear and shield. In no way concealing his wish to annihilate Creon's heirs, Lycus relishes his evil plot to kill Megara and her children. Amphitryon is quick to dispute Lycus. He upholds Hercules' reputation for bravery and daring, and he labels Lycus' murderous plot a cowardly attempt to terrorize innocent people. Sadly, he doubts that his own feeble strength can protect the children from harm. The chorus murmurs support for Amphitryon.

Lycus, overblown with arrogance and audacity, calls for wood so that he can burn the family alive. In his pride, he flaunts his ill-gotten power over the old men of Thebes. The chorus leader staunchly rejects Lycus' denigration and longs for relief from the foreign usurper who takes advantage of a city torn by inner squabbles and bad advice. Megara thanks them for their support, but she begs them not to jeopardize their welfare by tempting Lycus' evil temper.

Understandably fearful of death by fire, Megara fears more an ignoble end, and thus she steels her children to face certain death without lowering themselves to beg for exile. The chorus leader regrets that he lacks the strength to defend her. Amphitryon asks one favor of Lycus – that he and Megara be killed before the children are slain. Megara adds a second request – that her children be allowed to enter the palace to don suitable robes for their execution. Lycus grants both wishes.

Bitter and frustrated, Amphitryon chastises Zeus for betraying Hercules' children. The chorus then chants a paean to Hercules' twelve labors, including killing a lion, a race of centaurs, and a hind; taming Diomedes' man-eating horses; executing Cycnus and the dragon that guarded the golden apples; supporting the firmament on his shoulders; fetching the girdle of the Amazon queen; slaying the Hydra and a three-bodied shepherd monster; and daring to enter the underworld on a final quest.

Megara and the children return, dressed for the slaughter. She bemoans the fate of each child and the empty promises of future prosperity and influence. She ends her speech with an invocation to Hercules' spirit – that he will appear and frighten away their cowardly enemy. As Amphitryon makes a final prayer to the gods, Megara glimpses Hercules and cries out with joy. To Hercules' consternation, she explains their tenuous position in Lycus' kingdom. He vows to decapitate the traitor and throw his remains to the dogs.

Amphitryon warns Hercules to avoid haste, for Lycus has villainous friends to back his claim to the throne of Thebes. He sends Hercules home and promises that all will work out if Hercules controls his temper. Hercules agrees, but he stays long enough to answer his father's questions about the journey into Hell, explaining that he delayed after subduing Cerberus in order to release his friend Theseus, who returned to Athens. Hercules draws his children to him and enters the palace with his family. The chorus ends the scene with a hymn decrying the sufferings of old age.

Lycus returns and demands the victims' presence. Amphitryon refuses to fetch Megara lest he become an accomplice in her murder. Lycus enters the palace to fetch mother and children. Amphitryon follows the hapless Lycus into the trap. The chorus bursts into a song of joy, which is intermixed with cries of woe from Lycus.

As the chorus ends its victorious tune, Iris (handmaid of the gods) and the spirit of madness appear from above. Iris reminds the chorus that, according to Hera's law, Hercules must suffer the penalty for killing a relative. His punishment is a fit of insanity which will cause him to murder his children. The spirit of madness tries to dissuade Iris, but she will not listen to reason. As Iris flies away in her chariot, the chorus laments "hell's confusion" within Hercules' house.

A messenger reports the carnage to the chorus: just as Hercules and Megara were readying the purifying fire by Zeus' altar, madness seized Hercules. To his servants' terror, he wandered through the house, frothing at the mouth and hallucinating that he was on the road to Eurystheus' palace to kill his old enemy. Although Amphitryon tried to stop Hercules and his family cried for mercy, Hercules aimed his bow and club at his children and wife. Before Hercules could dispatch his father, however, Athena's messenger struck Hercules in the chest with a rock, and Hercules collapsed on the ground. Then Amphitryon and the servants bound him so that he could do no more harm.

Like a clucking nurse over a sleeping infant, Amphitryon lulls his fallen son, while the chorus chants their despair, both for Hercules' misfortunes and for the pitiful old man. Hercules awakens and, understandably, he wonders if he has entered Hell a second time. Amphitryon displays compassion in gently leading Hercules to rationality and to a gradual awareness of his awful deed. Distraught by his terrible loss, Hercules longs for death.

Theseus arrives to assist Hercules against the usurper, Lycus, and is stunned by the awful butchery in Thebes' royal house. Amphitryon explains the situation, and Theseus comprehends Hercules' plight. Yet, he refuses to abandon his friend. In order to justify his view of fate, Hercules expounds on his wretched beginnings which have cursed his existence with a bad foundation. Claiming Zeus as his sire, he holds no hard feelings against Amphitryon; instead, he blames Hera, Zeus' jealous wife, who makes a practice of punishing her husband's hapless offsprings. The chorus leader concurs. [Some words have been lost from the connecting speech.]

Theseus advises Hercules to abandon suicide as an escape from his wretchedness. He agrees that both gods and men are victims of misfortune. His chief advice is for Hercules to leave Thebes and go with Theseus to Athens, where Theseus will divide his land holdings with Hercules. Hercules rejects Theseus' summation of the gods' faults; however, he accepts Theseus' generous offer of refuge in Athens. Mourning his unspeakable deed, Hercules bids farewell to Amphi-

tryon and invites Theseus to accompany him as a guardian to Argos,
where Hercules anticipates a reward for bringing Cerberus from Hell.
To combat the effects of trauma, Theseus undergirds his friend with
courage and understanding. Hercules promises to fetch Amphitryon
to Athens so that he can bury his old father. Rejoicing in the love
of friendship, Hercules and Theseus take their leave.

Ω

─────────────── ION ───────────────

Like other of Euripides' works, the play *Ion* is undated but probably belongs near the end of his canon. An unprecedented choice of
subject matter in comparison with other extant Greek dramas, the
play deals with the story of Creusa, queen of Athens, whose marriage to Xuthus, an Achaian, is marred by childlessness. Some critics
assess the happy ending as an example of New Comedy, although
some uncharacteristic elements, such as melodrama and intensely
negative emotions, suggest otherwise.

The play opens at sunrise in Delphi before the temple of Apollo.
Hermes (messenger of the gods) speaks the lengthy prologue in which
he explains the background material of the plot as well as the outcome. According to Hermes, Creusa, daughter of Erechtheus (son of
Zeus and king of Athens), was seduced and overcome by Apollo and
bore an illegitimate son. In adherence to accepted practice, Creusa
abandoned the boy in a cave near Athens, so that her shame could
remain secret from her father, the king of Athens.

Apollo sent Hermes to rescue the child and leave him as a foundling at Apollo's shrine. The child, wrapped in Creusa's clothes and
lying in a wicker basket, found favor with Apollo's priestess, who
suspected that a nymph had borne him. When the boy grew up, he
assumed the role of caretaker of Apollo's treasures. It was during this
period that Creusa married Xuthus, a war hero from Achaea in the
northern Peloponnesus who distinguished himself in the conflict with
Euboea.

As the play opens, Xuthus comes to Delphi to consult the oracle about his lack of an heir. According to Hermes, Apollo plans to give him Ion, Apollo's own illegitimate son, who will claim the throne of Erechtheus and establish Greek colonies on the coast of Asia Minor.

Hermes vanishes. Ion enters, accompanied by temple attendants, and he chants a ceremonial hymn describing his sacred duties. Although the attendants leave, Ion continues to sing at length about his ritual offices and about the arrival of spring at Delphi. He stresses his gratitude to Apollo, who has been like a father to him, and, in his eagerness to preserve the dignity of the temple, he discourages a swan from soiling the god's shrine. A chorus of Creusa's hand-maidens joins him in a song of praise to the rising sun and to the heroic deeds pictured on the temple walls.

The chorus then asks permission to enter the inner sanctum; Ion refuses their request. They ask him if the temple is the center of the earth; Ion replies that it is. He explains how they must approach the oracle if they seek its wisdom. As Ion is asking the name of their mistress, Creusa approaches. He greets her courteously, noting her tear-filled eyes. Creusa describes her family background in great detail, explaining how her father killed his other daughters when Creusa was a baby and how Poseidon punished him with a stroke of the trident.

To Creusa's dismay, Ion asks insistent questions about Macrai, the place where her father was killed and also the place where Apollo seduced her. She continues supplying information – about her marriage to Xuthus, their journey to Delphi, and their desire for children. Creusa, charmed by Ion, asks his mother's name. Ion explains that he was found, brought to the temple priestess, and tenderly nurtured, but that he lacks tangible evidence that can link him to his real mother.

Warming to the sensitive lad, Creusa reveals that, while Xuthus presses the oracle for an answer, she, too, wishes a secret answer from Apollo. She seeks information about "an unnamed friend" who was seduced by Apollo. Despite the fact that "the friend" exposed her infant, she returned and found no trace of either the child or attack by a predator. If the child survived exposure, he would be about Ion's age. Ion and Creusa comfort each other for their mutual sorrows, but Ion is scandalized by Creusa's sacrilegious condemnation of Apollo.

As Xuthus approaches, Creusa quiets Ion. Xuthus fusses over Creusa, apologizing for his long absence, and says that he brings good news: the oracle has promised that Xuthus and Creusa shall not return home childless. He instructs Creusa to bear laurel boughs around the altar while he enters the temple to consult with the Delphian chiefs. Creusa departs to the outer shrines to propitiate the god.

Left alone, Ion puzzles over Creusa's hostility toward Apollo and concludes that gods, too, must respect moral law. The chorus sings appropriate stanzas, calling Athena to Erechtheus' aid, praising parenthood, and decrying the misfortune of Apollo's paramour. After Ion returns from sprinkling sacrificial water from a golden vase, Xuthus rushes through the temple gates and greets Ion as his son. Ion, fearful that Xuthus has gone mad, is astonished by the man's behavior and especially displeased that Xuthus has crushed the ceremonial garlands. He threatens to shoot Xuthus through the heart with an arrow.

Xuthus announces that, according to Apollo, Ion is his son. Ion suggests that Xuthus received a "dark answer," but Xuthus quotes a clear and understandable response: the first person whom Xuthus meets after exiting the temple will be his son. Eager to know the identity of his mother, Ion questions Xuthus about his extramarital exploits. Xuthus vows that, since his marriage, he has known no other women, but he confesses to foolish amours in his youth during Bacchanalian revelries, which occurred about the time that Ion was conceived.

Ion accepts the explanation of his conception, but he wonders why he was brought to the temple. Xuthus suggests that Ion's mother may have exposed the boy. Satisfied with his meeting with his newfound father, Ion accepts Xuthus; yet, he continues to ponder the identity of his mother. The chorus leader rejoices. Xuthus urges Ion to leave off his concern for his mother and anticipate the wealth and influence that await him in his new home. Ion, however, fears that his father's foreign birth and his own illegitimacy will mar his reception in Athens. He also frets that his residence in Xuthus' house will cause dissension because of Creusa's bitterness over her barren state. As Xuthus and Ion depart, the chorus echoes Ion's concerns.

Creusa enters and directs her aged tutor, a faithful servant of King Erechtheus, to ask the oracle whether she will ever bear children. He agrees to do so, but asks Creusa's guidance over the rough ground. As the chorus leader prepares Creusa for bad news, the tutor returns with a report that the oracle has given Xuthus a grown son, the boy whom Creusa saw sweeping the temple steps. Creusa mourns her unhappy fate.

The tutor stirs up resentment in Creusa by describing Xuthus in unfavorable terms – a foreigner who married into a royal household and who now plots to pass on his wife's inheritance to a baseborn son. The tutor adds to his own embellishments, linking Xuthus with deliberate deception in foisting on Creusa the son of his paramour, a lowly slave. He urges Creusa to kill Xuthus and Ion before they can murder her and gain control of her inheritance. Volunteering to kill Ion in the nearby grotto where Xuthus and the boy celebrate their new relationship, the tutor pledges loyalty to Creusa. The chorus leader echoes his sentiments.

Unable to contain her festering secret, Creusa unburdens herself and tells the story of her seduction and the son whom she abandoned to die in a cave. The chorus leader and the tutor commiserate. At the tutor's urging, Creusa elaborates on the details. The tutor urges her to take immediate action. Creusa reveals the existence of two drops of gorgon's blood, one medicinal and the other lethal, which were passed down to her by her father and which she carries in her bracelet. She suggests that her palace is a good location for Ion's murder, but the tutor urges her not to delay. Creusa agrees and gives the old man the poison, warning him of its power. They depart together. The chorus chants a song to Persephone, queen of the underworld, in anticipation of the murder.

An attendant, searching for Creusa, announces to the chorus leader that Delphian rulers, warned by Apollo, plan to stone her to death for plotting against Ion. According to the messenger, Xuthus left Ion to erect a tent while Xuthus sacrificed to Dionysus. Ion, perceiving evil afoot after the tutor had secretly poisoned his wine cup, ordered all wine to be poured on the ground and fresh drinks prepared. A flock of doves sipped from the pools of discarded wine. One dove died from the effects of drinking the wine that was meant for Ion, who immediately suspected the murder plot. The tutor, caught in his heinous plot, admitted everything. Ion raised an uproar, and the Pythian council commanded that Creusa should be killed.

As the chorus grieves her fate, Creusa rushes in, terrified by the verdict. At the chorus leader's suggestion, she seeks sanctuary near Apollo's altar. Ion enters with guards and the Delphian hierarchy and labels Creusa a sorceress. He and Creusa debate her premeditated crime. Then Ion reaches toward Creusa to remove her bodily from the now-polluted altar of Apollo when a priestess, Ion's foster mother, intervenes and chastises him for his intended violence. Speaking at the command of Apollo, she presents the basket in which Ion was found shortly after his birth, and she urges him to accept the god's will that he leave Delphi and accompany Xuthus to Athens. Ion is excited because the basket provides him some clue to his mother's identity. The priestess bids him farewell and departs.

Weeping at the sight of the basket, Ion opens it and finds the hand-embroidered clothing that Creusa wrapped him in. Meanwhile, Creusa abandons the safety of the altar and reaches out to Ion, whom she recognizes as her son by the symbols of the gorgon and serpents embroidered on his baby clothes. Fearing a trick, Ion demands further evidence. Creusa identifies, first, a golden necklace picturing two dragons and then the unfaded olive branch that she wrapped around him.

Ion acknowledges his mother and embraces her; he credits Apollo with their reunion. Creusa rejoices that Erechtheus will have a male heir. Ion regrets that he was baseborn, but Creusa assures him that he is the offspring of Apollo.

Athena appears above. Explaining that Apollo has summoned her to justify Ion's present situation, Athena commands Creusa to conduct Ion to Erechtheus' throne, where Ion shall establish himself as a tribal leader. Ion's four sons will establish new seats of power along the seacoast and among the islands of the Aegean Sea. The Ionian influence shall spread to the plains of Europe and Asia, bringing honor to Ion. A natural son, Dorus, shall be born to Xuthus, and his offspring, the Dorians, shall achieve power in Achaea. Athena ends her speech by justifying Apollo's plan for Creusa's life, which is now restored to good fortune. Both Ion and Creusa accept their part in Apollo's scheme. The chorus concludes that only those who revere the gods can find happiness.

$$\Omega$$

IPHIGENIA IN TAURIS

Composed around 414 B.C., this play explores two important variations on the legends concerning the House of Atreus. First, Euripides
fabricates an end to Orestes' wanderings and reunites him with his
sister Iphigenia. The second and more important alteration of the
original legend involves a miraculous rescue by which the goddess
Athena saves Iphigenia from death. Critics denigrate Euripides for
his frequent use of the _deus ex machina_ device, but, according to critic
Edith Hamilton, an examination of the historical milieu may justify
the romantic conclusion. Because the Athenians were battling the
Spartans for mastery of the Greek world, Euripides may have imposed
a reassuring conclusion on the tragedy as a means of uplifting his
countrymen.

The play opens outside a temple in Tauris, on the shore of a pro-
jection of land in the northern Black Sea connected by a slender
isthmus to the Ukraine. Iphigenia, daughter of Agamemnon and Clytemnestra and high priestess of Artemis, stands alone on a staircase
and speaks an introductory soliloquy. She explains how her father,
following the orders of Calchas, the seer, in order to rescue Helen
from her captor, attempted to sacrifice Iphigenia on an altar near the
bay of Aulis, a seaport of Boeotia north of Athens, where the Greek
fleet gathered to set sail for Troy.

Iphigenia blames Odysseus for his wily words that lured her from
her mother. Her brush with death ended just as the knife was raised
over her; Artemis deceived the onlookers and substituted a deer in
Iphigenia's place; then she whisked her through the air to safety. From
that time on, Iphigenia has served Artemis in Tauris, a land of "savage
men ruled by their uncouth king, Thoas." In her present capacity, her
chief task is the preparation of foreigners for blood sacrifice. Although
other hands do the actual killing, Iphigenia says that she regrets being
a part of such unholy rituals.

She then descends the steps into the court and narrates a dream
from the previous night, a dream in which she was again at home
in her bed at Argos on the eastern shore of the Peloponnesus. Thunder
sent her running outdoors where she observed the royal palace in
ruins. Only one pillar remained, a symbol which took the form of
a man, her brother Orestes. Iphigenia, fearful that the dream foretells
his death, weeps for him. Resigned to her brother's fate, she returns
to the temple to look for the Greek serving women who assist her.

Orestes and Pylades, his companion, enter along the path by the bay. Having left Argos in search of the shrine of Artemis, at their destination they find evidence of human sacrifice. Orestes, sated with violence and bloodshed in his own household, cries in despair to Phoebus Apollo, who sent him to Tauris to steal Artemis' statue and return it to Attica. Fearing the task is impossible, Orestes urges Pylades to return with him to their ship. Pylades fears that they will be captured if they return to the shore. He encourages Orestes to persevere, and he suggests that they hoist the wooden statue of Artemis through the beams in the temple roof. Orestes, his courage returned to him, agrees.

After the pair withdraw to wait for the cover of darkness, Iphigenia rings the temple bell to summon the temple maidens, who assemble in the courtyard and perform a hymn to Artemis. While they sing, Iphigenia exits the temple carrying a heavy golden urn containing sacrificial wine, milk, and honey which mourners offer the gods for the souls of the dead. She tells her companions of her inauspicious dream and grieves for her lonely life, far from her family and friends in Argos.

A herdsman, who has been tending his cattle on the beach, runs up the path and announces news of a ship from Greece that has evaded the Symplegades, the clashing rocks that destroy approaching vessels, and the arrival of two young men who waded ashore and were captured for sacrifice. He knows the name of one, Pylades, but he did not hear the other's name. Iphigenia is surprised to learn that a Greek has been captured.

The herdsman also describes how the unnamed captive battled the herdsmen until they knocked the young man's sword from his hand with rocks. Then the two Greeks were taken to the king. The messenger is pleased to have taken a Greek, whom he blames for Iphigenia's near-sacrifice in Aulis. Iphigenia sends the herdsman for the two foreigners.

Unsettled by her dream, Iphigenia finds herself unable to pity the captives whom she must prepare for sacrifice. She wishes that the victims were Helen and Menelaus, whom she blames for robbing her of her promised marriage to Achilles. Vivid memories of her pleas for mercy lead her to question Artemis' role in blood sacrifices. She concludes that the Taurians blame the innocent goddess for their own savagery. A chorus of maidens echoes her sentiments and prays for a savior.

Soldiers lead the two Greek captives to the temple, and Iphigenia orders their chains removed and the altar be readied for the sacrifice. She asks the prisoners about their families. Orestes rejects her pity and refuses to reveal his name. He indicates that he is from Mycenae in Argos. Iphigenia is bursting with questions about home and about the war in Troy. At his mention of Helen, she spits out her hatred. Orestes answers questions about other Achaians, including Calchas, Odysseus, and Achilles, Iphigenia's former fiancé who died at Troy.

Iphigenia's concern for Agamemnon, the "happy king," and her hatred for the queen, who was killed by her own son, leads Orestes to blame the family's sufferings on a "wicked war for a wicked woman." When Orestes explains that Agamemnon's son is not dead, Iphigenia calls her dream a lie. Orestes accuses the gods of being "blinded, confused, and ignorant as we." Iphigenia offers freedom to this young man if he will take a letter back to Argos. Orestes refuses to send Pylades to his death as a sacrifice and insists that Pylades be saved to take the letter to Argos. Impressed by this loyalty to a comrade, Iphigenia agrees to the proposal.

After learning the nature of the sacrificial rite, Orestes wishes that his sister could tend his remains. Iphigenia promises, in place of the stranger's sister, to pour the sacrificial oil. Leaving the captives in the charge of soldiers, she goes to fetch the letter. The temple maidens ponder the predicament of the two captives, one of whom will live and the other will die. Intrigued by Iphigenia's knowledge of Argos and the Trojan War, Orestes discusses her questions with Pylades. Pylades is more concerned with their fate than with the priestess' knowledge of Argos. Orestes requests that Pylades return home to his wife, Electra, and name a son in honor of Orestes. Pylades promises to obey.

Iphigenia returns with the letter and promises Orestes that she will persuade the king to grant Pylades safe passage from Tauris. She tells Pylades the contents of the letter in case something happens to it on the voyage home. Orestes, incredulous, listens to her narration and recognizes his sister. Excitedly, they exchange memories of the past and embrace, and Iphigenia calls their reunion a miracle. She urges Orestes to outrun his captors and escape to the sea.

Before Pylades can lure Orestes into an escape plan, Orestes shares some crucial information with Iphigenia: Pylades is Electra's husband, Clytemnestra killed Agamemnon, Menelaus usurped Orestes' rightful place as king of Argos, and the Furies now possess Orestes in punishment for his mother's murder. He explains in detail how he sought relief from his madness at the tribunal of Ares and how Phoebus Apollo persuaded Pallas Athena to cast the deciding vote for acquittal. Orestes ends his narrative with a plea for Iphigenia's help in stealing the statue so that he may be free of the avenging Furies. Iphigenia fears that the king of Tauris will kill her for her complicity in the theft, although she does not think a woman's death important.

Orestes alters his plan and proposes that they kill the king. Iphigenia counterproposes that she denounce Orestes as a matricide so that he, Pylades, and the statue will have to be cleansed of defilement in deep seawater. Iphigenia begs her assistants' help in carrying out the plot; the temple maidens pledge their silence and loyalty.

King Thoas arrives to attend the sacrifice, and Iphigenia stops him at the door, claiming that the goddess turned away from impure sacrifices and shut her eyes. She compounds her lie with false information that Agamemnon is alive and prospering.

Iphigenia convinces Thoas that she must purge the statue and the victims in deep seawater. To make her request sound more reasonable, she insists that the men be bound with ropes and their heads covered with cloth. To maintain secrecy, she orders the Taurians to remain indoors until the rites are complete. She leaves Thoas in charge of purifying the temple with pine smoke. The procession of priestess, idol, and victims moves toward the sea. Soldiers rush back to the temple and interrupt the attendants' hymn honoring Phoebus; they announce the escape of the captives and Iphigenia and accuse the temple maidens of complicity.

Overhearing the din, Thoas appears at the door and questions the soldiers. They explain that, fearing that the captives overpowered the priestess and murdered her, they disobeyed her orders and ran to the beach, where the threesome were making their escape. Orestes announced his identity and struck a soldier in the face. As the soldiers ran for safety from the Greek archers, Orestes placed his sister in the ship where she prayed to Artemis for safe passage to Greece. At last sight, the Greek ship was in danger of rough seas and sharp rocks.

Thoas screams with rage and sets out in pursuit. The goddess Athena appears, quieting Thoas and explaining the reason for Orestes' theft of the statue. She calls to Orestes to continue on his way to Greece and to stop at Athens to build a temple to house the image so that he may be free of the avenging Furies. In remembrance of Orestes' deed, temple priests shall draw a single drop of blood from the throats of future victims.

Athena then calls to Iphigenia and commands her to assume the post of keeper of the keys at Artemis' shrine at Brauron. Athena then commands Thoas to send the temple maidens home and establish a new law: tie votes at the Tribunal must be counted in favor of the petitioner. Thoas, mindful of the goddess' power, accedes to her wishes.

Ω

HELENA

Written around 412 B.C., this alternate tale of Helen's captivity has received various interpretations by critics, some of whom consider the work a parody. Because the play bears a resemblance to the situations in *Iphigenia in Tauris* and because its plotline veers so far from the more popular version, there is some merit in minority opinions that perhaps Euripides meant *Helena* as a spoof of his earlier tragedies.

Euripides appears to have been influenced by Stesichorus, a sixth-century poet who is reputed to have fostered the notion that Helen was innocent of complicity in her abduction after he suffered blindness for writing bitter poems about her. He regained his vision only after recanting in his famous *Palinode*, a poem which exonerates Helen and blames the gods for sending a wraith to impersonate her at Troy. The real Helen was supposedly transported to Egypt to await the arrival of Menelaus at the end of the war. Herodotus, too, records a story of Helen in Egypt, as told to him by Egyptian priests.

The play opens outside the palace of Theoclymenus, king of Egypt, near the tomb of his father, Proteus. Helen stands as a suppliant before the tomb and ponders the Nile River and the reign of Proteus. She compares the story of Proteus' daughter, Theonoe, a prophetess, to the Spartan legend of Leda, Helen's mother, who was seduced by Zeus in the shape of a swan. Helen unfolds her own misery by recounting the judgment of Paris and Aphrodite's promise that Paris, the youthful judge of the famous beauty contest, should have Helen as his reward if he chose Aphrodite as the fairest of three goddesses—Aphrodite, Hera, and Athena.

Helen declares that the envious Hera gave Paris a wraith as his reward. Zeus further confused matters by initiating the Trojan War so that the Greeks might have a proving ground for their courage. To save Helen from ill repute, Zeus transported her to Egypt, where she was to wait out the war until Menelaus returned for her. Helen, mindful of the blame attached to her name, regrets the grand deception and relies on the word of Hermes that she will once again be rejoined with Menelaus. She says that she enjoyed safety as long as Proteus ruled Egypt, but after his death, his son, Theoclymenus, pressed his suit for Helen's hand.

Teucer, a Greek warrior and a veteran of the Trojan War, enters and is startled to see Helen, whom he blames for causing the hostilities between Troy and Greece. He regrets that he is on foreign soil and cannot kill the despised woman. After Helen replies graciously to his angry words, he softens his tone and explains how Telamon, his father, has exiled him for neglecting to follow his brother, Ajax, in suicide after Ajax failed to win Achilles' armor.

Teucer indicates that the war has been over for seven years and that the walls of the city are destroyed. He relates how Menelaus came for his wife and dragged her away by her hair, yet never reached home with her. The Greeks assume that Menelaus is dead. Teucer relates more bad news: Leda hanged herself in grief for her daughter's sin. In addition, her brothers have become gods in the likeness of stars after committing suicide because of Helen's shame. Teucer explains that he has come to consult a seer, Theonoe, to learn the way home to Cyprus, where Apollo has designated he should go. Helen urges him to flee from Theoclymenus, who hunts down every Greek stranger and kills him. Teucer is grateful for her advice, declaring that so kind a lady bears resemblance to the despised Helen in body only.

When Teucer departs, a chorus of captive Greek women enters and sings a duet with Helen, lamenting Helen's numerous sufferings and her famed beauty, which has caused so much woe. The leader cautions Helen not to believe the stranger's assertion that Menelaus is dead and urges her to ask Theonoe the truth of the matter. Helen is grateful for this support, but nevertheless contemplates suicide as an end to her troubles.

After the women depart into the palace, Menelaus enters, alone and tattered. He narrates his adventures following his successful military career: at the command of the gods, he was shipwrecked near a strange land. Leaving Helen in a cave in the care of his trusted companions, he has wandered hungry, ragged, and dirty. Leery of all Greeks, the portress shoos him from the gate. But she answers his questions, telling him he is in Egypt, a land ruled by Theoclymenus, who hates Greeks. Before she can explain fully, she indicates that Helen dwells in the palace and that everyone is in an uproar.

Menelaus is confused that a woman named Helen, who is the daughter of Zeus, came from Lacedaemon to live in Egypt. He settles the matter with the statement that there are many people in the world who share the same name. Depending upon his military fame to protect him, Menelaus determines that he will not cower before hostile Egyptians, but will demand food and shelter.

Helen and the chorus enter. In their enthusiasm for the prophetess' words, they take no notice of the ragged beggar. Helen is delighted with the possibility that Menelaus is still alive, wandering the seas in search of his homeland. She spies the beggar and thinks him a suppliant. When he detains her, she fears that he will take her to Theoclymenus. They recognize each other, but Menelaus rejects her, believing that the real Helen resides in a nearby cave. Helen explains Hera's evil plot to substitute a phantom in her place, but Menelaus is unconvinced.

A messenger arrives and announces a strange portent – the phantom Helen has disappeared from the cave into the air. The messenger sees the real Helen and instantly identifies her as the true daughter of Leda. The reunion of husband and wife is joyous and touching. Helen shares information about her captivity in Egypt and mourns their daughter Hermione, who remains unwed in Sparta. Menelaus includes the faithful messenger, who attended them on their wedding day, in their conversation.

Helen begs information about their friends who fought in the war, but Menelaus demurs, wishing to spare himself the pain of recounting their sufferings. He indicates that the war lasted ten years and that he has wandered for seven more. Helen regrets that he has come to hostile territory where he will surely be killed. She indicates that, although Theoclymenus desires marriage with her, she has kept herself pure for her husband. Fearful that Theoclymenus will kill Menelaus, Helen urges him to conceal his identity until she can win Theonoe to their cause. Menelaus, believing that "women deal best with women," leaves the arrangements to Helen. Helen swears that, if their plan fails and Menelaus is slain, she will kill herself with the same sword. They seal a death pact.

Theonoe, carrying firebrands for purification, enters with her handmaidens. She indicates that she knows Menelaus has returned and that Hera and Aphrodite are at war – this time with Hera on Helen's side and Aphrodite opposed lest Helen return to Greece and reveal that the beauty contest was rigged. Helen implores Theonoe to keep Menelaus' presence a secret; she reminds her that Proteus intended to keep his pledge to Hermes. Menelaus stops short of tears, but humbles himself sufficiently to beg for an opportunity to save his wife, whom he has sworn to kill if they are captured.

Theonoe weighs the alternatives and chooses in favor of the newly rejoined couple. She promises to keep their plan a secret from her brother out of respect for her dead father. After she withdraws into the palace, Helen and Menelaus resume making plans for escape. They consider several possibilities and decide to pretend that Menelaus has died at sea. Helen will ask for a vessel so that she can drop funeral offerings into the waves. Menelaus will pretend that he is the sole survivor of the wreck. Helen enters the palace to don the robes of mourning and to cut her hair and scratch her cheeks, as is the Greek custom. Meanwhile, Menelaus hides at the tomb of Proteus.

As the chorus ends a woeful dirge mourning the sufferings of the past seventeen years, Theoclymenus enters with his hunting companions. He reveals that he has heard of a Greek stranger's approach, and he vows to kill him lest he steal Helen. Noticing that Helen has deserted her post at the tomb, Theoclymenus assumes that she has been captured by Greeks and leaps into action. He halts when he catches sight of her, dressed in funeral garb. Helen sets her plan in motion, spinning a woeful tale of Menelaus' drowning and her own plans to mourn his death before wedding Theoclymenus.

Helen pretends to end her grudge against Theoclymenus. He, like-

wise, pledges to assist her in proper Greek burial customs to honor
Menelaus. They call on the ragged survivor for particulars of the rite.
Menelaus goes to great lengths to describe the blood sacrifice, empty
coffin, and bronze armaments which are cast overboard after the ship
is out of sight of land so that the burial offerings will not wash up
on shore. He indicates that only a mother, wife, or child is eligible
to perform the rites. Theoclymenus promises clothing and food to the
wretched survivor; in return, the survivor promises to clear Helen's
name of its former taint.

After they withdraw, the chorus dedicates a song to Demeter.
Helen returns alone and exults over the cunning scheme, by which
Theoclymenus has provided Menelaus with arms. Now he eagerly
awaits the funeral ceremony so that he can marry Helen. Helen promises the chorus that, if all goes well, perhaps they can return to rescue
the Greek women from captivity. Menelaus and Theoclymenus return
and make ready the funeral offerings. At the last minute, Theoclymenus instructs Helen to remain behind lest she be overcome with
grief and drown herself. Helen convinces him that she has all intentions of returning to marry him. Theoclymenus ardently anticipates
preparations for the wedding, which will follow the ceremony honoring Menelaus.

After the chorus sings a song of encouragement, a messenger
arrives, announcing Helen's escape. At the shore, it is related, Helen
and Menelaus were joined by the other ill-clad survivors. The Egyptians were suspicious, but kept silent and did as their king commanded. Having coaxed the sacrificial animals aboard, they rowed
to a suitable place, and Menelaus made the sacrifice to Poseidon. A
spurt of blood jetted into the sea, an evil omen that revealed the
intended treachery of the Greeks. While Helen cheered them on, the
Greeks attacked the Egyptian crew, who leaped overboard and swam
for home.

In anger at the double deception of Helen and Theonoe, Theoclymenus vows to punish his sister. A servant intervenes and tries to
reason with the king. After the servant offers to die in Theonoe's place,
the Dioscuri, Helen's twin brothers, appear above and quell Theoclymenus' anger. They announce that the will of the gods must prevail
and that Helen must return to Greece with her husband. They predict
that, after her death, she will be worshipped as a deity and that

Menelaus shall enter the island of the blessed. Theoclymenus yields to the sons and daughter of the noble Tyndareus.

Ω

———— *THE PHOENICIAN WOMEN* ————

Euripides apparently pleased the theatergoers of Athens with this play, a compact retelling of the entire Oedipus myth, first presented about 409 B.C. Judging from the interpolated lines and passages, most scholars believe that the play was probably altered and lengthened, a sign that it may have returned to the stage by popular demand. The play opens before the royal palace of Thebes. Jocasta, wife of King Oedipus, addresses Apollo and recaps the story of her marriage to her first husband, Laius, who ignored the oracle's advice and, in a moment of drunken lust, begat a son destined to bring bloody destruction on the house of Cadmus.

Mindful of the god's warning, Laius gave the infant to shepherds to expose on Mount Cithaeron. The child, whose ankles were pierced by iron spikes, was named Oedipus ("swollen-foot"). Polybus' horse-keepers took pity on the child and brought him to their mistress for suckling. The boy was accepted as the offspring of Polybus until something raised a question in his mind. Ironically, he journeyed to Apollo's shrine for answers to his origin at the same time that Laius returned to the oracle for information about his long-lost child. At the branching of the road toward Phocis, Laius' charioteer ordered Oedipus to yield passage. The two men fell to blows, and Oedipus killed Laius. Oedipus then returned to his foster-father with Laius' chariot.

When the sphinx caused great trouble in Thebes, Jocasta's brother, Creon, offered his sister as a prize to the man who could fathom its riddle. Oedipus answered the riddle and became king of Thebes and husband of Jocasta. The couple, unaware that they had transgressed society's law against incest, produced two sons, Eteocles and Polyneices, and two daughters, Antigone and Ismene. When Oedipus perceived his great sin, he scratched out his eyes with Jocasta's golden brooch. Oedipus lived on in the palace, demented and raging against his sons. After Eteocles and Polyneices erected a shaky balance of power, the rule of Thebes fell to Eteocles while Polyneices chafes in exile.

As the play opens, Polyneices and his seven-man team storm the gates of the city; Jocasta sends a messenger offering a negotiated truce. After Jocasta departs the stage, an old servant appears on the roof and points out the armed figures, including Polyneices. Spotting a crowd of women approaching the palace, the old servant sends Antigone, who has joined her, to the safety of her room.

The chorus of Phoenician women sings of their journey from Tyre to the temple of Apollo, where they will serve the god as ministrants. They lament that they have arrived in the midst of warfare. Polyneices, peering anxiously over his shoulder, takes this opportunity to approach the palace. The chorus leader introduces herself and asks the reason for the hostilities. When she learns Polyneices' name, the leader calls for Jocasta to welcome her son.

Pulled in two directions by maternal love and anxiety, Jocasta expresses genuine happiness, but she scorns her son's choice of a foreign bride. Despite his regrets at his family's hopeless political attitude toward him, Polyneices greets his mother warmly and mourns the loneliness and poverty of exile. Jocasta indicates that a god is "plaguing the race of Oedipus." They enter a fruitful discussion, and Jocasta learns of Polyneices' trip to Argos, where he married Adrastus' daughter and formed the band of warriors that now sit like vultures outside the walls of Thebes.

Eteocles enters and agrees to arbitration with his brother regarding who shall rule Thebes. Jocasta urges the two brothers to face each other and to concentrate on the situation at hand – Polyneices' complaints about the distribution of power. Polyneices reminds Eteocles of their original agreement: Polyneices willingly withdrew for one year and returned to assume his rightful place on the throne. Eteocles counters that he can never give up the scepter to his brother in the face of his brother's armed Argive mercenaries. Jocasta grieves that Eteocles is ruled by ambition, "that worst of deities." She urges him to "prize equality that ever links friend to friend, city to city, and allies to each other." Likewise, she chastises Polyneices for falling under

Adrastus' evil influence and for threatening to bring disaster on his homeland.

At this point, the arbitration fails. Eteocles pushes Polyneices into a do-or-die situation. They bicker and part company, vowing to fight to the death. Despairing for the future of her family, Jocasta withdraws. The chorus chants a narrative of the family's bloody past.

Eteocles summons his uncle Creon; the two discuss strategy. Because the Argive host is so numerous, Creon urges Eteocles to select seven leaders to confront the attackers at the seven watchtowers. Anticipating his own death in the coming battle, Eteocles thanks his uncle for his advice and commends Jocasta to Creon's care. In addition, Eteocles sanctions the marriage of Antigone to Haemon, Creon's son. Eteocles sends Creon's other son, Menoeceus, to fetch Teiresias, the blind seer. The chorus ends the scene with an ode addressed to Ares, god of war.

Teiresias enters, his path of darkness made safe by his daughter. He wears a victory crown as a result of his recent journey to aid Cecrops' sons. Creon requests guidance for Eteocles' war with the seven attackers. Teiresias grudgingly predicts a terrible conclusion to the fray – death for both brothers at each other's hands. There is only one way out of the tragedy – but Teiresias declines to say more.

Creon insists, so Teiresias divulges the rest of the prophecy in the hearing of both Creon and his son Menoeceus – Creon must sacrifice Menoeceus. Appalled at the seer's words, Creon begs him not to repeat them in the hearing of Theban citizens. Teiresias indicates that he is honor-bound to reveal the prophecy to all, for Creon must end Ares' grudge against the house of Cadmus. The choice is clear – Creon must choose his city or his son.

Unable to carry out the cruel deed, Creon sends his son into exile to Dodona's house in Aetolia, to the northwest of Thebes. The boy sets out to find Jocasta, who breast-fed the boy after his own mother's death, to bid her farewell. However, as soon as Creon departs, Menoeceus conceives another plan: he will sacrifice himself on the city's battlements to escape false slander about his cowardice. The chorus sings of Oedipus' victory over the sphinx and praises noble sons.

A messenger enters and calls for Jocasta. He allays her fears that her sons have initiated their duel and announces Menoeceus' suicide – a sword to his throat. He describes how the battle began, favoring Eteocles' forces until Tydeus ordered an assault on the gates. Periclymenus circumvented their attack, but the rush of battle moved on to other gates. Capaneus, leading a party to scale the walls, was hit by a thunderbolt from Zeus. Dismayed that Zeus took sides with the Thebans, Adrastus regrouped his Argive troops. The Thebans took advantage of the moment and led their charioteers in fresh assaults on their enemies.

Jocasta rejoices that her sons are still alive, but she stops short in her joy to mourn Creon's dead son. She perceives that the messenger is hiding bad news and demands to hear the rest. The messenger describes how Eteocles stood on the battlement and demanded single combat with Polyneices in an effort to end the war. The messenger urges Jocasta to halt their contest lest she lose both sons. As Antigone enters, Jocasta shares the information, urging Antigone to help her stop the duel. They hurry toward the battle scene, leaving the chorus to decry the fate of Thebes.

Creon enters with the corpse of his son and searches for his sister to perform the ritual bathing. The chorus leader repeats the news that Eteocles and Polyneices are about to clash and that Jocasta and Antigone hope to halt the hostilities. Before Creon can act, a messenger arrives with woeful news—both Jocasta's sons are dead. He elaborates with details of Polyneices' tearful prayer to Hera and Eteocles' prayer to Athena for victory. Both men fought equally well until Eteocles failed to protect his leg and suffered a wound and Polyneices did likewise and received a spear in his shoulder. Reduced to using swords, Eteocles tricked his brother and plunged his weapon into Polyneices' abdomen. Brazenly dropping his defense, Eteocles prepared to despoil the body and suffered a blow to the heart.

Eteocles died before speaking any parting words, but Polyneices uttered regret for killing his only brother and begged to be buried in the soil of his homeland. Insane with grief, Jocasta snatched a sword from a corpse, drove it into her throat, and fell upon her sons' bodies, her outstretched arms enfolding both in death. As the enemy continued their squabble over which brother gained the advantage, Antigone stole away. The Thebans seized the initiative and bested their aggressors. Antigone then brought her brothers home for the ritual mourning.

Antigone enters with the bodies of her mother and both brothers. The multiple traumas suffered by her family seem more than she can bear. Oedipus responds to her shrieks and asks how the three died.

Antigone complies and describes the bloody scene. Creon quiets the chorus leader's wails and takes charge of the dismal situation, declaring Haemon the rightful successor to the throne and banishing Oedipus from Thebes to end the awful plague of catastrophes brought on by the gods. Creon then hardens himself against Oedipus' entreaties and decrees that Polyneices shall lie unburied beyond the city gates. He commands Antigone to put off her mourning and prepare for the next day's nuptials.

Creon and Antigone enter into controversy over his harsh dicta. Their debate leads to a schism between niece and uncle, Antigone vowing to abandon marriage with Haemon and share her father's exile. Creon exits imperiously with the body of Menoeceus. Oedipus embraces Jocasta one last time. Antigone continues to grieve for Polyneices. Oedipus recalls the oracle of Loxias which has predicted that Oedipus will die in Colonus after a "life of wandering." Bowed with the manifold tragedies of her family, Antigone mocks Oedipus' vows to endure. She pledges to bury her brother, despite Creon's harsh decree. Glorying in better days when he triumphed over the sphinx, Oedipus accepts the fate decreed by the gods.

Ω

ORESTES

In 408 B.C., about five years after composing *Electra*, Euripides returned to the story of Agamemnon's tragic family with a retelling of the story of Orestes, which was apparently a popular subject with Greek audiences. The play begins with Electra's prologue before the royal palace at Argos on the sixth day after Orestes killed his mother, Clytemnestra, and her lover, Aegisthus. Bowed down by the sufferings of her family, both in the dim past and during her own lifetime, Electra justifies Orestes' act by blaming Phoebus Apollo for goading him to commit matricide. Electra also acknowledges the part which she and Pylades played in abetting the atrocity, and she grieves for her brother, who lies nearby, prostrate with mental torment.

Madness, imposed by the gods, has seized Orestes' mind. He neither eats nor washes himself. Huddled in his cloak, gripped by manic ravings, he exists in a limbo of lunacy. The city of Argos wastes no pity on the children, who are outcast from all human compassion until the city fathers can decide whether stoning or decapitation is the more appropriate death for mother-killers. Electra clings to the only hope she has – the arrival of Menelaus' fleet from Troy to the harbor at Nauplia. Helen, the children's aunt, has already taken refuge in the palace lest she confront any citizen who bears a grudge against her, the cause of Greece's protracted war with Troy. Helen mourns Clytemnestra's death, but takes solace in Hermione, her daughter.

Helen enters, but she keeps her distance to ward off contamination from her blood-sullied niece and nephew. She halfheartedly consoles Electra and inquires about Orestes' health. Electra replies that her brother finds no relief from his torment. Helen begs a favor: to protect herself from the censure of the town, she wants Electra to carry the sacrificial offering of hair and wine to Clytemnestra's tomb. Unconvinced by Helen's smooth words, Electra offers a tart rejoinder, and Helen replies in kind. Electra proposes that Hermione perform the task and, at the same time, repay her aunt's kindness for assuming motherly duties during Helen's long absence. Helen accepts the suggestion and exits to find Hermione. Electra groans aloud that Helen has paid the merest lip service to tradition, trimming only the ends of her smart hairdo to honor her dead sister.

A chorus of young Argive women tiptoes by, joining in a subdued, plaintive duet to avoid waking Orestes. Orestes revives, refreshed by his lengthy slumber, and he questions Electra about the details of his retreat into madness. She busies herself by ministering to minor needs, brushing his matted hair and wiping his face. Her news that Menelaus has beached his fleet in Nauplia sparks hope in Orestes, yet he regrets that Helen, too, has come home to Argos. In an instant, the Furies take control of Orestes' senses, and he is once again raving. Wearied by days of tending to his needs, Electra returns to the palace while Orestes reclines on his sickbed.

The chorus remonstrates over Orestes' fateful journey to the earth's umbilicus, the seat of Apollo's oracle, and begs for Zeus' pity. Menelaus, joyful to be home again, but saddened by news of Agamemnon's and Clytemnestra's deaths, longs to greet his beloved nephew. Orestes struggles to get off his couch. He greets Menelaus, not as a favorite uncle, but as the only savior who can come to his rescue. Orestes explains that conscience gnaws away his reason. Menelaus demands particulars of the onset and nature of the symptoms. Orestes tells how he, accompanied by his friend Pylades, was watching by Clytemnestra's funeral pyre when three dark phantom females, whom both men decline to name, took command of his brain. Bereft of assistance from the gods, from Agamemnon's spirit, or from the community, Orestes has been unable to cleanse his hands of the polluting blood. Now he is ringed by armed men who prevent his fleeing from punishment which is expected any time.

Orestes' old grandfather, Tyndareus, totters up, deep in mourning for his daughter, and asks for Menelaus. No sooner do the two men make contact than Tyndareus spies his wretched grandson and spits out his loathing. A law-abiding man, Tyndareus laments the way in which the successive family crimes lead to more deaths in a never-ending cycle of blood and mayhem. He regrets that Agamemnon did not exile Clytemnestra with his dying breath to fend off the spiral of revenge that now encircles the royal house of Argos. He turns to revile Orestes a second time and regrets again the misfortune his two daughters have brought him.

Orestes tries to set the matter straight by recalling Clytemnestra's evil alliance with Aegisthus, who defiled Agamemnon's bed and plotted his slaughter. He turns the tables on Tyndareus and blames the old man himself for siring such viperous offspring. His direct questions to his grandfather spark more vituperation. Tyndareus sets out to turn the village council against Orestes and Electra, and as he stomps off the stage, he warns Menelaus to stand aside and let Orestes suffer whatever comes his way.

Orestes turns his persuasive oratory on Menelaus, who paces and wrings his hands in uncertainty. Calling on the spirit of Agamemnon as a means of softening Menelaus, Orestes touches a responsive place in his uncle's heart. Menelaus follows Tyndareus into town to act as a voice of moderation in the deliberations. Behind his back, however, Orestes despises his uncle, whom he describes as a traitor and a false friend.

Pylades is distraught by the news that the citizens are assembling to execute Orestes. He presses his friend for information about Menelaus' response to his nephew's plight. Orestes disgorges spite and loathing for his uncle (whom he expected to champion his cause without reservation) and for his vengeful grandfather as well. Pylades confides that his own father, Strophius, has banished him for his complicity in the double murder. Orestes fears that Pylades will also suffer at the hands of Argos, but Pylades feels safe in that he is a citizen of Phocis, well out of Argive jurisdiction. Pylades decides that the best way to help his friend is by bearing Orestes' weakened body through the town. Orestes utters thanks for a faithful friend.

As the chorus ends a grim retelling of Clytemnestra's death, Electra returns to her brother's couch and finds him missing. The chorus explains that he has gone to stand trial. A messenger interrupts their exchange with news of the verdict. Following a windy introduction, he narrates how he saw Pylades shouldering Orestes through the mob and heard Talthybius, an old war comrade of Agamemnon, favor condemnation. Diomedes spoke next, urging exile as a safer path. The crowd reaction was divided. At the urging of Tyndareus, an outsider spoke up, advising the citizens to stone both Orestes and Electra.

At this point, a member of the working class offered a counter proposal—that Orestes be crowned king of Argos for avenging Agamemnon's murder. The feisty spokesman damned all men who stay home and seduce the wives of patriotic warriors who leave their families untended while they fight wars in foreign lands. Orestes then took this opportunity to build on the momentum of this speech, reminding the citizens that he helped purify Argos from the taint of a regicide. His tactic failed. Pylades guided him toward home, weeping that both Orestes and Electra must now consider suicide as a means of escaping the vengeful fury of the town.

Electra scores her cheeks with her nails and cries out in frustration. Orestes shushes her "womanish lamenting" and pleads with her to accept their fate with fortitude. Her fears, however, have him on the brink of tears. She begs him to help her die. Her request fills him with dismay at the thought of plunging his hands once more into the blood of a family member. They embrace and weep piteously. Electra asks what action Menelaus took to save them. Orestes, contemptuous of Menelaus from the start, replies that their uncle absented himself from the proceedings in contemplation of his own rise to power as the next king of Argos.

Though Orestes depends on Pylades to provide a decent burial, Pylades rejects the notion and pledges to end his own life rather than remain alive without Orestes. Pylades then heaps himself with blame for abetting the crime against Clytemnestra. Together, he and Orestes plot against Menelaus. Pylades proposes that they kill Helen, who scandalizes Greece by her adoption of Phrygian ways. Electra interjects a helpful thought – they should seize Hermione on her way back from pouring the libation over Clytemnestra's grave. Orestes is impressed by Electra's manly wisdom.

The two men withdraw, leaving Electra to intercept Hermione. Electra divides the chorus into two groups, one on the main road and the other at the path. Helen's screams break the peace; Electra, in support of the deed, chants "Cut, stab, and kill." Hermione arrives, alarmed by the cries within. Electra explains that the cry came from Orestes, a suppliant at Helen's knees. Hermione sorrows for her cousins, whose fate she has just learned, and agrees to join Electra and Orestes in a petition to Menelaus. As she enters the palace, her cries indicate that she has been captured.

The chorus' gloating over Helen's demise is interrupted by the arrival of a Phrygian eunuch. He describes how Orestes and Pylades postured before Helen as she twisted flax on her distaff in preparation for an embroidery project in Clytemnestra's honor. Orestes requested her to take a seat at Pelops' altar so that he could make a formal request. Pylades, meanwhile, was shutting the Phrygian guards in other rooms to keep them out of the way. The two executioners assailed Helen with sword blows, Orestes administering the *coup de grace* with one hand while his other clutched her golden tresses. Just as Pylades was dispatching Helen's slaves, Hermione appeared at the door. When they turned their attention from Helen, she disappeared from their fingers into thin air.

Orestes advances on the surviving Phrygian, a gutless menial who prostrates himself in terror and praises Orestes for killing a woman who surely deserved death. Disgusted by the girlish eunuch, Orestes scorns his cries for mercy, but lets him live, turning his attention toward a worthier foe, Menelaus. The divided chorus debates its part in the matter. Stunned by news of his wife's death, Menelaus enters as Pylades and Orestes appear on the roof, Hermione in hand.

Menelaus agrees to a parlay. Orestes, by now desperate in his thinking, threatens to kill Hermione and burn the palace to deprive Menelaus of his chief object. Menelaus bandies bold words with his nephew, but fails to dissuade him from his intended savagery. At this point, Menelaus despairs of rescuing Helen. Orestes orders Electra to set fire to the palace.

As flames leap into view and Menelaus yells for help, Apollo appears above with Helen. He commands Menelaus to seek another bride; Helen, marked for godhood, must join the Dioscuri in heaven as a guide to mariners. Apollo then dispatches Orestes to Parrhasia in Ephesus for a year and thence to the hill of Ares in Athens, where he will be tried for matricide by the "Avenging Three." After Orestes' case is decided, he will marry Hermione. Pylades will wed Electra. Apollo settles the matter of rule by placing Orestes over Argos and Menelaus over Sparta. Assuming blame for Orestes' crime, Apollo establishes the means of reconciliation.

Orestes hails the words of Apollo and agrees to marry Hermione. Menelaus, too, accedes to the god's wishes, blessing Helen in her new role as goddess and setting his cap for a new wife. Apollo takes his leave to escort Helen to the throne of Zeus, where she will join her brothers and dwell in the company of Hera and Hebe.

Ω

THE BACCHAE

This play was written in Macedon during Euripides' last years, which he spent with King Archelaus, (408–406 B.C.) and was produced posthumously in Athens in 405 B.C. Reflecting the playwright's disillusionment with corruption in Athens, it contains Euripides' most severe criticisms of ancient Greek religion, particularly the excesses of fanaticism as evidenced by the annual Dionysiac festival. Because it is marred by omissions, interpolations, and spurious passages, the play is one of Euripides' most neglected works.

Set before the royal palace at Thebes near the shrine of Semele, the play begins with Dionysus' prologue, then gives a detailed explanation of his birth to a woman named Semele, Dionysus' wanderings in Asia, and his return to Greece. The sisters of Semele, Dionysus' mother, he drove mad because they claimed that Dionysus was the son of a mortal rather than the son of Zeus. In fact, Dionysus forced all Theban women to wander distraught under the fir trees as proof of his power.

Cadmus, Semele's father and former king of Thebes, chose Pentheus as his heir; Pentheus opposes the rites of Dionysus. Dionysus proposes to demonstrate his powers in such a way that Pentheus will believe. Afterward, Dionysus plans to carry his cult to other cities. If the Thebans revolt against the cult, Dionysus will lead his maenads against them in battle.

At this point in his narrative, Dionysus calls to the chorus of bacchae, fifteen women devotees from Lydia in Asia Minor who are dressed in white robes and fawn skins with ivy twined in their loose curls. Some carry timbrels, some pipes and other musical instruments, and some carry the ivy-twined thyrsus, the sacred staff of Dionysus. As they enter, Dionysus sets out for Mount Cithaeron to join the bacchants in revelry. Various members of the chorus sing stanzas of a hymn of dedication and exuberant worship.

Teiresias, a blind old man dressed in festive garb, totters onto the stage and summons Cadmus, who is even older and also clothed in ritual costume. As Cadmus warms to the festive atmosphere, he seems to draw strength from his devotion to the god. The two set out for the mountain road to join the cultists as Pentheus and his bodyguard dash on. Pentheus objects to the Theban women's participation in Dionysus' frenzied, erotic rites. To stop the drunken, amorous activities of their women, the Theban men pursue them and chain them in the dungeon. Pentheus has heard that a stranger from Lydia leads the women in their revelry and vows to decapitate him.

At the sight of the old prophet, Teiresias, and his own father, Cadmus, in ritual dress, Pentheus chafes in anger and impatience. He blames Teiresias for fostering the new religion. Teiresias encourages Pentheus to accept the two fertility gods, Demeter and Dionysus, who are responsible for feeding and uplifting human beings. As proof of Dionysus' divinity, Teiresias reiterates the story of his supernatural gestation: after Zeus destroyed Semele with a thunderbolt, he rescued her unborn son and hid him in a fold of his own flesh so that Hera could not harm the child. Teiresias exhorts Pentheus not to be beguiled by his own earthly power, but to accept and worship Dionysus as a god.

Although Cadmus, too, urges his son to join the throng, Pentheus condemns their folly and dispatches a band of troops to destroy the sylvan altar and to locate the stranger who preys on the Theban women. After the king's departure, Teiresias draws Cadmus away from the king's party, warning of dire reprisals on the city of Thebes for Pentheus' sacrilege.

The guards return, escorting Dionysus in restraints. One guard regrets having to bind Dionysus, but happily reports that the women imprisoned in the royal dungeon have been miraculously freed of their bondage and returned to the woods to frolic. Pentheus calls the guard insane and orders him to loosen Dionysus' manacles. Dionysus regards the king with fearless, kind eyes. Pentheus accuses him of having a "woman's eye." Jeering at the stranger's long curls, light skin, and soft, rosy cheeks, Pentheus launches an interrogation.

The stranger claims to be a Lydian and a disciple of Dionysus. Pentheus inquires about particulars of Dionysus' appearance and the order of worship, but the stranger deftly avoids specifics. Before sentencing the prisoner, Pentheus orders a soldier to shear the curls from Dionysus' head. Pentheus confiscates Dionysus' staff and orders him bound. Dionysus warns Pentheus that he will suffer a calamity for binding one whom the gods favor, but Pentheus scoffs and has Dionysus, bereft of hair and wand, led to the stable to lie in the dark.

The maidens sing a querulous hymn; then a distant voice, identifying himself as the child of Zeus and Semele, replies with comforting words. The voice calls down lightning and fire on the house of Pentheus, and the maidens throw themselves on the ground. Dionysus appears, unbound. He describes how, from his vantage point next to the stall of a sacrificial bull, he watched Pentheus thrown down by earth tremors. Pentheus enters and rails at Dionysus for daring to appear unbound before the royal gates. He orders the gates barred to keep Dionysus from escaping.

A messenger arrives from Mount Cithaeron and announces that the women who worship Dionysus, including Autonoe, Ino, and Pentheus' mother, Agave, are performing strange deeds. Awakened from their slumber by approaching herds of cattle, the worshippers decked themselves in ritual dress, bound with hissing snakes, which they fed with the milk of their breasts. To the amazement of shepherds and drovers, miracles occurred—a stream of water jetted from a rock, and red wine bubbled from a staff set in the earth. Milk gushed from springs, and wands ran with drops of honey.

The messenger and his companions hid and watched the worshippers, among whom was the king's mother. The messenger tried
to seize Agave, but he soon fled in terror when Agave called to her
companions. The carnage of bulls torn apart and blood dripping from
pine boughs was too much for the messenger, who beat a hasty retreat.
The cultists continued on their way, invading the corn fields along
the Asopus River, snatching up untended babes, handling fire, yet
suffering no wounds. Even the weapons of outraged villagers failed
to harm them. After quelling their attackers, the women returned to
their original haunts on the mountain slope and washed and redecked
themselves. The messenger concludes from his experiences that any
harm toward the stranger will bring doom on Thebes.

Pentheus reacts with kingly bravado, ignores Dionysus' warnings,
and charges out the gate, calling for the worshippers' blood. Dionysus
calls him back and offers to lead the women home to Thebes. Pentheus spurns the offer. Dionysus wrests control of Pentheus' spirit
and guides his words. Pentheus offers Dionysus all the gold of Thebes
for the women's return and asks to hide in the undergrowth and
observe them at their prayers. He also agrees to follow Dionysus, but
balks when Dionysus suggests he forego armor in favor of a linen
robe, snood, fawn skin, and staff. Dionysus wins out over Pentheus'
objections. While the chorus sings a hymn describing the happiness
of submission to god's will, Dionysus dresses Pentheus in the palace.

Pentheus returns to the gates garbed like a female cultist and
aglow with zeal. In his frenzy, he perceives a bull's horns on Dionysus'
head. Pentheus stands patiently while Dionysus rearranges his tresses.
They go off toward Mount Cithaeron, from which Pentheus plans to
return with his mother. Pentheus leads the way, with Dionysus trail-
ing behind, presaging doom for Pentheus. The chorus decries the
watcher who hides in the rocks to spy on their devotions. They predict
his subsequent downfall.

A messenger returns from the mountain and raises a hue and cry
for Pentheus. The chorus exults over his demise and pants for details.
The messenger, miffed that the maidens rejoice over the death of their
king, describes how the watchers approached the maenads, but Pentheus was unable to see them clearly. Dionysus caused a pine tree
to bow down so that Pentheus could be lifted up in its branches for
a better view. Dionysus disappeared, yet his voice exhorted the

maenads to avenge themselves on the spy. Agave led the women as they uprooted the tree with their hands and dislodged Pentheus.

Despite Pentheus' pleas for mercy, Agave vented her fury by yanking his arm from the socket. Ino, too, tore at his flesh. Autonoe joined the fray as the women dismembered the Theban king. After the frenzied participants scattered his severed parts through the glen, Agave claimed the head and set it on her wand. The messenger, sickened with the barbarous sight, ends his speech and withdraws into the palace. As the chorus chortles with glee, Agave, demented with righteous transport, carries the head onstage. The chorus is struck dumb with horror. Agave croons insane lyrics and strokes the head of her son. The chorus leader is unable to share her enthusiasm for the savage deed. Agave searches for a proper perch on which to hang her trophy, which she imagines to be a lion's head.

Cadmus returns with Pentheus' remains. He encounters his crazed, gory-fingered daughter and grieves for her and her fearful burden. Cadmus doubts that Agave will ever return to sanity, but his probing questions strike a responsive chord in her and she trembles as her mind approaches rationality once more. She lifts the covering over Pentheus' body and knows her sin. [A page is missing from the extant manuscript. Apparently, Agave makes her speech and Dionysus appears overhead to judge the daughters of Cadmus who denied his divinity.]

After Dionysus ends his lament for the sufferings of disbelievers, Agave begs forgiveness. Cadmus laments his hard lot – that he must lead the raging maenads over Greece. Agave bewails her homelessness. Dionysus reminds them that "bitter was the shame yet did me, when Thebes honored not my name." Agave wanders off, opposite Mount Cithaeron, where she can never again join the maenads in their wild bacchanals.

$$\Omega$$

IPHIGENIA IN AULIS

King Agamemnon restlessly paces in front of his tent on the shores of Aulis. He looks to the heavens, then calls to an old man and asks him what star he sees. The old man answers, noticing Agamemnon's terrible agitation.

Agamemnon says that he is envious of men who are obscure and unknown. Men like himself, men of high honor, must of necessity live dangerously close to the brink of grief – grief because of the whims of the gods and men. The old man reminds Agamemnon: you are human; therefore, your life is full of a mixture of joy and sadness. Then the old man asks Agamemnon why he seals, unseals, and then seals again the letter he is holding.

Agamemnon explains that his wife, Clytemnestra, is a sister of the fabled Helen, and that many years ago, young men from all parts of Greece came as suitors for Helen. They all desired Helen so much that they threatened to murder the other suitors. To resolve this problem, Helen's father, Tyndareus, convinced the suitors to take an oath: if Helen were ever kidnapped after she was married, she would be rescued by all of the suitors. That is, after Helen was married, if she were stolen by another man, all of her present suitors would be honorbound to attack the kidnapper's town and sack it.

As it happened, the Trojan prince Paris stole Helen away one day, and Menelaus immediately invoked the oath binding Helen's former suitors. A fleet was assembled, and Agamemnon was chosen as commander-in-chief. Since then, however, the fleet of Greek ships has remained anchored in the harbor of Aulis because there has been no wind to fill the sails.

Calchas, a prophet, has stated that if Agamemnon's daughter Iphigenia were sacrificed, the sails would be filled and the Greeks would be victorious over Paris and the Trojans. Initially, Agamemnon agreed to sacrifice Iphigenia, but then he realized that he could not bring himself to sacrifice his daughter.

Menelaus argued strongly in favor of the sacrifice: Helen must be reclaimed. Thus, reluctantly, Agamemnon finally agreed to honor Calchas' order, and so he wrote to Clytemnestra, asking that she send Iphigenia to Aulis "to be married to Achilles" – which, of course, was a lie.

Now, Agamemnon has written another letter to Clytemnestra. In this letter, he tells her *not* to send Iphigenia – but he does not tell

Clytemnestra why. This is the letter that Agamemnon gives the old man to deliver, and he tells the old man that if he meets Iphigenia on the road to Aulis, he must turn her back toward home.

Shortly thereafter, Menelaus chases the old man onstage. Menelaus has seized Agamemnon's letter, he has read it, and he has discovered Agamemnon's plan to avoid sacrificing Iphigenia. Agamemnon, of course, is furious that his letter has been intercepted and that its seal has been broken.

Menelaus accuses Agamemnon of being treacherous and disloyal. He reminds him that not long ago, Agamemnon was eager to become commander-in-chief of the vast fleet of Greek troops. At that time, Agamemnon was ecstatic at the possibility of conquering Troy. Menelaus says that when they arrived at Aulis and discovered that the sea remained calm, Agamemnon was unhappy, fearful that he might never have the chance to command the Greek army. In fact, Agamemnon was so depressed, fearing that he might lose the chance for making his name immemorial, that he agreed to call for Calchas the prophet. At that time, he gladly agreed to Calchas' solution concerning the sacrifice of Iphigenia. Now, however, Agamemnon is unwilling to sacrifice Iphigenia; he is willing to allow the reputation of Greece to become a mockery.

A messenger arrives with news that Iphigenia, Clytemnestra, and her infant son, Orestes, have arrived. Naively, the soldiers assume that because of Agamemnon's great love for Iphigenia, he has sent for her.

Agamemnon sends the messenger away and begins sobbing. He blames Paris and Helen for this terrible misfortune. He admits to Menelaus that he is defeated. Menelaus confesses that he too is brought to tears because of Agamemnon's painful dilemma, and he pleads with him, "Do not slay the child." To do so, he says, would enable Menelaus to regain Helen – but it would destroy Agamemnon. To sacrifice Iphigenia in order to regain Helen would be to exchange excellence for evil.

Agamemnon expresses fear that the armies may call for Iphigenia's death; he is sure that Calchas will report his prophecy. To solve that problem, Menelaus proposes to have the prophet killed, but Agamemnon reminds Menelaus of the ambitious and cunning Odysseus who will certainly spread word of the prophecy and hunt Agamemnon down and kill him if he does not carry out the prophet's orders.

Sighing, Agamemnon confesses that he has no choice: he must carry out the will of the gods. He asks Menelaus one favor: keep Clytemnestra away until after Iphigenia is sacrificed.

Unexpectedly, Clytemnestra and Iphigenia enter. Iphigenia is smiling and laughing as she greets her father, and she immediately notices his sorrow. When Agamemnon explains that they will soon be separated for a long time, Iphigenia urges him to remain at home — forget about conquering Troy and forget about Menelaus' problems. Agamemnon concedes that Menelaus' problems will surely destroy others. Iphigenia says that she would like to go on her father's voyage, but Agamemnon answers that soon Iphigenia will be going on a trip — alone. Then he sends her into the pavilion.

Agamemnon turns to Clytemnestra and apologizes for his excessive sorrow. Clytemnestra says that she too sorrows, but that time will soften sadness. After questioning Agamemnon about her daughter's intended husband, the warrior Achilles, Clytemnestra is satisfied that he will make a good husband for Iphigenia. Then Clytemnestra questions Agamemnon about the ceremonial sacrifices and the marriage plans. He insists that Clytemnestra must return home to Argos. Clytemnestra objects: it is a mother's duty to give her daughter away in marriage. She refuses to leave and vows to do what is proper for Iphigenia's wedding to Achilles. At this, Agamemnon leaves.

Achilles arrives at Agamemnon's tent. He has come to say that if the troops do not sail soon for Troy, the army should be sent home. Clytemnestra comes out of the pavilion to greet Achilles, but he nervously turns to leave. He doesn't know who this beautiful woman is, but he knows that he should not be talking to her in an army camp. He is further confused when Clytemnestra dismisses his anxiety and explains that he will soon marry her daughter. Achilles assures her that he is unaware of any marital plans; in fact, he has never courted her daughter.

Clytemnestra is humiliated. She starts to withdraw into a tent when an old man calls to her. He identifies himself as a servant from her dowry. He says that because he feels more loyalty to her than to her husband, he must reveal that Agamemnon plans to kill Iphigenia as a sacrifice in order to bring winds that will fill the sails of the Greek fleet. Then he also reveals that Agamemnon tried to prevent Iphigenia's coming to Aulis — that is, Agamemnon sent a letter telling Clytemnestra not to bring Iphigenia to Aulis, but Menelaus intercepted that letter.

Clytemnestra begs Achilles to protect Iphigenia, and he vows to do so. Achilles then urges Clytemnestra to go to Agamemnon one more time and beg him not to kill Iphigenia; perhaps he will be in a saner mood. If Clytemnestra fails, they will agree upon a meeting place where they can make further plans. Clytemnestra agrees, assuring Achilles that if indeed there are gods in heaven, he will be rewarded; if there are none, all their anguish has no meaning.

Clytemnestra enters. She says that Iphigenia is weeping because she has heard about her father's plans to kill her. Agamemnon enters in a good mood, and he asks Clytemnestra to call Iphigenia. Iphigenia, holding little Orestes in her arms, enters. Agamemnon realizes that she is crying, and he asks why. Clytemnestra challenges Agamemnon with a question: does he intend to kill Iphigenia? Agamemnon explodes with wrath – an evil demon haunts him. He is destroyed – someone has betrayed his dark secret.

Clytemnestra then reveals to Agamemnon that she married him against her will – after he tore her baby from her breast and murdered Tantalus, her first husband. Now, however, matters have changed – Clytemnestra has grown to love Agamemnon, and she has produced four children for him, but she warns him: she might now be forced to become an evil woman if he leaves her, kills their daughter, and goes to war in quest of Helen "who has sinned against her husband's bed." She suggests that, as an alternate solution, the army cast lots and decide whose child should be a victim. The sacrifice, she says, should not be Iphigenia; the sacrifice should be Menelaus and Helen's daughter.

Iphigenia speaks and begs her father not to kill her. But Agamemnon explains that if he doesn't sacrifice Iphigenia, Menelaus cannot reclaim Helen, and furthermore, if he doesn't sacrifice Iphigenia, there is a strong possibility that the Greek army will come to Argos and slaughter them all. It is not Menelaus, he emphasizes, who requires Iphigenia as a sacrifice – it is Greece. Greece demands the sacrifice of Iphigenia. It is a "fated thing."

Agamemnon leaves, and Iphigenia turns to her mother. Desperately she says that she wishes Paris had never been born and that the breath of Zeus had not stilled the Greek fleet of soldiers who are "maddened" to sail to Troy.

Iphigenia sees Achilles approaching, and she covers her face in shame, but Clytemnestra stops her. This is no time for delicacy. Achilles reports that the soldiers are shouting for Iphigenia. He risked his life trying to speak on her behalf, yet still they want to sacrifice her.

Iphigenia says that she stands before a "helpless doom." To defy the soldiers now would only assure Achilles' ruin. Her fate is to die — murdered by her father. She announces her intention to die for her country. It is wrong, she says, to love life too deeply. She will not oppose divine will. She will give her body as a sacrifice so that the Greeks can conquer the Trojan barbarians.

Achilles gazes upon Iphigenia. He envies Greece because Greece has claimed her. The more he sees of Iphigenia's noble and generous nature, the more he wishes that he could claim her for his wife and fight for her. He tells her that although he knows that she is determined to sacrifice her life for Greece, it is possible that she may change her mind. Thus, he vows to bring his weapons to the sacrifice, and he will save her — in case she changes her mind at the last minute.

Achilles leaves, and Iphigenia turns to her mother. She makes her promise not to cut her hair or dress herself or Iphigenia's sisters in mourning clothes. Furthermore, she asks her mother to nurture Orestes and see that he grows to strong manhood in memory of Iphigenia. As for Agamemnon, Iphigenia tells Clytemnestra that she must not hate him; all of these tragic events have happened against his will. Clytemnestra, however, accuses him of taking part in a treacherous, unkingly plot. Then in spite of Clytemnestra's begging and crying, Iphigenia bids farewell, and the chorus speaks of the sacrificial sword that will soon sever her lovely neck, her blood flowing in streams upon the altar.

In an appendix, Euripides inserts a divine rescue of sorts — if we believe it. A messenger sent by Agamemnon announces to Clytemnestra that at the very moment that Iphigenia's throat was struck, she disappeared and a deer was slain instead. Clytemnestra does not believe the messenger, but Agamemnon enters and assures her that the story is true: Iphigenia now dwells with the gods.

Ω

THE CYCLOPS

Several years ago, Silenus set out to rescue Bromius from pirates. His ships were wrecked, and he and his sons were captured by Polyphemus, one of the wild and vicious Cyclopes. Now, Silenus and his sons are slaves. Silenus' sons watch the Cyclops' sheep and goats, while Silenus cleans the Cyclops' cave and prepares the meals.

Silenus' sons and a chorus, dressed like satyrs, enter. They are singing and driving before them a flock of goats and sheep. Silenus stops their singing because he sees the Greek sea captain Odysseus and his oarsmen approaching. Odysseus identifies himself and asks if he and his men might buy food; he says that the storm drove them off-course and left them without provisions. Silenus warns them that this island is inhabited by a man-eating race of wild Cyclopes.

Silenus agrees to give Odysseus and his men some meat, cheese, and milk in exchange for some wine, "Dionysus' drink." Odysseus agrees to the barter, and Silenus is ecstatic—until he sees how little wine Odysseus' wineskin holds. He dismisses the bargain, saying that the wineskin will hold no more than a swallow of wine. Odysseus then explains that for every swallow taken, the wineskin will give two more.

Silenus is so overjoyed at this revelation that he refuses Odysseus' money and even offers Odysseus and his men the Cyclops' entire herd of animals as food. Silenus tastes the wine. It is superb and it immediately quickens his sexual appetite. In his delight, he goes off to the Cyclops' cave in search of good food for Odysseus and his men.

The chorus leader asks Odysseus a question: since it is said that the fabled Helen enjoys great variety in men, did all of Odysseus' men take turns having sex with her after they took her away from the Trojans?

At that moment, Silenus reappears with some choice food and gives it to Odysseus in exchange for more wine. Suddenly, the Cyclops arrives, and Silenus orders everyone to run into the cave. Odysseus refuses. He says that he and his men were heroes at Troy and that they would rather die with honor than run from a Cyclops.

The Cyclops demands his dinner from Silenus and then discovers the Greek sailors near his cave. Fearing for his life, Silenus accuses Odysseus and his men of trying to steal the Cyclops' food. The Cyclops roars with hunger: he has not eaten human flesh for some time. Odysseus cries out that it was Silenus who traded the Cyclops' food in exchange for wine. Silenus, in turn, pledges that his children may die if ever he committed such an act. The chorus, however, refuses to lie. They agree with Odysseus' statements.

The Cyclops decides to question Odysseus: what country does he come from? Odysseus explains that he comes from Ithaca and that his ship was driven to the Cyclops' island after the sacking of Troy. The Cyclops disapproves of going to war for a woman (the Trojan War began when Paris seized Helen from her husband, Menelaus).

Odysseus reminds the Cyclops that a god was to blame for the Trojan War, and that Greece is now safe because of its many devoted soldiers. He reminds the Cyclops that it is a Greek custom that ship-wrecked sailors should be clothed and protected. Silenus says that if the Cyclops eats Odysseus' tongue, he will become clever and elo-quent. The Cyclops dismisses such claims and says that the only thing he cares about is indulging himself with good food and drink. He chases Odysseus' crew into the cave with threats of boiling them in a cauldron, and Odysseus, praying to Athena for help, reluctantly follows the man-eater into the cave.

Moments later, Odysseus rushes out of the cave. The Cyclops, he says, prepared an enormous fire, grabbed two of Odysseus' huskiest men, slit the throat of one and smashed the other one's head against a rock. Then he hacked the men's choicest flesh away in scallops, roasted it on the coals, tossed the remainder of the men in a pot to boil, and uttered a loud belch.

Odysseus has an idea: get the Cyclops drunk enough to fall asleep and then attack him. Accordingly, he offers the Cyclops cup after cup of wine, which the Cyclops eagerly accepts. The plan is working.

Odysseus will use a sword to sharpen the trunk of an olive tree, heat it on the coals, then shove it into the Cyclops' eye and blind him.

Very drunk, the Cyclops comes onstage. He says that he would like to share the wineskin with his fellow Cyclopes, but Odysseus urges him to keep the liquor to himself. Before long, the Cyclops becomes drowsy and lies down. Silenus tries to hide the bowl of wine so that he can drink it in secret, but the Cyclops catches him.

The Cyclops then demands to know Odysseus' name. Odysseus replies that he is called "Noman." The Cyclops is satisfied; he says that he will dine on "Noman" last. The Cyclops and Silenus continue to drink, and finally the Cyclops decides to drag Silenus into the cave to have sex, remarking that he has always liked lads better than wenches. Silenus shrieks.

Meanwhile, Odysseus prays to Hephaestus, asking for help. The chorus offers to try to confuse the Cyclops, but Odysseus silences them: not one sound until the Cyclops' eye is burned blind.

Another shriek comes from the cave, and a blinded Cyclops staggers out, trying to guard the entrance so that Odysseus and his men cannot escape. The Cyclops says that "Noman" has blinded him. The leader of the chorus mocks him, claiming that Odysseus and his crew are under cover of the rocks, which allow them to escape the cave. The Cyclops panics and falls, gashing his head. Odysseus now reveals his true name. He is not "Noman." He is the mighty Odysseus, and he celebrates his victory over the Cyclops.

The Cyclops reveals that an old oracle is now fulfilled; the oracle predicted that Odysseus would blind the Cyclops following the Trojan War. Odysseus dismisses the last part of the oracle, which states that he will be forced to wander over the seas for many years.

The Cyclops goes into the cave to find a boulder to crush the men and their ship, and the chorus exits, escaping with Odysseus and his crew.

$$\Omega$$

GREEK COMEDY

- **Aristophanes**
- **Menander**

ARISTOPHANES

- *Lysistrata*

- *The Birds*

- *The Clouds*

- *The Frogs*

- *The Wasps*

- *Peace*

ARISTOPHANES

LIFE AND BACKGROUND

   Proclaimed as one of the most inventive, audacious comic writers of all time, Aristophanes, (*ca.* 450–385 B.C.) holds first place in the ancient world for buffoonery, satire, puns, wit, parody, burlesque, mummery, caricature, farce, whimsy, travesty – in short, the entire arsenal of feathers and fluff that tickle the human funny bone. Born of Athenian parents, a fact that was at one time unsuccessfully contested by his detractors, Aristophanes began writing humorous, biting plays before the age of eighteen and continued at a swift pace, producing fifty-five comedies, of which eleven, along with nine hundred and eighty-five fragments, are still in existence. In honor of Dionysus, he competed at the major Athenian festivals – the Lenaea in midwinter and the City Dionysia in early spring – and he won five awards: one first place, three second places, and one third place.

   Aristophanes exemplifies the style known as Old Comedy – the wildly exuberant farce which yanks an audience out its apathy and demands response. To feed his humor mill, Aristophanes relied on imaginary subjects as well as myths and the absurdities of everyday life. Underlying the loosely constructed plots were satires of the abuses, excesses, sham, and chicanery of contemporary politicians and self-important notables. He adorned his outrageous humor with lyric passages, intrigue and love plots, parodies of tragic themes, burlesques of mythological situations, and an overlay of coarse, sometimes obscene belly laughs. The goal of much of his lampooning was the stuffy, overly serious city life in Athens and its reverence for sophistry, educational innovation, ponderous religiosity, and high-sounding philosophy. Unfortunately for modern readers and audiences, the fast-paced puns and allusions to local scandals can never be translated without tedious footnotes and a lessening of impact.

   Aristophanes was a product of the Periclean era – a time which was a bit beyond the golden years of Greek drama. Born in the

225

borough of Cydathenaeum about the time that construction of the Parthenon was begun, he grew up in Athens, but may have moved to the island of Aegina, south of Piraeus, where he eventually owned land. Most certainly, he was alert to the tenor of the times, for his eyes and ears absorbed a wide array of gossip and political undercurrents and his pen exploited it all, to the delight of Athenian theatergoers. Rather than support a particular political party, he chose to belabor the political establishment in general; his personal position, however, remained conservative with a decided slant toward pacifism.

Not wholly given to cynicism and scorn, Aristophanes took part in local affairs as a member of city hall. His persistent irreverence suggests that he was an atheist. A family man, Aristophanes fathered three sons; Ararus is the only one identified by name. The few remains of Aristophanes' art were preserved as models of Attic lore rather than for their literary value. The first to be produced was *The Banqueters,* a parody of modern educational philosophy and the influence of sophistry. The play received a second place prize in 427 B.C.

According to record, Aristophanes chose not to produce his own works and hired Callistratus to direct *The Banqueters,* as well as *The Babylonians, The Acharnians, The Birds,* and *Lysistrata.* In subsequent performances, Philonides performed this task, although Ararus directed *Cocalus.* In reference to his lack of interest in stagecraft, Aristophanes addresses the need for a separation between the playwright and audience in *The Knights.* He cites a difference between the talents of writing and directing as his reason for absenting himself when a play went into production.

Notable among the objects of Aristophanes' invective was Cleon, successor to Pericles, whom Thucydides describes as a violent, calculating, but persuasive demagogue. Cleon's vanity and unrefined tastes were open game for the playwright's lampoons, which rained down incessantly during Cleon's short, controversial career. Aristophanes gloried in frontal assaults against the war-mongering plutocracy which lured Athens from its intellectual moorings into the treacherous waters of power politics. Although Aristophanes was playing fast and loose with a dangerous crowd, he seemed to thrive on danger as audiences leaned forward in their seats to catch every nuance of the ribald, slapstick routines. Tradition maintains that in lieu of a brave actor to play the role of Cleon in *The Knights,* Aristophanes himself undertook the task, smearing his face with wine residue to ridicule Cleon's love for drink.

Rather like the cartoonists of our own time, Aristophanes held a mirror for Athens to study itself and draw its own conclusions. His titillating drollery spared no folly, overlooked no foible, using every "in" word, every fad that caught the attention of Athenians. Aristophanes protected himself by eliciting gales of laughter from his audiences, against whom discomfited lampoonees were helpless. According to one source, the great Socrates entered into the fun by standing during a revealing segment of *The Clouds* so that the audience could view the real thing alongside the parody. The equivalent of modern funny papers, Aristophanes' comedies rocked Athens with healthy, restorative humor, similar in nature to tragedy's cathartic purging of pity and fear.

Unfortunately for scholars, nothing remains of his rivals' works, some of which were certainly on a par with Aristophanes' efforts, but the structure of fifth-century comedic style is discernible in the eleven extant plays. The prevailing mode allotted only three actors. The chorus concluded each skit with song-and-dance routines and often intruded into the dialogue. The author freely addressed the audience by imposing long speeches which spoke directly to the matter under scrutiny, although names and local references were altered or disguised in puns. Aristophanes relied on the intelligence of an alert, well-read audience who could easily fill in the blanks in the rapier-sharp banter. As a result of his scurrilous, scatological, and derisive jests, Aristophanes holds a permanent place among the world's funnymen.

Ω

LYSISTRATA

The most controversial piece of literature from ancient Greece, Aristophanes' *Lysistrata*, written in 411 B.C., is also one of the most frequently revived of all classic plays. Set in front of the Acropolis in Athens in early morning, Scene 1 begins with an exchange between the title character, whose name means "she who disbands armies," and Calonice, an earthy Athenian woman. Lysistrata is miffed that no one has arrived from Sparta or Boeotia to attend her anti-war conference. She believes that a coalition of women can stop senseless militarism and save Greece.

Calonice doubts that women have the strength to overcome the male urge to fight. Lysistrata points out that women, by means of their winsomeness and beauty, can turn weakness into might. Before she can elaborate on her plan, delegates arrive from Sparta, complaining about the early hour. The Athenian women admire their neighbors' clothes and curvaceous bodies until Lampito, leader of the Spartan women, calls a halt to the examination and turns their attention to business.

Lysistrata presents her plan: in order to bring husbands and lovers back to the important business of sex, women must lure them away from war. Her method is straightforward: until peace reigns, there will be no more sex. Women are to dress in their most alluring robes and apply makeup and fragrance skillfully, but refuse all amatory advances. If they are forced, they must not willingly cooperate, thereby lessening the men's pleasure.

Lampito, disdaining the "Athenian rabble," assures the assembly that Spartan women can maneuver their men into making peace, but she objects to the Athenian advantage of a strong navy. To allay her fears, Lysistrata proposes the other half of her two-pronged attack: the matrons of Athens, under the guise of religious piety, will occupy the Acropolis, commandeer the Treasury, and cut off financial support to the military, thus stymying the Athenian advantage over Sparta.

Seizing the initiative, Lysistrata pushes for a vote. She inverts a war shield, fills it with wine, and entices the thirsty assembly to pledge an oath to abandon their part in further sexual liaisons until war is eradicated. On adjournment, the visiting delegates return home. The Athenian women then sequester themselves behind the locked gates of the Acropolis.

A chorus of old men arrives with sticks and fire to burn the women out of their stronghold, but they succeed only in choking themselves on the smoke. A counter-chorus of old women appears with jugs of water to douse the flames. Belittling the old men's withering masculinity, they dump hot water on their adversaries' heads. The men are utterly perplexed by this unforeseen ploy. A local magistrate intervenes, decrying the waywardness of women who have grown bold and promiscuous while their husbands are away at war. Despite his disapproval, he keeps a safe distance and orders his attendants to force open the gates.

Lysistrata calls for a truce and an application of sense rather than violence. The magistrate orders her arrest, but his officer retreats from so menacing a foe. The two sides mass forces, and the women quickly best the men. Humiliated by his defeat, the magistrate holds a parlay with Lysistrata, who explains her vision of peace for Athens. To assure themselves that corrupt warmongers will not profit from militarism, the women propose to administer public funds in the future. The men are outraged that women would usurp their traditional role.

Lysistrata calls for silence and continues. Comparing the status of public policy to a ball of wool, she declares that the women will cleanse and unsnarl the strands of military affairs, discard the briars, and weave the fibers into a "good stout cloak for the democracy." In answer to the magistrate's sneer that women cannot manage warfare, she reminds him that it is women who suffer most when hostilities flare between nations. The magistrate, quick with an unflattering remark, finds himself dressed like a corpse and headed for the underworld. Degraded and ridiculed, he beats a hasty retreat.

The two choruses doff their outer garments and launch a pitched battle, which ends in victory for the old women. Lysistrata, out of patience with her comrades for sneaking back to their husbands, announces that an oracle has proclaimed that victory is at hand. The two choruses sing comic songs about male/female relationships.

Cinesias, Myrrhine's husband, obviously uncomfortable from lack of sexual release, approaches the Acropolis. After bandying words with Lysistrata, Cinesias puts on a display of anguish, even pinching the baby to make it cry. Myrrhine agrees to talk with Cinesias and entices him to greater heights of desire. Before surrendering to his embrace, she asks if he will vote for peace. Cinesias' half-hearted support nets him empty arms as Myrrhine rushes back to the women's stronghold. The choruses, avid spectators of the foregoing scene, take sides and wrangle over the outcome.

When a messenger, also afflicted with lust, brings word that Spartan women are using similar tactics to bring an end to warfare, the magistrate suspects collusion. He hastily assembles a council of Spartan and Athenian graybeards to end the sexual boycott. The leaders of the opposing choruses reconcile and sing in unison a song of compromise and harmony.

Suffering the pangs of abstinence, representatives from both city-states arrive and court Lysistrata, the only person who can end their misery. Assembling the two embassies to her right and left, she sets before them a nude female statue representing Reconciliation. She reminds Spartan and Athenian alike that Greeks worship the same gods, yet they threaten the welfare of the entire nation by engaging in a constant struggle for supremacy. Her ultimatum provides a reasonable solution to everyone's problem: Athens and Sparta should cease fighting each other and join forces against their common enemy. Although they squabble over minor points of rule, the men eagerly end hostilities in exchange for the return of their bedmates.

For a more comprehensive, in-depth analysis of this work, consult Cliffs Notes on *Lysistrata & Other Comedies*.

Ω

THE BIRDS

A product of unsettled times during the Great Peloponnesian War, Aristophanes' *The Birds* (414 B.C.) depicts the restlessness and unbridled ambition that threatened Athens' future. In Scene 1, Euelpides and Pisthetairos, two elderly Athenians who have grown weary of petty politics, follow their pet birds, a raven and a crow, to a land of peace and contentment. Arriving at an uninviting stretch of wasteland, however, they regret having followed the birds to so forlorn a place. Then they realize that the house before them belongs to Epops, the Hoopoe bird.

After they are admitted to his presence, Euelpides and Pisthetairos rejoice in Epops' advice. Like them, Epops says, he was once plagued with creditors, but the gods changed him into a bird, and now he views the mortal struggle on earth from his bird's-eye view. Excited by the prospects of such a metamorphosis, the two Athenians ask a favor of Epops: could he find them a town where true friendship reigns over snobbery and where the enjoyment of sex is encouraged?

Epops describes the perfect city to fit these specifications – a place near the Red Sea. Although the men do not take readily to a seaside environment, Epops whets their enthusiasm with the news that money does not exist in this particular town. Pisthetairos suddenly concocts a plan to build an exciting utopia – a town in the sky where birds can enjoy happiness. In Cloudcuckooland, birds would hold sway over human beings. Pisthetairos elaborates: "Your air is the boundary between earth and heaven . . . and when men propose a sacrifice to heaven, you can impose a boycott, refusing to transmit the smoke of their offerings and forbidding any transit through your land until the gods agree to pay you tribute."

Before Epops agrees to the plan, he insists on talking it over with the birds. Suspicious of anything that smacks of human intervention, the birds upbraid Epops for considering cooperating with people, and they threaten to dismember Euelpides and Pisthetairos. Epops, however, persuades them to shield their talons until they hear the entire proposal. Leery of the menacing assembly, the two Athenians choose their words carefully, emphasizing their belief in the superiority of birds. Pisthetairos strokes their egos with grandiose reminders of a golden era when birds ruled over people.

The proposal – that the birds contain the heavens with a high wall and cut off communication between humans and their gods – would strengthen the birds' position, rendering humanity helpless against them. Pisthetairos rounds out his speech with stark reality: at present, birds are powerless and must hustle just to survive. The chorus of birds agrees that the gods have indeed usurped the lofty position they once held, before the creation of human beings. If the birds succeed in humbling humanity, they can reclaim their rightful rule from Zeus; if they fail, they will launch a holy war against Olympus. An alternate method of reining in the haughty gods is to forbid free passage to earth, where gods are notorious for wenching.

The birds doubt that they can control money, which is humanity's greatest concern. Pisthetairos assures them that they can manipulate human greed by revealing the location of hidden treasure and by relaying accurate weather information and thereby lessen the number of shipwrecks. His closing remark wins them over: "[The birds] demand no marble temples intricate with golden doors . . . their highest gods live in the sanctuary of olive trees." In unison, the birds proclaim their fealty and swear death to the gods.

Seizing upon momentum, Epops urges quick action. He invites the two Athenians to his nest and suggests an herb which will enable them to fly. After the chorus sings a paean to the noble history of all feathered creatures, Pisthetairos and Euelpides return, newly outfitted in wings, feathers, and beaks, and very ill at ease with the change. Nonetheless, they set to work on the walls of Cloudcuckooland and summon a priest to offer prayers for its success. The priest, though, subverts their efforts by inviting predatory birds to the feast. At this point, Pisthetairos takes charge, ousts the clergyman, and prays his own prayers.

Other profiteers arrive, including a poet and a prophet, but Pisthetairos rejects their services and concentrates on erecting a foundation. A third meddler, Meton the surveyor, receives a similar response to his offer of assistance. Two more charlatans, an inspector and a legislator, offer their expertise, but Pisthetairos offers them short shrift. After a second choral interlude, a messenger reports that the wall is complete.

Before the birds can enjoy their success, though, a second messenger announces that a god has already breached their barricade. As Pisthetairos arms himself for a shooting war with heaven, the chorus bemoans a conflict that pits god against bird. Before Pisthetairos launches his attack, Iris appears and reminds the birds that they owe reverence to the gods. Pisthetairos retorts that birds have merely reclaimed their rightful place in their relationship to the gods. Despite Iris' warnings of dire consequences, Pisthetairos threatens both Zeus and his messenger, whom he vows to ravage if she returns to Cloudcuckooland.

A messenger returns from earth with satisfying news: human beings are offering a golden crown in praise of Pisthetairos' wisdom. Soon thousands of visitors will arrive, for whom Pisthetairos must provide wings. He distributes a set to each of the first two arrivals, a potential patricide and a poetaster, but he refuses to equip the third man, an informer, with wings. Then, disgusted at the quality of his first three visitors, Pisthetairos collects the remaining wings and takes them inside.

The fourth visitor, Prometheus, humanity's mythic champion, warns Pisthetairos that Zeus is mobilizing for retaliation. Prometheus advises him to spurn all peace offers until the birds obtain the best offer and Pisthetairos receives Basileia as his bride. Upon Prometheus' departure, the peace delegation from Olympus arrives, consisting of Poseidon, Hercules, and Triballus, a barbarian god. Pisthetairos ignores the intimidation and Poseidon's display of *noblesse oblige.*

Munching on delicacies and disdainful of lesser proposals, Pisthetairos holds out for his original plan – supreme power for the birds. Using the same powers of wisdom with which he charmed the birds, Pisthetairos persuades them to acquiesce to a "rule by bird." The play ends with the marriage of Pisthetairos and Basileia, king and queen of birdland, whom the birds honor with a dance and recitations.

For a more comprehensive, in-depth analysis of this work, consult Cliffs Notes on *Lysistrata & Other Comedies.*

Ω

THE CLOUDS

One of Aristophanes' early works, *The Clouds* (423 B.C.), a notable farce that satirizes Socrates and the sophists, is set on the street in Athens before the home of Strepsiades and next door to Socrates' school. While his son, Phidippides, snores and mutters in his sleep, Strepsiades tosses and turns. Suddenly he sits bolt upright, debating with himself how to cope with his topsy-turvy life. The Peloponnesian War threatens his country, and on the home front, his son wastes enormous sums on fast horses. Strepsiades shuffles through a pile of correspondence and discovers a bill for yet another thoroughbred horse and chariot.

Clearly, Phidippides is still ignoring his father's complaints and dreams of ever-faster race horses. Strepsiades resigns himself to one frail jest – that some day he will die and leave an enormous pile of debts to Phidippides. He curses the matchmaker who introduced him to Phidippides' mother. In his bachelor days, he enjoyed a bucolic life among his flocks. Now he has only worries, brought on by a spendthrift wife and her equally free-spending son. He recalls Phidippides in infancy. Strepsiades wanted to name him Pheidonides, "son of thrift," but his wife chose a loftier-sounding name and spoiled Phidippides, encouraging his penchant for fine robes and fast horseflesh.

Awakening his son, Strepsiades offers to pay the tuition if the boy will enroll in Socrates' academy and learn logic so that he can outwit the daily horde of bill collectors. Phidippides shudders at the thought of associating with the eggheads and milquetoasts who make up Socrates' following. Strepsiades loses his temper and orders his wastrel son out of the house, and so Phidippides takes refuge with Uncle Magacles, who shares his nephew's appreciation for fine horses.

Dismayed at being bamboozled by his son, Strepsiades, prepared to learn logic himself, approaches the academy and knocks. A snooty student opens the door and berates him for "improper knocking." Strepsiades, cowed by the young man's effrontery, looks so forlorn that the student reconsiders and invites him into the "mysteries" of Socrates' academy.

The scene shifts to Strepsiades' first day in class. The students gaze intently at the ground while Socrates floats above them in a basket. They explain to their new classmate that they are trying to ascertain what is under the ground. As they train their eyes on earth, their rumps point skyward and contemplate the mysteries of the heavens. Spying Socrates in his basket, Strepsiades hails him as "Sweet Socratesicles!" The master's high-sounding mumbo jumbo impresses Strepsiades, who explains his financial predicament and begs for a solution.

Socrates performs an incantation to the clouds. He is answered by a rumble of thunder. A chorus of clouds hovers at the rear of the stage and sings a song about life in the heavens. Strepsiades quivers in fear at the majesty of the clouds. Socrates assures him that clouds are the only true gods. Strepsiades is shocked that Socrates disputes the existence of Zeus. The philosopher then calms his pupil's fears with a distorted bit of logic, and the clouds promise that Strepsiades will soon master the art of eloquence and will be besieged by other men who also seek to evade their creditors.

After the clouds perform a bit of interlude doggerel, Socrates bursts from his school and bemoans his luck in enrolling so inept a dolt as Strepsiades, who has failed to learn metrics, rhythm, and grammar. Because Socrates despairs of him, Strepsiades turns to the clouds and begs their advice. They propose that he persuade Phidippides to enroll. This time, Phidippides accedes to the wishes of his father, who he assumes to be insane. Socrates introduces his new pupil to Right Logic and Wrong Logic, and the two allegorical characters start arguing over which approach is best for young scholars. Wrong Logic wins out over his opponent and takes charge of Phidippides' education.

After a second short interlude, Strepsiades appears with a gift for Socrates for improving his son's mind. Then, imitating what he supposes is logic, Strepsiades battles two moneylenders, Pasias and Amynias, and drives them away with his foolishness. The cloud chorus is appalled at his gibberish and predicts a bad end for Strepsiades. Phidippides begins berating his father for senility, and Strepsiades begs the clouds to intercede, but they refuse. In anger, the old man torches Socrates' academy and ends the philosopher's reign in Athens.

For a more comprehensive, in-depth analysis of this work, consult Cliffs Notes on _Lysistrata & Other Comedies._

Ω

THE FROGS

One of Aristophanes' last comedies, _The Frogs_ (405 B.C.) is set before Hercules' house in Athens. Dionysus, wearing a lion skin over his gown, and his slave, Xanthias, laden with enough baggage for a lengthy journey, arrive at Hercules' front door. After exchanging pleasantries with Hercules, Dionysus explains that, since seeing the play _Andromeda,_ he longs to meet the playwright Euripides, and he is now traveling to the underworld to find him. Hercules, eager to dissuade him from the dire journey, suggests that he content himself with a living dramatist, but Dionysus insists there is none to compare with Euripides. The reason for his stopover in Athens is to acquire information about the underworld, which Hercules visited in the last of his twelve labors. Hercules directs him via the quickest route and describes the passage over a forbidding lake and through a malodorous, snaky swamp.

Dionysus sets out, and at the shores of the Infernal Lake, he meets Charon, who waits for his passengers. Bigoted and officious, Charon refuses passage to Xanthias, a slave, and orders Dionysus to row. To the frogs' chorus of *Brekekekex koax koax,* Dionysus plies the oars, blistering his hands and sharpening his temper. On the opposite shore, he rejoins Xanthias, who urges him to follow Hercules' advice and leave this dismal place. Despite his fears of monsters, Dionysus crouches by the lake and waits for a chorus of initiates to pass.

The procession, bound for their annual appearance at Eleusis, sings paeans to Athena and Demeter. Then Koryphaios, the chorus leader, sings to Dionysus, the "adorable god who leads us all in our dancing." After the chorus launches a scurrilous attack on Archedemos, Cleisthenes, and Callias, three disreputable Athenians, Dionysus creeps out of his hiding place and asks Koryphaios for directions to Pluto's abode. Koryphaios is happy to oblige.

Arriving at the palace door, Dionysus, disguised as Hercules in a lion skin, trembles at the doorman's hostility and switches identities with Xanthias, who claims to be braver than his master. Persephone's maid welcomes them inside and tempts them with nubile young girls. Dionysus, eager once more to assume the role of Hercules, dons the lion's skin, but after Plathane, a young waitress, accuses him of gluttony, Dionysus is again eager to give it back to Xanthias.

The doorman, armed with a whip, escorts three constables onstage and urges Hercules' arrest for stealing Cerberus, the three-headed dog of Hades. Xanthias, now disguised as Hercules, suggests that they torture, instead, his "slave" (Dionysus). Dionysus, however, claims that his status as a god prevents his feeling the pain of torture. The doorman orders both interlopers to strip and suffer the whip until one of them admits that he is mortal. Both men undergo the test and cry out verses from Sophocles and other playwrights to cover their suffering. Giving up his original test, the doorman decides to let Pluto and Persephone decide which man is the deity. An interlude concludes the scene.

As Scene 5 begins, Xanthias is conversing with one of Pluto's servants, who clearly admires Xanthias. In the background, a dispute breaks out between Aeschylus and Euripides over which one deserves the seat of honor next to Pluto. Like the boisterous frogs of the Infernal

Lake, the two rivals have at each other, no holds barred. To settle the matter fairly, they decide on a poetry contest. Although Aeschylus receives slim backing, Pluto agrees to the contest and names Dionysus the judge.

Following the usual baiting of opponents, Aeschylus and Euripides break off their bickering and settle down to business. Dionysus announces the rules: they must emphasize elegance and exclude decoration and imitation. Euripides renews his tirade against Aeschylus, noting that, like Aristophanes, he himself relies on realism, as opposed to the high-flown trumpery of Aeschylus' plays. The arguing between playwrights goes on at length, with Dionysus switching loyalty from Euripides to Aeschylus and back again at each new attack. They settle the matter by weighing each dramatist's verses on a cheese-scale. Aeschylus wins three rounds, trouncing his opponent.

Pluto arrives and listens to Dionysus' complaint that the choice is impossible. Pluto insists that Dionysus make up his mind and accompany the winner back to earth. Dionysus chooses Aeschylus. Euripides grumbles over his reward for second place—permanent residence in the underworld. Aeschylus then leaves his chair at Pluto's throne to Sophocles, who is "second among the serious poets." The chorus ushers Aeschylus back to earth and urges him to "heal the sick State, fight the ignoble, cowardly, inward foe and bring us peace."

For a more comprehensive, in-depth analysis of this work, consult Cliffs Notes on *Lysistrata & Other Comedies.*

Ω

THE WASPS

Produced at the Lenaean festival of 422 B.C. under the pen name of Philonides, *The Wasps,* a political satire, won Aristophanes a third victory only a year after his great disappointment over the reception of *The Clouds.* Set before the house of Philocleon, which is swathed in a huge net, the play opens at dawn with two slaves onstage, Sosias on guard duty and Xanthias sleeping nearby. Bdelycleon, Philocleon's son, sleeps on the roof. (Bdelycleon's name means "hater of Cleon," the Athenian demagogue; Philocleon's name is the opposite, "lover of Cleon.")

Xanthias relates the details of his curious dream – he saw an oversized eagle seize the shield of Cleonymus, the Athenian coward, and carry it away. Sosias, too, narrates a dream in which sheep sit in the people's assembly in the Pnyx and a whale harangues the citizens and weighs oxfat on a scale. Xanthias interprets the whole affair as a comment on the state of Athens, where the citizens are beset by a ravenous beast.

Xanthias turns to the audience and speaks a belated prologue. He explains that Bdelycleon stands guard over his father, who is an habitué of the law courts. If his son does not stop him, Philocleon will spend every waking moment participating at trials. Bdelycleon interrupts Xanthias to warn that Philocleon is "ferreting about like a rat in his hole" and may try another escape through the bath drain.

Philocleon rails at his captors for preventing his attendance at court. He pleads with Bdelycleon to allow him freedom to sell a donkey. Philocleon fetches the animal and sets out for market. Xanthias warns him that the wily old man, in the manner of Odysseus, is clinging to the donkey's underside. Intercepted once more in another plot to elude his captors, Philocleon carries the ruse to extreme, calling himself "Noman," as Odysseus did.

Bdelycleon warns Xanthias that the other jurors will soon arrive to accompany Philocleon to the courthouse. "As terrible as a swarm of wasps," they are equipped with stingers and are capable of inflicting grievous wounds, he notes, which "burn like so many sparks." Xanthias brags that he can drive them away with stones.

In the half-light of early morning, a chorus of old men in wasp costumes enters, lifting their lamps before them to light their way over the mud. They sing outside Philocleon's house to summon him from his bed. From an upper window, Philocleon begs his compatriots to free him from unjust captivity. They give him moral support while he gnaws through the net and slides to the ground on a rope.

Bdelycleon and Xanthias catch Philocleon in the act of escaping. As Bdelycleon shoves his father back into the house, the chorus threatens to attack. The two guards drive them away. Bdelycleon, weary with his charge, attempts to reason with the old man to convince him that his obsession with jury duty is ridiculous. They agree to a formal debate.

In answer to Bdelycleon's charge that the prestige of the juror is illusory, Philocleon raves on about his many triumphs: "We are the only ones whom Cleon, the great bawler, does not badger. On the contrary, he protects and caresses us; he keeps off the flies . . ." Bdelycleon scoffs at his father's boasts with scurrilous rejoinders. Philocleon turns his bombast against his son: "You yourself are afraid of me, yea, by Demeter! you are afraid. But may I die if *you* frighten *me*."

Bdelycleon counters his father's arguments with sense – the juror, despite his imagined power and prestige, earns only one hundred and fifty talents per year, less than a tithe of the state revenue, while the mob is courted with "dishes of salt fish, wine, tapestries, cheese, honey, sesame-fruit, cushions, flagons, rich clothing, chaplets, necklets, drinking-cups, all that yields pleasure and health." Philocleon begins to see the light. Bdelycleon concludes with winning words: "That is why I always kept you shut in; I wanted you to be fed by me and no longer at the beck of these blustering braggarts."

The chorus leader is impressed with Bdelycleon's offer to care for his father and urges Philocleon to accept. Yet Philocleon, aggrieved at his imprisonment, chafes to return to the court chamber. Bdelycleon proposes a compromise, that Philocleon practice his hobby at home on his own slaves. To assure him all the comforts, Bdelycleon assembles a chamber pot, a fire, beans for a snack, a rooster to awaken him, and a statue of Lycus, patron of the courts.

Xanthias provides the first offender – Labes, the family dog, who forced his way into the kitchen and devoured a whole cheese. Philocleon sets up the pig trough as a bar; the chorus sings a solemn invocation to Apollo; and the first offender is brought before the judge. A second dog states his case against Labes, who not only gobbled up the cheese, but refused to share it.

To humor his father, who is enjoying the mock trial, Bdelycleon speaks on behalf of Labes, whom he excuses as "wretchedly ignorant; he cannot play the lyre." Philocleon's firmness begins to waver. Bdelycleon assails him further by calling on Labes' puppies to "yap, up on your haunches, beg and whine." Philocleon relents and acquits the dog. Overwhelmed by his son's charade, Philocleon agrees to live at home in peace and submission.

After the chorus presents a short interlude on the importance of poets to society, Philocleon and his son return and quarrel over Philocleon's cloak, which the old man soils with greasy fingers. Bdelycleon insists that his father give up the cloak in favor of a simple tunic and that he wear slippers and walk like a rich man. He exhorts Philocleon to mingle with enlightened men and tell witty stories about his youthful feats, but the old man refuses to pander to the rich and powerful.

Bdelycleon convinces Philocleon to give his plan a try. After they depart to share a meal with Philoctemon, the chorus sings in praise of talented, jovial table companions. Xanthias returns from the dinner with bruises and lumps as a result of Philocleon's drunken scene. Behind him comes Philocleon, still in his cups and groping the nude form of a flute-girl. The other guests are outraged at his behavior and threaten lawsuits. Philocleon gives Bdelycleon his comeuppance, continuing his bawdy, frivolous behavior by breaking into a wild dance.

Ω

PEACE

Often proclaimed to be Aristophanes' wittiest, most delightful, and most satisfying comedy, *Peace*, which won second prize at the Great Dionysia of 421 B.C., was bested by Eupolis' *The Flatterers*. Filled with double entendres, puns, scatological humor, and allusions to local scoundrels and ne'er-do-wells, the play is rollicking and fast-paced. The setting focuses on three locales—Trygaeus' farm to the right; at center, a cave sealed by a great boulder; and to the left, Zeus' palace. As the play opens, Trygaeus' slaves are toiling busily, shaping pones from dung and tossing them to a ravenous dung-beetle. Doubting their master's sanity, they wonder at Trygaeus' new pet.

From within comes the master's cry. One of the servants hints at Trygaeus' aberration—he has tried to build a ladder to heaven, but now he is determined to fly straight to Zeus on the beetle's back. Trygaeus appears overhead astride the enormous insect. The servant worries that his master will come to harm, but Trygaeus assures him that his efforts are necessary in order to save Greece from the Medes. Trygaeus' little girls appear and reach out their hands to their father in supplication. He calms their fears, quoting Aesop as the source of his inspiration.

The beetle's precipitous flight ends at Zeus' door, where Hermes greets the visitor with harsh, demanding questions. Hermes explains that the gods, angered at the Greeks, recently moved to the "furthest end of the dome of heaven" and left War to punish them as he pleases. Trygaeus demands the reason for such ill treatment. Hermes replies that the Greeks deserve retribution for preferring War to Peace.

War, now in ascendance, has cast Peace into a deep pit and piled stones on top. To oppress the Greeks further, War has procured a huge mortar bowl. He enters, hauling his mortar and relishing more war-torn cities. War orders his servant, Tumult, to locate a pestle so that he may grind in a bit of garlic. Trygaeus worries that the pestle will enable War to "amuse himself with pounding all the towns of Hellas to pieces," but he is relieved that Tumult is unable to locate a pestle in either Athens or Sparta. Out of sorts with his ineffectual servant, War exits to make his own pestle.

In his absence, Trygaeus encourages all Greeks to work together to get Peace out of the pit. The chorus, made up of laborers and farmers from all parts of Greece, rush to aid him and dance with delight. As Trygaeus organizes his motley crew, Hermes catches him redhanded and condemns him to death for trying to rescue Peace. The chorus raises a hue and cry and softens his heart. Trygaeus tricks Hermes with an absurd lie – that the Sun and Moon are plotting to deliver Greece into barbarian hands. Further tempted by a golden libation cup, Hermes lends a hand with the digging.

Hermes and Trygaeus spout out a series of invocations as the work progresses. The chorus tugs in rhythm. Despite mutterings of disunity, they manage to extricate Peace along with Opora and Theoria, goddesses of the harvest and festivals, respectively. Trygaeus and the chorus hurry to the fields to enjoy the bounty of Peace.

The chorus leader interrupts the revelry to inquire where Peace has been. Hermes tells how Phidias' exile caused local spats which led to War and the disappearance of Peace. They blame all their troubles on Cleon the tanner. Without Peace to bless their husbandry, farmers flocked to the cities in fear for their lives. No one planted or harvested, and people soon went hungry. Trygaeus encourages Peace to speak, but she is so angry at all Greeks that she will only whisper into Hermes' ear.

Hermes reports her message. Peace claims that she brought baskets of truces to the Greeks, but they ignored them. Now, guided by Hyperbolus, the lampmaker, they grope about in better light. Hermes gives Trygaeus Opora for a wife, whom Trygaeus accepts with kisses, and sends Theoria to lodge with the Senate. Because Zeus has commandeered the beetle as a draft animal, Trygaeus must rely on the goddess to return him to earth.

The chorus sings a brief interlude about War in Athens and about the poet's attempt to bring Peace. At the end of their presentation, Trygaeus limps up the street with Opora. He is greeted by his servant, whom he leaves in charge of nuptial arrangements. Before joining in the festive preparations, Trygaeus searches for someone to take charge of Theoria. He introduces her to the ruling council, and proclaimed the savior of humanity, he enjoys the limelight.

Trygaeus prepares a sacrifice to honor Peace. Hierocles, a local soothsayer, eager for his share of the roasting flesh, interrupts, gets in the way, and insults Trygaeus with oracular nonsense. Hierocles announces that War will not stop "until the wolf uniteth with the sheep." He and Trygaeus engage in a war of words, Trygaeus quoting Homer to offset Hierocles' skill with priestly mumbo-jumbo. Trygaeus resorts to violence and verbal abuse and drives away the seer.

Trygaeus returns to the wedding feast, where a sickle maker enters to thank Trygaeus for creating a demand for farm tools, thereby driving up the price. The cask maker has also met with better business. They are followed by the crest maker, armorers, a trumpet maker, and a lance polisher, each of whom bemoans the collapse of War and their loss of trade. Trygaeus ridicules their war paraphernalia. They leave in a huff.

The son of General Lamachus arrives to sing for the wedding. He opens with a hymn to young warriors, but Trygaeus stops him and asks for another song. The boy can think of nothing suited to the theme of Peace. Another singer sings lines from Archilochus' famous poem about desertion, and the guests begin the banquet. The bride appears, and Trygaeus is carried in triumph as the chorus chants, "Oh! Hymen! oh Hymenaeus!"

Ω

MENANDER

- *The Shearing of Glycera*

- *The Girl from Samos*

- *The Arbitration*

- *Dyskolos (The Grouch)*

MENANDER

LIFE AND BACKGROUND

An Athenian from the borough of Cephisia, Menander (*ca.* 342–291 B.C.) is remembered as a handsome ladies' man, elegant of manners, contented with his life, and, although living in the exciting era of Alexander the Great, decidedly apolitical. He was aptly trained for drama by Theophrastus in a direct line of scholarly descent from Aristotle and the Peripatetics. The modern reader can learn much about Menander from the people he fraternized with, including the politician and lawgiver Demetrius and the prolific comedy writer Alexis of Thurii, who has been called Menander's teacher and was possibly his uncle. Menander's association with Epicurus, who was his contemporary and an army buddy, provided the patina of social grace that lends an air of refinement and *savoir faire* to his work, perhaps the most endearing of his qualities.

A believer in the goodness of human beings, Menander led a peaceable, scholarly life in his villa at Piraeus, southeast of Athens, under the watchful eye of his mistress, Glycera, and later his lover, Thaïs. In her letter to another courtesan, Glycera indicates that Menander is a stouthearted lover, one whom she intends to hang on to. A homebody at heart, he once declined an invitation to visit Ptolemy I in Alexandria, preferring the familiarity and ferment of Athens. He is said to have died while swimming near Piraeus.

Menander's first production was the *Orge* in 321 B.C., although dates for his plays are, at best, approximations. His extensive body of work, numbering 108 plays at the rate of three to four per year over a thirty-year span, charted a new path for comedy from the phallic jokes, vaudeville antics, and pointed satires of Aristophanes a hundred years earlier. His gracious, tasteful comedies, however, often appeared poor also-rans in the company of the works of his contemporary, Philemon, who followed the buffoonery and virulent wit of his predecessors and garnered most of the praise. Over the years,

245

however, it is Menander who had the most influence on later dramatists, particularly the best of Roman writers of comedy, Plautus and Terence.

Although little of his work remains, including the 900 one-liners featured in school texts of his day, one entire play, *Dyskolos* (*The Grouch*), produced at the January Lenaea in 316 B.C. when Menander was twenty-five, was discovered piecemeal in 1898, 1905, and 1957, written on strips of papyrus which had served as packing for legal documents in Egypt. It was published in 1959.

Another play, *The Curmudgeon,* was added to the canon in the mid-1900s in Switzerland. In addition, readable chunks of *Samia* (*The Girl from Samos*), *Epitrepontes* (*The Arbitration*), *Periceiromene* (*The Shearing of Glycera*), *Aspis* (*The Shield*), and *Sicyonius* (*The Sicyonian*) give some credence to suppositions about his skill as a dramatist. For some scholars, these few scraps plus the close imitations by Roman comedy writers provide a hint of the original style and structure of Menander's comedies.

Menander dipped into what is now called the treasured stock of middle-class comedy — that is, stereotypical characters (the warm-hearted prostitute, the stony-hearted old moneybags, the conniving slave, the self-centered fop, the bloodsucking relative, the grumpy father, the macho military man, the sweet young thing, and the honest but simple-witted son), coincidence, mistaken identity, unfortunate accidents, recognition of highborn foundlings, thwarted love, maidens in distress, and the obligatory kiss-and-make-up ending. Yet, Menander masks the artificiality of stage convention with his attention to detail, individualization of stock characters, and skillful management of balance and harmony. He wrote rapidly and well, commenting on the feast of Dionysus for which he was to provide entertainment, "My comedy is finished: I've got the whole plan of it in my head — all that remains is to write the words."

Menander was much admired by ancient audiences, which are said to have preferred *The Arbitration* as a favorite for stage revivals. In addition, Menander received worthy tributes. St. Paul quotes him in I Corinthians 33, "Evil communications corrupt good manners." He was honored with a bronze portrait bust, which was rendered by Praxiteles' two sons and placed in the Theater of Dionysus. Notable critical opinion, including Plutarch and Aristophanes of Byzantium, establishes him among the best in his field, although the latter's claim that Menander's poetic talents should reside next to Homer's seems extreme.

$$\Omega$$

—— THE SHEARING OF GLYCERA ——

Although over half the play is missing and the rest is in tatters, Menander's Shearing of Glycera offers enough of a contrast to his other works to intrigue a reader's interest. The first act probably began with the actual cutting of Glycera's hair. Glycera, an orphaned twin of Moschion, as well as Polemon's mistress, argues with her lover, a stereotypical braggart warrior who earned his fortune in the Macedonian wars. Returning to Corinth unexpectedly, Polemon walks in on an apparent tryst between Glycera and Moschion, her neighbor. Outraged at the cozy twosome's dalliance, Polemon deals with the situation in standard macho style—he slices off Glycera's locks with his sword. The local folks mock and deride Glycera for her denuded scalp.

The allegorical figure of Misapprehension speaks to the audience, explaining how twins—a boy and a girl—were abandoned. A poor woman found them and nurtured Glycera, but placed Moschion in the care of Myrrhine, a rich lady. Hard times continued for Glycera's guardian, and so when Polemon fell in love with Glycera, the woman encouraged their liaison as a welcome relief from financial hardship. Before dying, Glycera's foster mother revealed to her alone how she found Glycera and her brother. The old woman achieved two purposes in her revelation—she assured Glycera of a direct tie with a wealthy kinsman, and at the same time, she prevented the development of an incestuous relationship between Glycera and the harddrinking neighborhood playboy.

According to Misapprehension, the old woman died; Polemon bought a house in Corinth next door to Moschion, who was unaware that Glycera was his twin sister. Glycera hoped to profit by her brother's good fortune; he, on the other hand, was attracted to his

pretty neighbor and employed a frontal assault, falling on her with
unforeseen kisses and caresses. Polemon approached at the height
of Moschion's passion and misinterpreted their embrace. Misapprehension claims to have engineered the muddle, sending Polemon into
a rage. Now, Misapprehension plans to tidy up loose ends and bring
together lover and mistress as well as brother and sister. She defends
her godlike right to intervene in human affairs, and she departs with
a cheery farewell.

Polemon's sergeant, Sosia, sent to spy on Glycera under the pretext
of fetching a sword and cloak, leaves Polemon's house at the beginning of Act 2 and describes the gallant warrior, prostrate and tearful
over Glycera's shearing. Glycera, traumatized by Polemon's boldness,
seeks help from her neighbor, Myrrhine. As Doris, Glycera's slave,
leaves to deliver the message to Myrrhine, Sosia catches sight of her.
Doris apparently gains entry at Myrrhine's house, and Glycera exits,
leaving behind her clothing and Doris, both belonging to Polemon.

Moschion is not at home when Glycera moves in with Myrrhine,
but his slave, Davus, takes in the whole situation and departs to find
his master. Meanwhile, revellers perform an entertaining intermission.

Moschion, doubtful of Davus' boast of how he masterminded the
girl's change of residence, returns with his slave. Davus expects reimbursement for luring Glycera into Myrrhine's house. (Moschion promises to set him up in business as his reward.) While Moschion preens
for his meeting with Glycera, Davus goes within and reports back
that lunch is ready. Moschion sends Davus in a second time to accept
the luncheon invitation and continues his self-promoting monologue,
fantasizing how Glycera will simper and shrink from him and how
he will soften up his mother with courtly manners and attention.
Davus returns, downcast. He explains that Myrrhine does *not* welcome her son during the two women's tête-á-tête. Moschion realizes
that Davus misrepresented the girl's coming. He quarrels with his servant, but lets Davus escape unscathed.

Polemon, unaware that Glycera has moved out, sends Sosia to
gather more information. Sosia enters the house; Doris slips out. She
worries about her master's reaction when he arrives home and finds
his mistress gone. Sosia reappears, clucking over Glycera's disappearance and blaming the servants in a surly voice. He assumes that
Glycera has moved in with Moschion, her lover. Before Sosia can
knock at Myrrhine's door, Davus accosts him. Sosia accuses Davus

of complicity in Glycera's kidnapping. Davus ridicules his charges. Sosia pretends to call to a comrade who can attest to the abduction. Davus, leery of the violent mercenary's threats, disappears within.

Sosia spots Doris coming out of hiding and accuses her of arranging Glycera's disappearance. Doris claims that Glycera sought refuge with Myrrhine, not Moschion. [A major portion of the text is missing.] Sosia, backed up by a band of mercenaries and a camp follower, Habrotonon, makes a belligerent display of liberating Glycera from Myrrhine's house. Pataecus, an elderly man, acts as mediator, but insists that the army back off.

Pataecus quells Sosia's boisterousness and mulls over the situation. He questions Polemon about particulars – whether Glycera is his lawful wife, whether she has been misused, and whether Polemon intends to use force to get her back. As proof of his good intentions, Polemon drags Pataecus into his house to examine Glycera's gorgeous wardrobe.

Moschion appears, armed and ready. He yells at the retreating figures, who are unaware of his presence. Bemoaning his misery, he describes how he withdrew to a small room in Myrrhine's house, sent Davus to announce his arrival, and prepared a speech. [Another large segment is missing. It appears that Moschion overheard his mother and Glycera discussing the girl's mistreatment and realized that she loves Polemon. Pataecus, serving as go-between, encounters Glycera and hears her side of the story.] Glycera makes point after point in her favor, punctuating her phrases with gestures and frantic tone of voice. Pataecus urges her to return to Polemon. Still offended that he so unceremoniously lopped off her hair, Glycera refuses.

[Glycera offers to send for items that prove her birth and entreats Pataecus to speak in her defense. He suspects that she is his own daughter.] Glycera dispatches Doris for a basket of embroidered baby clothes. [Another textural lapse. Glycera and Pataecus examine the remnants of her past. Pataecus tries to decipher the figures embroidered on the garments.] Pataecus recognizes the stag and the winged horse as belongings of his wife. Moschion eavesdrops, cursing the fate that makes Glycera his sister. Glycera provides other tidbits of proof – about the woman who rescued the twins and about the shaded brook where they were exposed.

The story rings true with Pataecus' version, which he got from the slave who left the children to die. Because Glycera recoils at his insensitivity, the old man justifies his wretched choice, citing his wife's death in childbirth and sudden impoverishment when his shipping business collapsed after his only ship sank in the Aegean Sea. Glycera pities his fate. They continue discussing the items left with the infants — a necklace decorated with engraved gems, a silver girdle patterned with dancing girls, a sheer wrapper, and a gold fillet. [Moschion joins the twosome; they share a three-way reunion, father with son and daughter. Glycera's fortunes improve.]

[At the beginning of the next scene, Polemon is talking with Doris.] Doris soothes Polemon's fears that Glycera will never love him again and discourages talk of suicide. Doris exits; Polemon verbally kicks himself for seeing harm in Moschion's brotherly kiss. Doris returns, rejoicing that Glycera is preparing to return and is dressing up for the pleasure of her rediscovered father. Before Glycera and Pataecus appear, Polemon loses his nerve and withdraws.

He returns and allows Pataecus to betroth him formally to Glycera. Pataecus insists that Polemon change his ways, give up soldiering, and mind his temper. Polemon promises to try. Polemon then invites Pataecus to join their feast, but Pataecus has other plans. He sets out to arrange Moschion's marriage to Philinus' daughter. To the side of the stage, Moschion groans in protest. [The fragmented play breaks off at this point.]

Ω

—————THE GIRL FROM SAMOS—————

Similar in plot and format to Shakespeare's *Comedy of Errors*, Menander's *Samia*, or *The Girl from Samos*, exemplifies the Greek sense of delight in confusion. The play opens before Demeas' house. He creeps out the door, pondering some enigma, and explains to the audience how he has gotten caught up in the frenzied preparations for the wedding of his son, Moschion, and the girl next door, Plangon.

Demeas also describes what has just occurred within his house: Moschion's former nurse, an old maidservant who has obtained her freedom, passed through the weaving room and picked up a crying infant, murmuring to it about Moschion's growth to manhood. [The text is faulty at this point.] The nurse then passed the baby to Chrysis, a slave girl, who scolded the noisy old woman for speaking loud enough to disturb the master. Demeas exited the domestic scene at this point.

Demeas notes that the slave who is nursing the child is a girl from Samos, an island east of Athens on the coast of Asia Minor. He indicates that the baby boy may be his. At this point, Parmeno, leading a queue of menials bearing goods from the market, interrupts Demeas' chatter about the baby. He quarrels with the cook, who carries kitchen knives into the street. Demeas calls to Parmeno and indicates to the audience that Parmeno is nosy.

Exasperated with Parmeno's dawdling, Demeas explodes in fury. He demands information about the baby's parentage, which he believes is being kept from him. Parmeno replies that the baby is the child of Chrysis and Demeas. Demeas disputes his word, insisting that Moschion is the father. Parmeno concedes that Moschion is the father. Demeas drives Parmeno from the stage with threats of whipping and branding.

Demeas cries to the heavens, withholding blame from Moschion, who has proved his innocence by agreeing to marriage. He charges Moschion with attempting to escape Helen, who caught Moschion in a drunken indiscretion. In consternation at the state of affairs, Demeas decides to cast out Chrysis, the girl from Samos. As the cook exits through the door in search of Parmeno, Demeas pushes through, forcing Chrysis, the nurse, and the baby into the street.

Chrysis and Demeas argue. The cook butts in; Demeas drives him back into the house with angry words. Demeas turns on Chrysis, reminding her that at one time, she earned her living by cadging meals. He slams the door in her face.

Niceratus, the father of the bride-to-be, enters with a skinny sheep, which he intends to sacrifice as part of the wedding ritual. He asks Chrysis why she stands so forlornly in the street. Chrysis explains that Demeas is angry because she kept the baby rather than leave it to die in the wild. Niceratus is surprised because Demeas was not at first upset about the child.

[There is a major gap in the text. Niceratus probably takes Chrysis into his home, where his wife and daughter, Plangon, attend the baby, who is really the son of Plangon and Moschion. Moschion evidently explains the baby's true parentage to Demeas, who is glad to put the matter behind him so that he can turn his attention once more to Chrysis, his mistress, and to Moschion and Plangon's nuptials. But when Niceratus learns that he is sheltering his own daughter's illegitimate child, he boils with rage. Yet, fearful that Moschion plans to break his engagement, leaving Niceratus to support his daughter's infant, Niceratus rushes away.]

Demeas panics when he hears Niceratus calling for fire to burn up the baby. Niceratus then rushes into the street, complaining that his wife and daughter have conspired to keep information about the baby from him. Niceratus even considers murdering Chrysis and chases her out of his house with a stick. Chrysis, still cradling the infant, shrieks in panic. Demeas shoos her back toward his house. As Chrysis cowers behind him, Demeas tries to reason with his irate neighbor. Meanwhile, the slave girl scurries to safety in the house.

Demeas seizes Niceratus. They argue over the baby, which Demeas identifies as his own. Niceratus is incredulous at the admission. The two men calm their voices, and Demeas suggests that Zeus may have slipped through the roof and fathered the child, but Niceratus refuses to be cozened. Gradually, though, he accepts Demeas' advice to forget the argument and go on with the wedding. [The act ends with the traditional revelry.]

Moschion appears onstage, angry that his father suspects him of fathering an illegitimate child. He considers running away to Bactria or Caria (parts of modern Afghanistan) to join the military, but decides that his love for Plangon is too great. Parmeno interrupts. Moschion sends him for a cloak and sword so that he can pretend he is leaving home. Parmeno returns without the items and urges Moschion to join the wedding ceremony. Moschion hesitates, worried that his father will agree to his son's departure. (The text ends here.)

Ω

THE ARBITRATION

A more thought-provoking play than Menander's *Samia, The Arbitration* resembles Shakespeare's problem plays in that there is the potential for tragedy, although the story ends happily. The first act, which exists in bits and pieces, contains the exposition, probably outlining how Pamphila, the winsome, pampered daughter of Smicrines, a grouchy, penurious Athenian businessman, married Charisius five months earlier. We learn that five months before the wedding, during a night celebration at Tauropolia, a drunk youth raped Pamphila. Five months pregnant when she married Charisius, she bore a son while Charisius was absent from home and sent the child to be exposed in the fields.

Charisius, formerly a frugal, priggish, cerebral sort, has suddenly begun throwing his money around and carousing in the streets. His transition occurs after his servant, Onesimus, informs him that Pamphila has borne an illegitimate child. To give his wife a chance of rejecting him, and thereby save her honor, Charisius goes on the prowl in the honky-tonks of Athens. His father-in-law is outraged by the change in Pamphila's new husband, whom he selected precisely because of his tightfisted, fuddy-duddy ways. As Smicrines departs to chastise Pamphila for her husband's profligate behavior, Chaerestratus, one of Charisius' friends, goes to warn Charisius of the situation.

In Act 2, Smicrines, unaware of his daughter's illegitimate child, rails at Charisius' irresponsible behavior. On his way into town to get advice, Smicrines encounters two men – Syriscus, a coal-burner and Chaerestratus' slave, and Davus, a goatherd – clad in rough skins and involved in a noisy argument. Davus' wife, carrying a baby, accompanies them. They choose Smicrines at random to arbitrate their dispute. Davus explains how, a month earlier, the two men found an abandoned baby boy wearing a necklace and other trinkets. Although Davus was sympathetic with the child's plight, he passed the burden of raising a child to Syriscus, who recently suffered the death of his own child.

In addition to the foundling, Syriscus also claims the items which Davus found with the child. Syriscus, in a long, eloquent speech, describes instances in which foundlings have been identified as the offspring of noble families. If Davus retains and sells the trinkets that may link the baby with a rich, prominent family, the child will never come into his rightful inheritance. Smicrines decides that the trinkets belong to the child and the child to Syriscus. Davus grouses over the verdict; Syriscus makes an accounting of each item.

Onesimus, Charisius' servant, appears and observes Syriscus examining the trinkets—a toy ax, an iron ring banded with gold, a necklace, a bit of red cloth, and a seal in the shape of a bull or a goat and identified by Cleostratus' mark. Onesimus identifies the ring as a duplicate of his master's ring, which he lost during a drinking bout, and grabs it from Syriscus' hand. Too busy for legal involvement, Syriscus yields, since both men are entering Chaerestratus' house where Charisius is giving a party.

At the beginning of Act 3, Onesimus returns to the street, talking about the ring, which he hesitates to show to his master. His last revelation—that Pamphilia had borne a son—proved so devastating to Charisius that Onesimus is loathe to impart any more news. Suddenly, a scuffle breaks out between Habrotonon, the harp girl, and some guests as a result of Charisius' rejection of the girl. Onesimus ignores the harpist and pursues his own thoughts, which have connected his master's drunkenness with the abandoned baby: Onesimus realizes that Charisius is probably the child's father.

Syriscus leaves Onesimus to settle his own quandary. Habrotonon, overhearing the circumstances surrounding the child's conception, claims that she, too, attended the festival of Tauropolia, where she played the lute. Habrotonon declares that she could recognize the rich, beautiful girl whom Charisius raped, but she chooses not to make a statement until she knows more about the episode lest there be some other explanation for the loss of the ring. Habrotonon concocts a scheme whereby she will pretend that she was the victim so that Charisius will confess if he is, in fact, the baby's father.

Onesimus congratulates himself for his coup—he has started the intrigue without divulging his part in it. [More of the text is pieced together at this point.] Smicrines returns from town, convinced that Charisius is wasting money and besmirching his daughter's good name by his crass indiscretions. Habrotonon, in the meantime, has stirred up a hornet's nest within, where Charisius acknowledges the foundling as his own. The party breaks up; the cook and his entourage stomp out in a snit. Smicrines learns that Charisius plans to buy Habrotonon's freedom and raise the child, in violation of his marriage contract with Pamphila. The guests gossip over the change in Charisius, from a high-toned moralist to a drunken rowdy and sower of wild oats. Smicrines vows to end the ill-famed marriage.

When Act 4 opens, Smicrines attempts to drag his daughter home. But Pamphila, loyal to her husband, rejects her father's arguments about wasted money and the mistress and insists on staying with Charisius. Smicrines strides out in search of someone who will physically remove Pamphila from her home. Pamphila's strength drains away. She withers by the door, crushed by the truth of her husband's philandering. As Habrotonon strolls by with the baby, Pamphila shrinks from contact with her rival.

Habrotonon recognizes Pamphila—not as Charisius' wife but as the rape victim at the festival. At the same moment, Pamphila identifies the trinkets the baby is wearing. Habrotonon confesses that she only pretends to be the child's mother. To Pamphila's delight, Habrotonon reveals that Charisius is the father. [Charisius, who overheard Pamphila's conversation with her father, is humbled by his wife's loyalty and outraged that she has suffered needlessly. Onesimus, fearful that Charisius will blame him for meddling, tiptoes out.]

Onesimus assumes that Charisius is insane. He ponders his master's muttering and breast-beating, but can make no sense of the situation. When Charisius comes in sight, Onesimus hides from possible punishment for involving himself in his master's personal business. Charisius debates aloud how to resolve his marital dilemma and opts to continue his marriage to his faithful, long-suffering wife. Habrotonon accosts Charisius, confesses that she is not the baby's mother, and she unleashes another tirade from Charisius. In his anger at being hoodwinked, he collars Onesimus, who lurks nearby to catch every word. Habrotonon separates the two men and names Pamphila as the baby's mother.

[Charisius and Pamphila are reunited. Habrotonon is probably set free and given a worthy position, in compensation for her wisdom and honesty. Smicrines, the complicator of the plot, returns with Pamphila's nurse, Sophrona, who was also the midwife at the baby's birth. Sophrona attempts to calm the old man during one of his comic outbursts.] Smicrines threatens to duck Sophrona in the pond all night for butting in.

Smicrines pounds at Charisius' door; Onesimus bars the way, sneering at Sophrona, whom Smicrines hauls along in a tightfisted grip. Onesimus mouths a pious admonition and invites Smicrines to enter and see his (Smicrines') grandson. Smicrines is dumbfounded by the news. Sophrona corroborates Onesimus' account of the child's conception the night of the Tauropolian festival. [The concluding lines are missing.]

Ω

———DYSKOLOS (THE GROUCH)———

First published in English in 1959, the discovery of a complete, if slightly fragmented, comedy by Menander has greatly enhanced the world's knowledge of ancient humor. In contrast to the three more seriously fragmented plays which had previously made up the canon, this discovery is a twentieth-century Rosetta Stone for scholars who attempt to piece together a thorough examination of Greek drama.

Menander wrote *Dyskolos* for the Lenaean festival of 317 B.C. and garnered first prize for his efforts. The play delighted the audience with a glimpse of New Comedy at its best, featuring coincidence, the motif of love at first sight, stereotypical wily servants, and the standard struggles between Athenian nobility and country folk, and also between the older generation and their offspring.

Set near a cave in Phyle, a rural district on the outskirts of Athens, the play opens at the shrine of Pan, who speaks the prologue. He points out two houses which dominate the scene. The one to the right is owned by Knemon, a grouchy misanthrope in his sixties who married a widow, but he eventually drove her away by his perpetual crabbiness. Although the couple had a daughter, Myrrhine, Knemon could find no happiness with his family. To escape the carping grouch, his wife fled to the house on the left, the nearby farm of her son, Gorgias, who was fathered by her first husband.

Myrrhine, innocent and dutiful, continues to live with her cranky father and devotes herself to Pan's shrine. In return for her attentions, Pan tends to a developing romance between the girl and Sostratos, a wealthy young Athenian who saw Myrrhine while he was on a hunting trip and immediately fell in love with her. Pan hints that he is responsible for their auspicious meeting.

Sostratos returns to Phyle to woo Myrrhine. He is accompanied by Chaireas, a parasitic companion. As they draw near the shrine, Pyrrhias, Sostratos' servant, runs toward his master in an attempt to escape a madman. Sostratos questions Pyrrhias' peculiar behavior and learns that Pyrrhias, in order to make discreet and proper inquiries about Knemon's daughter, approached an old man who was crawling about in his wild pear garden. Angered by the unwanted visitor, Knemon suddenly began throwing dirt at Pyrrhias. The attack escalated as Knemon hurled stones, mud, and pears.

Sostratos berates Pyrrhias for cowardice. Chaireas, who has come along to help Sostratos with his courtship of Myrrhine, proposes that he approach the old farmer the next day and departs. Sostratos, who doubts that Chaireas really intends to help, is venting his frustrations on Pyrrhias when Knemon appears. Pyrrhias, eager to avoid a second encounter with the crusty old grouch escapes.

Knemon is in a froth over the number of trespassers who disturb his solitude. He wishes that he could change them all to stone and convert his farm into a sculpture garden. Timidly, Sostratos says that he is not a trespasser; he is "waiting for a friend," but the acid bite of Knemon's ill humor disturbs him. Cowed by the old man's railing, Sostratos contemplates seeking assistance from Geta, his father's slave.

A noise interrupts Sostratos' thoughts. Myrrhine enters, fretting over the loss of a bucket which the nurse dropped down the well. Transfixed by her beauty, Sostratos is enraptured, breathing a triple oath to Apollo, Castor, and Pollux. As Myrrhine debates with herself the best way to avoid Knemon's ire, Sostratos offers to fetch water for her and carries her proffered jug to the cave.

A noise erupts from Gorgias' house next door. It is Daos, Gorgias' slave, who bewails the ill luck that binds his master in poverty. He observes Sostratos returning with the water and suspects that Sostratos is taking advantage of Myrrhine, a poor country lass whose father locks her away from society. Vowing to tell her half-brother, Gorgias, Daos enters the house as drunken revelers approach the shrine of Pan. (This interlude provides light entertainment between Acts 1 and 2. In standard Greek style, the interlude has little connection with the plot.)

Daos returns with his master, who berates his servant for failing to take decisive action against Sostratos. Gorgias emphasizes his position as Myrrhine's protector, but Daos reminds him that Knemon is a feisty adversary, one he prefers to avoid. [The text of this speech is garbled.] Sostratos, unable to locate Geta, returns and encounters Gorgias in the street. Acting on his hunch that Sostratos is up to no good, Gorgias warns him that no hanky-panky will be tolerated.

Sostratos professes his love for Myrrhine with a solemn oath to Pan. Gorgias, impressed with the young Athenian's sincerity, apologizes for his hasty judgment, identifies himself as Myrrhine's half-brother, and offers his help. Although Gorgias describes in detail Knemon's foul temper, Sostratos cannot escape love's spell and refuses to give up hope of winning the girl.

Gorgias proposes a test of Knemon's state of mind. While the three men await Knemon's return by his usual route, Sostratos agrees to change into humble work clothes so that Knemon will think him a simple farmer. [Again, parts of Gorgias' lines are garbled.] Daos, sneering at Sostratos' soft, city lifestyle, suggests that they work him so hard that he will sprain his back and not return to Phyle. As Sostratos sets to work with a pick, Daos and Gorgias exit.

Sikon, a cook, plods onstage, dragging an unruly sheep toward the shrine. He calls to Geta, who trails behind with a load of baggage. [Another section is indecipherable.] At Sikon's urging, Geta describes his mistress' prophetic dream in which Pan snares Sostratos, dresses him in farmer's clothes, and forces him to do menial farm work. The family plans a sacrifice to avert this terrible omen. Sikon promises to relieve Geta's worries about the ominous dream with a gourmet meal.

Following a second choral interlude, Act 3 opens on Knemon, who snarls at his maid, Simiche, bidding her to keep the door locked until he returns after dark. He spies Sostratos' mother and sister, Plangon, moving toward the shrine. Cursing the interlopers, Knemon disparages their preparations for the sacrifice, which he describes as a "picnic." Meanwhile, Geta greets his mistress, and Parthenis pipes a hymn to the god. When Geta accosts Knemon for staring, the crotchety old man spews a stream of invective. In his frustration with the worshippers' infringement on his solitude, Knemon threatens to tear down his residence and rebuild on less popular ground. He retreats into his house.

Lacking a pot for the sacrifice, Geta pounds on Knemon's door and braves his wrath to borrow a vessel. Knemon is so unpleasant, however, that Geta hastily withdraws his request and departs. Knemon stomps back into his house. Sikon ridicules Geta's fruitless efforts to obtain a pot and, banking on his skill in manipulating strangers, he himself knocks at Knemon's door. Knemon is so enraged at this further disturbance that he calls for a whip and seizes Sikon. After Sikon manages to free himself, Knemon disappears into his house. Sikon ponders how the situation got so out of hand. He decides to roast the sacrifice and forget about borrowing a pot.

Meanwhile, Sostratos, weary and dirty from digging, wanders up, muttering about his sore muscles but undeterred in his desire for Myrrhine. He meets Geta, who is also muttering complaints about hard work. [Sections of Geta's speech are unreadable.] Cheered by the news that his mother has arrived to prepare a meal at the shrine, Sostratos plans to invite Gorgias and Daos to the feast.

Simiche exits Knemon's house, wailing that she dropped both a bucket and a pick down the well. She freezes in terror as Knemon roars onstage, threatening to tie her up and drop her down the well. She hastens back indoors. Then, in a sudden change of character, Knemon sinks into self-pity. Geta attempts to relieve his dismal mood by offering a rope and a hook to retrieve the lost objects. Snapping back into his usual mood, Knemon curses him and stomps off in a huff.

To Geta's amazement, Sostratos returns with a common laborer and a slave, Gorgias and Daos. As Gorgias and Sostratos enter the shrine, Daos hurries back to see to Gorgias' mother's needs. A choral interlude rounds out Act 3.

Act 4 begins with Simiche, again lamenting her ill luck. Sikon exits from the shrine and offers grudging assistance. This time, Knemon himself, the old grouch, has fallen down the well. Sikon chortles with glee and suggests that Simiche finish him off with a rock. Simiche calls for Gorgias, who rushes out of the shrine to her aid. As Gorgias and Sostratos follow Simiche to the well, Sikon snickers that Knemon deserves the gods' punishment for his stinginess. [Another section is marred. The two rescuers apparently get Knemon out of the well.]

After Sikon returns to his duties in the shrine, Sostratos leaves Knemon's house, expostulating about his adventure. According to Sostratos, Gorgias jumped down the well while Sostratos remained at the top and comforted Myrrhine. Overwhelmed by Myrrhine's beauty,

Sostratos forgot to hold the rope and dropped Gorgias and Knemon three times before the rescue was completed.

Sostratos is so caught up in puppy love that he is tempted to dash back and kiss Myrrhine. Before he can move, though, Knemon, Myrrhine, and Gorgias enter. [Knemon is apparently wheeled in on a bed.] Knemon is greatly subdued by his harrowing tumble down the well and speaks kindly to Myrrhine, an act that is completely out of character for him. Gorgias urges him to change his lifestyle and live with a companion. [Some segments are missing, during which Gorgias' mother arrives.]

Knemon extols Gorgias' virtues as a rescuer and a gentleman and vows to adopt him. Knemon also entrusts Myrrhine to her brother and asks him to find a suitable husband for the girl. As the former grouch settles back against the pillows, content that a strong, youthful pair of hands will provide for him and Myrrhine, Gorgias interrupts his reverie and introduces Sostratos, who assisted with the rescue. Knemon is impressed that Sostratos is a tanned farmer rather than a wealthy idler. [More lines are missing here. Knemon apparently agrees to a wedding between Sostratos and Myrrhine.] Knemon is wheeled out.

Gorgias lauds Sostratos for his worthy attitude. As they talk, Sostratos' father, Kallippides, hurries to the feast and enters the shrine. Sostratos follows his father to the shrine. Gorgias plans to talk with Kallippides after Kallippides has eaten his share of the sacrificial meal. A choral interlude ends Act 4.

Act 5 begins with a conversation between Sostratos and his father in which the two disagree about marriage plans. Kallippides, however, accedes to Sostratos' wish to marry a poor girl, but he balks at the suggestion that he give his daughter to Gorgias, an obvious pauper. Sostratos softens his father with wise words: "A friend in sight is far more valuable than hidden wealth, which you keep hoarded up." Kallippides warms to his son's point of view and agrees to accept Gorgias as a potential son-in-law.

At first, Gorgias hesitates to betroth himself to a noble wife, but at Sostratos' insistence, he agrees to marry Plangon. Kallippides offers three talents as a dowry, and Gorgias offers a talent for Myrrhine, which is the worth of his land. Kallippides gently refuses, insisting that Gorgias keep his land.

The two families plan to celebrate the weddings the next morning.

Gorgias goes to Knemon's house to try to coax the old man out, but he returns empty-handed. The two families enter the shrine for an all-night drinking bout. Simiche enters the empty stage, muttering over her shoulder at her cranky owner, who declines to join in the prenuptial festivities. As flute music drifts from the cave, Geta leaves the party.

Geta calls to Sikon and suggests that they take their revenge on Knemon, who is sleeping in his house. Drunk and foul-mouthed, Sikon anticipates the sweetness of vengeance. He awakens Knemon and asks to borrow pots, a bowl, seven tripods, and a dozen tables. When Knemon declines to lend his household goods, Sikon accepts his refusal and sends Geta to harass the old man. Geta demands nine mats and a hundred-foot Oriental rug. Pushed to the limits, Knemon abandons his recently gentled spirit and erupts into his former curmudgeonly state.

While Knemon shouts impatiently for Simiche, Sikon takes advantage of the old man's weakness and accuses him of antisocial behavior and misogyny. [Parts are garbled here. Sikon apparently renders a lyrical description of the festivities that Knemon is missing.] Geta and Sikon force Knemon to join the party and summon a slave to support him as he hobbles into the cave. Geta decks the grouch with a garland and tosses a gesture of farewell over his shoulder to the audience.

Ω

GREEK PROSE WRITERS

- **Lysias**
- **Demosthenes**
- **Aesop**

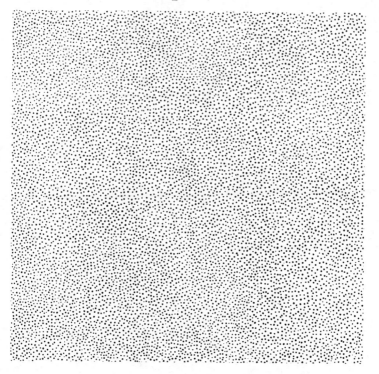

LYSIAS

Lysias, a noted Athenian orator and professional speech writer, who was born about 445 B.C. and died about 380 B.C., was the son of Cephalus, a native of Syracuse, a prosperous manufacturer of shields, a close friend of Pericles, and a noted orator honored by Plato in the *Republic.* Despite his alien birth, Lysias was brought up among the elite of Athens. At fourteen, he and his brother, Polemarchus, went to Thurii in southern Italy to study philosophy and eloquence. Later, he assembled his own school, but he was surpassed by Theodorus, another teacher of oratory, and so he shifted his energies to writing speeches, thirty-four of which are extant.

The brothers returned to Athens in 411 B.C., operated their father's arms factory, and for a time, lived a comfortable life. However, after Polemarchus became a victim of envious political forces and was forced to drink hemlock, Lysias, whose life was in danger and his finances in ruin, escaped to Megara near Corinth, where he supported the return of the democrats.

When the democrats again seized power in 403, Lysias returned to Athens and earned his living by writing forensic speeches for peasants, merchants, artisans, and other inexperienced speakers to deliver in the lawcourts. He himself was involved in lawsuits over his lost fortune for years after the restoration of democracy. Despite a strong movement to extend him citizenship, all his life Lysias retained the designation of *metic,* or resident alien.

In his fragmentary *Olympicus,* an elaborate, impressive speech read at the Olympic celebrations of 388 B.C., Lysias advocates political unity among Greeks against tyrants like Dionysius I of Syracuse. Mobs, in reaction to the speech, looted the gaudy marquee of the Syracusan embassy. The only speech which Lysias himself delivered, entitled *Against Eratosthenes,* demands that his brother's murderer be punished. Its style, according to critics, is moderate, sensible, sometimes ironic, but lacking in fire.

Another of his narrative speeches, *On the Murder of Eratosthenes,* is reminiscent of the amorous tales of Boccaccio. Lysias attempts to exonerate Euphiletus, an Athenian who killed his wife's lover. Euphiletus wins his case by explaining how his wife's seducer first sees her at Euphiletus' mother's funeral. The domestic details, which explain how Euphiletus' wife eludes detection and locks her husband in his room during her adultery, give a realistic picture of fourth- and fifth-century Athenians.

In contrast, *Against Simon* reveals the sordid details of two aging males' rivalry for the affections of a youth named Theodotus. In contrast also, *For the Invalid* concerns a disabled client who petitions craftily and humorously for the council to reinstate his pension. In other speeches, Lysias makes a case against Alcibiades the Younger, a self-promoter and turncoat military leader, who was exiled after transferring his loyalties from Athens to Sparta. Different in style and content from his other speeches, *On the Olive Tree* defends a client who was brought before the Areopagus for the crime of offending the enclosure around a sacred tree.

Lysias is known for his ability to identify with clients and typify their station, lifestyle, and idiosyncrasies with application of suitable examples and logic. This skill fostered his reputation as an unprincipled opportunist; however, his survival amid the political climate of his day demanded adaptability. Under the guise of utter simplicity, his subtly calculated speeches give modern readers a picture of ordinary litigation. His prolific works served as models of clarity and style for his contemporaries, many of whom imitated him.

Respected for his grace and charm, Lysias was admired for breaking with the sophists, writers of ornate, specious argumentation. In contrast to their stiffness, pomposity, and convoluted logic, Lysias wrote in unaffected, natural prose which won his clients' cases by its simple appeal.

Ω

DEMOSTHENES

Remembered as a staunch supporter of Athens and the most vigorous, earnest, and skillful orator of his time, Demosthenes (384–322 B.C.) holds a place among the great speakers of history. The son of a wealthy arms manufacturer and investor, he was orphaned at the age of seven. Having been withheld by his mother from wrestling and other vigorous sports, he was too delicate and sensitive for the military and dedicated himself to an ascetic, scholarly life.

Demosthenes studied under Isaeus and learned rhetoric and law, skills which he applied at the age of eighteen during lawsuits against his three guardians, who embezzled and squandered his inheritance. His method of overcoming a lisp and shortness of breath is legendary: withdrawing to a cave, he practiced before the roar of the surf while he held pebbles in his mouth. Greatly influenced by his reading of Plato, Pericles, and Thucydides, Demosthenes earned his living as a teacher of rhetoric and a writer of speeches rich in idealism, historic allusion, and rhythmical structure, sixty of which are still in existence.

One of his earliest speeches, *On the Symmories* (354 B.C.) advocates an increase in the number of citizens liable for taxation to support naval units and reveals his concern for military preparedness and the survival of Athenian independence, the most important themes of his work. His interest in foreign policy led to numerous influential speeches in the assembly and lawcourts over a thirteen-year period during which he tried in vain to rouse Athens from its apathy and complacency. He delivered repeated complaints concerning the rise of Philip II of Macedon, who threatened the grain supply and united northern kingdoms against Athens.

Inflamed by the pacifism and isolationism of his contemporaries, Demosthenes delivered the first of his *Philippics* in 351 B.C. Although these historic orations lack humor, they are models of oratorical power, idealism, and ardor. The first speech urges: "Observe, Athenians, the height to which the fellow's insolence has soared: he leaves you no choice of action or inaction . . . he is always taking in more, everywhere casting his net round us, while we sit idle and do nothing."

Like the controversy stirred by Senator McCarthy's personal battle against communism or William Jennings Bryan's testimony against creationism, the uproar created by Demosthenes' repeated denunciations led to hasty, but ineffectual action. An Athenian coalition with Thebes and increased spending for the military proved to be too little, too late; Athens never regained her former glory.

In 334 B.C., Demosthenes attacked Aeschines, one of Philip's supporters, for mismanaging an embassy to Macedon. Both sides displayed powerful oratory; Aeschines barely escaped conviction. The personal animosities between the two enemies continued, leading to Aeschines' accusation of impropriety against Demosthenes when Ctesiphon proposed a gold crown to honor Demosthenes, a move which Aeschines countered in a personal diatribe entitled *Against Ctesiphon.*

Demosthenes' rebuttal, *On the Crown,* is an impassioned defense of his principles: "I swear by your forefathers – those who met the peril at Marathon, those who took the field at Plataea, those in the sea fight at Salamis, and those Artemisium, and many other brave men who repose in the public monuments, all of whom alike, as being worthy of the same honor, the country buried, not the successful only or the victorious! Justly! For the duty of brave men has been done by all: their fortune has been such as the Deity assigned to each." As a result of Demosthenes' powerful rhetoric, Aeschines had to leave Athens.

Following Alexander's accession after Philip's death, Demosthenes continued to support coalition with Thebes against the growing menace of Macedon. Although Alexander, after destroying Thebes, spared Athens, he demanded that Demosthenes be turned over to him. Subsequent turmoil, which centered on Harpalus, Alexander's governor of Babylon from whom Demosthenes accepted a bribe in the form of a gold cup filled with twenty talents, resulted in Demosthenes' public embarrassment, an exorbitant fine of fifty talents, and his self-imposed exile to Troezen. He returned to Athens after Alexander's death in 323 B.C., but never regained his former influence or position.

In a final rally of Athenian strength against Macedon, Demosthenes was countered by Antipater. After the Athenian navy was defeated at Amorgus and the army at Crannon, Demosthenes escaped to the island of Calauria and swallowed poison before he could be captured. He was eulogized by an ancient critic as follows: "Our orator, owing to the fact that in his vehemence, – and in his speed, power, and intensity, – he can as it were consume by fire and carry away all before him, may be compared to a thunderbolt or a flash of lightning."

Although he earned the nickname Batalus (an effete flute player) in his youth, Demosthenes came to be called Argas (the snake) for his savage, quick-witted oratory. However, it is his late title, "the orator," which establishes his place among ancient Greeks. On the base of the brass statue which Athenians dedicated in his honor was engraved: "Had you for Greece been strong, as wise you were,/ The Macedonian had not conquered her."

Ω

AESOP

The semi-legendary writer and/or collector of 350 fables, Aesop (620?–560? B.C.) was a slave from Phrygia, or Lydia, who served Iadmon on the island of Samos before being freed. After extensive travels, he is thought to have been thrown from a cliff at Delphi after envious Delphians, angered by his ironic tales, hid a golden bowl in his luggage and accused him of theft. The city is said to have suffered a plague and was forced to pay blood-money to Iadmon's grandson to atone for its savagery. However, this story, like most episodes attached to Aesop's name, contains the elements of legend.

An ancient biography of Aesop pictures him as a Greek Uncle Remus – a jolly teller of tales and dispenser of homespun wisdom who confounds the learned men of his day with common sense. The bits of orally transmitted folklore, proverbs, and yarns attributed to Aesop were probably written down around 300 B.C. by Demetrius Phalereus. The collection known as "Aesop's Fables" is the product of Phaedrus (ca. 15–50 A.D.), a Roman slave of the Christian era who compiled books of pointed, satiric verse which got him into difficulty with the Emperor Tiberius.

Four overlapping manuscripts contain a series of animal fables as well as stories of men and gods, particularly the mythic narratives about Hermes the Trickster. For the purpose of educating young readers, each story ends with an explicit moral, such as "To change place is not to change your nature"; "The greedy who demand more lose all"; "Danger often comes from where we least expect"; and "There is always someone worse off than you." The stories were used as classroom exercises in composition and declamation and as illustrations by many orators, including Abraham Lincoln. Whatever the truth of Aesop's life, it is obvious that he was respected and loved, as indicated by the statue in his honor in Athens.

Ω

GREEK LYRIC POETS

- Sappho
- Pindar
- Alcaeus
- Lesser Lyric Poets

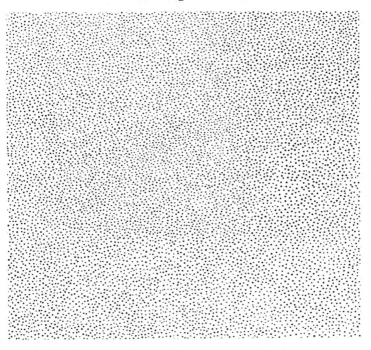

SAPPHO

The most famous Greek poet and a particular favorite of the ancient Romans, Sappho, whose name is sometimes given as Psappho, lived in the late seventh century, B.C. According to Eusebius, her work flourished from 600 to 594 B.C. The daughter of Scamandronymus and Cleïs, she was born on the island of Lesbos off the coast of Asia Minor, but little of her personal life can be established with certainty except what biographical data she reveals in her poems. She came from an aristocratic background and spent most of her life in Mytilene. She appears to have enjoyed a freedom not known to mainland girls – a freedom which encouraged personal growth, education, and artistic expression.

Sappho's father died when she was six, leaving her in the care of her mother and three brothers, Larychus, Charaxus, and Eurygius. One of the three, Larychus, poured wine in the council chamber on holidays. According to Herodotus, her brother Charaxus was a merchant sailor who traded wines in Naucratis, a Greek city in the Nile delta, and he became enamored of Doricha, a hetaera or courtesan. He spent large sums of money on Doricha, bought her freedom, and caused his sister embarrassment because of his devotion to a woman of questionable honor. Sappho gently upbraids Charaxus in a poem which prays to Cypris (Aphrodite) for his safe return. Sappho begs him to abandon his tawdry affair, which has robbed him of reputation and wealth, and to reestablish his dignified position in the community.

Sappho was married to an Andrian merchant named Cercolas, and she mentions with affection a blonde daughter, "Cleïs, my beloved," whom she advises to accentuate her fair hair with a garland, rather than the purple band more suited to brunettes. Her devotion to the child is evident in the verse which states, "I have a small daughter called Cleïs, who is like a golden flower; I wouldn't take all Croesus' kingdom, with love thrown in, for her." Concerning her own looks, Sappho laments having a short body and dark complexion. Another

273

poem that mourns the passing of her youth indicates that she may have lived well past middle age.

Sappho clearly aligns her loyalties with the Muses, rather than with religious worship or political ideology. Although she makes little mention of politics, her life was affected by civil wars and the political turmoil of Mytilene. She was exiled by Pittacus, one of the Seven Sages of ancient Greece, and she lived in Sicily from *ca.* 604–595 B.C. During this troubled but creative period in her life, she wrote short lyrical verse about girls who struck her fancy; hymns to her favorite deities, notably Aphrodite and Hera; and traditional *epithalamia,* or marriage hymns, which were performed by a chorus to the accompaniment of the lyre at the threshold of the couple's home or outside the bridal chamber.

Historians have mused for centuries over Sappho's relationship with the refined young girls mentioned in her more intimate lyrics. One explanation of their association is that, having been abandoned by the males of Lesbos during wartime, this group of women – Eunice, Anagora, Gyrinno, Dika, Atthis, Anactoria, Mnasidica, Praxinoa, Gongyla, Hero, Timas, Arignota – formed a supportive league or club, which was led by the strongest female intellect of the island. Sappho lavished love and attention on her young friends, relishing their delicacy, femininity, and grace. Probably they were not a finishing school or religious cult, but their exact position in Sappho's affections can not be ascertained without more evidence. Whatever the organizing principle of their circle, such a coterie was neither rare nor scandalous in ancient Greece.

Legend embellishes the events surrounding Sappho's death. Menander alludes to a tradition that Sappho loved a mythic ferryman named Phaon, a conceited Adonis figure, allegedly favored by Aphrodite, who transported passengers from Lesbos to Lydia. Sappho mentions him frequently in her love poems. Following her unsuccessful attempt to win Phaon's love, Sappho is reputed to have leaped into the Ionian Sea from a cliff on Leucas, an island off the west coast of Greece.

Sappho's exquisite marriage of form and feeling set a precedent in literature. In her honor was named the sapphic stanza pattern, consisting of three verses of eleven syllables each ($'-|''|'--|'-|'-$) called hendecasyllabics and a fourth verse of five syllables ($'--|'-$), which many English poets have attempted but only a few, notably Swinburne and Pound, have mastered.

Other of her verses stray from sapphic style, featuring instead dactylic rhythms, folk motifs, or epic language. These poems, one of which details Andromache's arrival at Troy for her marriage to Hector, imitate the high romance of Homer, but maintain the dialect of Aeolia and Sappho's own short sentences, musical phrasing, and liquid vowel sounds. Overall, most of Sappho's poetry follows a single pattern – personal experiences revealed through flowing verses accompanied by the lyre. Her tone is upbeat, loving, generous. Sappho reflects the open spirit of one who risks pain and sorrow for the rewards of love and beauty.

The *epithalamia*, idealized celebrations of the lucky groom's choice of a beautiful bride, record Sappho's execution of a traditional Greek verse form. Their fresh, wholesome imagery honors matrimony, as demonstrated by this tribute to a not-so-young bride: "Like a rosy apple on a high branch is the maiden; the pickers have forgotten her – no, not forgotten: they have simply not been able to reach her." In another example, the bride reflects wistfully on her girlhood: "Maidenhood, maidenhood, whither goest thou from me?" A third example depicts a laconic maiden who cannot concentrate on her spinning wheel for thoughts of her absent lover.

Sappho's style is pleasantly straightforward and simple: "Awed by her splendor, stars near the lovely moon cover their own bright faces when she is roundest and lights earth with her silver." Sappho avoids the more intricate strophes which are characteristic of Greek poetry, and she stresses sincere expressions of love and appreciation of beauty couched in the Aeolian dialect of Lesbos. Her genius for sound and sense, unfortunately, cannot be translated. Sappho was widely read, influencing writers of her own period as well as later masters. Strabo referred to her as a "wonder"; Plato named her the "tenth muse."

Most Greeks considered her poetry first rate, in a class with Homer's. Dionysius of Helicarnassus admired her ability to weave a poem into a unified whole by the "natural affinity of the letters." Solon declared that he could not die in peace until he had memorized her verses. Lucretius, Catullus, and Ovid borrowed from her work, as did Racine, Baudelaire, and Boileau; Plutarch, Aristotle, and Longinus quoted her; and Horace imitated her distinctive stanzas frequently.

Bits and fragments of her verse are preserved in quotations by ancient critics, grammarians, dramatists, orators, and historians.

Collections of her poems filled nine books in ancient times; however, only two long poems have survived, through quotation by Dionysius and Pseudo-Longinus. Some epigrams are preserved in *The Palatine Anthology*. Other fragments, obtained from papyri, complete the body of her work that is available to modern readers.

As revealed by her verse, Sappho places no overt trust in an afterlife. When she mentions separation or death, her buoyant faith in memory, which is aided by poetry, restores her joy in people and nature. One of her verses notes, "You may forget but let me tell you this: someone in some future time will think of us." The beauty which Sappho captured in her poems becomes her bid for immortality, through the enjoyment of those who live after her and who take pleasure in her poems.

Ω

PINDAR

A well-traveled aristocrat and a member of the noted Aegidae family, one of Sparta's royal houses, the poet Pindar (518–442 B.C.) was born a half mile west of Thebes in Cynoscephalae, Boeotia, the native country of Hesiod. Despite a lack of formal education and polish, he studied poetry in Thebes under Corinna, a distinguished poet whom he surpassed late in his teens. In Athens, he continued his studies under Apollodorus and Lasus of Hermione, and he quickly earned fame and a respectable living from his lyric verse.

From the age of twenty, Pindar earned large commissions from competitors from all corners of the Mediterranean world who participated in the pan-Hellenic games and paid to have their victories commemorated in song. He numbered among his patrons Hieron I, ruler of Syracuse and supporter of the arts, at whose court Pindar spent four years. As a result of his prolific verse, he amassed much wealth from gifts and commissions and was known for his generosity.

Buoyed by an adoring public, Pindar thought well of himself, as he illustrates when he calls himself a "prophet-priest" and the "tuneful prophet of the Muses." He addressed notables as equals. Ignoring the privilege of their rank, he spiced his praise of them with advice, admonition, and even criticism. On a visit to Athens, one of the many cities that invited him, he wrote a dithyramb for which he received the honorary title of envoy, a gift of ten thousand drachmas, and a statue in his honor. Pindar felt especially at home on Aegina, the triangular island southwest of Athens, and he dedicated eleven poems to its people. To the residents of Sicily, he dedicated fifteen odes.

Pindar was married, had a son and two daughters, but he followed the Greek penchant for young men. He loved Thrasybulus and Theoxenos, whom he eulogized late in life. Of young men he confesses: "The beauty of boys in the freshness of youth wakes the fire in my heart." He was reputed to have died at the age of eighty in the theater at Argos, resting his head on Theoxenos' shoulder.

Pindar experimented with a variety of forms, including hymns, paeans, dirges, dithyrambs, eulogies, threnodies, partheneia, skolia, processionals, panegyrics, choruses, and forty-four *epinicia*, or victory songs, the last comprising most of his extant works. One of his earliest successes, the *Tenth Pythian Ode*, describes Hippocles' victory at Delphi, where priests heaped honors on Pindar and provided him with a stipend. From the beginning, his verse was marked by conservative tastes in theme, a willingness to experiment with form (particularly the accepted forms which Homer had established), and deep religious convictions.

Pindar's considerable reputation as a lyricist rests upon his output of *epinicia*, or liturgical odes, at four great pan-Hellenic games — the Olympian, the Pythian, the Isthmian, and the Nemean. The events covered the range of Greek athletic skills: chariot races; foot races extending 200, 400, and 1200 yards; wrestling; boxing; discus and javelin throwing; and the pentathlon, which included running, jumping, wrestling, and the discus and javelin throw. The victor at these contests was showered with adulation and awards, including processionals and banquets, and the recitation of an ode especially in his honor. The Greek thirst for praise led to the lionizing of any word-smith who could capture in verse the cult of the athlete.

These odes comprise the four books of Pindaric odes, which were sung by a male choir made up of the victor's friends to the accompaniment of a lyre, or a lyre and flute. Pindar himself directed whenever he was present at the ceremony, which took place before the victor's house or in a hall or temple. When Pindar was unable to attend, he carefully selected an alternate *didaskalos,* or choir director.

Although his poems follow no set pattern, Pindar tends to include certain standard features – the victor's name and lineage, the athletic feat, the location of the contest, and often a familiar scene from a mythic victory which parallels the accomplishment. Because Pindar believed that aristocrats inherited talent from their noble strain, he pays particular attention to the country and family of the victor. To save the champion from the deadly sin of pride, Pindar balances his praise with reminders that success must be tempered with humility, moderation, and gratitude to the gods, who make all things possible.

The opening lines of his *Olympian, I* illustrates Pindar's ability to select images that set a noble, dignified tone:

> Though water be the first of all the elements, yet gold, sparkling like a flame in the night, overshadows all other treasure with its proud opulence. Would you sing of the Games, O my heart? Then seek not in the desert of the noonday sky a star more dazzling than the sun, nor hope to celebrate a contest more glorious than Olympia's.

His use of color and light add more than sense impression, for both gold and light are sacred to Apollo, god of the sun, healing, and creativity.

In the *Pythian, II,* Pindar tends toward a monotheism that echoes David, the Hebrew psalmist, when he intones:

> God alone shall accomplish everything in accordance with his hopes: God, who outsoars the eagle in its flight and overtakes the dolphin in the sea, bends the proud man to his will, while to others he bequeaths imperishable glory.

Thus Pindar, always mindful of his debt to the gods, combines the elements of nature with religious significance to elevate his verse and infuse it with the dignity of worship.

His outlook in difficult times suggests a humble stoicism, as revealed by a poem inspired by an eclipse of the sun:

If thou bringest foreboding of war or failure of crops or unspeakably heavy fall of snow or destroying strife or emptying of the sea over the land or freezing of the earth or a wet summer-heat drenched in ceaseless rain, or if thou wilt flood the earth utterly and make a new race of men entirely, I make no moan, for with all men shall I suffer.

Pindar, despite his great fame and high position, maintains a realistic view of success, which the gods can destroy at will.

After a cursory account of an athletic event, Pindar usually enlarges at length on his own insights into philosophy, religion, current events, ethics, and morality. In the *Pythian, VIII,* he exhorts his audience to think on the human condition:

Ephemeral creatures that we are! Who shall say what each man is, and is not? For man is but the shadow of a dream. Yet if the gods bestow upon him but a gleam of their own radiance, bright flame surrounds him and his life is sweet.

Like Macbeth's comparison of life to a "walking shadow," the poet dwells on human fragility, yet his conclusion reflects a positive interpretation of God's purpose:

All men who have had the energy, during their triple sojourn in this world and the next, to keep their souls pure of all evil, shall follow to the end of the path of Zeus that leads to the castle of Cronus. There, where the Islands of the Blest are cooled by ocean breezes, from the splendor of golden flowers, some on the branches of magnificent trees springing from the earth, some nourished by the water, shall they weave themselves garlands and crowns.

Like Wordsworth in "Intimations of Immortality," Pindar believes that humans are reflections of a great light, one that beams from the creator. The only requirement for happiness is meticulous care for right behavior and a proper attitude toward the gods.

Breaking with old, traditional forms, Pindar employs a disciplined triadic structure, composed of similar stanzas—the strophe, antistrophe, and epode. The meters are loosely connected and complex, but they never inhibit the flow. Horace, an admirer of Pindar, compares his rapid transition of images to a precipitate mountain stream overflowing its banks. For example, in *Pythian, IV,* Pindar describes the woodsman:

> What though the ax an oak tree's branches clove,
> And all their beauty marred, the forest sire,
> Though never fruiting more, will surely prove
> His own great heart, when to the winter fire
> He cometh in the end,
> Or when in alien chambers he fulfills
> A menial service, resting on a base
> Of soaring columns, and his own old place
> Knows him no more among the lonely hills.

Critics note the freshness of his diction as well as his emphasis on abrupt contrasts. Because the music for Pindar's lyrics no longer exists, the modern reader can only guess at the inflection of the lyrics that combined to form these majestic, sonorous hymns.

The Pindaric odes have been imitated through the ages in the works of Callimachus, Horace, Quintilian, Ronsard, Du Bellay, Milton, Goethe, Gray, Shelley, Wordsworth, and Hugo. The care with which the odes have been preserved and passed on to later generations suggests that they were the masterpieces of Pindar's art. Dionysius of Helicarnassus, in the first century A.D., credits Pindar with lines that are "vigorous, weighty and dignified." He adds, "They are slow in their rhythm and present broad effects of harmony; they exhibit, not the showy and decorative prettiness of our own day, but the severe beauty of a distant past."

Although he was a contemporary of Aeschylus, the founder of Western drama, Pindar obeyed a different muse. In addition to his belief in aristocratic ideals and in the gods, Pindar held dear a third belief—the importance of poetry. He credited the gods with giving him an innate gift for words and music. He realized that life possesses more bad than good, but he chose to praise the good, as reflected in athletic victories. For him, myth contained the ultimate lessons—the ideal harmonies which provide humans with achievable goals.

Ω

ALCAEUS

Alcaeus, a contemporary and admirer of Sappho, was born in Mytilene about 652 B.C. In contrast to the lines in which he expresses tender regard for his colleague, whom he calls "pure sweetly-smelling Sappho of the violet hair," his poetry usually espoused a rowdy, swaggering, masculine point of view:

Let no soft fear lay hold of anyone;
Before us lies a great task to be done.
Remembering the past and how
We suffered, prove our manhood now!

In one of his encomia, he honors his brother Antimenidas, a soldier who fought in the Babylonian army of Nebuchadnezzar, although the exaggerations of his verse suggest a humorous or sarcastic tone. In another, Alcaeus describes how, in the revolution of 612 B.C., he abandoned his shield and fled from the field of battle, like Shakespeare's Falstaff; he was obviously pleased to have come out of the war alive.

Alcaeus, a member of the Aeolian upper class, was a vocal partisan during a period of history when social change was weakening the solidarity of the aristocracy. He involved himself in a territorial dispute between the Athenians and Mytilenians. As a result, he and his brothers were exiled to Egypt. Later, Alcaeus was allowed to return home, where he led an unsuccessful coup against the democrats in order to restore the nobles to power.

Alcaeus took an active role in Pittacus' defiance of the tyrant Myrsilus. In celebration of Myrsilus' demise, Alcaeus penned an outspoken toast:

Now let us drink our fill and get drunk
For Myrsilus is dead!

Alcaeus later turned against Pittacus, his former oath-sworn ally, who gained control of Mytilene. One fragmented poem describes Alcaeus' strong convictions about friendship and his disillusionment with Pittacus, one of the Seven Sages who is best remembered for doubling the penalty for any infraction of the law committed under the influence of alcohol.

A staunch defender of the aristocracy, Alcaeus came to regard Pittacus as a traitor and a personal enemy, even though Pittacus pardoned him and graciously overlooked his rather pointed verses. In a condescending tone, Alcaeus sneers:

> This peasant's son, Pittacus, everyone joins in acclaiming him,
> and now they have set him up as the tyrant of our comely
> and ill-starred town.

Relentlessly, Alcaeus bore his grudge, rejected the amnesty offered by his one-time friend, and returned to Lesbos only after Pittacus' abdication.

Alcaeus' apostrophe to his friend Melanippus underscores a "carpe diem" philosophy:

> While we are young. Now is the moment, now,
> To take what happiness the gods allow.

A devotee of the good life, Alcaeus indulged in the privileges of his class—wine, women, political rivalry, and horseracing. During his exile, Alcaeus expressed through verse his wretchedness in a foreign land, far from the marketplace and council chamber of Lesbos. A member of a close circle of comrades, Alcaeus suffered from the politically imposed separation from his close friends. He implores Apollo, the "son of Zeus and grandson of Cronus," to hear his prayers and take action against Pittacus, a false friend.

Alcaeus' lyrical verses cover a range of topics: contemporary politics, war, love for both women and young boys, drinking, friendship, and the worship of Pythian Apollo, Athena, Aphrodite, Eros, and Hermes. The original ten volumes of his works, edited by Aristophanes of Byzantium, have been lost. Only fragments of his two- and four-line stanzas remain.

Alcaeus' poems reveal the stress he suffers from rainy days, cold or heat, and the sorrows of age, disease, and death. Rather than lighthearted drunkenness for its own sake, his drinking songs encourage partaking of wine for the relief of human miseries, a quality which Horace approved and admired:

> To woe the heart must not give in.
> In grief's no help. One medicine,

My friend, alone is fit —
Wine — and get drunk on it.

Alcaeus believed that alcoholic consumption can bring out truth, particularly the truth concerning which of his companions were honest and trustworthy friends.

Apart from the rowdy, restless life of drinking buddies and political intrigue, Alcaeus earned fame for a single image, his poem which depicts the ship of state, tempest-tossed and struggling to stay afloat. The much-imitated metaphor notes:

We in the good black ship
Between the opposing waves are hurled, and wage
A desperate struggle with the darkling storm.
The straining sails grow clamorous; they rip
And fly in rags. The foaming waters burst
Into the hold. The anchors loose their grip.
And now a billow, greater than the first,
Rushes upon us, fraught with perils grave,
While the ship plunges deep into the wave.

Obviously, Alcaeus had more to offer than the few extant fragments of barroom songs and war stories. The graphic beauty of this poem suggests a greater poet, one capable of artistic vision and dignified themes.

Ω

LESSER LYRIC POETS

Not as famous as Sappho, Pindar, and Alcaeus, the three giants of Greek lyric poetry, the minor lyricists — Archilochus (*ca.* 650 B.C.),

Theognis (*fl.* 544–541 B.C.), Anacreon (*fl.* 550 B.C.), and Simonides (556–468 B.C.)—deserve mention for the diversity, inventiveness, and influence of their work.

Archilochus, a widely traveled soldier of fortune, achieved fame for inventing iambic meter and the epode, a short couplet appended to the ode, and for honing his invectives so well that he caused two victims of his satire to hang themselves. He was the illegitimate son of Telesicles and a slave girl, Enipo; he enjoyed Greek citizenship, but worked as an ox-herd and lived in poverty because he had no right of inheritance. Born on the island of Paros, he emigrated with his family to a better life on Thasos, an island south of Thrace.

A legend describes how Archilochus, like Hesiod, met the Muses and received his poetic gift in the form of a lyre. Telesicles consulted Pythia about his son's strange experience and learned:

> One of your sons, Telesicles, shall become
> An immortal poet upon earth, he who shall first
> Salute you on your return to your own country.

When Telesicles arrived back at Paros, Archilochus ran out to greet him.

In general, Archilochus' poems lack the high moral tone of Hesiod, the reverence of Pindar, and the refinements of Sappho. In contrast to those writers, he speaks the straightforward, often crude language of an untutored craftsman whose gut instincts guide his pen. Of his brothers-in-law, who died in a shipwreck, he notes:

> Since weeping will not cure my grief,
> Pleasure and feasting cannot make it worse.

To a courtesan, nicknamed Pasiphile or "Dear to All," he dedicates a couplet:

> Fig tree of the rocks, where many rooks delight to feed,
> How sweetly, Pasiphile, you make your guests at home.

To Neoboule, the object of his passion, he pours out these lusty thoughts:

> Hair and breast steeped in perfume, she would wake desire
> in an old man. . . . Now am I tamed by the longing that turns
> the bones to water: no longer am I moved by feasting or the
> delights of poetry . . . O that I could seize Neoboule in my

arms, fling myself upon this burning wine-skin, thrusting
belly against belly and thigh against thigh!

Unfortunately, the girl's father, Lycambos, ended the engagement
when he learned of Archilochus' illegitimate birth.

In his anger at father, daughter, and rival, the poet taunts his
former love with bitter invective:

No longer is your body in the freshness of its bloom; your
skin has begun to fade, and the plough of old age is digging
its furrows there.

Vowing that "this man shall pay for all he has done to me," he continues goading Neoboule and her father with spiteful verses and with
a fable about a fox and an eagle. Fragments indicate that Archilochus
married a courtesan, but never found happiness in wedlock.

Stung by his experience, Archilochus joined a mercenary band
and developed his artistic gift with themes from the battlefield. He
dedicated a couplet to his weapon:

It is on my lance that I depend for my ration of black bread
and my wine of Ismaros, and it is on my lance that I lean
as I drink it.

He found no haven in war, however, and readily acknowledged the
waste of bloodshed. On one occasion, he abandoned his shield and
ran. His words, as noted earlier, echo the sentiments of Shakespeare's
Falstaff:

Today my shield is the pride of a Seian. Despite my intentions, as soon as I found a suitable bush, I quit our admirable
army. But I saved my life. Why should I worry about an old
shield? All the worst for it: I can buy myself a new one, just
as good.

Archilochus died in a battle between the armies of Thasos and Naxos
around 604 B.C. According to legend, Pythia ejected his killer, Cal-
ondas, from the temple of Apollo.

Above all a pragmatist, Archilochus espouses none of the usual
high-sounding sentiments of more well-known poets. In addition, the
fact that his poems were popular suggests that he was not the only
Greek who spurned the romantic notions of Homer. Archilochus
typifies the spirit of a new breed which undermined the foundations

of power for the privileged by challenging traditions and exposing inequities.

In contrast to Archilochus' support for the common man, **Theognis of Megara,** who wrote his best work in the mid-sixth century B.C., supported the nobles against the rise of democracy, which he hated and distrusted. Equally averse to peasants and the rising merchant class, his verse stresses a belief in pure genetic strain, as illustrated by these lines to his pupil:

> Look, Cyrnos: we select true-bred rams, donkeys, and stallions to mate with pure-blooded females, yet there are men of quality who do not scruple to marry women simply for their wealth, with the result that good blood is mixed with bad.

His often bitter temperament led him to write cold, vengeful, didactic, sometimes cynical lines, of which around 1400 are still in existence.

Unlike the outspoken verses of Archilochus and the joyless works of Theognis, **Anacreon's** poems sing of love, fellowship, and pleasure. Anacreon was born in Teos, but fled to Thrace when the Persians menaced his homeland. From there, he migrated to the courts of patrons – to Polycrates on Samos and eventually to Hipparchus in Athens. He is said to have lived into his eighties.

More cosmopolitan than the preceding two poets, he is described as a Dionysian, a reveler, courtier, and ladies' man who eased the hearts of his listeners with graceful, elegant verse. Of his frivolous lifestyle, he reports:

> Whose after-supper tattle's ever bent
> On fights and frays, he's not the friend I choose;
> But he that minds him of true merriment
> And mingles Aphrodite with the Muse.

An appreciator of wine and good company, Anacreon urges restraint in indulgence:

> Wine goes in and tongues let out.
> Gentlemen observe a mean,
> Tippling with good songs between.

His light-spirited poems, which found renewed interest during the Renaissance, influenced the work of Ronsard, Goethe, and Herrick.

A wanderer and seeker of the great, **Simonides** holds a lesser position among his peers, but he earned a reputation for perfecting his art. He was born in Ioulis, the capital of Ceos, and, like Anacreon, he journeyed north to the court of the ruler Hipparchus. After his patron's murder, Simonides made himself at home in Thessaly with various appreciators of the arts, including Crannon, Pharsalus, and Larissa. Well into his eighties, he retired in Sicily at the court of Hieron of Syracuse, where he associated with two other poets, Pindar and Bacchylides, Simonides' nephew.

Simonides demanded large fees for his commissioned works, which ranged from dithyrambs, paeans, funeral epigrams, and threnodies to epinicia, which he is credited with inventing. His reputation for charm and grace seems justified by his lines which honor the Greek dead at Thermopylae:

> The ground is holy: here the brave are resting,
> And here Greek Honor keeps her chosen shrine.
> Here too is one the worth of all attesting—
> Leonidas, of Sparta's royal line,
> Who left behind a gem-like heritage
> Of courage and renown,
> A name that shall go down
> From age to age.

$$\Omega$$

GREEK HISTORIANS

- **An Introduction to the Classical Historians**
- **Herodotus**
- **Thucydides**
- **Xenophon**

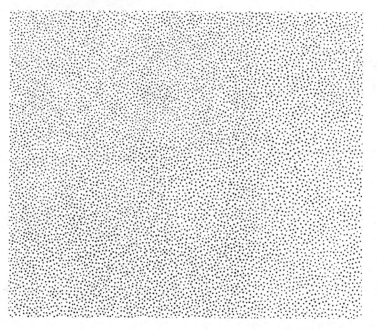

AN INTRODUCTION TO
THE CLASSICAL HISTORIANS

The word *history* comes from the Greek *historia,* which meant research, investigation. The Greeks, Herodotus in particular, created this discipline as we know it. Other ancient peoples had records of their past, but their style and philosophy differed from that of Greek historians. The Egyptian and Middle Eastern chronicles glorified dynasties by recording their deeds. Hebrew history was a form of theology that accounted for national victories and defeats by how faithful the people were to their covenant with God.

In contrast, the Greeks were the first to inquire into the past and minimize the traditional elements by stressing the importance of rational cause and effect. They also were unique in that they applied reason to contemporary events in the writing of history. In this, as in other fields, the Greek achievement was unique and profoundly influential—not only to Roman historians, but also to succeeding historians of the West.

The development of history as a literary form began in Ionia in the Greek cities on the western coast of Asia Minor. The port of Miletus had been a center of philosophical and scientific speculation since Thales, who lived around 600 B.C. This speculation had introduced rational skepticism toward myth, which had been the prevailing version of the past in Greece for countless generations. The Ionians, dependent on trade and shipping, had opportunities to visit foreign ports and learn about different traditions. Moreover, they were subject to rule by Eastern kings, first Lydian and then Persian, whose influences increased the cosmopolitan quality of their cities and stimulated their curiosity about foreigners. In such circumstances, it was natural for independent-minded Greeks to question the validity of their own myths, thus preparing the way for a secular view of history.

Around 500 B.C., Hecataeus of Miletus wrote his *Travels,* a geography book containing much historical, ethnographical, and biographical material. This work undoubtedly provided a model for the earlier portions of Herodotus' *Histories,* although only a few fragments of Hecataeus' *Travels* have survived. Other writers, too, produced quasi-historical works, such as Ion of Chios. However, Herodotus was the first author to write history, as we understand it today. His style left a deep and lasting imprint on later historical writing.

In addition to Herodotus, another ancient historian who was influential in shaping historiography was Thucydides. He and Herodotus wrote approximately one generation apart, Herodotus from about 450 to 428 B.C. and Thucydides from 430 to 399 B.C. Essentially, however, they established guideposts—in research technique and in prose style—for future historians to follow.

Because war usually decided whether a city or nation maintained its independence, Herodotus established war as the primary subject of historical writing. His *Histories* presented the Greek and Persian Wars as an epic conflict between two opposing civilizations, a conflict which proved conclusively the superiority of Greek character and institutions over those of the Persians. Herodotus' example in choosing his subject has been followed by historians from Thucydides to the present.

Herodotus also showed an interest in comparative politics, an interest that became pronounced in his successors, who often devoted long passages to analyses of political constitutions. The Greeks and Romans regarded war as an inevitability, a constant fact of life, but they also believed that governments could be changed and improved upon. In classical history, these two subjects frequently balance each other.

Because Herodotus was dealing with events that had taken place thirty years and more before he wrote, he often had to weigh questionable reports of what happened. Thucydides, in contrast, limited himself to events that he himself witnessed or about which he could obtain trustworthy information. Later historians also kept to contemporary or near-contemporary events. Or, as with Livy, they borrowed from earlier writers and reinterpreted them. For the most part, ancient historians did not bother with antiquarian research into old documents and inscriptions.

Another contribution of Herodotus was his treatment of history as a literary prose narrative with a beginning, middle, and end. In addition, the fact that history was read aloud in public meant that it had to be stylistically pleasing. To accommodate his audience, Herodotus introduced fictitious speeches to give the narrative dramatic interest and to present critical issues in a sharp, telling manner.

Thucydides adopted this device, and later historians did the same. Thus, literary ability became a prerequisite to the success of Greek and Roman historians.

In addition, Herodotus concentrated on individuals as movers of history. In this innovation, Herodotus anticipated Plutarch, Suetonius, Xenophon, and others. Thucydides, in contrast to Herodotus, was an expert on mass movements and used this approach to advantage. But Herodotus was justified in his approach because he knew that important decisions were made by a small number of people.

Perhaps the most significant influence which Herodotus had on later historians was his recognition of the moral value of history. Even today, events frequently display a pattern that perceptive men can locate and from which they might benefit. Herodotus found this pattern in the struggle for power, a struggle that led men to overreach themselves and bring disaster on themselves and on their nations. His accounts of Croesus, Cyrus, Polycrates, Cambyses, and Xerxes are all studies focusing on how the gods punish *hubris*, or excessive pride. Again, in contrast, Thucydides, with his emphasis on mass behavior, believed that human nature was everywhere the same. Accordingly, when he wrote about the Peloponnesian War, it was clear that he believed that he was recording universal patterns of action that would repeat themselves throughout time.

Between Herodotus and Thucydides, the writing of history was definitively shaped for the next eight hundred years. Subsequent historians may have had fresh events to record, an individual point of view, or idiosyncrasies of style and presentation, but they wrote in the tradition of these two masters.

The Greek historians provide an excellent introduction to a study of Greek and Roman classics. They cover crucial events in the classical world, events that helped to determine the future of Western civilization, and their ideas and aims illuminate the cultures from which they came. In their works, we see vital issues being decided by politics, by individual men, and by war, and we see the reactions of intelligent men to the outcome. War was brutal and men and politics were often corrupt, but the reactions were not too different from ours – frequently a mixture of bewilderment, contempt, and dismay. While reading the works of classical historians, we can sense a kinship with them and the classical world that transcends two thousand years.

Ω

HERODOTUS

LIFE AND BACKGROUND

"The Father of History," as Cicero called him, was born about 484 B.C. at Helicarnassus in southwest Asia Minor, which was then under Persian rule. The son of Lyxes and close kinsman of Panyassis, the epic poet, Herodotus had the advantages of close ties with the aristocracy and a sound Greek education. As a young man, he was exiled from his native city because his family opposed Lygdamis, the ruler of Helicarnassus; consequently, he went to Samos and, in time, to Athens. At some point in his early manhood, he began extensive travels that led to his life's work – a history of the conflict between the small, disunited city-states of Greece and the mighty Persian empire, a work that has been called one of the high points in Western literature.

To collect material, Herodotus journeyed to Macedonia, Thrace, Scythia, Asia Minor, Phoenicia, Syria, Babylonia, Egypt, Libya, and Greece. He did a great deal of sightseeing and interviewing, but he was hampered by the fact that he knew only one language – Greek – and thus he had to depend on interpreters. He had little or no access to Middle Eastern documents; in addition, Greece had almost no records. Nevertheless, he gathered a huge amount of facts, legends, gossip, and curiosities in his travels that he included in his *Histories of the Persian Wars*. The scope of that work is vast because Herodotus found cultural, geographic, religious, ethnographic, political, and military matters interesting and relevant to his great themes.

His purpose, as he states it in the opening paragraph, is threefold: (1) "in order that the actions of men may not be effaced by time, (2) nor the great and wondrous deeds displayed both by Greeks and barbarians deprived of renown, and (3) amongst the rest, for what cause they waged war upon each other." Herodotus actually tried to create an epic in prose similar to Homer's *Iliad* about the confrontation of the Greeks and Persians. But he had acquired some of the rational skepticism of the Ionion philosophers, as well as their inquiry after truth. Thus he tried, as far as he was able, to distinguish between fact and fiction. He single-handedly set forth the beginnings of a new discipline by his example. Moreover, he named this incipient field *historia* and determined some directions it would take.

Since he had to rely on oral testimony about the Persian Wars, which had occurred a generation earlier, Herodotus frequently states the nature of his evidence – whether he witnessed it himself in his journeys; whether it was firsthand testimony, secondhand, or hearsay; or whether his information was corroborated by independent sources or, in some cases, if he is presenting conflicting accounts. The material he uses ranges from the credible to the preposterous. When he gives scientific or factual information, he attempts to assess its truthfulness, but when the material appeals to the imagination, he usually presents it at its face value in his capacity as a recorder of unusual lore. Herodotus is quite open about the way he selected and weighed his information. His single requirement was only that it be of interest. When versions of a story conflicted, he gave each variant, often stating his own preference.

Despite his *Histories* being highly readable, however, Herodotus has serious limitations as a "historian," as we understand the term today. Herodotus' lack of interest in documents, his knowledge of only one language, his presentation of legend for its own sake, his belief in oracles, omens, and divine intervention, his military inexperience, and his obvious inaccuracies (such as the colossal size of Xerxes' army) all tend to cast doubt on his credibility. Likewise, his characters, often the victims of fate, ambition, and/or the sin of pride, suffer like actors in a Sophoclean tragedy rather than function like actual historical figures.

But against every likelihood, Herodotus wrote a great history, and of particular note is the fact that archeologists have discovered evidence that supports some of his information. In addition, his account of the Greek and Persian Wars is splendid in the way it contrasts and balances two important rival civilizations. Naturally, Herodotus sides with the Greeks, and his bias in favor of the Athenians is noticeable, but loyalty did not prevent him from trying to understand the enemy barbarians or from liking them. His *Histories* are a monument to his accomplishment as a determined, energetic, intelligent, and enthusiastic innovator of a new genre.

In retrospect, it is clear that it was more as a literary artist than as a historian that Herodotus gained his reputation. In contrast, Thucydides' rigorous and critical approach to history tended to discredit Herodotus, who in antiquity was regarded not only as a fine stylist and storyteller, but also as an unreliable source (mainly for the reasons given above). Yet, Herodotus' writing ability and charm are undeniable. His prose is lucid, brisk, and colorful and emphasizes Herodotus' genius in organizing his vast amount of heterogeneous material.

Broadly, the *Histories* have a three-part structure: (1) The first three books treat Persia's westward expansion by conquest until the empire was adjacent to Greece. (2) The next three books deal largely with resistance by Scythia, Ionia, and Greece to Persian imperialism, a time when Athenians vanquished the Persian king Darius at Marathon and succeeded in repelling the Persians. (3) The final three books cover Persia's repeated invasion of Greece ten years later under Xerxes and the empire's defeats at Salamis, Plataea, and Mycale. The *Histories* has an epic form that accommodates numerous digressions, but near the middle it starts to build toward a powerful climax.

A history in antiquity had to be readable in public in order to survive, and Herodotus had the necessary brilliance to make his work last despite widespread doubts about his reliability. Around the middle of the fifth century B.C., Herodotus began to give public readings from his *Histories* in Athens, and he made prominent friends in the Periclean circle, including Sophocles. Then around 443 B.C., he emigrated to Thuria, a Greek colony on the instep of Italy. Except for brief trips abroad, he probably spent the remaining years of his life there and undoubtedly revised his work then.

Herodotus probably died around 428 B.C., after the Peloponnesian War had started, and his *Histories of the Persian Wars* presumably appeared between 435 and 420 B.C. They amply testify to the tolerance, good humor, shrewdness, and vivacity of Herodotus, who found much to marvel at among the accomplishments of human beings.

Ω

___HISTORIES OF THE PERSIAN WARS___

Book One sets forth a prominent theme – the instability of power. During the course of the *Histories,* Croesus, king of Lydia, and Cyrus, the Persian king, are devoured by their lust for empires. In their pride, they overreach themselves. They are aware, however, that divine forces are at work. Croesus consults Pythia, the Delphic oracle, about the outcome of a war with Cyrus. Her famous answer, "that if Croesus should make war on the Persians, he would destroy a mighty empire," fails to deter his enthusiasm.

After making a fruitless alliance with Sparta, Croesus initiates combat with Cyrus, finds his own Lydian army inadequate, and re-treats to Sardis. Before Croesus can muster allies, Cyrus boldly lays siege to Sardis and captures it. Croesus, a prisoner of his sworn enemy, is saved from being burned alive by a miraculous rain. The kingdom he unwittingly destroys is his own. Too late, he comprehends Solon's advice to "count no man happy until his life is ended."

Cyrus, believing himself divinely favored, begins conquering neighboring lands. He captures much of Asia Minor from Croesus and takes Babylon. Then he challenges the Massagetae, and after kill-ing a third of Queen Tomyris' troops, among them the queen's son, Cyrus himself falls in battle. The vengeful queen abuses his corpse, stuffing Cyrus' head into a sack of blood to let him "drink his fill."

Throughout this section of the *Histories,* Herodotus balances the themes of vanity and ambition with lighter material – Near-Eastern legends, anecdotes, customs, and geography. Some of his gems of information include the fact that the Massagetae ate the corpses of their aging relatives, that Babylonian women had to take turns serving as sacred prostitutes, and that Queen Nitocris had her coffin placed above a city gate with an inscription that the wealth inside was only to be taken in case of great need. This is the stuff of which popular speakers are made, and it is said that Athens paid Herodotus a huge sum for his lectures.

Book Two introduces another great Persian leader, Cyrus' son, Cambyses, who is preparing to invade Egypt. At this point Herodotus appends a short social and religious history of the Egyptians (who trace their kings back eleven thousand years), along with an explanation of the Nile's annual flooding. The Egyptians' ancient gods are the proto-types for Zeus (Amon), Dionysus (Osiris), and Hercules. Egyptian society is stratified into four main classes – farmers, craftsmen, war-

riors, and priests. Above these classes is the king, and at the bottom
are the swineherds.

Ritual plays an important part in Egyptian life, particularly funeral
and memorial ceremonies. At fashionable banquets, full-size wooden
coffins are displayed to remind the guests of their mortality. Mummi-
fication, a common practice, is available in several forms. For the
wealthiest customers, the organs are carefully removed with iron
hooks through natural orifices. Then the outer body is soaked in myrrh
and cassia and steeped in natrum for seventy days before being
wrapped in flax strips, smeared with gum, and stored in a wooden
case. A medium-priced embalming involves infusing the body with
oil of cedar, steeping it in natrum, and draining the dissolved tissue
before the administration of last rites. The cheapest preparation is
much simpler—the abdomen is rinsed in syrmaea and the entire body
steeped in natrum for seventy days.

The kings of Egypt build great and lasting monuments: temples,
huge stelae, pyramids, and a canal connecting the Nile to the Red
Sea. Herodotus highlights some of the more interesting kings—Sesos-
tris, conqueror of much of the Near East, Scythia, and Thrace; Cheops
and Chephren, who began the fashion of pyramid-building; Sethos,
who is rescued when a plague of field mice overrun the enemy; and
Amasis, a shrewd, hard-living commoner who gains the throne by
rebellion. Amasis is king when Cyrus' son, Cambyses, decides to
invade Egypt.

Book Three begins with two versions of the story of the Persian
king's demand for Amasis' daughter—one version reporting that the
king was Cambyses and the Egyptian version declaring that it was
Cyrus himself. In the first version, Cambyses, wishing to surpass his
father, allows his pride to overrule good judgment. He defeats the
Egyptian army, humiliates the king and his nobles, and plans expeditions farther into Carthage and Ethiopia.

After his plans falter, Cambyses goes mad with egomania, committing outrages against the Egyptian religion, murdering his own
brother and sister, and inflicting hideous torments on his closest advisers. On his way home to Persia, Cambyses dies of an accidental
wound on his thigh, which is similar to the wound which Cambyses
made on the Egyptian calf-god, Apis. He is succeeded by a deceitful,
ruthless upstart, Darius, who imposes regular taxation on subject

peoples and engorges his treasury with wealth from Libya, Egypt, a portion of Ethiopia, Syria, Asia Minor, Assyria, and eastward to India.

Book Four details Darius' unbridled ambition. Spurred by the traditions of Cyrus and Cambyses, Darius pushes Persian forces to attack the cunning, nomadic tribes of Scythia (now southern Russia), who are notorious for scalping enemies, blinding slaves, cannibalism, and other barbaric practices. Cunningly, the Scythians use guerrilla tactics and lure the Persians deep within their territory. When supplies dwindle, Darius moves quickly to extricate himself from a losing situation and barely escapes across the Danube to safety.

Book Five reveals a change in Darius. No longer motivated by mindless vengeance, he employs statecraft and generosity in his dealings with the Greeks. He accepts the advice of knowledgeable subordinates and appears to learn from past failures. After the Scythian fiasco, he does not accompany his troops into the field, and he extricates himself from all previous military involvement before beginning a new campaign against Ionia and captures one city after another before turning his attention toward Athens.

In **Book Six** the description of the climactic events of the Battle of Marathon form Herodotus' greatest achievement. In 492 B.C., Darius' push into Greece meets disaster when a storm wrecks his fleet and his army is caught off-guard by a Thracian tribe. Darius then hones his forces for a second assault against Sparta and Athens, the two most powerful Greek states. This time, his ships sail across the Aegean instead of taking the northern route, and they attack at Eretria. Traitors hand over the city, and Persia enslaves its inhabitants.

The Persians, guided by Hippias, an exiled Athenian tyrant lusting for a return to power, push on to Marathon, a plain near Athens where the Persian cavalry believe that they can successfully maneuver. The Athenian generals send Pheidippides, a long-distance runner, to Sparta to enlist aid, but for religious reasons the Spartans must wait until a full moon before sending help to Athens. Meanwhile, Plataea, an independent region, sends troops to Athens, and together the armies rush to Marathon to halt Darius.

Miltiades, experienced in Persian military tactics, takes charge of the Athenian military. He allows the Persians to break through the center of his line of defense and then presses in from the right and left flanks. The Persians are defeated, but they sail for Athens, hoping to take the city by surprise. The Athenian army, however, manages to save the city, and the Persians sail home, salvaging only their Eretrian captives, whom Darius resettles on Persian soil. The Greek victory is a tribute to intelligence, courage, and self-control.

Book Seven finds Darius preparing a third assault on Athens, but he dies before he can initiate it. His son, Xerxes, demonstrates his style of rule by mercilessly crushing a revolt in Egypt and launching a five-year preparation for an all-out war on the whole of Europe. He raises an awesome force of 2,500,000 men and 1,200 ships. Xerxes then encounters a series of bad omens, but arrogant to a fault, he ignores the gods' intimations of disaster and pursues his maniacal vision of glory.

The Greeks make their stand at Thermopylae, a narrow pass dividing Thessaly from Greece. Xerxes, although he lost a third of his fleet in a storm, is encouraged when he finds only five thousand Greeks awaiting the invasion, but he is unable to deploy his full army because of the narrowness of the pass. Then he is dumbfounded when the Greeks easily stymie his forces for three days. A traitor shows Xerxes another route, and Xerxes advances into Greek territory and clashes with Leonidas, leader of the Spartans and Thebans. They battle until the Thebans desert and Leonidas falls. The Greeks are massacred. Xerxes, outraged at the strength of Greek resistance, desecrates Leonidas' body.

In **Book Eight,** Xerxes persists against Greece on two fronts. As the Greeks head south to stop Persian ships at Salamis, the Persian army invades Greece and destroys all the towns that resist. Xerxes orders the Acropolis burned to repay a burned temple at Sardis; by a miracle, however, Delphi is saved from his "scorched earth" policy. The Greeks make a stand in the narrow straits of Salamis and trounce the Persians by means of luck and superior seamanship. Xerxes' army, shaken by defeat and plagued by dysentery and starvation, limps back to Sardis. His face-saving excuse is that he succeeded in one goal – he punished Athens for helping to burn Sardis.

Book Nine describes the defeat of Mardonius, Xerxes' commander, who remains behind in Macedonia and initiates new hostilities the next spring. Mardonius marches on Athens, burns the city, and erects a wooden fort near Thebes. The Greek army swells to 100,000 against the Persians, who are three times more numerous, and engages them at Plataea in 479 B.C. Although the Persians inflict serious losses, heavily armed, seasoned Greek fighters succeed in killing Mardonius and routing the enemy. A large Persian detachment escapes north, but the rest are annihilated.

$$\Omega$$

THUCYDIDES

LIFE AND BACKGROUND

If Herodotus fathered history as a serious art, Thucydides raised it to an astonishing level of maturity in a mere generation. Thucydides was born about 465 B.C. to a propertied Thracian father, Olorus, and a distinguished Athenian mother. He is thought to have been the grandson of Miltiades, hero of the Battle of Marathon, and a kinsman of Cimon, a heroic general at the Battle of Salamis.

The facts we have of his life are few. He is said to have shown great feeling for history in his youth when he was moved to tears by one of Herodotus' public readings. It is likely that Thucydides took part in some early engagements of the Peloponnesian War, which broke out in 431 B.C., when he was around thirty. He contracted the plague that ravaged Athens in the early years of the war and was one of the few to recover.

Although young and virtually unknown, he was elected to the post of general and in 424 B.C. was stationed at Thasos, an island in the far north of the Aegean Sea. On learning of the Spartan general Brasidas' attempt to capture Amphipolis, an Athenian colony in north-eastern Greece, Thucydides led a fleet of seven ships to the rescue but arrived too late to prevent its surrender. Because of this failure, Cleon turned public opinion against him, although, according to Books IV and V of his *History of the Peloponnesian War,* Thucydides' exile from Athens was voluntary. Thucydides lived in Thrace until the establishment of a general amnesty at the end of the war in 404 B.C., twenty years later.

No doubt he traveled widely, as evidenced by detailed information in his work, particularly about the colony at Syracuse in Sicily, but nothing indicates where or for how long. He is thought to have returned to Athens in the last years of his life. Local legend, capitalizing upon his abrupt conclusion to Book VIII, indicates that he was murdered and buried in Thrace, but other information suggests that his tomb in the family plot in Athens is not a monument in memory of him.

Exile proved a great advantage, affording Thucydides time to reflect on world events and to work on his *History*. It also gave him access to enemy informants, who helped him achieve the necessary detachment and balance in his account of the war. The inheritance of gold mines near Strymon in Thrace provided him with a comfortable income.

When Thucydides died around 399 B.C., his work was unfinished, breaking off with the events of 411 B.C. and lacking the characteristic polished speeches that he regularly put into the mouths of his characters. His daughter is credited with the completion of the eighth book as well as with the preservation of the entire text. Later historians took up his *History* where he left off, but Xenophon's continuation, the *Hellenica,* is the only one that has survived.

When the war between Athens and Sparta began, Thucydides correctly surmised that it would be prolonged and terrible, a "world war" involving the whole of Greece and many of the rest of the Mediterranean countries as well. He decided that he would record the history of the war as it happened. The idea was original and had great impact on future historians. Thucydides understood that to ascertain the truth about the past is difficult, and that the best way to grasp historical truth is in the present, where firsthand information is available.

This concept in itself was remarkable enough, but what distinguished Thucydides's *History* from Xenophon's mediocre performance is Thucydides' rigorous intellectual integrity, his single-minded attempt to uncover the general truths that underlie the specific events of the Peloponnesian War. He wanted his work to be a lasting possession for humanity, rather than a partisan effort of the moment. In addition, he knew that in order to achieve lasting prominence, his work must carry a lasting validity, arising from permanent truths about war.

Herodotus had arrived at general conclusions about human nature, but Thucydides concentrated on a far smaller range of human behavior – specifically, human action in war and in wartime politics. Spurning the techniques of his predecessors – Homer, who embroidered the truth with poetry, and Herodotus, who wrote to entertain an audience – Thucydides allowed full play to his brilliant, searching mind that worked and reworked the raw events of the war to discover meaning and relevance. His aim lay beyond the moment: Thucydides tended to compose a handbook of war for future statesmen to read and study.

The one quality which Thucydides valued in a leader was a keen, decisive intelligence. Unfortunately such intelligence was rare in the men who governed Athens during the Peloponnesian War, particularly during the final years. Only Pericles had the penetrating political insight needed to uphold the Athenian empire effectively, and he died shortly after the war began.

Whereas Herodotus regarded arrogance and impiety as the major sources of disaster, Thucydides felt that stupidity was the primary cause. In power politics, Thucydides, like Machiavelli, saw morality as a negligible factor: expedience was essential. In practice, what counted was foresight – the ability to calculate accurately the likely consequences of decisions.

Beyond intelligence, a leader needed courage, energy, and dedication to the interests of the state. Chance, of course, affected the welfare of any state, but an intelligent ruler made the most of whatever chance offered, while fools were overwhelmed by it sooner or later. To Thucydides, intelligence and logic were indispensable in the building and management of an empire. Rationality was required to perceive the specific principles that applied in any situation, and Thucydides did his utmost to extract those principles from the events of the Peloponnesian War.

Thucydides' emphasis on reason may be traced to the influential sophist movement in fifth-century Athens, in which reason was applied to human problems. His relentless dissection of politics and economics and his attention to the causes, course, and results of social disorders have a parallel in the medical methods of Hippocrates, the father of medicine and Thucydides' contemporary. Despite the obvious influence of his forerunners, Hecataeus and Herodotus, Thucydides chose to alter his predecessors' methods. The resulting style, heavy with antithesis, irony, and ponderous phraseology, is uniquely his own.

Thucydides' informants, his methods of gathering information, the variants that he rejected, and all the necessary means by which he arrived at his final version of the first twenty years of the war shall remain a mystery. But his *History* was so authoritative that no one after him attempted to modify or correct his version. Later historians simply took up at the point where he ended. Another credit to his name is the fact that only Thucydides and Aristotle are quoted by later generations as unimpeachable sources of information about the ancient world.

Thucydides' prose continually yields fresh, surprising illuminations, and his concentrated application of reason to events, plus his straining to grasp the significance of history through human political behavior, all reveal an original intelligence at work. The principles he found operating in history, however, were not the kind to prove useful to rising statesmen; they were principles that revealed the political deterioration of a crumbling empire. Thucydides' genius provides us with the most incisive autopsy of a democratic empire ever written. He was the originator of modern political-military history and one of the greatest historians of all time.

Ω

THE HISTORY OF THE
——————PELOPONNESIAN WAR——————

Thucydides introduces his work with a clear statement of purpose and belief. Because the Peloponnesian War was the most decisive and far-reaching conflict in the history of Hellas and surrounding nations, Thucydides sets out to record the events as they occur. He also appends a miniature history of ancient Greece.

After the settlement of minor internal difficulties and the defeat of the Persians, who were the only serious impediment to Greek dominion, two factions, Sparta and Athens, begin to develop separate identities. Thucydides characterizes them as "perpetually fighting or making peace, either with one another or with their own revolted allies; thus they attained military efficiency and learned experience in the school of danger." An inevitable conflict arises from their rivalry.

Pericles, the strongest spokesman in Athens' hour of decision, urges his countrymen to stand firm against the Peloponnesian threat. Outlining the economic expediencies that will determine the timing and nature of the conflict, he concludes that a ready stance befits Athenian dignity: "We must be aware however that war will come;

and the more willing we are to accept the situation, the less ready will our enemies be to lay hands upon us."

With **Book II,** the carnage begins in earnest. Thucydides notes that a fourteen-year truce ends when two power-hungry Thebans lead a sudden raid on Plataea. When Athens rushes to aid its stricken ally, the long-anticipated war breaks out on two fronts between the super powers: the Spartans march on Attica, and the Athenians, ever dependent upon naval preparedness, raise a fleet to attack the Peloponnesus.

During the first winter, the Athenians hold a mass funeral to honor citizens killed in the war. Thucydides describes their preparations — a tent to house the bones of dead warriors, private offerings from family and friends, a single chest of cypress for each tribe's dead, a single honorary litter in memory of unrecovered bodies, and a choice spot outside the city wall for interment. Pericles, a man of "known ability and high reputation," delivers an appropriate eulogy.

Thucydides characterizes the high moral tone and lofty sentiment of Athenian funeral oratory in Pericles' words. His idealization of Athens becomes the focal point of the summary:

> . . . I say not only that our city as a whole is a model for all
> Greece, but that in my opinion there is no other place where
> the individual can develop independence and self-reliance so
> easily, so gracefully, and in so many directions. That all this
> is not a matter of boastful talk for this occasion, but of plain
> truth, is proved by the fact of our power, which we acquired
> because we possessed those qualities. Athens alone, in our
> time, is greater than her own fame. . . . The reason why I
> have dwelt at length on Athens is that I wanted to demon-
> strate to you how much greater is our stake in this struggle
> than theirs who do not share our advantages, and also to give
> force to my eulogy of the dead by citing real evidence.

In the eyes of some historians, this speech is the pinnacle of Athenian greatness, from which it was destined to fall.

The following summer, a devastating plague sweeps Attica. The disease is so virulent, so deadly, that medical science is helpless; supplications to the gods prove "so futile that people finally gave them up of their own accord, in utter despair." Thucydides details the symptoms: fever; red, burning eyes and throat; strong-smelling breath; sneezing and hoarseness; chest pain; and great abdominal distress, including cramps, ulceration, flux, and dry retching. Even predatory birds and dogs die from eating contaminated carrion. His description, presaging Defoe's graphic scenes of an outbreak of plague in seventeenth-century England, depicts tormented victims hurling themselves down wells to escape its ravages.

In **Book III,** the war spreads to outlying islands. The people of Lesbos revolt and appeal to Sparta for help, but surrender to Athens to escape starvation. The Athenians resist their initial urge to slaughter all men of Mytilene and enslave the women and children; instead, they kill only the leaders and subjugate the rest. Rebellion spreads to Corcyra (Corfu), Megara, Aeolus, Messina, Leucas, and Ionia. The Plataeans surrender to the Spartans. The leaders are executed and the city burned to the ground. Thucydides spares no detail in chronicling the waste of unbridled violence.

Books IV and **V** reveal a favorable turn of events as Athens rallies and Spartan morale ebbs. Yet the shift in the balance is shortlived when Sicily turns its back on Athens and the Spartan commander Brasidas encourages rebellion in principalities on the north shores of the Aegean Sea, including Amphipolis and Torone. When Athenian troops attempt to conquer Boeotia, they suffer two serious setbacks at Delium. In 423 B.C., the Athenians agree to a one-year truce in order to restructure their alliances. After infractions of the peace on both sides renew the fray, the two city-states, worn thin with losses, sign the Peace of Nicias in 421 B.C.

The Athenians lack strong leadership after the death of Pericles and fall prey to the strategems of impulsive, war-mongering self-seekers like Cleon and Alcibiades. The shaky peace treaty succumbs when both parties violate its injunctions. Athens allies itself with Argos and marches on Epidaurus. Sparta, angered at Athenian effrontery in renewing the scramble for allies, harasses the Argives so severely that Argos breaks off its support of Athenian insurgents.

One of the most vicious episodes of the war is the Athenian expedition against the island of Melos, a Spartan colony in the southern Aegean Sea. Athenian spokesmen try to subdue the citizens into submission by refusing to recognize their request for neutrality. Thucydides records their intense dialogue:

> **Melos:** It may be your interest to be our masters, but how can it be ours to be your slaves?

Athens: To you the gain will be that by submission you will avert the worst: and we shall be all the richer for your preservation.

Melos: But must we be your enemies? Will you not receive us as friends if we are neutral and remain at peace with you?

Athens: No, your enmity is not half so mischievous to us as your friendship; for the one is in the eyes of our subjects an argument of our power, the other of our weakness.

Bent on vengeance and destruction, the Athenians overrun Melos. The Melians surrender, the men are put to death, and the women and children are enslaved.

Books VI and **VII** attest to folly on both sides. Despite the steadying influence of Athens' two great generals, Nicias and Demosthenes, and the brilliant leadership of Sparta's Brasidas, the two antagonists continue to pursue unrealistic policies, overreach their abilities, delude themselves with schemes and wishful thinking, and underestimate the risks involved in escalating the war. The Athenians send an expedition to Sicily in hopes of adding its resources to Athens' dwindling supplies. The Spartans acquire Alcibiades, who flees Athens when he is recalled from Sicily and tried for treason. Alcibiades convinces Sparta that Athens intends to conquer the whole Hellenic world.

Sparta renews its attacks on Attica and takes notice of the Athenian intervention in Sicilian politics. In 414 B.C., Athenian troops attack isolated sections of Sicily and build a fortress above Syracuse. With Spartan help, the Sicilians thwart the aggressors in notable sea battles. Morale reaches a new low when the Sicilians succeed in trouncing the Athenians, who desert their ships in the harbor and retreat by land. Syracusans force Demosthenes' retreating army to surrender and trap Nicias at a narrow pass. Both leaders are executed and the remaining soldiers sold into slavery.

Athens' final effort to defeat Sparta begins **Book VIII.** Rebellion and desertion decimate the Athenian forces. Oligarchy supplants democracy in Athens. The government of the Four Hundred struggles to effect a truce. Panic spreads throughout the Attic world when a Spartan fleet menaces Athenian shores.

Thucydides' account of the Peloponnesian War ends after Athens wins a small victory in a naval engagement with Sparta at the Helles-pont. Yet, the small surge in morale cannot compensate for the moral blows that Athens has suffered. The account leaves off in 411 B.C., omitting the inevitable dissolution and subjugation of the Athenian empire.

Ω

XENOPHON

LIFE AND BACKGROUND

Noted for essays on history, philosophy, and biography, Xenophon began his writing career late in life and wrote of his varied experiences – as an Athenian cavalryman during the Peloponnesian War (431–404 B.C.), a hired soldier for Cyrus in Asia Minor, a philosophy student of Socrates, and a gentleman farmer in Elis. The son of Gryllus, he was born in Erchia near Athens to a land-rich family, and from an early age, he devoted himself to horses and riding.

His life was a peculiar mix of opposites – the leisurely pleasures of a country gentleman and the thrill of action and adventure on foreign battlefields. Legend describes how he fell from his horse during the battle of Delium and was rescued and carried off the field by Socrates, who became his friend and mentor. Yet Xenophon, despite his devotion to his teacher, was never able to duplicate Socrates' contemplative powers; instead, he chose a soldier's life, for which he was more aptly suited.

Discouraged with the destruction of the Delian League after Athens established peace with Persia, Xenophon joined his mercenary forces to the army of Cyrus the Younger, who was making war on his brother, King Artaxerxes. After Cyrus' death, Xenophon led the retreat of 10,000 Greek survivors through the Armenian highlands from Cunaxa to Chrysopolis on the Black Sea. With consummate leadership and strategy, he managed to cover over 4,000 miles in fifteen months and to salvage half his forces.

Because of his alliance with Persia, Xenophon was banished from Athens. Therefore, upon his return to Greece in 399 B.C., he served with a Spartan expeditionary force against Persian despots in Asia Minor, for which King Agesilaus II, his military idol, awarded him a consulship and a pleasant country estate near Olympia in Elis, where Xenophon lived for twenty years with his wife, Philesia, and two sons,

Gryllus and Diodorus. A pious man, Xenophon dedicated a shrine there to Artemis from his share of the loot.

He spent his days riding, farming, hunting, entertaining, and writing until 371 B.C., when his estate was captured by the Eleans. He fled to Corinth. Athens, having formed an alliance with Sparta against Thebes, restored his citizenship in 369 B.C., and Xenophon subsequently sent his two sons to serve in the Athenian cavalry. Gryllus, who died fighting at Mantinea in 362 B.C., received many epitaphs, partly for his bravery and partly in honor of his noted father.

The most famous of Xenophon's fourteen works include the following: the *Anabasis* (the Military Expedition), a seven-book description of Cyrus' abortive campaign and the Greek retreat from Cunaxa; the *Hellenica*, a seven-book history of Greece from 411 to 362 B.C.; and the *Cyropaedia*, an idealized biography of Cyrus the Great (559–529 B.C.), the founder of the Persian monarchy.

His other works – the *Polity of the Lacedaemonians, Agesilaus, Hipparchicus* (Cavalry Commander), *On Horsemanship, Cynegeticus* (A Hunting Manual), *Hieron, Symposium* (Banquet), *Oeconomicus* (House Manager), *Socrates' Apology, Memorable Facts about Socrates, On Revenues,* and *Polity of the Athenians* – cover a variety of topics, including Spartan institutions, biography, military tactics, breeding and training of hunting dogs, his philosophy of happiness and friendship, Athenian finances, agriculture, and country life.

Critics praise Xenophon's industry, graphic descriptions, simplicity, and clarity of detail and his ability to empathize with the common foot soldier. Yet, he is given to repetition, superficiality, imitation, subjectivity, and moralizing. According to most historians, his comments on Socrates' life and defense are inferior to Plato's and his political analyses are spotty. Apparently, Xenophon commits no gross errors or inaccuracies; his major fault lies in omissions and lapses. He tends to favor Sparta in all his reportage, despite the fact that he was Athenian born.

$$\Omega$$

ANABASIS

Based on personal experiences with the army of Cyrus the Younger (423–401 B.C.), Xenophon describes the unsuccessful military expedition into which his friend Proxenus lured him. As a kind of freelance soldier, Xenophon probably took daily notes on his march from Sardis to Babylon and back to the Greek coast and completed his book by 394 B.C., but he did not publish it until 370 B.C.

The *Anabasis* is valuable for information concerning the strength of a democratic mercenary force that quashed the legendary Persian war machine on its home turf. In addition, Xenophon outlines creative tactics to enable the successful retreat of an army through hostile, mountainous country. The turn of events puts Xenophon in command of Greek forces far from home without a military goal, supplies, or money. However, modern critics question the subjectivity which turns Xenophon into a model commander and an instant hero.

Book I outlines the conflict between Cyrus and Artaxerxes after the death of their father, Darius. Xenophon justifies Cyrus' side of the brothers' altercation, describing Cyrus as a charming host who sent guests away "more devoted to him than to [Artaxerxes]." After securing Peloponnesian mercenaries, Cyrus sets out from Sardis with his army, encountering intermittent fighting along the way. In a battle near the Euphrates River, Cyrus is killed after a javelin strikes him under the eye and he is set upon by the enemy.

Xenophon, who serves as a major character in the narrative, eulogizes the fallen leader. He notes that when Cyrus was compared to other youths, "he was regarded as the best of them all in all respects." As a man, Cyrus is remembered as a wise administrator, dependable soldier, faithful friend, and generous ruler. Cyrus' body is mutilated by enemy forces, who cut off the head and right hand.

After Clearchus, a Spartan exile and Cyrus' second-in-command, conducts serious discussions with the Greek forces, the verdict is clear: "But since Cyrus is dead, we are neither contending with the king for his realm nor is there any reason why we should desire to do harm to the king's territory or wish to slay the king himself, but rather we should return to our homes, if no one should molest us." In Book III, Xenophon, after making sacrifice to Apollo, begins the long trek home.

$$\Omega$$

GREEK HISTORIANS

HELLENICA

Xenophon's main historical work, the *Hellenica* relates the political climate of Greece from 411 to 362 B.C., beginning when Xenophon was twenty and describing the next fifty years of his life. The work provides a valuable service to modern readers—it completes the account of the Peloponnesian War (431–404 B.C.) which Thucydides began but died without finishing. Xenophon appends the events that follow the war: Athens' internal disorders (404–401 B.C.), Sparta's war with the Persians (399–387 B.C.), the Corinthian War (394–387 B.C.), and twenty-five years of struggles with the Greek states to attain a balance of power among themselves and against Persia.

Part I, including Book I–Book II, section 3, carries the reader through the end of the Peloponnesian War, which Xenophon describes as follows:

> And Lysander gave over the city and everything therein to the former citizens, and appointed ten rulers to guard it; then he dismissed the naval contingents of the allies to their several cities and sailed home with the Laconian ships to Lacedaemon, taking with him the prows of the captured ships, the triremes from Piraeus except twelve, the crowns which he had received from the cities as gifts . . . and whatever else he had obtained during the course of the war.

At this point, Athens, ruled by the Thirty, begins to reestablish a peacetime government. Their most pressing tasks are framing a constitution and arresting and punishing informers.

Part II ends with the so-called "Peace of Antalcidas" (Book V, section 1) which was consummated with the seal of King Artaxerxes and the pledges of all Greek states. From this point to the end of Book VII, Xenophon deals with Thebes' threat to the balance of power, ending with the battle of Mantinea (362 B.C.) in which Theban forces win the war but lose Epaminondas, their great commander.

Ω

CYROPAEDIA

Xenophon's attempt at a biography of Cyrus the Great (600–530 B.C.) has been called a historical romance, the first work of its kind in the Western world. Although he commits several "indiscretions" with the facts, the most remarkable being a confusion of the Persian constitution with that of Athens, he does present a fascinating world of Eastern manners and customs with precision and clarity. Xenophon's tribute to Cyrus includes not only Cyrus' education, as indicated by the title, but also his entire life, his administrative style, and his military conquests.

In Book I, Xenophon, after considering the human condition and the task of governing, sets the parameters of his book:

> . . . we were inclined to conclude that for man, as he is constituted, it is easier to rule over any and all other creatures than to rule over men. But when we reflected that there was one Cyrus, the Persian, who reduced to obedience a vast number of men and cities and nations, we were then compelled to change our opinion and decide that to rule men might be a task neither impossible nor even difficult, if one should only go about it in an intelligent manner.

Xenophon ends section 1 with a direct purpose in mind: to account for Cyrus' success by cataloguing his family, talents, and education.

$$\Omega$$

MEMORABILIA

An anomaly among the more sensible, straightforward works of Xenophon, his defense of Socrates suffers two major flaws—Xenophon was absent from Athens during the trial and execution of his former master, and his rebuttal of the charges against Socrates are based not on court proceedings, but on a literary work by Polycrates, written while Xenophon was living on his farm in Elis. Furthermore, Xenophon repeats segments from the *Cyropaedia, Anabasis,* and *Hippar-*

chichus, a fact which suggests deep personal involvement in his defense and a subjective interpretation of events he did not know firsthand.

Book I begins with a statement of the indictment: that Socrates was guilty of impiety and of corrupting young minds. Xenophon builds a strong case for Socrates by logic and by example, pointing out his regular sacrifices, openness, humanity, civic-mindedness, and upright behavior. The remainder of Book I and **Book II** enlarges upon Socrates' virtues – his piety; self-discipline; respect for law, the family, and friends; and his generosity.

Book III is a loose arrangement of dialogues and aphorisms on the subject of civil and military service. Concerning the education of a soldier, Xenophon puts this speech into the mouth of Socrates:

> Did you never reflect that all the best we learned according to custom . . . we learned by means of words, and that every other good lesson to be learned is learned by means of words; that the best teachers rely most on the spoken word and those with the deepest knowledge of the greatest subjects are the best talkers?

In **Book IV,** where he praises Socrates the teacher, Xenophon uses model dialogues to describe the lessons which encouraged individual students to realize their own innate wisdom. Socrates encourages them to "become skilled in discussion" so that they will not mislead either themselves or others. Xenophon concludes from the preceding examples that "[Socrates] seemed to be all that a truly good and happy man must be."

$$\Omega$$

GREEK PHILOSOPHERS

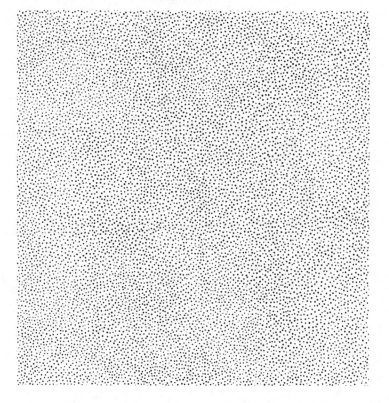

- **Plato**
- **Aristotle**

PLATO

- *Euthyphro*

- *Apology*

- *Crito*

- *Phaedo*

- *Meno*

- *Ion*

- *Symposium*

- *The Republic*

PLATO

The Athenian philosopher Plato (428–347 B.C.) distinguished himself in two respects – as a spokesman for Socrates, the quintessential teacher and humanist, and as the author of lively dialogues. The son of Ariston and Perictione, both members of established and influential families, young Plato was well schooled in mathematics, literature, and music. His early life was marred by the death of his father and the remarriage of his mother to Pyrilampes, an active participant in the political milieu of Periclean Athens.

After choosing politics as his life's work, Plato veered from his initial goal after becoming disillusioned with the conduct of Athenian dictators during the chaotic rule of the Thirty following Sparta's defeat of Athens in the Peloponnesian War. He was first put off by the brutality and dishonesty of politicians in 404 B.C. when he saw at close range the corrupt machinations of his second cousin, Critias, and his uncle Charmides. However, he pursued political ambitions until the hypocritical trial and poisoning of his friend and mentor, Socrates, in 399 B.C. curtailed his enthusiasm for the political arena.

Plato left Athens, visited his friend and fellow philosopher and the man whom today we revere as the father of geometry, Euclid, in Megara, on the isthmus of Corinth; there, Plato devoted himself to the private realm of research and writing. He never married, preferring celibacy, and he had little to say about the institution of marriage. After his brief military service from 395 to 394 B.C., he is reputed to have traveled to Egypt to study astronomy and to have settled in Cyrene, a city in north Africa, to study mathematics with Theodorus. For the remainder of his life, he gave up all interest in political life, dismissing the accomplishments of Miltiades, Themistocles, and Pericles as nothing more than "harbors and dockyards and walls and tributes." To Plato, the ideal was not government but order, managed by the best of society's thinkers and moralists.

A follower of monotheism, Plato believed that good people attain their reward for goodness in another world. His blend of mystical and empirical wisdom denied scientists their place in the rational scheme of things, for, in his view of nature, phenomena should be contemplated rather than observed, measured, manipulated, and explained. His preference for thought over action was a rejection of the Athenian world, won at great cost by the doers who established the first democracy. To Plato, liberty meant little; poetry, even less. He is said to have written dithyrambs and tragedies, but to have torn them up after his first meeting with Socrates. Plato based his idealized society on a transcendent never-never land, far from the realities of war, treachery, and cups of poisonous hemlock.

Traveling to the court of Dionysius I in Syracuse in 388 B.C., Plato found his opinions to be greatly out of favor. After humiliating treatment, he was deported on a Spartan vessel and marked for sale on the slave block in Aegina where Anniceris rescued him by negotiating a price with the auctioneer. Undaunted in his wish to see the Mediterranean world, Plato continued on to Tarentum in southern Italy, where Archytas, the famed mathematician and follower of Pythagoras, served as mayor.

Influenced by Archytas, who believed that the principles of mathematics would one day serve society as a valuable tool, Plato returned to Athens. He taught at the gymnasium called Academea, and in 387 B.C., on the outskirts of the city near Colonus, he founded and administered his own school, called the Academy, the prototype of the modern university. He taught there for thirty-eight years. Over the door to the Academy was inscribed a single requirement: "No one shall enter who knows no geometry." Men and women from all parts of the Mediterranean world came there to pursue various studies, notably mathematics, logic, and astronomy.

In 367 B.C., when Dionysius II succeeded his father as dictator, his uncle, Dion, entrusted the boy's education to Plato, who made a second voyage to Sicily. Plato's attempt to educate Dionysius according to the model of the philosopher-king proved disastrous — Dionysius not only developed an aversion to philosophy, but he also accused Dion and Plato of plotting his demise.

Once more, Plato returned home; in 361 B.C., he returned to mediate the growing contretemps between Dionysius and Dion. Again unsuccessful, Plato was forced to flee Athens. Meanwhile, as a result of Dion's invasion of Syracuse, Dionysius fled to Corinth. A year later, Dion was assassinated. As a result of his involvement in court politics, Plato worked out his frustrations in his *Letter VII* and *Letter VIII*, in which he extricates himself from complicity.

Plato's Academy enjoyed a whiff of fresh air in the stimulating and challenging work of Eudoxus, one of Plato's pupils. Eudoxus devoted himself to mathematical inquiry, particularly as it applies to conic sections and the early principles of calculus. His theories of planetary movement involved an array of concentric circles with the earth in the center, a concept later supplanted by Copernicus' theory of a heliocentric universe in the Middle Ages. In addition to these principles, Eudoxus contemplated an ethos based on rational hedonism and a metaphysical theory of the relationship of time and space. Diametrically opposed to his student's logic, Plato, who believed that the universe was based on numerical relationships, refuted Eudoxus' notions in *Parmenides* and *Philebus*.

During a final trip to Sicily, Plato, at the request of political leaders, constructed a model system of laws for use in colonial governance. He was actively engaged in refining his system when he died, at the age of eighty. Much to the dismay of Aristotle and Xenocrates, Plato's nephew, Speusippus, son of Plato's sister, Potone, replaced him as owner and administrator of the Academy until 339 B.C., when Xenocrates began his quarter century as headmaster. The school continued in operation until 529 A.D., when it was closed by Justinian.

One of the chief aims of Plato's writings was the vindication of Socrates, whose social criticism led to his arrest and subsequent death at the hands of Athenian reactionaries. Plato's *Apology*, a forthright attempt to clear his friend of the charge of impiety, has the wise old philosopher speaking in his own defense. In addition, Plato penned forty-two dialogues and a total of thirteen letters, all of which survive in their entirety. Plato spent the major portion of his life contemplating reality. He deplored dogma and favored a sincere, arduous search for truth, a system which reflects his own inner questioning of the true and just path. His conclusions about the nature of the ideal life has influenced succeeding generations of thinkers, including Aristotle, Plotinus, St. Augustine, Kant, Nietzsche, and Husserl.

Ω

EUTHYPHRO

In this dialogue between Socrates and Euthyphro, which takes place at the porch of King Archon shortly before Socrates faces his accuser, Meletus, in a court battle over Socrates' alleged impiety, Plato describes how Socrates characterizes the virtue of piety, or fulfilling one's obligation to god and humanity. In order to prove that Athenians do not understand the nature of either piety or impiety, Socrates deliberately chooses for debate a sophist, one who claims to have wisdom and who devotes his life to teaching morality as it applies to politics and practical matters. Socrates, professing to be ignorant, makes no claims about his own wisdom.

Both Socrates and Euthyphro are involved in legal matters at the time of the dialogue. Socrates, charged with poisoning the minds of the young with impious thoughts, faces Euthyphro, the plaintiff in a murder case in which Euthyphro's father is charged with the crime. The facts are as follows: a dependent of Euthyphro's family killed a slave. Euthyphro's father commanded that the killer be bound and thrown into a ditch and remain there until messengers could procure a religious interpretation to settle the matter. By the time the messengers returned, the killer had died of starvation and exposure. As a result, Euthyphro's father was charged with causing his death.

Socrates is impressed that Euthyphro is pursuing justice, even though he must oppose his own father, but he deserts the details of the case to discuss the abstract question "What is piety?" Euthyphro describes the term from his own point of view: piety is exactly what he represents in involving himself in the murder trial against his father. Socrates acknowledges Euthyphro's virtue in ignoring a personal relationship while seeking justice, but he rejects a single example of piety and delves further for a clear definition that will cover all instances.

Euthyphro makes a second attempt at definition: "Piety is what is dear to the gods and impiety is that which is not dear to them." Socrates counters that the answer is still inexact, given that Euthyphro has not explained what is "dear to the gods," since different gods respond to different endearments. Euthyphro insists that piety consists of what is dear to all gods. For example, he points out that murder is offensive to all gods. Socrates challenges his statement, pointing out the differing circumstances under which murder takes place.

Approaching the question from another angle, Socrates asks

Euthyphro if all pious people are just. Euthyphro agrees, but points out that the corollary – that all just people are pious – need not be true. Socrates asks whether piety is a part of justice, and if so, what part. Euthyphro separates justice into two areas – that part which affects god and that part which affects human beings. Socrates again questions the word "affects," demanding a clearer definition in view of the fact that "affects" implies "bettering," a possibility with humans and animals, but not with gods. Euthyphro states that human beings can minister to gods, but he does not have the time to substantiate his claim.

Socrates, declaring that Euthyphro failed to clarify his point, repeats his earlier need for a definition of piety because the matter is important to anyone making a decision involving moral conduct. The dialogue ends without a satisfying answer. Socrates encourages Euthyphro to continue his search for the meaning of piety. Without a credible definition, Euthyphro can make no claim to a just cause in the matter of his father's guilt or innocence.

For a more comprehensive, in-depth analysis of this work, consult Cliffs Notes on Plato's *Euthyphro, Apology, Crito, & Phaedo*.

Ω

APOLOGY

Plato's *Apology*, believed to be the most authentic, extant account of Socrates' defense of himself, allows the main character to speak at length, possibly in the actual words he used at his trial in 399 B.C. Accused of impiety and the corruption of youth by Meletus, Anytus, and Lycon, the seventy-year-old educator and philosopher made a stirring plea for acquittal. The court, composed of 501 citizens, had no judge or jury; rather, they returned a majority vote, finding Socrates guilty, 281 to 220, and condemning him to death. After a short period of confinement, Socrates died as a result of drinking poisonous hemlock. According to one tradition, Plato, Socrates' pupil and ardent admirer, was ill and could not attend the trial, but evidence within the text indicates that he did attend.

The *Apology* opens with an introductory statement in which Socrates explains his style of speaking. This is followed by an account of the specific accusations made with reference to his life and daily activities. Socrates replies at some length to each of the charges brought against him. After reporting Socrates' defense, Plato gives an account of Socrates' attempt to mitigate the penalty imposed on him. Finally, Socrates makes a prophetic rebuke of the judges for supposing they will live at ease with untroubled consciences after pronouncing the death sentence.

In the opening argument, Socrates explains the colloquial style in which he will be making his defense. His accusers have warned the citizens to be on their guard lest they be deceived by his oratory when he attempts to establish his innocence. Socrates insists that he is neither an orator nor a rhetorician. Rather, he is accustomed to clothe the truth in plain language so that all can follow his logic. He concludes that his hearers should consider his cause rather than his manner of speaking.

Within his defense, Socrates replies to two kinds of accusations: the first, the older, more generalized accusation, and the second, the current charge made by the three accusers in the courtroom. He dreads the first charge more than the second charge because he cannot face his accusers when he is refuting rumor and innuendo. The complaints against his conduct have accumulated over a number of years: he is said to be a "criminal and a busybody, prying into things under the earth and up in the heavens, and making the weaker argument the stronger, and teaching these same things to others."

Socrates declares that these assertions are false. In his defense, he mentions Aristophanes' comedy *The Clouds,* in which a character named Socrates claims he can walk on air. This silly scenario, however innocent in intent, he says, has contributed to his bad reputation. Another rumor alleges that he investigates supernatural matters, both above and below earth. He assures the assemblage that he has never taken an interest in physical science, although he admires physical scientists and refuses to place blame on their work. Socrates insists that his main interests lie in moral conduct and the soul's welfare.

Another instance of negative feeling came about, he says, when Chaerephon claimed to have heard the Delphic oracle say that Socrates was the wisest of men. Disturbed by such a bold allegation, Socrates questioned a group of wise men to determine if they were indeed wise. The method of his research led to enmity and suspicion in one politician whom he investigated and among others who heard about Socrates' probings. At this point, Socrates concludes that the oracle was right: whereas others are unaware of their limitations, Socrates at least knows and acknowledges his own ignorance. Further investigations involving poets and artisans led Socrates to deduce that many Athenians who consider themselves wise are more foolish than lesser men. Despite the wisdom Socrates gained from his research, the bad ultimately outweighed the good, as he was afterward disrespected and ridiculed for asking such questions.

In addition, some of Socrates' students have inadvertently besmirched his reputation by their enjoyment of his denouncement of the wisdom of others and by inept attempts to imitate his methods. Spreading false information that Socrates enjoys ridiculing people, his students have engendered much hatred based on half-truths and downright falsehood. It is this state of affairs that has led Meletus, Anytus, and Lycon to charge him on behalf of poets, craftsmen, statesmen, and orators.

Socrates' defense then narrows to the specific accusations of his chief accuser, Meletus. He cross-examines Meletus concerning the charge that he, Socrates, is evil, a corrupter of youth, and an atheist who seeks to establish his own deities. Through Socrates' skill in questioning, Meletus trips up on his own words. It is obvious to members of the court that Meletus has not thought through his accusations and their possible ramifications. On the matter of atheism, Meletus again confuses his allegations, seeming to accuse Socrates both of atheism and of inventing new deities.

At this point, Socrates considers another important point — whether he should change his style of inquiry and instruction to ward off the possibility of execution. He compares the situation to his honorable record on the battlefield when he served in the army. To Socrates, death is preferable to disgrace. He chooses to live according to god's command in order to fulfill his mission as a philosopher. To disobey god in order to save his own life would be the real disgrace. For Socrates, the straight path leads to an inquiry into wisdom, truth, and the "greatest improvement of the soul."

In a direct summation of intent, Socrates speaks directly to Athens:

". . . either acquit me or not; but whatever you do, know that I shall never alter my ways, not even if I have to die many times." He mentions the many students whom he has taught, who, if they had indeed been corrupted, would join Meletus and Anytus in their accusations. Socrates boasts that his pupils are among his most devoted friends and loyal supporters, several of whom he points out in the audience. Furthermore, he refuses to make a display of sympathetic family members in order to sway judgment in his behalf. Socrates rests his case on truth.

After the vote, Socrates expresses surprise that the majority did not go more heavily against him. By Athenian law, Socrates could propose an alternative punishment, such as a heavy fine, banishment, or other methods of paying his debt to society. Socrates rejects the obvious alternative and requests that the court impose a sentence that would provide at public expense for one who has dedicated his life to public service and the education of young minds.

To the suggestion that Socrates might escape the death penalty if he would stop his dialogues, which tend to arouse suspicion and controversy, Socrates notes again that he would disobey divine authority by holding his tongue. Instead, he promotes a life of inquiry into virtue, stating that the "unexamined life is not worth living." He asks only one favor – that the court watch over his growing sons and punish them if they become materialistic, pretentious, or vain.

His defense completed, Socrates warns the court not to congratulate themselves upon ridding Athens of a troublemaker. They will receive no peace or honor from their choice, for Socrates' execution will bring more harm to them than to their intended victim. In Socrates' opinion, the avoidance of death does not supercede the avoidance of unrighteousness. His parting sentence expresses his life's philosophy: "And now it is time to go, I to die, and you to live; but which of us goes to a better thing is unknown to all but God."

For a more comprehensive, in-depth analysis of this work, consult Cliffs Notes on Plato's *Euthyphro, Apology, Crito, & Phaedo.*

Ω

CRITO

Plato records a conversation between two old men – Crito, a fervent supporter of Socrates' ethical teachings, and his friend Socrates, who has spent a month in an Athenian prison cell awaiting execution. Crito appears at the cell early in the morning two days before Socrates is to be executed. Socrates has slept soundly; Crito explains that he has waited until his friend awoke so as not to disturb his rest. He is surprised that Socrates can sleep so calmly, as his time is short. Socrates' execution has been postponed until a particular ship returns from Delos, and Crito indicates that the ship, which has left Cape Sounion, should arrive in Athens the following day.

Socrates reveals much of his philosophy in his reply: if God wills his death, Socrates is ready. Yet, he interprets his dream of the previous night to mean that he can expect to live at least one more day. Offering money from his own coffers as well as from Simmias the Theban and Cebes, Crito pleads with Socrates to escape from prison and go to Thessaly. He gives two reasons for his advice: if Socrates is executed, Crito will lose an irreplaceable friend, and many Athenian citizens will condemn Crito, calling him a coward for failing to help Socrates in a time of extreme need.

Rejecting the latter argument, Socrates refuses to concern himself with so uncertain a matter as public opinion. Crito suggests that Socrates declines to accept help in escaping because the law would punish his abettors by confiscating their property. Socrates replies that the consideration has crossed his mind, but greater factors carry more weight.

Crito attempts to relieve Socrates' worries and encourage him to make the attempt. He assures Socrates that a little money will grease the wheel and offers to underwrite whatever amount is necessary for bribes and expenses. Crito lists other inducements, mentioning Socrates' enemies, who rejoice at his incarceration, and his family, who will grow up without a father's nurture and leadership and may become victims of evil habits without Socrates to guide them. In his final exhortation, Crito accuses Socrates of taking the easy way out and of putting his friends in an unfavorable light, allowing people to accuse them of not coming to Socrates' assistance.

Socrates divides Crito's arguments into two categories – rational and emotional. He acknowledges his old friend's zeal, but he faults his logic. Citing long-established principles based on rational, non-emotional thinking, he begins to refute Crito, item by item. First, Socrates rejects public opinion as a standard by which one should judge an action. Using analogies from gymnastics and medicine, Socrates illustrates how a majority opinion could mislead him in matters concerning justice. Crito agrees with his logic, but insists that the majority, which has the power to put Socrates to death, must receive some consideration.

Socrates counters with a distinction between life at all costs versus the good life, based on honor and justice. Under the heading of opinions of the majority, Socrates lumps together three of Crito's inducements to escape—money, diminished reputation, and the education of his children. Socrates reduces Crito's arguments to a single query: is it right or honorable to allow friends to use bribes or other unlawful means in helping Socrates escape? Socrates deduces that escaping from a duly imposed prison sentence would be wrong and would jeopardize the principles for which he has stood.

Crito, still unconvinced, counters that the law itself is unjust and that Socrates has an obligation to break it. Socrates replies that evil for evil is an unjust exchange. Comparing his life in the state to that of a child living with its parents, Socrates declares that he has a duty to Athens and must pay back the benefits he has obtained by yielding to the judgment of its courts. In Socrates' estimation, obedience to the law will be the supreme test of Socrates' lifelong philosophy. In order to prove his point, he must not avoid death at the cost of principle. Socrates concludes that escape would not benefit either him or his friends. As an exile, he would carry the taint of his accusers into Thessaly, where Crito urges him to flee. When Crito can make no further arguments, Socrates asks that his friend leave him to obey the will of god.

For a more comprehensive, in-depth analysis of this work, consult Cliffs Notes on Plato's *Euthyphro, Apology, Crito, & Phaedo.*

Ω

PHAEDO

In the town of Phlius in the Peloponnesus, sixty miles from Athens, an undetermined time after Socrates' death, Phaedo narrates for Echecrates an eyewitness account of the philosopher's execution. Echecrates begins the dialogue by asking if Phaedo saw Socrates drink the poison. Phaedo replies that he was present, and he names fourteen people who were there, excluding Plato, who was ill at the time.

The visitors at the death cell discussed Socrates' views on the soul, seeking reassurance on the day that their beloved teacher was to be executed. They asked specific questions: what proof is there of the soul's existence? How does the soul relate to the body? Where does the soul go after the body dies? Are souls immortal? Are souls influenced by the body? Are there good and bad souls? Are souls rewarded or punished in a future life? Socrates attempts to provide clear, convincing answers to their questions.

Echecrates questions Phaedo about Socrates' last words. Some people heard that Socrates was condemned to drink poison, but they lacked details of the execution. Phaedo explains that the execution was delayed until a certain ship arrived from Delos. He indicates that he did not pity Socrates because Socrates bore himself nobly and fearlessly to the end and appeared to be blessed by the gods.

Phaedo then launches into a reproduction of the final conversation on the morning of Socrates' last day. Having been released from the chains imposed by "The Eleven," Athens' rulers, Socrates sits with his wife, Xanthippe, who clutches their son and weeps. He directs Crito to find someone to take Xanthippe home. Cebes asks Socrates why he rejects the notion of suicide. Socrates explains that human beings, who belong to the gods, may not destroy possessions of divine beings and therefore should not commit suicide. At the prompting of more questions from Cebes and Simmias, Socrates describes how the soul finds good company with the gods and the souls of other departed people, although he can offer no positive proof of his belief.

Crito interrupts with a message from the jailer – Socrates should not overheat himself by talking too much, thereby interfering with the action of the poison, which sometimes must be administered more than once. Socrates tells Crito to ask the jailer to mind his own business and prepare himself to administer the poison several times, if need be.

Socrates returns to the subject of death and dying, affirming his belief that "he who has lived as a true philosopher has reason to be of good cheer when he is about to die, and that after death he may hope to receive the greatest good in the other world." Dying, he declares, is the pursuit of the true philosopher because death separates the soul from the mundane pleasures of the body, such as eating, drinking, and wearing fine clothes. A cessation of life frees the soul from the enslavement of the body.

The body knows pleasure through the senses, whereas the soul gains wisdom through the intellect. Truth, the ultimate end of philosophy, can be achieved only when the soul is no longer deceived by sensual pleasures. The philosopher's soul, longing to be free of bodily wants, desires an escape from the body's entrapment. From the body's lusts and fears come fighting, greed, and war, but from the intellect come justice, beauty, and goodness. People who love wisdom look forward to death; people who love power and money fear death.

Cebes is skeptical that the soul survives after the body dies. Socrates refers him to the Heraclitean doctrine of opposites. According to this concept, the world is constantly changing—night into day, sleep into consciousness, life into death. As opposites regenerate each other, Socrates deduces that life must be reborn from death in an endless cycle of regeneration.

At the request of Simmias, Socrates agrees to explain the doctrine of reminiscence. Cebes comments that the mind is capable of answering any question if the question is phrased in a proper form. The only source for this profound knowledge must be a prior life. Socrates illustrates the matter by describing human knowledge of equality, an absolute state that also proves a prior existence of the soul.

Simmias pursues further proof that the soul continues to exist after the death of the body. Socrates reiterates earlier statements about life being created out of death, but Cebes and Simmias demand stronger justification. In reply to Cebes' suggestion that the soul may be destroyed, Socrates replies that, whereas compounds may change and dissolve, pure matter, such as beauty or justice, truth or goodness, is not compounded. The soul, which rules over the body, reflects the divine, in contrast to the body, which is mortal. Because the soul remains pure, it does not decay with the body, but departs to an invisible realm and lives in happiness, free of mortal error and folly.

Concerning the matter of good and evil souls, Socrates continues with supposition alone, acknowledging that there is no proof to substantiate his assumption. Employing myths from various cults, he explains that the soul pollutes itself by association with the body. Contaminated souls, therefore, must wander in the afterlife until they expiate their former crimes. Some return to life as lower beings, some as mortals, but only the pure dwell with the gods.

After a few moments of silent contemplation, Simmias confesses that he still has questions. Socrates commends their open minds and tries to reassure both Simmias and Cebes with more logic. Comparing the soul to harmony from the lyre, Simmias notes that when the lyre is destroyed, harmony vanishes. Likewise, he extends his example to the body: when the body dies, the soul, too, vanishes. Cebes refutes his thinking, insisting that the soul is strong, more resilient than the body. Yet, he too wonders if the soul, like a coat, can outlast several wearers before falling to pieces.

To convince Cebes that the soul does not die, Socrates describes his own developing wisdom in the matter. Beginning with his study of physical matter in his youth, Socrates studied the human form, but rejected the premise that answers can be found in a study of anatomy. Since life excludes both death and the soul, and death excludes life, then the soul must be immortal. Therefore, human beings should avoid wickedness, since they must one day face punishment in the endless passageways of the underworld.

When Socrates comes to a stopping point, Crito asks if he has any last requests. Socrates begs them all to live justly and honorably by the principles he has taught them. He refuses to take seriously their concerns for burial, joking with them before concluding, "do with that as is usual, and as you think best." Socrates then bathes and, in the presence of Crito, bids farewell to his family. Dismissing them, he returns to the group and takes the poison that the jailer brings. As he begins to feel its effect, he uncovers his face and reminds Crito to pay his debt, a cock, to Asclepius. Crito promises to carry out his wishes. In a few moments, Socrates lies dead. Crito smooths the eyelids and the jaw. Phaedo remarks, "This was the end of our comrade, Echecrates, a man, as we would say, of all then living we had ever met, the noblest and the wisest and most just."

For a more comprehensive, in-depth analysis of this work, consult Cliffs Notes on Plato's *Euthyphro, Apology, Crito, & Phaedo*.

Ω

MENO

This dialogue between Socrates and Meno, a wealthy young noble-man from Thessaly, a section of Greece south of Macedonia, concerns virtue. Meno opens the discussion with a direct question: can virtue be taught? Socrates, who introduces his reply with extensive cour-tesies, replies that he cannot answer the question because he does not understand the nature of virtue. Meno suggests that Gorgias, a Sicilian sophist who lectured in Athens, may have had the answer.

Declining to accept the answer of an absent rhetorician, Socrates urges Meno to find the answer within himself. Meno makes a two-part reply: first, he says, a man's virtue is his ability to manage public business, help his friends, hurt his enemies, and keep out of trouble; a woman's virtue involves managing her home, keeping the stores, and obeying her husband. Meno adds that there are other virtues which apply to different circumstances, such as age, sex, and condi-tion of servitude.

Socrates' answer to Meno is in the form of an analogy. He asks Meno if bees are all alike. Meno replies that they are similar in their beehood. Socrates then explains that virtues, although differing in quality, reflect core characteristics, namely temperance and justice. Thus endowed with these virtues, human beings are able to rule justly. Using examples of color and shape, Socrates leads Meno to a clearer definition of virtue: it is the desire for beautiful things and the ability to provide them.

At this point, Socrates examines the corollary, that some people desire bad things, even when they know that the objects are harmful. Yet, there are people who desire bad things without knowing the harm that they do. Socrates clarifies the issue somewhat. Since nobody wants misery, nobody truly desires bad things, which will lead to wretchedness. Therefore, it appears that everyone desires good, although some people are better at providing it than others. By this logic, virtue is the power to get good things. He who acquires good things justly is virtuous, but he who acquires them unjustly is evil.

As Socrates seeks to establish the nature of pure virtue without chopping it into fragments, such as temperance, justice, and piety, he quotes inspired poets, including Pindar, who believed the soul to be immortal. If the soul has seen all that is on earth and in Hades, what appears to be learning is really remembering. To prove this point, Socrates summons a young slave and shows him the diagram of a square. The boy's logical answers concerning the length of lines indicates that he has some knowledge of geometry. Socrates probes further into the matter of size, asking the boy to make deductions about diameters of squares. Although the slave claims not to understand, Socrates stirs up his logic and leads him to a correct answer.

Socrates draws a worthy conclusion from his questions, declaring that "if the truth of things is always in our soul, the soul must be immortal . . ." Comparing the contemplation of virtue to the study of geometry, Socrates proposes that the original question be rephrased in hypothetical terms: if virtue is a quality of the soul, can it be taught? He deduces that virtue is a form of wisdom. In order to be taught, it must be a form of knowledge.

As Socrates ponders whether there can be teachers and learners of virtue, Anytus, (who will be among the faction that will charge Socrates with impiety), a young man of worthy upbringing, joins the two men. Using Anytus as a sounding board, Socrates asks how a man might learn medicine or shoemaking. Anytus replies that each should go to an expert physician or shoemaker in order to be trained. Socrates suggests that Meno should seek out an expert in virtue — that is, he should seek out a sophist if he wants to learn about virtue.

Anytus swears an oath and declares that sophists have a bad reputation for spreading false ideas in exchange for hefty fees. He suggests that Meno would do well to consult any Athenian gentleman rather than put himself in the hands of greedy charlatans. Socrates inserts a disclaimer at this point, noting that many worthy gentlemen in Athens produce sons of lesser virtue. Since these notables would surely have passed on knowledge of virtue if such could be taught, it appears that virtue is not learned. Anytus, misunderstanding Socrates' meaning, leaves in a huff, certain that Socrates has maligned the nobles of Athens.

Meno admits that he is still unsure whether virtue can be taught. Socrates reassures him by admitting that many notable people, including the poet Theognis, ponder the same question. It seems, since there are no true teachers of virtue and no learners, that virtue cannot be taught. Comparing the teaching of virtue to giving directions, Socrates at first assumes that right opinion in a matter may be as valuable as knowledge. However, he refines his premise by concluding that right opinion, when maintained over a period of time, becomes knowledge and that both right opinion and knowledge perform good and useful functions.

Recapitulating their debate, Socrates reestablishes an earlier premise, that the politicians who guide cities use right opinion rather than knowledge. He compares their occasional brilliance to the godlike truth that comes from babbling oracles, prophets, poets, and artists in that ordinary men may speak divine truth without realizing the source. Therefore, virtue is a divine gift. Socrates takes his leave of Meno and assigns him the task of mollifying Anytus by explaining to him the nature of virtue.

Ω

ION

In a dialogue between Socrates and Ion of Ephesus (a *rhapsode*, or reciter), Socrates refutes Ion's boasts. Socrates greets Ion, who returns victoriously from the reciters' contest at the feast of Asclepius at Epidaurus. Overjoyed by his first prize, Ion looks forward confidently to a win at the Panathenaea at Athens. Socrates admires the reciter for his close association with the great poets, particularly Homer. Ion agrees with Socrates' comments, noting that he speaks of Homer "better than any other man alive." Intrigued by his claims, Socrates asks for a demonstration and promises to find the time to attend.

Socrates inquires if Ion is as good at reciting other poets, such as Hesiod or Archilochus. Ion claims to have mastered only Homer. By drawing out a comparison between Homer and the lesser poets, Socrates leads Ion to confess that anyone could distinguish between the best and the merely good. Ion himself is bored by discussions of other poets, but at the mention of Homer, his attention is galvanized in an instant. Socrates leads Ion to consider painters, both good and bad, as well as sculptors, pipers, harpists, and singers. In all cases, experts in each field can discuss artists of all levels. Ion agrees, but sticks to his original boast that he discusses Homer better than any man alive.

Socrates is moved to make an observation – Ion must receive divine inspiration. Like a magnet attracting stones, the muse must inspire by direct contact. Therefore, poetry is *not* the result of art, but of a godlike possession, through which "God himself is the speaker." Ion eagerly accepts Socrates' premise, acknowledging further that interpretation, too, is an emotional act, causing the audience to experience sadness and terror through the powers of the *rhapsode*. Socrates returns to his image, declaring that Ion is like the middle ring, a ring that draws its power from the magnet, which represents God. Because of his possession by the muse, Ion is "Homer's great encomiast."

Ion applauds Socrates' comments, but notes that he does not always appear possessed by godlike inspiration. Citing the example of the horse race at Patroclus' funeral, Socrates notes that Ion cannot know every incident mentioned in Homer's verses because he is not an expert in all arts. Continuing his argument with passages about medicine, fishing, and prophecy, Socrates asks Ion to select passages about recitation. Ion claims that all of Homer's poetry is about recitation.

Socrates reminds Ion that he earlier admitted that other types of artistry exist in Homer, such as the skill of the charioteer. Bombarding Ion with his own examples of specialists – the ruler, the pilot, the slave, the oxherd, and the wool-spinner – Socrates digs deeper into Ion's logic, noting that just as a horseman is no judge of a harpist, a reciter is likewise no judge of military matters.

Socrates then reaches the concluding point of his argument: is Ion, a reciter of military matters, therefore the best general in Hellas? Ion, swept along by his own ego, agrees that, through knowledge of Homer, he is indeed the best general in Hellas. Socrates inquires why Ion practices the art of recitation rather than the art of warfare. Ion replies that Ephesus, under the command of Athens, needs no foreign general. Socrates reminds Ion that Athens often chooses foreign generals, such as Phanosthenes of Andros and Heracleides of Clazomenai.

Socrates ends the argument by accusing Ion of misleading him with his inflated claims of greatness. Like Proteus, Ion can change himself into many forms and is thereby cheating Socrates, unless, in truth, he is divinely inspired. He leaves Ion a choice – either he is a deceiver or a mouthpiece of the gods. Ion decides that it is "finer to be considered divine!" Socrates concludes that Ion is a spokesman of the gods rather than an artist.

Ω

SYMPOSIUM

Plato's *Symposium* describes a banquet that takes place in Agathon's house in 416 B.C. to honor his first victory at the dramatic festival in the Theater of Dionysus in Athens. The story, which is told second-hand through a conversation between Apollodorus and Plato, relates a lively discussion which involved twelve guests, including Socrates and four other prominent Athenians—Phaedrus, Plato's friend; Pausanias, a disciple of the sophist Prodicus; Aristophanes, a dramatist; and Alcibiades, an eminent statesman and admirer of Socrates.

On his way from the public bath, Socrates, dressed for a formal occasion, encounters Aristodemus and invites him to come along. Agathon, the host, whose name means "gentleman," welcomes them, greeting Aristodemus warmly and offering Socrates a seat of honor at Agathon's left. After the guests do homage to the gods and exchange pleasantries, Eryximachus, a physician, introduces the evening's discussion topic, love. The guests speak in orderly fashion clockwise around the table until each member of the symposium has contributed.

Phaedrus speaks first, noting that love "is at once oldest, and most precious, and has the most power to provide virtue and happiness for mankind, both living and dead." Because of its worth to humanity, love should guide mortals throughout their lives. The second speaker, Pausanias, takes the symposium a step further. He asserts that love is not one deity but two, common and heavenly, both of which he characterizes in a lengthy speech enhanced with many references to familiar myths.

Because Aristophanes excuses himself until his hiccups abate, Eryximachus speaks out of turn and claims that love exists in all living things. Basing his philosophy upon his practical experience as a doctor of medicine, he notes: "For the healing art, to put it shortly, is knowledge of the body's love for filling and emptying, and one who distinguishes the beautiful and the ugly love in these things is the most complete physician . . ." He concludes that mortals must preserve love as a whole, which "has great and mighty power, or rather in a word, omnipotence . . ."

Opening with a one-liner on the subject of sneezing, Aristophanes takes his belated turn and pursues a different approach. Love, he insists, has received too little praise from mortals. After describing the history of love, he proposes that each person is half of a complete love relationship. "So when one of these meets his own proper half, whether boy-lover or anyone else, then we are wonderfully overwhelmed by affection and intimacy and love, and . . . never wish to be apart for a moment." In response to this perfect union, Aristophanes insists that people owe great praise to the god who blesses them with love and happiness.

Counter to those who have preceded him, Agathon maintains that the gathering should turn its attention from the human point of view and turn toward the gods themselves, whose Love is the most beautiful and happy of all. The reason for Love's virtues is obvious: ". . . Love wrongs not and is not wronged, wrongs no god and is wronged by none, wrongs no man and is wronged by none." If people emulate Love, they will rid themselves of violence, estrangement, and ill will. Agathon takes his seat amid hearty applause on all sides.

Socrates, humble and unassuming as always, engages Agathon in a dialogue, questioning whether Love always has an object, which, of necessity, must be something that the lover lacks. Agathon agrees that these suppositions are true. Socrates concludes that Love lacks both beauty and truth, despite Agathon's earlier assertions to the contrary. He next tells a long story about his conversation with Diotima, which leads to a satisfying moral: anyone who perceives beauty with the soul shall "be the friend of God, and immortal if any man ever is . . ." As he closes, he reiterates the common theme that Love deserves honor. He begs them to receive his speech as a "eulogy to Love."

A ruckus at the door interrupts the group, and Alcibiades, drunk and insistent, is led to the banquet table. They wave him toward a couch next to Agathon, where the host provides all courtesies and welcomes him to the feast. Looking hazily about him, Alcibiades is startled to find Socrates on his left and chastises his fellow diner for making advances. He realizes that the other men are still sober and encourages them to join him in drunkenness. Eryximachus invites Alcibiades to add his comments to their symposium, but Alcibiades hesitates to address men who are still in control of their senses. Eryximachus good naturedly suggests that Alcibiades speak in praise of Socrates.

In imitation of a popular game, Alcibiades speaks in similes. He compares Socrates to Silenus, the mythic player of panpipes, pointing out that Socrates bewitches through his skill with words. To protect himself from sure seduction, Alcibiades always runs from Socrates, whom he accuses of having a "loving eye for beauty." He confesses that he once pursued Socrates and believed that Socrates "would talk to me as a lover would talk to a darling in solitude . . . [but] nothing came of it, nothing, he just talked as usual . . ." On a second occasion, Alcibiades invited Socrates to dinner and engaged him in late-night conversation, but Socrates again brushed aside Alcibiades' overtures.

Alcibiades continues to deck Socrates with praise and concludes: ". . . none could ever be found to compare with him, neither modern nor ancient, unless he is to be compared to no man at all, but to the Silenuses and satyrs to which I have compared him—him and his talk." He warns the gathering that Socrates has been courted by other worthy men, but their experience has been the same as his—rejection.

Perplexed by Alcibiades' skillful tirade, Socrates accuses him of pretending to be drunk, for the intricacy of his words suggests that he has a devious purpose in mind. Alcibiades apparently wants both Socrates and Agathon as lovers and is merely trying to stir up enmity between the two so that he can have them to himself. Agathon agrees, offering as proof the fact that Alcibiades deliberately chose a seat between them.

Socrates vows to follow the pattern that Alcibiades has started and laud the man on his right; therefore, Agathon changes seats so that he can bask in Socrates' praise. Alcibiades chafes at Socrates' clever evasion, but before he can raise a row, more revellers join them. Soon, everyone is sleeping off his wine except Agathon, Aristophanes, and Socrates, who discuss tragedy and comedy until the wee hours. When his two companions fall asleep at daybreak, Socrates tiptoes out, bathes, and goes about his usual routine.

$$\Omega$$

THE REPUBLIC

Plato's *Republic*, his most famous work, is a compendium of thoughts on the ideal life. Written in the form of a dialogue and set in the house of Cephalus, a wealthy retired businessman, on the festival day of the Thracian goddess Bendis, the conversation of the dozen well-known Athenian guests covers a range of topics, all of which relate to the central idea – the ideal conditions under which the perfect life would flourish. For convenience in discussing the dialogue, scholars have arbitrarily divided it into ten books.

BOOK I

Socrates, who speaks in the first person, accompanies Glaucon, Plato's older brother, to Piraeus, a seaport a few miles south of Athens, for the first celebration of the festival of Bendis. After observing the procession and performing devotions, the two men meet Polemarchus and learn that there is going to be a relay race on horseback. Tempted by the event, they decide to stay for dinner and watch the show. They accompany Polemarchus home and meet other guests there. Cephalus, Polemarchus' aged father, welcomes Socrates courteously.

The dialogue opens on a friendly exchange between Socrates and Cephalus. As they discuss old age and wealth, they reach a difference of opinion concerning the part that money plays in the attainment of happiness. Cephalus maintains that a comfortable income increases the likelihood that a person will enjoy life and follow moral precepts. Socrates disagrees, insisting that Cephalus has oversimplified morality as "telling the truth" and "paying your debts." He states the hypothetical case of the borrowed knife: it would be morally right to return the knife to its owner, but if the owner demonstrates a vicious, spiteful spirit, returning the knife might lead to a violent act. In this case, returning borrowed property would not be morally right if it led to harm.

Cephalus becomes bored with the finer points of argumentation and turns his attention toward the performance of sacred rites, but his son, Polemarchus, takes up his father's side of the discussion, offering three separate definitions of justice. First, he claims that doing right means "giving everyone his due." Socrates questions him further; Polemarchus refines his statement to "giving everyone what is appropriate to him." Socrates inquires how this definition applies to enemies.

Polemarchus replies that it is appropriate to cause harm to enemies. Therefore, justice consists of benefiting friends and doing harm to enemies.

By way of discussion, Socrates extends this definition to specific examples, noting that the doctor, the navigator, and the bricklayer are best equipped to benefit friends and harm enemies in matters of health, travel, and building. In meting out justice, the just man, in contrast to these experts, is least likely to achieve his goals. Therefore, justice seems virtually useless.

Socrates builds his case by adding a further disclaimer: people are often wrong in identifying who is a friend and who is an enemy. If a person chooses bad people for friends and good for enemies, it would seem more fitting to do ill for friends and good for enemies. Polemarchus, stymied in his first argument, retrenches, stating his definition in clearer terms: justice consists in benefiting friends who are truly good and harming enemies who are truly evil.

Again Socrates criticizes his rule, arguing that evil for evil does not produce good ends. Using a horse as an example, he notes that harming the horse will only make him a more disagreeable animal. Likewise, harming human beings does not benefit them, but only makes them worse. By applying Polemarchus' rule, the just would make evil people even more abominable. Socrates concludes that evil is never just, regardless of the circumstances.

Polemarchus accedes to Socrates' argument, but Thrasymachus, a sophist, or professional teacher of morality, succeeds in interrupting the debate and rudely demands a clear definition of justice from Socrates. Socrates, never one to push his opinions on others, admits that he has no answer and only wishes to learn the definition of justice from the other guests. Thrasymachus, reluctant to proffer his opinion until he is offered a fee, states his own thinking in the matter: justice is what benefits the stronger party. For example, a ruler makes laws that benefit himself. His subjects, the weaker party, are obligated to obey the laws.

Socrates points out that rulers can make mistakes, creating laws that are not beneficial to them, but which may benefit the populace at large. Thrasymachus strenuously objects to Socrates' logic, insisting that rulers, by definition, are faultless, just as mathematicians, by nature of their title, are error-free in their calculations. Socrates counters with an important consideration, that the function of a ruler is to serve the people's interests and not his own. He uses the doctor as an example, asserting that the doctor cures the patient in order to benefit the patient. In respect to his medical knowledge, he receives no benefit, but in respect to his need for wages, he receives some benefit. Likewise, the ruler receives money or honor for his work, but the chief purpose of his work is the welfare of his subjects and not personal gain.

Thrasymachus interposes personal commentary about his view of life. He sneers that justice is a virtue for fools and dolts. People lead moral lives because they lack intelligence or because they are afraid of the consequences of immorality. In contrast, intelligent people, who are stronger and bolder, find immorality more beneficial and line their pockets by evading taxes, embezzling public monies, and enjoying a more successful existence than just people. The best way to succeed at injustice, he claims, is to launch a full-scale operation and to threaten the public, who will become slaves to the tyrant.

Thrasymachus attempts to leave at this point without giving Socrates the courtesy of rebuttal, but others convince him he should continue the debate. Socrates refutes his opponent on three issues: that the unjust man is more intelligent, that injustice strengthens, and that injustice produces happiness. Again referring to various trades and professions, Socrates claims that only a fool will challenge a person who is obviously more talented. A good musician, on the other hand, recognizes skill in a better musician and avoids competition. Therefore, the unjust person, who tries to outdo everyone, is less intelligent.

Concerning the second error in Thrasymachus' thinking, Socrates remarks that even criminals are just in their relations with other criminals. Otherwise, they could not conspire together if they lacked mutual trust. To have unity, people must have some semblance of justice. Therefore, complete injustice is not a source of strength, but of anarchy and chaos.

On the third faulty assumption, Socrates states that everything has a function and a virtue. The pruning knife prunes trees; if it possesses clear vision, then it functions as it should. Socrates extends his analogy to human life. The function of human beings is living; the virtue, possibly the only virtue, of human beings is justice because justice allows humans to live well. If people do not live well, they cannot be happy. Injustice by definition, cannot bring happiness.

Thrasymachus wilts at this point. By nature of his role as sophist, he is not convinced, but he realizes he has been bested. Socrates agreeably thanks Thrasymachus for his company, but regrets that he has not paid enough attention to the food. Like greedy people grabbing at every passing dish, Socrates claims that he has advanced to other subjects without thoroughly covering the nature of justice.

BOOK II

After Thrasymachus falls silent, Glaucon and Adeimantus, Plato's older brothers, take up the discussion. Glaucon is the first to express his dissatisfaction with the previous argument. He declares that he would like to believe that the just life is better than the unjust, but he requires more convincing evidence. Restating Thrasymachus' position, he leads Socrates into a second debate.

Socrates, believing that justice is good in the same way that knowledge and health are beneficial, avers that justice, like knowledge and health, is beneficial in and of itself, regardless of rewards or consequences. Glaucon, quick to disagree, takes an opposite stance, comparing justice to hard work or medical treatment. Whereas work and medication are beneficial, both are unpleasant. Justice, too, is unpleasant, even though it brings valuable rewards.

In defense of his position, which he contends is the popular view, Glaucon attempts to explain the origin of justice, to account for most people's decision to be just, and to prove that justice is not valuable in its own right. In the beginning, he claims, there was no law or justice. People did as they pleased and stole from each other at will. They realized that a rapacious lifestyle caused more suffering than happiness because no single individual had the power to impose his will on others without suffering dire consequences. To stem the mutual hurts within society, people agreed to avoid harm to each other. They created laws to protect themselves. What was lawful was right; what was unlawful was wrong. Therefore, justice and morality were born out of necessity: they exist only because people fear each other.

In defense of his second premise, Glaucon explains that people seek justice out of necessity, not because they value justice for its own sake. He proposes two hypothetical cases, a just man and an unjust man, who are allowed to do anything they please. If each has a magic ring that, when turned on his finger, makes him invisible, both men would respond to the magic in the same way. They would break into houses, steal, and do as they wished with impunity, although their reasons would differ. The unjust man would be continuing in his normal habits; the just man would take up criminal habits because he no longer has a reason to avoid crime. Glaucon emphasizes that the just man would be a fool to continue in his moral ways and miss the opportunity to be unjust without fear or reprisal from the law. Therefore, Glaucon concludes, people are just only because they fear the consequences of being unjust.

To prove his final point, Glaucon concludes that if justice is its own reward, then the life of the just man should always be better than that of the unjust man. However, circumstances vary. For example, if a wicked man is clever enough to hide his misdeeds, he will have a spotless reputation. To his neighbors, he will seem just, even though he is evil. On the other hand, a just man, deprived of everything except his sterling character, never does wrong, but is blamed for everything, thereby marring his reputation. Glaucon concludes that it is absurd to imagine that the just man is happier than the unjust man. Yet, according to Socrates' reasoning, the just man should always be happier, under *any* circumstance. In the final view, it is much better to *appear* just than to *be* just.

Before Socrates can reply to Glaucon's assertions, Adeimantus, as noted, another older brother of Plato, speaks in support of Glaucon. He offers examples of what people say when they praise justice and condemn injustice. Fathers urge their sons to be just, not to build character, but to enhance reputation and social prestige. They commend not justice, but the respectability that accompanies it. An intelligent son will surely realize the difference and come to value good reputation over virtue so long as he profits by it.

In addition, Adeimantus believes that fear of a god's punishment is a poor deterrent to wrong, since poets show that the gods can be bribed by sacrifices. It would seem, therefore, that Thrasymachus is correct. If one is powerful and rich and can maintain a good reputation while leading an immoral life, he is better off. Adeimantus ends his commentary with a request. He wants Socrates to override popular opinion and prove that justice is inherently good, regardless of rewards, punishments, or reputation.

Socrates introduces his reply with a comparison: a near-sighted person, when presented two notices, would do well to read the one in larger print. In this way, people seem near-sighted in that they look for the quality of justice in the individual, but cannot see it clearly. Justice, he claims, is a property of communities as well as individuals. Since the community is larger, it is easier to find justice there. Once Socrates establishes justice in the community, he can return to the individual. Glaucon and Adeimantus agree with his logic.

Socrates examines the manner in which a state begins. In a hypothetical situation, people come together to form a community because they are not self-sufficient and cannot supply their needs for food, shelter, clothing, and other necessities. The best way to satisfy these needs is for each citizen to practice a trade according to individual talents and skills. To enhance the community, each citizen should follow the trade for which he or she has an aptitude. The community, when fully developed, should afford happiness and contentment for its citizens.

In answer to the question what makes this community just, Glaucon declares that it is fit only for pigs, not human beings. Material needs do not comprise the whole life; there should be comforts, luxuries, and entertainment. Socrates admits that he thought he had covered enough of the community's wants for the purpose of debate, but he complies with Glaucon's suggestion and, for the sake of discussion, he extends his model.

To provide society with comforts, luxuries, and entertainment, there must be artists and servants. Because people will make themselves sick by overindulging, they will also need a full staff of medical people to look after them. These new demands will cause the state to swell to the limit and extend into neighboring territory; neighboring states, also undergoing growth, will invade the hypothetical state. This overextension will lead to war and establish a new need for specialized people to fight the wars.

Professional soldiers, as guardians of the community, must be carefully selected and trained. Their bodies must be strong, their spirits courageous and warlike. But these traits make them a danger to the people they protect. If they are to discriminate between friend and foe, they must have knowledge and the love of knowledge, which Socrates characterizes as a "philosophic temperament."

Socrates elaborates on the education and training of the guardians of the state, noting that their upbringing must predispose them toward morality. In childhood, they must hear proper stories of gods and heroes, not the more unsuitable literature current in Socrates' day. Homer and other poets would be unsuitable, for their poems tell of tricky, cruel gods. Since the gods, by definition, are incapable of wrongdoing, these stories must be false.

The perfect soldiers must grow up without fear of death so that they will be brave and willing to die for their country. Therefore, Hellas must rid itself of gloomy, terrifying stories of the underworld so that brave men will not be affected. In summary, soldiers, during their formative years, must hear only stories that will have a good moral effect. The purpose of education – to mold their minds and characters so that they will become good leaders – requires positive, character-building material.

_____ **BOOK III**

Socrates enlarges on his theme of education by describing proper physical training, expounding upon dietary needs and the avoidance of excess. Returning to the subject of the ideal state, Socrates divides the guardians into two classes: rulers, or those that govern, and auxiliaries, or those that execute the decisions of the governors. He maintains that only the best should rule the state. They should be older men who are endowed with experience and wisdom. In addition, they must be intelligent, capable, and public-spirited. Their entire lives must be devoted to the public good. In order to attune themselves to public need, rulers must avoid bribery and propaganda. To assure itself of the best rulers, the public must test future rulers in their youth for weakness.

Beneath the first two classes – rulers and their auxiliaries – are tradesmen, who, in compliance with the original premise that each must follow the trade for which he is most fitted, take no part in government or military affairs. Under this category come doctors, farmers, and builders, who carry on necessary trades and professions. At this point, Socrates asks how the state can guarantee that each level of society will not meddle in the work of the other two. In answer to his own query, he hesitates to propose a method to insure harmony and stability. Glaucon interjects his own supposition – that Socrates is suggesting the formulation of the Myth of the Metals, a great and noble lie that will convince each social level that it has reason to be content.

According to the myth, all citizens are brothers, created by the gods from the same raw material. Some, however, have gold in their veins, namely the rulers. Others, obviously the auxiliaries, have silver. The third class, the tradesmen, are made of iron and bronze. As would be expected, gold-veined parents produce similar children. Likewise, silver-veined parents produce silver offspring, and people of baser metal bear children of iron and bronze. If, by chance, a golden child is born to silver parents, the child must be removed from his home and repositioned in the appropriate class for the good of the whole community. Socrates acknowledges that citizens will be inclined to doubt the myth, at least for the first few generations. Ultimately, however, he hopes that the myth will lead to stability and loyalty.

Socrates ends Book III with a fuller description of the lives of guardians — that is, the people in the upper two levels. If the rulers and auxiliaries receive a proper education, they should avoid corruption and abuse of fellow citizens. Yet, the community requires further precautions, lest guardians be tempted to ride roughshod over people of lesser strength and intelligence.

To avoid the creation of tyrants, society must insist that rulers and their facilitators live together in barracks, exist on the barest essentials, and reject private ownership of possessions and money. This method is the only way to prevent jealousy. Therefore, citizens must agree to support the guardians with food and clothing in return for their performance as guardians.

BOOK IV

Though Glaucon agrees with Socrates' logic up to this point, Adeimantus objects vigorously that Socrates is not necessarily establishing happy lifestyles for the citizens of his hypothetical state. The rulers of other states live in grand, showy style. How can Socrates hold to the belief that the rulers of this community will not seek greater benefits? Socrates concurs that, in his model state, rulers do not enjoy a lavish lifestyle. But he disagrees with Adeimantus' suggestion that their lives are not happy.

To Socrates, external goods do not create contentment. In addition, the hypothetical state was not founded to make rulers happy but to create a contented state as a whole. Returning to the original premise, the purpose of erecting this imaginary community is to explain the nature of justice. If the community serves only to make rulers happy by endowing them with riches, then the people at the lower end of the spectrum will certainly be discontent and jealous. In such a state of affairs where one class has all the advantages and the other class none, justice cannot exist.

Concerning the third class, the tradesmen, Socrates declares that there must not be extremes of either poverty or wealth. If a builder is too rich, he would not need to work and might become careless and lazy. If he were too poor, he could not provide himself with necessary tools. Without tools, his work would suffer and he would grow restive.

Socrates turns his attention to legislation, maintaining that there need not be many laws. If, as Socrates originally proposed, citizens receive a thorough education, they will develop self-discipline and behave reasonably. Therefore, in a well-run community, laws should be kept to a bare minimum.

When this ideal state is established, Socrates continues, it should exhibit four cardinal virtues—wisdom, courage, discipline, and justice. He sets out to identify these four virtues, beginning with wisdom, which he expects to find in the ruling class. Certainly, rulers will be wise, because they are the community's arbiters of right and wrong. In making these judgments, therefore, they establish what is wise.

Where, then, is courage to be found in the ideal state? Surely, courage belongs with the second class, the soldiers. The third virtue, discipline or temperance, is less easily located, for each of the three classes requires its own type of self-control. For a person to possess self-control, the better portion of his character must control the weaker part in order to rein in his desires.

Likewise, the state must be self-disciplined. The wiser elements must rule over the weaker parts. It seems reasonable that the discipline of the state is not to be found in a particular class, but the interrelatedness of the whole. The wise rulers hold sway over the other classes, but the craftsmen must allow themselves to be governed. Otherwise, there would be a constant struggle between ruler and ruled. In similar fashion, a human being cannot be called disciplined if his desires are in constant conflict with his reason. Socrates sums up this state of discipline as "natural harmony," an agreement between divisions whereby the lower class allows the wiser class to rule.

This leaves the fourth virtue undiscovered. Socrates assumes that if justice is the most important of the four cardinal virtues, it must therefore lie at the root of the other three and make their existence possible. In order for the state to be wise, courageous, and disciplined, the citizens must agree to the founding principle that every man should have one job. In conclusion, justice in the ideal state results from this simple fact – each citizen assumes one role, the role for which he is best suited.

To shore up his definition of justice, Socrates proves inversely that performing a single job is the fourth virtue, which is as important as the other three virtues. Furthermore, the greatest harm that could befall the state is the loss of this individual performance of responsibilities. If people began interfering with each other's roles, the situation would result in injustice. Therefore, the opposite must be true: if everyone performs his own job, the state will maintain justice.

Socrates now extends his model from the community to the individual. First, Socrates establishes the concept of parts whereby part of a human being can be involved in one exercise, while another part does something entirely different. As an example, he describes a man who is standing still while moving his arms. Part of the man is active, while part is at rest. He contends that the mind, too, can be divided into parts. A part of the mind may wish to do something, while another part refuses. This mental conflict between desire and reason proves that the mind possesses at least two parts.

Searching for a third part, to parallel the three classes of the state, Socrates proposes that emotions form the third part. In a situation where reason debates with desires, emotions can enter in, rendering a person angry with himself for wanting to do what is not reasonable. Socrates assumes that, in a good and enlightened person, reason will always control desires and emotions.

Socrates applies his tri-fold model to the tri-level state: reason is associated with the ruling class, emotions with the auxiliaries, and desires with the tradesmen. In addition, he expects to find in each person the four cardinal virtues: wisdom, courage, discipline, and justice. Wisdom and courage are the easiest to locate, for wisdom resides with reason and courage with the emotions. Applying the arguments concerning discipline in the state, Socrates finds discipline in any person who allows reason to control his emotions and desires.

The fourth virtue, justice, also follows the paradigm of the state. Where the three classes perform their proper tasks, justice exists. So with human beings, justice will prevail if the individual allows the three parts of his mind to function properly without interfering with each other. At this point, Socrates has attained his original goal. He has defined justice. Justice to the mind is like health to the body. A just man has an orderly mind; a healthy man has an orderly body.

_____ BOOK V

At this point, Glaucon and Adeimantus consider letting Socrates rest, but they decide instead to pursue the question of justice to the end. In order to prove that justice is always preferable to injustice, Socrates develops his definition of justice. He refers to justice as an internal harmony, whether in the state or in the mind. When the natural order is upset, injustice results. Such a disturbance could cause more than one type of injustice. The first occurs when the emotions control the reason, or the auxiliaries overpower rulers; the second, when desires control reason, or tradesmen take over the state. In conclusion, Socrates proposes that there is only one type of goodness, but several kinds of evil.

Before he can describe the different kinds of injustice, Polemarchus and Adeimantus interrupt and demand more information about life in the ideal state, particularly as it applies to women and children. To accommodate their need for more information, Socrates pursues a different course, applying his paradigm to the lives of women. Although women are physically weaker than men, they possess abilities and assume lighter duties which suit their aptitudes. Women fit each classification and can thereby serve the state as rulers or auxiliaries. Their education, like that of men, must prepare them for the demands of their class.

Since all the guardians live together in communes, the notion of a family unit must be abolished. However, the state must assure that people live together decently and morally, but must allow individuals to express their sexual needs. Also, the state must provide for child care. To maintain high standards for procreation, mating (like other aspects of civilized life) must be regulated.

Under Socrates' plan, the ideal state will hold marriage festivals. Individuals will have no choice in the selection of a mate. The state will breed the best possible future citizens by pairing the best men with the best women. To prevent rebellion among the youth, the rulers must arrange the festivals so that men and women will believe they have chosen each other on their own. The offspring of these marriages must be reared by the state. To prevent conflicts of loyalty, children should not know their parents' identities. Living together in a communal nursery, they will come to accept all children as their brothers and sisters. All men will be their fathers and all women their mothers.

Glaucon and his companions express doubts about Socrates' plan for the family and demand more proof that his ideas are practical. Socrates counters that his plan will insure stability and prevent internal disorder in the state. Families, by their nature, lead to family jealousy. Without families, everyone's allegiance will rest in the state. Since all property will be owned communally, no one will quarrel over possessions. As a single extended family, the state will share everyone's pleasures and trials and will foster love and respect for all.

When further dissension erupts among his listeners, Socrates reminds all of the original purpose – not to prove that an ideal state can exist, but to establish the true nature of justice. Socrates concedes that nothing can exist in reality as perfectly as on paper. To prove his point, he examines the current state of affairs and points out how real governments differ from the ideal. The most obvious difference is in rulers. According to Socrates, until philosophers rule the world or until kings become philosophers, an ideal state is impossible. Glaucon expresses surprise at this bold statement. To quiet his doubts, Socrates provides him with a definition of the "philosopher."

The philosopher is a lover of wisdom and learning. He is curious and open-minded. Glaucon objects, noting that many curious, knowledgeable people are not philosophers, citing examples among the theatergoers and music lovers of Athens. Socrates agrees, amending his original definition to state that the philosopher is one who loves truth. This alteration requires further definition of truth and knowledge.

Socrates opens his comments on truth by establishing that beauty exists and that it is a single entity. Music and theater lovers enjoy particular examples of beauty, but they are incapable of knowing the nature of beauty itself in its pure form. The person who can see beauty has knowledge, whereas the one who sees beautiful things exhibits belief.

In order for knowledge to exist, the basis of knowledge, or beauty, must also exist. But for those who merely believe in beauty, the object of their belief does not truly exist. The objects which art lovers treasure are less real. In a separate example, Socrates discusses appearances.

From one point of view, an object may appear large; from another, it may seem small. Yet the concept of size itself is real and unchanging. In Socrates' estimation, only abstract qualities can be really known.

Summing up his argument, Socrates insists that music and theater lovers pursue a belief, but do not pursue knowledge. Philosophers, on the other hand, reach for reality itself. The philosopher, who is attuned to a lasting truth, perceives palpable representations of beauty as fleeting, temporal objects. Therefore, only the philosopher can attain knowledge.

_____ **BOOK VI**

Having established what the philosopher is, Socrates must use his definition to justify his belief that the philosopher is the best possible ruler. Whereas a good ruler must administer justice, act for the good of the community, and exhibit good character, the philosopher can best fulfill these requirements, since he is disciplined to ignore frivolous pleasures. The philosopher will not be tempted by money or possessions, because his chief desire is for higher worth. Lacking a fear of death, the philosopher will be courageous. Overall, the philosopher possesses the four cardinal virtues.

Adeimantus, frustrated with Socrates' logic, interrupts, demanding to know why philosophers seem so useless in real society. To the surprise of all, Socrates admits that this accusation is true, but that the fault lies with society, not philosophers. Because citizens lack respect for knowledge and wisdom and follow instead politicians, who are men of baser motives, philosophers have no opportunity to influence the state. Why then are some philosophers villainous? Obviously, society corrupts them. Only in a nurturing environment can gifted thinkers flourish. In a bad environment, philosophers succumb to flattery and vanity, using their intellectual skills for selfish purposes.

Still, Socrates does not despair of the situation. A philosopher may someday gain political power and convince people of the value of wisdom. Likewise, a king may develop into a philosopher. In either case, the real world will move closer toward the realization of an ideal state.

Socrates continues his consideration of the philosopher-king, noting that the sum of good traits is not likely to occur in a single individual. Moreover, the best ruler must also have a well-rounded education, including music, literature, martial arts, and intellectual training in order to pursue the highest form of knowledge. Glaucon asks for a more thorough discussion of the "highest form of knowledge," to which Socrates replies that higher knowledge includes justice and beauty and also goodness. Without goodness, an individual cannot understand why justice and beauty are valuable. An awareness of goodness, therefore, is the highest of all attainments.

The obvious topic for Socrates to discuss at this point is goodness, which he is unable to define, but can illustrate. Using the analogy of sight, Socrates describes how the eye observes objects through the intervention of light. Goodness, like light, allows human beings to observe the objects of knowledge. Therefore, as sight depends upon light, truth comes from goodness itself.

At Glaucon's insistence, Socrates gives an analogy from geometry concerning the divided line, which represents reason, understanding, belief, and conjecture. Glaucon, comprehending his meaning, quickly establishes the connection. Socrates' conclusion leads to a more complex distinction — that there are two degrees of knowledge and two degrees of belief. The highest knowledge is knowledge of goodness. The lower level of knowledge is of lesser virtues, such as justice and beauty. Likewise, the first degree of belief is in material objects, whereas the second level of belief involves the accompanying mental attitude toward shadows and images of real objects. As with the divided line, he summarizes by dividing perception into four categories: goodness, lower virtues, ordinary objects, and shadows and images of objects. The first two examples are objects of knowledge and the last two are objects of belief.

BOOK VII

In the most famous of his analogies, Socrates narrates the cave allegory, a parable which illustrates the four states of mind — that is, the two degrees of knowledge and the two degrees of belief. He asks his audience to imagine an underground cave and a long passage leading to the outside world. The inhabitants of the cave are prisoners who have been chained to the ground and have observed one wall of the cave since childhood. Behind the prisoners is a road, where people pass in the normal course of living. Beyond the road is a fire. Although the captives have never been able to turn their heads to look directly at the people on the road, the fire has thrown shadows on the wall in front of them. In their limited view of the real world, they have mistaken the shadows for true representations of real people.

If one prisoner were released and turned to face the real world, he would suffer both fear and pain from the movement of his stiffened limbs and the glare of bright lights. If he were told that the people he sees on the road are real and the shadows on the wall are not real, he would reject reality and return to his shadow pictures, which he has viewed as real all his life. If he were dragged out of the tunnel into sunlight, he would be more frightened. Blinded by the sun, his eyes would grow accustomed to bright light. He would first study the moon and stars; then he would notice the shadows made by the sun and reflections on the water. Finally he would see nature in full daylight. At this point, he would realize the difference between shadows and reality and he would understand the importance of sunlight to human sight.

He would pity the other prisoners and value his freedom for the change it has made in his perception of things. If he were returned to the cave, his eyes would have to grow accustomed to the murky light and the shadows on the wall. His fellow prisoners would contend that his departure from the cave ruined him and would call him a fool for leaving the cave.

Socrates then illuminates each part of his parable. The cave represents the realm of belief; daylight is the realm of knowledge. The sun symbolizes goodness. Each move, from the realm of belief to the realm of knowledge, is painful for the prisoner, although at each stage he acknowledges the value of his suffering. Yet, his fellow prisoners call him foolish when he rejects his former shallow beliefs for enlightenment.

This experience of moving from the cave into the light corresponds to the training of philosopher-kings for the ideal state. In order to recognize knowledge and goodness, philosophers must pass through these stages of awareness. Furthermore, they must return to the cave and apply their knowledge to their deluded fellow prisoners. By accustoming themselves to the old world of shadows, they will better understand the shadows, having witnessed how they are formed. With their newly found wisdom, they will be able to guide fellow prisoners to a clearer perception of reality.

Glaucon, absorbed in the story, resents the fact that philosophers must return to the world of belief. Socrates reminds Glaucon that the life of the ruler is not directed toward self: the purpose of the ruler is the happiness of the whole community. Certainly, philosophers would prefer a life of intellectual absorption in truth and beauty, but they must shoulder the burden of politics if they are to guide others.

Socrates points out that educating future guardians of the state requires leadership into the light, out of the world of belief to real knowledge and ultimately to goodness. To do this, society must devise an education that surpasses literature, music, and martial arts. The future rulers must study pure mathematics and the practical applications of numbers to government. Socrates lists five areas of mathematics which are necessary for a thorough education: arithmetic, plane geometry, solid geometry, astronomy, and harmonics.

After mastering mathematics, future rulers will be able to think in abstract terms. From there, they must leave mathematics and develop a grasp of reality through dialectic, the science of logical argument. Unlike geometry, dialectic examines every aspect of reality in the search for truth. By achieving perfection in definition, philosophers can know a subject thoroughly. Therefore, dialectic, the final stage in the pursuit of true knowledge, is the crowning achievement for future rulers.

Socrates recapitulates his educational goals for future rulers. First, they must be bright and moral and possess additional traits, such as honesty, courage, and a willingness to work. While they are young (up to the age of eighteen), they should be trained in literature, music, elementary mathematics, and martial arts. Next comes two years of rigorous physical training. The third stage, when the students have reached the age of twenty, requires a winnowing out of inferior candidates and enrollment in a program of ten years' training in higher mathematics for those who qualify. At the age of thirty, the least likely to succeed are removed. Those who remain will study dialectic for five years. By the time they reach thirty-five, they will have become philosophers.

At this point, future rulers must acquire practical experience in government by assuming secondary roles in military and political life. After fifteen years of climbing the political ladder, the mellowed philosophers will be ready to rule and guide the state. By this time, they will have acquired the essential knowledge of goodness and will know what is best for the community.

BOOK VIII

Glaucon reminds Socrates that earlier, in Book V, he was about to describe the different kinds of injustice. Happy to oblige so attentive a listener, Socrates names four types of unjust societies: timocracy, oligarchy or plutocracy, democracy, and tyranny or despotism, in ascending order from least unjust to most unjust. Assuming a state of internal deterioration, Socrates asks his audience to imagine timocracy (the militaristic government based on honor which existed in Sparta and Crete in his time).

What would cause an ideal state to degenerate into a timocracy? According to Socrates, disagreement within the ruling class can cause such a degeneration. For example, if a mistake at the marriage festival results in an unsuitable match within the ruling class, the offspring of that union would likely grow up without the necessary aptitude for guiding the state. If defective personalities rise to the level of rulers, the state will decline. Ambitious men, lured by the prospect of wealth and property, will compete with each other for power, neglecting wisdom and intelligence in the execution of their tasks. The virtue of courage will supplant wisdom as the highest attainment. The auxiliaries, who comprise the military class, will rule.

If the same upset occurs in an individual, the individual will reflect the imbalance of the timocratic state. The timocratic man, fond of physical exercise and hunting, will value bravery and ambition above intellectual pursuits. He will grow greedy. Reason will no longer rule his emotional side.

The next worst state of a deteriorating society is oligarchy, a government based on wealth. With political power in the hands of the rich, the poor will suffer disenfranchisement. Timocratic rulers will succumb to the lure of money and property. Wealth will supplant honor as the greatest good. As timocracy becomes oligarchy, the rulers will be chosen for material wealth alone. Tension between the haves and the have-nots will increase as class unity dissolves. The rich, basing their lives on consumption of goods, will perform no useful function in society; likewise, many of the poor will become beggars or criminals.

In the individual, degeneration from timocratic to oligarchic man could lead a great general into a state of exile or loss of property. As a result, his son, frightened and embittered, would prefer money over honor and courage, cardinal values which his father admired. Although he might work hard in order to amass wealth and reestablish his family's position, his respectability would be false, for he would lack moral conviction. His dedication would be oriented toward base desires.

The third worst state, democracy (which was the form of government under which Socrates was executed), will result from a debtor nation. As people borrow at high interest from the oligarchy, they will suffer bankruptcy. Embittered, they will revolt against their plutocratic oppressors and either kill or exile them. The resulting democracy will come into being when all people receive equal rights. The lack of discipline within a democratic state, in which everyone has equal rank, will lead to weakness in the military. Politicians, with no training in leading the public, will cater to the whims of the people. Democracy, like anarchy, lacks unity because people work for selfish motives instead of the good of the state.

The oligarchic man, as he degenerates into the democrat, will be ruled by his desire for money. His offspring, having nothing to respect, will be easily influenced and will mix with people of base instinct. These children will grow up living lives of pleasure, and, lacking order and restraint in their lives, will be unable to distinguish between good and evil.

The final stage in the corruption of the state, the degeneration of democracy into tyranny, results from the democrats' desire for freedom at all costs. No one will respect authority. Children will despise their parents and teachers. As leaders of the democracy try to please the people, they will concern themselves more with popularity than government. They will rob the rich to placate the poor, leading to dissension among the wealthy. The resulting discontent will escalate into full-scale revolt.

To end the ensuing civil war, citizens will look to any leader for relief from chaos. This popular hero will, with complete support of the masses, execute or exile his rivals. To protect himself from retaliation, he will surround himself with a coterie of guards, which will grow into a small army. As he struggles to make good his promises, he will overtax the people. Distrusting intelligent and courageous men, who will be better equipped to rule, the tyrant will choose stupid, criminal types as companions and bodyguards. When he runs out of funds to pay his army, he will oppress the citizenry, reaching the lowest state of government, tyranny.

The human counterpart is equally unpleasant. The son of the democratic man, who is unable to distinguish between good and evil, may fall into bad company. Ruled by lust, he will try in vain to satisfy his base passions. Without convictions of any sort, the despotic individual will try to manipulate everyone, including his parents, to feed his desires. With no friend in the world, the tyrant's life is the bleakest of all.

BOOK IX

Basing his argument on the above description of the tyrant, Socrates builds his case for the true state of happiness in the life of the just individual. First of all, citizens in a tyrannical state are slaves. So, too, the tyrannical man is enslaved by lust. Happiness cannot exist in slavery. The just man, by way of contrast, has no internal monster to subdue. Guided by reason and knowledge, he controls his inner desires and subdues his emotions. Therefore, he knows more happiness than the unjust man.

Stage two of Socrates' argument is more complex. He returns to his division of the soul into three parts – reason, emotion, and desire – and he reminds his audience of three character types – the man controlled by reason, the man controlled by emotion, and the third, who is controlled by desire. The first of these examples, he maintains, is the just man, the second, the timocratic man, and the third is a combination of the oligarchic, democratic, and tyrannical man. Each man would claim that he is the happiest of the three. Therefore, it is safe to assume that there are three levels of pleasure – pleasures of knowledge, pleasures of success, and pleasures of gain and satisfaction of the flesh.

The just man, who has experienced all three levels of pleasure, is the only one capable of judging which level is best. He would surely choose knowledge over the other two alternatives. Based on his more complete experience of human pleasure, one can assume that happiness experienced by the just man is the best type.

In concluding his argument, Socrates declares that the pleasures of the just man are real pleasures, as opposed to the illusory pleasures of success, gain, and bodily satisfaction. Food and drink, for example, hoodwink the body into believing that it enjoys pleasure, but in actuality, they seem pleasant only because they relieve unpleasant states, namely hunger and thirst. The pleasures of knowledge are therefore the only real enjoyments, for the objects of knowledge are real, as Socrates proved in Book V.

Abandoning serious debate and playing with squares and cubes, Socrates attempts to prove that the just man is 729 times happier than the unjust man. Returning then to his original discussion with Thrasymachus, Glaucon, and Adeimantus, Socrates concludes that the unjust man has wronged himself by starving his reason. Neither wealth, reputation, nor pleasures of the flesh can rectify the fault, since injustice leads to more injustice. The craftsmen, citizens of the third level in the ideal state and perfect examples of happiness, will lead satisfying lives because they will be guided by the wisdom of the philosopher-kings.

BOOK X

Returning to the ideas at the end of Book II and the beginning of Book III, where he objected to poetry which portrays the gods in a bad light or frightens children with horror tales of the underworld, Socrates broadens his criticism of the visual and dramatic arts. In his opening statement, he claims that artists appear to create things, but actually, he says, they create illusions. Whereas painters make copies of real objects, writers paint word-pictures of reality. Developing an example of a painting of a bridle, he proves that the artist is twice removed from the object, coming second to the harness-maker, who follows behind the harness-user in knowledge of the real bridle.

Socrates asks why art appeals to people, since artists' creations are mere illusion. Because the artist must create a deceptive perspective, the resulting distortion appeals to the worst part of our minds, that which lacks reason. Both poetry and drama, as well as painting, appeal to lower elements because the creators of each appeal to our emotions and desires through excitement. Because this stimulus is irrational, it fails to reach the upper level of the mind.

In conclusion, Socrates labels the arts as morally corruptive, even in the best of people. He maintains that the audience's expression of pity and fear in the form of tears or emotional outbursts sets a bad example, leading to lack of control in real life. Socrates appears to let emotion dominate his own reason at this point, for he regrets his condemnation of Homer, whom he admires. Yet, stoicism offers the best solution, for, by putting aside a worthless passion, a person can strengthen himself. Socrates finds a place for only two types of poems in the well-ordered state – hymns to the gods and paeans to great men.

In retrospect to his lengthy dialogue, Socrates declares that the chief rewards for the just and good life come *after* death. Glaucon is surprised that Socrates believes that the soul survives the body. Socrates therefore illustrates his belief with proof. Given that the body decays, iron rusts, and wood rots, he deduces that each is destroyed by a characteristic evil, in that wood will not rust nor iron rot. What then is the evil of the soul? As he has proved, injustice is the soul's evil, but it does not consume the soul the way sickness eats up the body. Therefore, if the soul's evil cannot destroy it, then the soul is immortal and lives forever.

By this stage of the dialogue, Socrates declares his point proven in that he has established that the just life is better than the unjust life, regardless of external rewards. To illustrate that justice receives rewards, Socrates narrates the Myth of Er, a story of the afterlife. Er, a native of Pamphylia in Asia Minor and a brave soldier who died in battle, lay on a funeral pyre ten days after his death. Suddenly he came to life and told a tale of the underworld.

He said that after death, his soul traveled to a strange place where two great abysses pierced the earth. Above them were corresponding holes in the sky. Between the chasms sat judges who judged all souls and marked them with tokens: the just went into the upper right-hand chasm to heaven; the unjust entered the lower lefthand hole that led to the underworld.

Er was forbidden to enter either of the holes. Instead, he was chosen as a messenger to mortals. After observing the activity around the chasms, he noticed that souls appeared at regular intervals – some from heaven and some from earth. Those from earth were stained and weary with their journey; those from heaven were clean and bright. As they passed by Er, they told him their experiences. The souls from heaven told of happiness and joy. They had lived just lives on earth and had been rewarded tenfold in heaven. But the souls that came out of the earth had traveled a thousand years and had paid ten times for their sins. They described worse men, who suffered even more because they had been murderers and despots. Because of their great evil, they could never expiate their crimes.

The wandering souls stayed with Er for seven days before resuming their journey. Er went with them. After traveling a few days, they

arrived at the throne of the Fates—Lachesis, Atropos, and Clotho—
who gave them new lives as mortals. Each soul could choose the life
he preferred. Some made wise choices; others were foolish. The first,
a greedy soul, unaware of the suffering he would endure, chose the
life of a tyrant. Others chose lives as animals: Orpheus wanted to be
a swan; Ajax, a lion; and Agamemnon, an eagle. When Odysseus' turn
came, he remembered the miseries of his wandering and chose the
uneventful life of an ordinary citizen.

When the choices were made, the souls drank from Lethe, the
River of Forgetfulness, so that they would lose all memory of the past
life. Er was forbidden to drink. There was a great earthquake and
the souls disappeared to be born again into new lives. Er awoke on
the funeral pyre. Socrates urges Glaucon to be guided by the myth
and to choose the right and moral path so that he might receive the
rewards of virtue. In the end, Socrates concludes, "all may be well
with us."

**For a more comprehensive, in-depth analysis of this work, con-
sult Cliffs Notes on Plato's *The Republic*.**

Ω

ARISTOTLE

- *Nichomachaen Ethics*

- *Poetics*

ARISTOTLE

LIFE AND BACKGROUND

The emergence of Aristotle (384–322 B.C.) as one of the foremost philosophical minds in the history of the world reflects the positive conjunction of several factors. First, the boy, a native of Stagira, a Greek colony in Chalcis on the Thracian Sea, who is sometimes called "the Stagirite," was the offspring of Nicomachus, a member of the medical guild of Asclepius and court physician of Amyntas II at Pella, the capital of Macedonia. Under the influence of his father's prestige and vast knowledge of anatomy, Aristotle received encouragement to study biology and to develop the investigative techniques which were his most useful contribution to science.

At the age of seventeen, Aristotle came under a second great influence when he enrolled at Plato's Academy outside Athens. Under the guidance of one of the outstanding educators of the age, Aristotle, over a twenty-year period, polished his raw talents with a refined awareness of ethics, esthetics, and philosophy. Plato nicknamed his pupil "the reader" because of his encyclopedic knowledge, which he gained from constant and broad-based reading, and almost immediately made him an instructor of rhetoric. Despite anecdotes to the contrary, Aristotle held Plato in high esteem, even during the latter portion of his life when he turned away from Platonic theory to found his own Aristotelian school of thought.

Rounding out his sphere of interests in 342 B.C. was a tutorial relationship with Alexander the Great, who was then thirteen years old. During this period, which he spent in the royal palace at Mieza near Pella, Aristotle developed his interest in constitutions and government and wrote two treatises on political science for Alexander to use as textbooks. He strove to influence the boy's life by teaching him magnanimity, a basic tenet of Aristotle's philosophy, and assigned him the reading of Homer's *Iliad*. Alexander came under the spell of Homer and chose Achilles as the model for his later heroics.

The relationship between teacher and student was reciprocal in that Alexander endowed Aristotle's library and museum in Athens and contributed to his collection of flora and fauna with rare specimens from eastern Mediterranean lands. The impact of Aristotle's teaching inspired Alexander to initiate research projects, including a study of the flooding of the Nile River and the exploration of the Euphrates and Indus Rivers. Unfortunately, Aristotle broke off all correspondence with his former pupil when Alexander, by then converted to Persian ways, had Callisthenes, Aristotle's nephew and disciple, murdered for refusing to prostrate himself in the Oriental manner.

After Plato's death in 347 B.C., Aristotle made a break from the Academy and Plato's successor, Speusippus, citing as his reason an increased emphasis on mathematics, to the detriment of his first love, biology. Accompanied by his friend Xenocrates, he journeyed to Mysia, east of Troy in Propontis, where his guardian, Proxenos, lived. At the invitation of Hermias, the crafty, rapacious Bithynian eunuch who became tyrant of Atarneus, Aristotle enjoyed the status of special guest and court philosopher. In deference to Aristotle's liberal teachings, Hermias modified his views on governance from strict tyranny to democratic representation for the citizens of Atarneus.

In 339 B.C., at the age of forty-five, Aristotle married Pythia, Hermias' niece and adopted daughter. The marriage ended when his wife died bearing their only child, a daughter also named Pythia. Aristotle married a second time, choosing Herpyllis, a native of Stagira. They had a son, Nicomachus, named in honor of Aristotle's father. According to Aristotle's will, which Diogenes Laertius preserved for posterity, the philosopher devoted much time to his family and gave liberally to all, including his servants and their families, whom he freed at the time of his death. Although Aristotle refused to accept the equality of male and female, he took a strong stand in favor of the friendship between husband and wife and condemned the practice of pederasty as a loathsome, barbaric vice.

Aristotle organized his first group of disciples in Hermias' town of Assos in Mysia on the Troad, where he was joined by his nephew Callisthenes; Theophrastus, a fellow empiricist; and two Platonic scholars, Erastas and Coriscus. Aristotle expressed warm feelings toward Hermias for fostering their intellectual colony. When Hermias was crucified by Mentor, a Persian general, in 341 B.C., Aristotle was badly shaken. He honored his father-in-law with a memorial at Delphi and composed a hymn in his memory. After three years at Assos and another two at Mytilene on the island of Lesbos with Theophrastus, where Aristotle conducted biological research, he returned to Athens to begin educating others in his theories.

In 335 B.C., Aristotle opened the Lyceum in the sacred grove of Apollo Lyceus northeast of Athens. The school, which espoused a contradictory view of learning from Plato, nurtured a stimulating rivalry with Plato's Academy. His students earned the name Peripatetics from the covered walk, or *peripatos,* which extended about the Lyceum. A dynamic lecturer, Aristotle succeeded in his role of educator, but was forced out of Athens in 323 B.C. after public opinion turned against Macedonian influence following the death of Alexander. Under the charge of impiety for writing a paean to Hermias and wishing to spare Athens "another opportunity to commit a crime against philosophy," Aristotle avoided the grisly death suffered by Socrates and returned to his native land in 323 B.C. On a plot of land owned by his late mother, he spent his last years reading and studying mythology. He died of a stomach disease in Chalcis, a city in Euboea, north of Athens.

Aristotle is thought to have written some 400 scholarly works on education, scientific observations, and thoughts at large, of which fifty survive. Despite questions of authenticity concerning nearly half of these works, the canon of Aristotle's philosophy has had great influence on succeeding generations of thinkers, including Dante and Thomas Aquinas. He viewed the natural world through the eyes of the biologist and established principles of classification for all living things. He applied these biological principles to all spheres of human knowledge, from forecasting the weather to composing odes.

His logic is decidedly individual; although he was influenced by Plato, he departed from Plato's mystical idealism and relied more heavily on deductive logic as it applies to observable phenomena. In tone, Aristotle displays the cool, objective eye of the empiricist. In personal relationships he preferred tolerance and wisdom to harsh argumentation and prejudice. The entire structure of modern scientific inquiry owes much to his untiring exploration of universal truth.

Ω

NICOMACHEAN ETHICS

Aristotle's most popular and influential work, which has been named the *Nicomachean Ethics* from an old tradition that credits his son Nicomachus with arranging and editing his father's notes, deals primarily with the good life. The volume is divided into ten books, each of which contains individual chapters covering some aspect of the main topic.

BOOK I

Chapter 1 opens with a broad statement: "Every art and every scientific inquiry, and similarly every action and purpose, may be said to aim at some good." With meticulous logic, Aristotle proceeds to the task of separating different goals into a hierarchy. He begins with politics in Chapter 2, which he claims is the most comprehensive of the practical sciences, because its aim is the creation of the best possible conditions under which citizens can enjoy life. Because politics can best serve the community by achieving the greatest good for all citizens, individual needs must naturally be subordinate to the common good.

Chapters 3 and 4 establish the philosopher's methodology. He delves into unavoidable variations in the study of politics and ethics, which arise from the inherent imprecision of behavioral science, in contrast to mathematics, which is an exact science. Therefore, the philosopher must accept imprecision as inevitable.

Aristotle comments that politics and ethics, because of their lack of absolutes, require mature assessments and are therefore not suitable fields of study for the young. Another deterrent to Aristotle's study is the lack of a commonly accepted definition of happiness, which he sets out to remedy. Selecting between the deductive approach as opposed to inductive logic, he chooses the latter, because it is empirically sound. Therefore, he begins with observable facts and moves toward conclusions that will shed light on the matter of ethics.

Aristotle separates the good life into three classes in Chapter 5: happiness based on sensual pleasure, the vulgar, bestial goal of the common man; happiness based on honor, which is the goal of cultivated men; and true happiness, which results from the contemplative or philosophical approach to life. In order to quell the side issue of money, he concludes that businessmen, in their search for wealth, overlook the fact that money, even though it can buy pleasures, is not an end in itself.

In Chapter 6, the philosopher introduces Plato's notion of universal good. Hesitant to differ with his mentor, Aristotle claims that there can be no single, universal ideal; rather, good must be defined in terms of the needs, circumstance, and point of view of the individual. He emphasizes that Plato's idealized concept of good is impractical and therefore worthless for general application.

Aristotle turns to a refinement of terms in Chapter 7 and isolates the qualities of goodness. Noting that honor, pleasure, intelligence, and virtue are not ends in themselves, he concludes that happiness lies beyond them. Because happiness is the supreme goal, it is both final and self-sufficient. By comparing humans to plants and animals, Aristotle deduces that mere existence is not happiness, but that thought and action are the aspects of human life which lead humans to a fuller expression of their existence.

In Chapter 8, he puts his premises to the test by examining the evidence. It appears that good falls into three classes: "external goods as they are called, goods of the soul, and goods of the body." Since external and physical goods are incapable of satisfying humans completely, it can be deduced that goods of the soul are the highest order. Another important consideration is the relationship of happiness to virtue, for the rewards of virtue nurture the soul. At this point, Aristotle admits that external goods, such as ancestry, looks, and children, are beneficial in that their absence robs the virtuous man of happiness. Therefore, he includes good luck in his definition of happiness.

Advancing his discussion of happiness, the philosopher (in Chapter 9) considers how people may acquire happiness. Although happiness is one of the blessings of the gods, human beings must make an effort to secure happiness by following a regimen of training and education. Politics, the best of all endeavors, should be the concern of all who live in a community, for the purpose of politics is the creation of an environment in which reason and virtue may thrive. Because "happiness demands a complete virtue and a complete life," animals and children, by nature of their limitations, are excluded from its attainment.

Opening Chapter 10 with a reference to the writings of Herodotus, Aristotle contends that no one can be labeled "happy" until he dies because the vicissitudes of life can alter the outlook of the virtuous.

A truly happy person will endure bitter sorrow and hardship, maintaining both dignity and virtue. In summary, the virtuous will perceive the overall picture and will live their days in pursuit of the complete good. Their deaths will round out the harmony of their days, which have been devoted to making the best of whatever happens.

Aristotle settles two minor questions in the next two chapters. Chapter 11, a consideration of the influence of the dead upon the living, ends with a definite answer. Because the misfortunes of friends may or may not affect our lives and because it makes a great difference whether bad luck strikes before or after death, it is obvious that the dead lack the ability to determine the happiness or unhappiness of the living. The second concern, whether happiness should be praised, seems obvious. Since human beings praise lesser goods, the divine nature of happiness requires the highest form of approval.

Aristotle concludes Book I with Chapter 12, an inquiry into the nature of virtue. Since good men must understand the functions of the soul, one essential branch of ethics is psychology. The soul consists of two spheres, one rational and the other irrational. The irrational is composed of physical functions and emotions, which include "desire, anger, fear, pride, envy, joy, love, hatred, regret, ambition, and pity." Because the purely vegetative—that is, eating, sleeping, and breathing—does not affect virtue, only the emotions require consideration in that they relate to rational faculties and cause a person to obey or disobey reason. Likewise, virtue can be separated into two classes: the intellectual, including wisdom, intelligence, and caution; and the moral, including temperance and generosity.

BOOK II

Chapter 1 introduces the question of character building, which Aristotle divides into two parts—intellectual growth through learning and morality through practice. People are born amoral and must develop moral attitudes and habits. Whereas they can see and hear at birth and do not have to learn to use either their eyes or ears, they must learn to be moral by exercising good behavior. Politicians actualize this concept by passing good laws to encourage moral conduct.

The corollary is equally important—bad habits encourage bad behavior. Therefore, there will always be a need for teachers to foster positive actions so that people will develop justice, bravery, and temperance as opposed to cruelty, cowardice, and lack of restraint.

Aristotle underscores the importance of early childhood training, which he concludes "is not a light matter, but important, or rather, all-important."

In Chapter 2, he probes the methods by which ethical conduct is assessed. Because ethics is an inexact science, the discussion of moral conduct can only approximate the truths that lie at the heart of the matter. Taking into consideration this imprecision, Aristotle observes that character can be destroyed by deficiency or excess. The virtue of courage, for example, will not develop to the fullest if a person has too much or too little fear. An absence of fear leads to foolhardiness; on the other hand, a preponderance of fear leads to cowardice. Consequently, proportion is an important consideration in the molding of character.

To measure the strength of a virtue, Aristotle proposes in Chapter 3 that the pleasure or pain that accompanies the exercise of that quality be used as an index. The object of ethics is to learn to associate pleasure with virtue and punishment with vice. The philosopher expands the nature of our choices by dividing each into three categories: virtue, which includes noble actions, expedience, and pleasure; and vice, which encompasses the base, the harmful, and the painful.

The way in which virtue grows from good behavior is the subject of Chapter 4. According to Aristotle, a person cannot be labeled virtuous because he exhibits proper conduct. In order to achieve good character, the doer must fulfill three conditions: to be aware of the virtue in his actions, to favor good behavior over bad, and to act in response to a regular pattern of moral behavior.

It is false to assume that people of good character are analogous to musicians who play an instrument. A person who behaves well cannot be labeled virtuous in the same way that a person who performs well on the harp can be called a musician. The attainment of virtue requires a right attitude by which the doer realizes the worth of the act. Knowledge of morality, therefore, is only part of the process.

Chapters 5 and 6 outline a thorough definition of virtue. Of the three divisions of the human soul—emotions or feelings, capacities, and dispositions or characteristics—virtue belongs to the third class in that it is neither emotion nor capacity. To classify it further, Aristotle maintains that because virtue is a disposition, a person of character will govern his behavior with wisdom and common sense. The mark of virtue is to experience feelings at the appropriate time, toward the proper objects or people, for the right reason, and in the proper manner.

The philosopher cites the ancient principle of the Golden Mean — that is, a Golden Mean is neither excess nor deficiency. However, he cautions that it is absurd to gauge what amount is too much or too little in every instance. Some acts, such as adultery, theft, or murder, and some emotions, notably malice, shamelessness, and envy, are always inappropriate, regardless of the degree.

The remaining three sections of Book II, Chapters 7 through 9, deal with the mean and extremes. For his discussion of human behavior, Aristotle turns to specific examples, which he charts under five headings — feeling, action, excess, mean, and deficiency. The mean, which illustrates virtues, is flanked by objectionable extremes. The extremes, by nature of their excess, are more unlike each other than either is to the mean — for example, generosity resembles both extravagance and stinginess more than extravagance and stinginess resemble each other.

Aristotle summarizes his arguments concerning proper behavior in Chapter 9. Good character is a mean between two vices and emphasizes a middle point in emotions and actions. To accentuate virtue, a person should avoid extremes, either excess or deficiency; guard against natural inclinations; choose the lesser of two evils; and avoid pleasures that encourage deviation from the mean. The model is not easy to apply because human behavior is complex, but the result of its application — that is, sensible, worthy choices — is beneficial to anyone who prizes good character.

BOOK III

In his evaluation of moral behavior, Aristotle differentiates between voluntary and involuntary acts. Since praise falls only on voluntary deeds, it is necessary to distinguish between the two classes. Involuntary acts, he contends, either are performed under compulsion or result from ignorance. For example, when an external cause precipitates an action (as when an adverse wind forces the captain of a ship off course), the doer contributes nothing. Unfortunately, not all situations are so easily classified, as is the case with coercion. In order to spare family members, a person may commit an immoral act in obedience to a tyrant's command. In this instance, the person is voluntarily breaching a personal code of conduct, but, in all fairness, the situation must be evaluated outside the abstract moral principles that apply.

Acts committed in ignorance are not voluntary, but fall either in the class of involuntary acts or non-voluntary acts, depending upon whether or not the agent feels regret for the deed. Application of these principles should not be, however, used to exonerate an evil person from all knowledge of right and wrong. Acts committed in ignorance are blameless in so far as the doer is unfamiliar with the specific situation. On the other hand, when a person understands the circumstances in which an error is made, that agent is accountable for his misdeeds.

Aristotle discusses the definition of choice in Chapters 2 and 3, closely linking choice to virtue. Voluntary acts, such as those committed by children and animals, do not involve choice. Choice pertains to means and to the deliberative process by which the doer selects among several courses of action in order to achieve an end. Such deliberation is possible only when the perpetrator possesses a fully developed human mind.

In Chapter 4, Aristotle defines "wish," which is concerned with goals. Differing with both the Platonic school and some sophists, he insists that a person of good character will see the truth in any situation. The actions of noble people should, therefore, set the criteria for judging questions of behavior. The most crucial consideration in matters of volition is that the agent accepts responsibility for the act. The fundamentals of law are based on this principle in that moral acts receive rewards while crimes are punished. Where there are extenuating circumstances involving involuntary acts, the law may exonerate the doers, except in cases where the doers willfully render themselves senseless, as in the case of drunkenness.

At this point, Aristotle challenges the proverb that claims "None would will to be wicked, none would not be blessed." The idea of responsibility for one's actions is inherent in Aristotle's philosophy. He rejects any attempt to explain away a person's choosing to do wrong and emphasizes that "we cannot refer our acts to any other source than what lies in ourselves, then the act that has its sources in us must itself be in our power and voluntary."

Chapters 7 through 12 deal with two individual virtues – courage and self-control. Aristotle asserts that "nothing is so frightful as death, for death is the end, and when a man is dead, it seems that he is beyond the reach of good or evil." Yet, he adds, ". . . it is weakness to fly from troubles; nor does the suicide face death because it is noble, but because it is a refuge from evil . . ." A virtuous person, therefore, behaves admirably in the face of normal fears and faces the grim situations that beset every human life.

In contrast to the brave, the two extremes, cowards and daredevils, behave improperly in the face of danger. Whereas cowards fear everything, even poverty and love, and daredevils rush precipitately into danger, the valiant remain calm until there is need for action. When the time demands response, the stouthearted are prepared to display an appropriate amount of courage.

In Chapter 7, the philosopher lists five lesser degrees of courage. The first, civic courage, inspires bravery for the sake of honor and fame or the avoidance of disgrace. Another form is the courage of experience, like that displayed by the mercenary. Because the professional fighter knows how to respond to real danger, he exemplifies courage, yet a loss of confidence can quickly turn this kind of courage into cowardice.

The third level of courage, that which is prompted by blind emotion, such as anger or pain, resembles animal courage. Flowing from instinctive reaction, it lacks choice and moral purpose, but can develop into true courage if these elements are added. The last two degrees of courage are fleeting and undependable. The courage of rosy optimism or sanguinity fades rapidly in the presence of adverse conditions. Similarly, the simpleton's courage fades to cowardice when faced with facts.

Aristotle concludes the section on courage in Chapter 9, where he states that the happier a person is, the more painful death will appear because the joy of living is harder to give up. Yet the effect of facing a dangerous situation is beneficial in that it raises the level of bravery to new heights. As a result of daring encounters, the stalwart are even nobler and more virtuous.

Chapters 10 through 12 complete the section on virtue with a detailed examination of self-control. Temperance, according to Aristotle, holds sway over the bestial side of human nature—the physical urges to eat, drink, and enjoy sexual relations. He excludes sight, sound, and smell, which are intellectual pleasures, because humans differ from animals in their use of these senses. In humans, these faculties can give pleasure—for example, enjoying art objects, music, and perfume – whereas animals employ them only for functional purposes.

In Chapter 11, Aristotle explains that a person who lives within the mean avoids overindulgence, in contrast to the sybarite or voluptuary, who suffers when physical urges are not satisfied. The other extreme, lack of enjoyment, is less common, but may be found among ascetics, who take pleasure in austerity and self-denial. In the philosopher's estimation, "in a moderate and right spirit [the temperate person] will want all things that are pleasant and that at the same time make for health and a sound bodily condition, and whatever other pleasures are not prejudicial to these ends, or opposed to what is noble, or costly beyond his means."

To conclude the last seven chapters, the philosopher contrasts cowardice and intemperance, noting that the former is motivated by pain and the latter by pleasure. Because pain is more destructive than pleasure and therefore should be avoided, he deduces that self-indulgence is the more reprehensible of the two behaviors. Like wayward children, indulgent people allow appetites and desires to govern their lives and disregard the place of reason in their conduct.

_____ **BOOK IV**

The eight chapters of this section continue Aristotle's discussion of particular virtues. Beginning with generosity, which relates to money and possessions, he examines the two extremes – stinginess and waste. The wise use wealth by giving or spending for right reasons, at the proper times, to the right people, and for appropriate purposes. The amount that donors give is relative, depending on their resources and the spirit in which they give. The philosopher concludes that "It is reasonable then to regard greed as the opposite of liberality; for it is a greater evil than prodigality, and men are more likely to err on the side of greed than on the side of prodigality . . ."

Chapter 2 deals with ostentation or magnificence, an extension of the concept of prodigality. Depending upon the spender's means, showy displays of wealth reflect vulgarity and bad taste for ignoble purposes. In contrast, the shabby or pinchpenny spender cuts corners and grumbles before investing funds. In contrast to both extremes, the balanced person, who is often a connoisseur of art, spends "in a cheerful and lavish spirit, because minute calculation of expense is a mark of meanness. He will consider how the work can be made most beautiful and most suitable . . ."

Similar to magnificence is magnanimity, which is defined in Chapter 3 as loftiness of outlook or greatness of soul. This quality, when compared to its extremes, vanity and pettiness, marks the high-minded person, the citizen who is devoted to honor, public office, and respectability. Magnificence implies high standards of conduct, which set an example for the entire community.

Chapter 4 contrasts ambition with aimlessness, which are the extremes of a nameless mean that resembles high-mindedness. A careful balance of generosity and other worthy attributes, this nameless virtue includes a proper attention to and appreciation for honor. It is more easily perceived when compared to its opposites, self-aggrandizement and self-effacement or false modesty, both of which present a distorted picture of individual worth.

Gentleness or affability, the subject of Chapter 5, is the mean between irascibility or malevolence and apathy. The good-natured person possesses an appropriate amount of anger, and he expresses it in the right circumstances. Both extremes, feistiness and indifference, reflect an abuse of anger, either from unjustified or exaggerated application of anger or the opposite reaction, an inability to display feelings when the situation calls for righteous indignation.

Friendliness, a worthy characteristic which affects all human relationships, contrasts strongly with its extremes, obsequiousness and crankiness. The congenial person "will behave the same to strangers and to acquaintances and to people with whom he is and is not intimate, except that in each case his conduct will be suitable . . ." Avoiding both surliness and kowtowing, the sociable, neighborly person associates well on all levels and avoids giving pain, except in situations where it is misleading or inappropriate to do otherwise.

The truthful person is one whom Aristotle calls a "sort of plain dealer; truthful both in life and in speech; he owns to having what he has; he neither exaggerates nor underrates it." Shunning both bragging and self-deprecation, the straight-shooter prefers honesty for its own sake. Even in trivial matters, the veracious person avoids deception and falsehood, for probity is the cornerstone of character.

Aristotle turns to lighter considerations in Chapter 8 in his discussion of wit and tact. In conversation, a virtuous person delights with carefully chosen, well-bred humor. The extremes of wit are numerous, including buffoonery, indecent language, mockery, and cruelty. The tasteful, decorous companion contrasts with the clown, who "is a slave of his own sense of humor; he will spare neither himself nor anybody else, if he can raise a laugh, and he will use language that no person of refinement would use . . ." Likewise, the boor, who lacks sparkle and a sense of camaraderie, is easily offended and contributes nothing to social intercourse.

The last chapter deals with shame, which Aristotle characterizes as "more an emotion than a moral state." Shame is appropriate to young people because youth is an emotional time, filled with errors in judgment. The extremes are more difficult to describe. Although shamelessness is unquestionably a vice, a person who commits an indecent or immoral act cannot be called virtuous simply by expressing remorse. A well-behaved person, on the other hand, will not commit disgraceful acts, and therefore will not need to express regret.

_____ **BOOK V**

Aristotle devotes all of Book V to the study of justice. Defining the word *just* to mean either *lawful* or *fair*, he first sets about the study of social justice and reserves universal justice for a later discussion. In Chapters 2 through 4, he describes how justice applies to the individual. There are two types of particular justice – that which applies to equal distribution of honors, public office, or material goods, and that which applies to business transactions and crime. The first type involves two people and two things and requires fairness in the apportionment of those two objects, based on a merit system which complies with the type of government of the particular state – for example, democracy, oligarchy, tyranny.

The second type of individual justice relates to corrective or remedial justice, particularly contracts. Where there is discontent with distribution, a judge must render a verdict not to punish either party but to remedy disproportionate distribution. The law treats both parties as equals as it seeks to reestablish the equilibrium which existed before the transaction. To correct the inequality, the law takes unfair gain from one party and restores it to the second party to compensate an undeserved loss.

Chapter 5 probes the concept of reciprocity, which Aristotle admits is an oversimplification of distributive justice. Since both parties in a disagreement may not desire a simple exchange of goods to rectify the situation, money, which is more stable than goods, is a necessary medium by which right can be restored. Once a money value is placed on the inequality, "it is the effort of the judge to restore equality by the penalty he inflicts, since the penalty is so much sub- tracted from the aggressor's profit." Aristotle concludes that the just individual, choosing to uphold fair distribution in the community, observes proper proportion and supports the law of reciprocity.

Chapter 6 examines political justice, by which citizens live in a community and share its goods and services. Because justice is a desir- able state for civilized communities, law is necessary to prevent people from acting unjustly in their dealings with fellow citizens. Conse- quently, rule by one person predisposes a state to tyranny. In a just state, the function of a ruler is to preserve law and justice so that law itself is the actual ruler of the state.

The philosopher notes that domestic justice, which exists between parent and child or master and slave, is a relative form of justice which contrasts with the absolute justice which exists between ruler and subject. He differentiates further by claiming that marital justice is the only true form of domestic justice, but that it differs from both political and social justice.

In Chapter 7, Aristotle describes two forms of political justice, natural and conventional. The first type refers to laws which are valid in every society. The second covers those laws which reflect common consent, such as local ordinances governing ransom of a prisoner of war or religious strictures affecting the sacrifice of animals. Like stan- dardization of weights and measures, conventional law may vary from state to state, depending upon convenience. In contrast, natural law is absolute and cannot change. Yet local modification of natural law sometimes makes it difficult to differentiate between conventional justice and absolute justice.

Voluntary acts, which Aristotle discusses in Chapter 8, involve volition and knowledge of consequence. To differentiate thoroughly in matters of culpability, he divides wrongful acts into four categories, arranged in ascending order of injustice. First are accidents, the acts which people commit in ignorance and without malice. These situa- tions do not require punishment. The second level occurs through negligence. In these cases, the perpetrators are held responsible but are not criminally liable.

The last two categories concern more serious acts of injustice. The third level, unpremeditated wrong, occurs when a person commits a crime without deliberation—that is, out of anger. The perpetrator is judged as an offender, but is not labeled wicked or unjust. The fourth class of injustice, the deliberate infliction of harm on an innocent party, is the most serious wrong and should be condemned more severely than the three preceding types.

Aristotle notes in Chapter 9 that verdicts sometimes reflect injustice. For example, a judge may make a decision in ignorance of some detail and may render a verdict based on law, but in violation of universal justice. The judge is not responsible for the injustice in this situation. A far different circumstance is a judgment which is influenced by favoritism, revenge, or bribery. In this case, the judge commits a mixture of voluntary and involuntary injustice because his motive is greed or vengeance rather than injustice.

Chapter 10 elucidates the difference between equity and justice, which Aristotle claims are closely related. Although both principles reflect good, equity is the higher good in that it is the principle that corrects flawed justice. Since many cases do not fit law in the generalized or abstract sense, the failure of law to rectify the situation requires an application of equity to restore universal justice.

The last chapter attempts to answer the question "Can people be unjust toward themselves?" Aristotle notes that in its true sense, law applies only to social relationships between individuals. Crimes such as suicide or self-mutilation, lacking a second party, must therefore be construed as crimes against society since conflict between the rational and irrational parts of the soul does not constitute injustice in its true sense.

BOOK VI

His examination of moral virtues completed, Aristotle turns to intellectual virtues, which govern human choices between right and wrong and enable human beings to conform to proper standards of conduct. The soul is divided into two parts, one rational and one irrational. The function of the rational hemisphere is twofold: first, it enables the individual to understand invariables—for example, scientific phenomena; and second, it assists in deliberations involving contingencies or variables.

In Chapter 2, Aristotle notes that three elements of the soul control action and the awareness of truth: the senses, reason, and desire. He disdains to discuss sense perceptions, the bestial side of human nature, and moves directly to the last two elements. Making worthy choices depends upon the working of both reason and desire. Desire, which determines the results of an action, depends upon reason to provide the means to the goal.

To arrive at truth, the soul utilizes five faculties, as described in Chapters 3 through 7, all of which are infallible. First, there is pure science, followed by art or applied knowledge. Third in line is practicality or prudence. The last two modes are intuition or intelligence, and theoretical wisdom. Although conviction and opinion impinge upon human choice, they do not appear on the list because they can result in faulty logic.

Pure science, the first in importance, concerns eternal facts, such as the laws of physical science. Art enables the individual to create, both in the esthetic and the utilitarian sense. Practical wisdom encourages the individual to choose what is beneficial, such as health, and dominates such disciplines as political science, economics, housekeeping, and exercise. The fourth level, intuition or intelligence, is the home of induction, by which the individual examines experience and draws conclusions about universal truth. The last level, which Aristotle calls the most noble kind of wisdom, is theory. Proper use of theoretical wisdom allows the individual to combine the other types of knowledge and to contemplate the highest truths.

In Chapter 8, the philosopher explains how political wisdom evolves from practicality. The goal of practical wisdom is self-improvement, whereas the goal of political wisdom is the good of the state. Usually the two are synonymous, but there are important differences, particularly where the needs of the individual are not met by the community. Political wisdom is divided into legislative and administrative branches, and the latter branch divides again into judicial and decision-making faculties.

Chapters 9 through 12 concern themselves with other aspects of practical wisdom. According to Aristotle, practicality enables the individual to determine whether the means justify the goal. Understanding impinges upon practical wisdom by passing judgment upon the opinions of others. Good sense, an innate ability, allows the person to sympathize with and forgive the injustices of others. In combination with theoretical wisdom, which concerns the individual's relationship with reality, practicality contemplates the means by which people make themselves happy.

Although practical wisdom enables the individual to make right choices, it cannot exist apart from virtue. On this point, Aristotle differs with Socrates, who maintained that virtue was another word for wisdom. In Aristotle's view, it is virtue that assists the practical sense in choosing the mean and avoiding the extremes.

_____ **BOOK VII**

Aristotle begins Chapter 1 of Book VII with "three moral states to be avoided: namely, vice, lack of self-control and brutishness," which he contrasts to three opposites: self-control, virtue, and heroic virtue or saintliness. Because the extremes of the two lists, brutishness and saintliness, are rare, he deems them unworthy of lengthy discussion. Likewise, vice and virtue, the subjects of past chapters, require little comment. Aristotle therefore concentrates on self-control and its opposite, incontinence, two behaviors which he associates with knowledge of appetites and the will to resist temptation.

After a lengthy definition of each behavior in Chapter 2, the philosopher confronts the question "Do undisciplined people know they are doing wrong?" In answer to his query, Aristotle notes that knowledge can be forgotten or overlooked when an individual is removed from reality—that is, asleep, drunk, or insane. Also, the senses can mislead the individual when emotions overpower logic. Finally, in some rare instances, logic itself can lead the doer to commit wrongful acts.

Undisciplined behavior can be tempted by three categories of pleasures: worthwhile rewards, such as honor or wealth; things which should be avoided; and neutral pleasures, such as food and sexual gratification. The undisciplined personalities realize that their behavior is wrong, but choose to ignore good sense. In Chapter 5, Aristotle notes that perverted pleasures, such as cannibalism or depravity, are not enjoyable for normal people. Therefore, he removes from consideration habits that are obviously brutish or morbid.

In Chapters 6 through 10, Aristotle refines his concept of waywardness. He ranks incontinence in anger as less sinful than incontinence in desire of pleasure. To justify his conclusion, he reasons that anger is amenable to reason, common to human nature, overt, and accompanied by bad feelings. Consequently, lack of self-discipline in matters of desire is worse, particularly because it tends to brutalize its victims.

To clarify the picture of incontinence, Aristotle compares the wayward to the self-indulgent and the stubborn. In contrast to a self-indulgent person, who feels no moral twinge when making choices, the incontinent person is wracked with remorse and is therefore amenable to reform. In contrast to stubborn people, the person who lacks self-control "is not immovable. It is easy to persuade him on occasion, but the obstinate person resists the persuasion of reason."

The final section of Book VII, Chapters 11–14, investigates the nature of pleasure. Aristotle concludes that the "chief good will be pleasure of some kind, although most pleasures may in an absolute sense be bad." Real pleasure, the result of pleasant, stimulating activity, results in good health. When the human spirit is in proper balance, activities seem neutral, neither pleasurable nor painful. If human beings were perfect, the best activity would be immobility, a state that requires no change.

BOOK VIII

Aristotle turns his attention to friendship at this point, a virtue which he deems "indispensable to life." In Chapter 2, he declares that for friendship to exist, both parties must display affection, mutual goodwill, and understanding. In praise of friendship, he concludes, "We praise those who love their friends, and to have many friends is thought to be a fine thing. Some people hold that to be a friend is the same thing as to be a good man."

Chapter 3 describes three varieties of friendship, each being based upon the objects of affection. First, friendship based on utility requires both parties to be helpful to each other. However, because needs may change, this form of friendship may be short-term. The second bond, based on mutual pleasure, is purely social in nature and lasts only so long as the two parties prove mutually entertaining. Aristotle notes that the second type is common among young people.

The third type, which Aristotle terms "perfect friendship," results from people who "wish good for their friends because of their friends' sake . . ." This relationship, because it is based on virtue, is stable and lasting, "for it unites in itself all the right conditions of friendship." Also, the philosopher comments, "Friendships of this kind are likely to be rare; for such people are few." The establishment of so strong a bond as *agape* (the Greek term that approximates the Christian concept of *love*,) or perfect friendship, requires both time and intimacy.

Chapter 7 deals with friendships which are unequal in intensity, such as the relationship between father and son, older and younger people, husband and wife, or ruler and subject. Because each party performs a distinct role, the two cannot be adequately compared as either givers or receivers of friendship. The feelings generated in unequal friendships are proportional, depending upon an equilibrium between the superiority of one and the affection of the other.

Aristotle emphasizes an important point in Chapter 8: that "only where there is love in adequate measure, are friends permanent and their friendship lasting." In parent/child relationships, love does not flow equally in both directions. Because a mother may delight in giving love to a child, it is not necessary for the child to reciprocate love with the same intensity. In this instance, the parent feels satisfaction from seeing the child prosper, even if the child fails to reward the parent for offering love without demanding anything in return. It is only after "they have lived some time and gained intelligence or sense" that children perceive the good that their parents have freely given.

Chapters 9 through 11 extend the notion of unequal friendship to relationships under particular types of governments. In a tyranny, friendship and justice cannot exist between ruler and subject because the tyrant uses the subject as a tool, plow animal, or slave. "One cannot therefore be friends with a slave as slave," the philosopher deduces, "although one can with a slave as a man." He concludes that democracy, the type of government which maintains the greatest equilibrium among people, promotes true friendship and justice "because when people are equals they have most in common."

An analysis of three types of governments – monarchy, aristocracy, and timocracy – results in the following axioms: wicked monarchs tend to turn into tyrants, corrupt aristocracies lead to oligarchies, or rule by the rich, and timocracy (political power based on ownership of land) degenerates into democracy, the type of government which Aristotle judges least bad. In any perverted government, the importance of friendship decreases as justice decreases. Because democracy bases its rule on equality, friendship and justice are more likely to be realized in a democratic state.

Chapter 14 returns to the subject of friendship within the family. Parents, Aristotle contends, "love their children as parts of themselves, and children love their parents as the authors of their being." Because the parent considers the child a product, "as a tooth or a hair or anything to its owner," parents naturally love their children more than the children return that love. This fact is particularly true of mothers, who love their children more than do fathers.

Chapters 13 and 14 deal with mutual obligations between friends. Aristotle notes that in equal relationships, there exists a moral obligation for each party to provide equal love and support to what he himself has received. In unequal relationships, friction occurs most frequently in relationships based on utility, specifically when one party feels that he gives more than the other party. However, in friendships based on virtue, "friends are eager to do good to each other as a sign of their goodness and friendship."

BOOK IX

Aristotle continues his commentary on the nature of friendship in Book IX, beginning with two chapters on obligation. Because human values cannot be reduced to dollars and cents, unequal friendships can be evaluated only in terms of the participants' assessment of their worth to each other. In matters of divided loyalty, such as choosing between a father's advice and that of the doctor, the philosopher recommends that "it is our duty to render to each class the respect that is natural and appropriate to them." In other situations requiring comparison of loyalty – that is, whether a friend should "vote for the best soldier as general, rather than for his father," Aristotle contends that "we ought to repay services which have been done to us rather than confer favors on our comrades."

In Chapter 3, the philosopher describes circumstances which necessitate the breakup of a relationship. When a person's character changes, it is easy to end a friendship based on utility or pleasure, for when function or entertainment no longer exist, there is no reason to prolong camaraderie. For friendships based on character, the decision is harder to justify. Aristotle urges the wronged friend first to attempt to reform the other party. If the relationship still falters, the parties owe each other a certain respect. Provided the rift does not arise from some unspeakable crime, friends are still obliged to show some deference out of respect for the old relationship.

As Aristotle notes in Chapter 4, the basis of friendship is self-love. Because people desire the best for themselves and their community and because they promote virtue as an aspect of the good life, they choose friends who wish them the same. In contrast, "Wicked people seek companions to spend their days with and try to escape from themselves; for when they are alone, they recall too many disagreeable things . . ." He concludes that, to avoid so miserable a state, people must strive for good so they can approve of themselves and be friends with other good people.

In Chapter 5, Aristotle differentiates between good will and friendship. Good will is the "germ of friendship" in that it lacks "intensity of feeling or desire, which are the signs of love." Good will is a superficial, spontaneous kind of familiarity based on sympathy or support, as when athletic competitors feel good will toward each other. Generally, good will depends on some form of admiration and "arises when we regard someone as noble or brave . . ."

Likewise, concord and good deeds resemble friendship. Chapter 6 notes that unanimity or concord comes about when individuals share a common interest or support an important goal or policy. Good citizens, for example, share a harmony when they strive for a mutual end. Good deeds, on the other hand, result in an unequal relationship in that the benefactor wishes the greater good for the beneficiary. The receiver, who takes the role of debtor to creditor, feels a passive, less noble feeling more akin to profit than to love. Aristotle concludes, "as it takes no trouble to receive a kindness but a good deal to confer it, benefactors are more affectionate than the recipients of their generosity."

In Chapter 8, Aristotle returns to the concept of self-love, pondering "whether a man should love himself or someone else most." He separates the types of self-love, declaring that lust and greed are its negative extremes which originate in the irrational parts of the soul. The good man, in contrast to a self-seeker, "chooses nobility above everything," thereby garnering praise for worthy conduct.

Chapters 9 through 12 conclude the discussion on friendship. The philosopher concludes that "if it is more a friend's part to do good than to receive it, if acts of generosity are part of a good man and of virtue, and if it is nobler to do good to friends than to strangers, the good man will need someone to do good to." In answer to the question of how many friends a person would have, he replies that one should be content with a few good friends, since friendship requires intimacy and effort. Aristotle is convinced that friends are necessary, in good times and in bad, so that a virtuous person will have someone to share the good things in life. In conclusion, friends "seem to become better by acting together and correcting each other's faults."

BOOK X

The last book probes the relationship between pleasure and human nature. In Chapter 2, Aristotle states that "Pleasures are desirable, but not if they are immoral in their origin; just as wealth is pleasant, but not as a reward for turning traitor to one's country, or as health is, but not as the cost of eating any food, however disagreeable." Because life is so closely allied with pleasure, the two cannot be separated, for every activity depends on an end goal that pleases the doer.

In Chapters 5 through 7, Aristotle concludes that neither pleasure nor relaxation is the greatest good, but that they are an essential part of happiness. Rather, happiness comes from virtuous activities that result from intellectual pursuits. The ideal or divine state is perfect reason. To achieve the greatest enjoyment of living, an individual should enjoy what is best for him, for a "man's reason more than all else is himself."

Chapter 8 summarizes the advantages of the contemplative life, which seeks to understand universal truths. This godlike existence achieves purity and stability that is akin to blessedness. A lesser form of happiness, based on morality and practical wisdom, focuses on physical harmony, which is not so exalted a state, but which prepares the individual for the highest form of happiness. Also, when the greatest good lies out of reach, the lesser good is a suitable consolation. Aristotle declares that the person who is "most beloved of the gods" is the philosopher, who is able to achieve these heights of virtue.

Chapter 9 concludes the *Nicomachean Ethics* with a statement on action. "It is not enough to know what virtue is," Aristotle warns, "we must strive to have and use it, and try whatever ways we may to become good." Even though people possess innate dispositions toward good, they must receive moral education, which the state should provide. Learning should be individualized so as to strengthen the individual, but teachers should adhere to universal principles. The state, grounded in sound ethics, has an obligation to develop the character of its citizens.

[Note: Although he mentions wives and mothers, Aristotle clearly intends his broad statements about mankind to mean males. In keeping with the traditions of his day, he did not consider women of such importance that they should be included in a major philosophical treatise. Consequently, his use of the pronoun *he* is deliberately exclusive of women. ED.]

For a more comprehensive, in-depth analysis of this work, consult Cliffs Notes on *Aristotle's Ethics*.

Ω

POETICS

Aristotle's vast knowledge includes an appreciation of literature. He wrote two critical works on the esoteric arts—*Rhetoric* and the *Poetics*. The *Poetics* is divided into two sections, tragedy and comedy; unfortunately, only the first half (tragedy) remains. As a guide and influence for later schools of criticism, notably the neo-classicists, the work is a touchstone of thought on the unities of time, place, and action as well as the Greek concepts of *catharsis, peripeteia, hamartia,* and *hubris.*

Aristotle begins his discussion with a statement of the psychological basis of poetry: "Epic poetry and tragedy, comedy also and dithyrambic poetry . . . are all in their general conception modes of imitation." They differ in medium, object, and style of imitation and employ varying combinations of rhythm, melody, and meter to achieve the same end. In depicting people in action, writers may either represent them as "better than in real life, or as worse, or as they are." Comedy chooses to show people as worse, whereas tragedy aims to show them as better than in actual life. The writer may choose to narrate the action, as Homer does, or to present the characters acting out their own story, which is the dramatic method employed by Sophocles and Aristophanes.

Human beings differ from animals in that they have an instinct for imitation, harmony, and rhythm. Poetry, therefore, arose from this inborn gift and developed in two directions – comedy, which satirizes or lampoons the meaner actions of life, and tragedy, which takes drama to a more worthy level. Tragedy has since grown and changed: first, Aeschylus introduced a second actor and reduced the importance of the chorus; then Sophocles added a third actor as well as introduced painted scenery. Comedy, too, has altered since its inception, but it has "no history because it was not at first treated seriously . . ."

Tragedy is like epic poetry in that it deals with noble characters, but differs in its meter, dramatic form, and length. The length of the action in tragedy is confined to a "single circuit of the sun," whereas poetry has no limit of time. In essence, "tragedy, then, is an imitation of an action that is serious, complete, and of a certain magnitude; in language embellished with every kind of artistic ornament, the several kinds being found in separate parts of the play; in the form of dramatic action, not of narrative; through pity and fear effecting the proper purification of these emotions." To achieve its ends, tragedy must have six parts – plot, character, diction, thought, spectacle, and song.

According to Aristotle, plot is the most crucial aspect of tragedy, with character holding second place. Spectacle bears the least connection with the art of poetry and is "more a matter for the property man." To achieve its magnitude, the plot, like a living organism, must possess a "beginning, a middle, and an end," but it does not require a single person as the hero to achieve wholeness. Also, it must be long enough to move the sequence of events "from calamity to good fortune, or from good fortune to calamity." The true test of unity of action is the structural union of the plot. Therefore, anything that can be removed without disturbing unity is not necessary to the whole.

In comparison to history, which deals with the past, the subject of poetry is what *may* happen. Therefore, poetry is a "more philosophical and higher thing than history: for poetry tends to express the universal, history the particular . . ." The worst form of poetic plot is episodic, which is often written as a means of pleasing the audience and winning a competition. The best tragedy utilizes surprise, as a result of either reversal or recognition or both, to arouse pity or fear; also, its complexity arises from cause and effect, which propose to the audience a plausible rationale for the action.

There are other requirements for perfect tragedy, notably that the tragic hero must be a noble individual who brings about his own downfall "by some error or frailty." From the workings of the plot rather than from spectacle, the audience must "thrill with horror and melt to pity at what takes place." The characters themselves must be good. Aristotle notes that "even a woman may be good, and also a slave, though the one is liable to be an inferior being, and the other quite worthless." In addition, the characters' actions must be appropriate, realistic, and consistent. The plot itself must be probable without intervention of the supernatural into the realm of tragedy.

When a tragedy is properly constructed, there will be two distinct parts—"complication and unraveling, or *denouement.*" Poetry, too, should contain a similar rise and fall of action. For example, Homer, whom Aristotle calls "admirable in all respects," limits himself to a single episode of the Trojan War and builds his story on the character flaws of a single individual, Achilles. Moreover, he appreciates the narrator's role and imposes himself in the action as little as possible.

The philosopher concludes his comments on poetry with a question: which is the higher form, epic poetry or tragedy? Rejecting the notion that the epic is more worthy because it appeals to a more intellectual audience, Aristotle chooses tragedy for its emphasis upon a unified action and for the fact that it maintains its appeal whether it is read or acted. Because tragedy functions better as an art by producing an appropriate amount of pleasure, it "is the higher art, as attaining its end more perfectly."

Ω

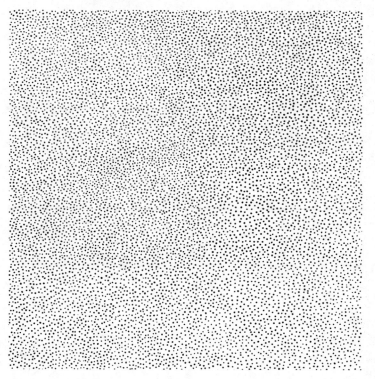

- **Glossary**
- **Timeline**
- **Selected Bibliography**
- **Index**

GLOSSARY

Aeschylus (es′ kə ləs)

Aesop (ē′ səp)

Alcaeus (al sē′ əs)

Anacreon (ə nak′ rē ən)

Archilochus (ar kil′ ə kəs)

Aristophanes (ar′ ə stof′ ə nēs)

Aristotle (ar′ ə stot′ l)

Demosthenes (di mos′ thə nēz)

Euripides (yoo rip′ i dēz)

Herodotus (hə rod′ ə təs)

Hesiod (hē′ sē əd)

Homer (hō′ mər)

Lysias (lis′ ē əs)

Menander (mə nan′ dər)

Pindar (pin′ dər)

Plato (plā′ tō)

Sappho (saf′ ō)

Simonides (sī mon′ i dēz)

Socrates (sok′ rə tēz)

Sophocles (sof′ ə klēz)

Theognis (thē og′ nis)

Thespis (thes′ pē əs)

Thucydides (thoo sid′ i dēz)

Xenophon (zen′ ə fən)

PRONUNCIATION KEY: ə = *a* in **a**bove, b**a**nana; **a**ct, d**ā**y, d**â**re, f**ä**ther; b**e**t, b**ē**at; t**i**p, **ī**ce; **o**x, b**ō**ne, **oi**l, b**oŏ**k, b**oo**t; **u**p, r**ü**le.

────────── TIMELINE ──────────

Homer (9th–8th centuries B.C.)
Hesiod (8th–7th centuries B.C.)
Alcaeus (7th century B.C.)
Sappho (7th century B.C.)
Archilochus (7th century B.C.)
Aesop (620?–560? B.C.)
Thales (*ca.* 600 B.C.)
Anacreon (*fl.* 550 B.C.)
Simonides (*ca.* 556–468 B.C.)
Theognis (*fl.* 544 B.C.)
Thespis (*ca.* 535 B.C.)
Aeschylus (524?–456 B.C.)
    The Persians (March, 472 B.C.)
    The Seven Against Thebes (468 or 467 B.C.)
    The Suppliants (463 B.C.)
    Oresteia (458 B.C.)
    Prometheus Bound (?)
Pindar (518?–438? B.C.)
Hecataeus (*ca.* 500 B.C.)
Sophocles (*ca.* 496–406 B.C.)
    Ajax (451? B.C.)
    Antigone (441 B.C.)
    Oedipus Rex (409 B.C.)
    Electra (409 B.C.)
    The Trachiniae (409 B.C.)
    Philoctetes (409 B.C.)
    Oedipus at Colonus (produced 401 B.C.)
Euripides (*ca.* 485–406 B.C.)
    The Cyclops (438 B.C.)
    Alcestis (438 B.C.)
    Medea (431 B.C.)
    The Heracleidae (*ca.* 428 B.C.)
    Hippolytus (428 B.C.)
    Andromache (*ca.* 427 B.C.)

   Hecuba (425 B.C.)
   The Suppliants (421 B.C.)
   Heracles (ca. 422 B.C.)
   Ion (ca. 417 B.C.)
   The Trojan Women (415 B.C.)
   Electra (413 B.C.)
   Iphigenia in Tauris (ca. 413 B.C.)
   Helena (412 B.C.)
   The Phoenician Women (ca. 410 B.C.)
   Orestes (408 B.C.)
   The Bacchae (405 B.C.)
   Iphigenia in Aulis (405 B.C.)
Socrates (469?-399 B.C.)
Lysias (458-380 B.C.)
Aristophanes (ca. 450-ca. 385 B.C.)
   The Acharnians (425 B.C.)
   The Knights (424 B.C.)
   The Clouds (423 B.C.)
   The Wasps (422 B.C.)
   Peace (421 B.C.)
   The Birds (414 B.C.)
   Lysistrata (411 B.C.)
   Thesmophoriazusae (411 B.C.)
   The Frogs (405 B.C.)
   The Ecclesiazusae (393 or 391 B.C.)
   Plutus (388 B.C.)
Plato (428-347 B.C.)
Herodotus (fl. 450-428 B.C.)
Thucydides (fl. 430-399 B.C.)
Xenophon (430-354 B.C.)
Demosthenes (384-322 B.C.)
Aristotle (384-322 B.C.)
Menander (343?-291? B.C.)
   Dyskolos (316 B.C.)

[NOTE: *ca.*, *circa*, about, approximately; *fl.*, *floruit*, flourished]

Ω

SELECTED BIBLIOGRAPHY

AESCHYLUS

BODKIN, MAUD. *The Quest for Salvation in an Ancient and a Modern Play.* New York: Oxford, 1941.

CONACHER, D. J. *Aeschylus'* Prometheus Bound. *A Literary Commentary.* Toronto: University of Toronto Press, 1980.

GAGARIN, MICHAEL. *Aeschylean Drama.* Berkeley: University of California Press, 1976.

LEBECK, ANNE. *The* Oresteia. *A Study in Language and Structure.* Washington Center for Hellenic Studies, 1971.

OATES, WHITNEY JENNINGS. *The Complete Greek Drama.* New York: Random House, 1938.

SANSONE, DAVID. *Aeschylean Metaphors for Intellectual Activity.* Wiesbaden: Steiner, 1975.

SHEPPARD, JOHN TRESSIDER. *Aeschylus, the Prophet of Greek Freedom. An Essay on the Oresteian Trilogy.* London: T. Murby, 1943.

SMYTH, HERBERT WEIR. *Aeschylean Tragedy.* Berkeley: University of California Press, 1924.

THALMAN, WILLIAM G. *Dramatic Art in Aeschylus'* Seven Against Thebes. New Haven: Yale University Press, 1978.

VELLACOTT, PHILIP. *The Logic of Tragedy. Morals and Integrity in Aeschylus'* Oresteia. Durham, North Carolina: Duke University Press, 1984.

WHALLON, WILLIAM. *Problem and Spectacle. Studies in the* Oresteia. Heidelberg: C. Winter, 1980.

AESOP

AESOP. *Aesop's Fables.* New York: Avenel Books, 1975.

CULLUM, ALBERT. *Aesop in the Afternoon.* New York: Citation Press, 1972.

ROCHE, PAUL. *New Tales from Aesop.* Tales retold by Paul Roche. Notre Dame, Indiana: University of Notre Dame Press, 1982.

ARISTOPHANES

BIEBER, MARGARETE. *The History of the Greek and Roman Theatre.* Princeton: Princeton University Press, 1961.

BONNER, ROBERT J. and GERTRUDE SMITH. *Justice From Homer to Aristotle.* Chicago: Chicago University Press, 1938.

CORNFORD, F. M. *The Origins of Attic Comedy.* Garden City, New York: Anchor, 1961.

DEARDEN, C. W. *The Stage of Aristophanes.* London: Athlone Press, 1976.

DOVER, K. J. *Aristophanic Comedy.* Berkeley: University of California Press, 1972.

EHRENBERG, VICTOR. *The People of Aristophanes. A Sociology of Old Attic Comedy.* Oxford: Blackwell, 1943.

ELDER, OLSON. *The Theory of Comedy.* Bloomington: Indiana University Press, 1968.

HENDERSON, JEFFREY. *The Maculate Muse.* New Haven: Yale University Press, 1975.

LORD, LOUIS E. *Aristophanes: His Plays and His Influence.* New York: Cooper Square, 1963.

MCLEISH, KENNETH. *The Theatre of Aristophanes.* New York: Taplinger, 1980.

NORWOOD, GILBERT. *Greek Comedy.* New York: Hill and Wang, 1963.

OLSON, ELDER. *The Theory of Comedy.* Bloomington: Indiana University Press, 1968.

PICKARD-CAMBRIDGE, SIR ARTHUR. *The Dramatic Festivals at Athens.* London: Oxford University Press, 1968.

SPATZ, LOIS. *Aristophanes.* Boston: Twayne, 1978.

STRAUSS, LEO. *Socrates and Aristophanes.* Chicago: University of Chicago Press, 1980.

SUTTON, DANA FERRIN. *Self and Society in Aristophanes.* Washington: University Press of America, 1980.

USSHER, ROBERT GLENN. *Aristophanes.* Oxford: Clarendon, 1979.

WEBSTER, THOMAS BERTRAM LONSDALE. *Monuments Illustrating Old and Middle Comedy.* London: Institute of Classical Studies, 1978.

_____. *Monuments Illustrating New Comedy.* London: Institute of Classical Studies, 1969.

ARISTOTLE

ACKRILL, J. L. *Aristotle the Philosopher.* New York: Oxford University Press, 1981.

ADLER, MORTIMER J. *Aristotle For Everybody.* New York: Macmillan, 1978.

ALLAN, DONALD J. *The Philosophy of Aristotle.* London: Oxford University Press, 1970.

BARNES, JONATHAN. *Aristotle*. New York: Oxford University Press, 1982.

BRENTANO, FRANZ C. *Aristotle and His World View*. Berkeley: University of California Press, 1978.

BURKE, KENNETH. *Dramatism and Development*. Barre, Massachusetts: Clarke University Press, 1972.

BUTCHER, SAMUEL H. *Aristotle's Theory of Poetry and Fine Art*. New York: Dover, 1951.

CLARK, STEPHEN R. L. *Aristotle's Man: Speculations Upon Aristotelian Anthropology*. Oxford: Clarendon Press, 1975.

EDEL, ABRAHAM. *Aristotle and His Philosophy: A Contemporary Reading*. Chapel Hill: University of North Carolina Press, 1982.

EVANS, JOHN DAVID G. *Aristotle's Concept of Dialectic*. New York: Cambridge University Press, 1977.

FERGUSON, JOHN. *Aristotle*. New York: Twayne, 1972.

FORTENBAUGH, WILLIAM W. *Aristotle on Emotion: A Contribution to Philosophical Psychology, Rhetoric, Poetics, Politics, and Ethics*. London: Duckworth, 1975.

GRENE, MARJORIE. *A Portrait of Aristotle*. Chicago: University of Chicago Press, 1963.

HARTMAN, EDWIN. *Substance, Body, and Soul: Aristotelian Investigations*. Princeton: Princeton University Press, 1977.

MORAVCSIK, J. M. E., comp. *Aristotle: A Collection of Critical Essays*. Garden City, New York: Anchor, 1967.

VEATCH, HENRY BABCOCK. *Rational Man: A Modern Interpretation of Aristotelian Ethics*. Bloomington, Indiana: Indiana University Press, 1962.

DEMOSTHENES

ADAMS, CHARLES DARWIN. *Demosthenes and His Influence.* New York: Cooper Square, 1963.

GOLDSTEIN, JONATHAN A. *The Letters of Demosthenes.* New York: Columbia University Press, 1968.

JAEGER, WERNER WILHELM. *Demosthenes. The Origin and Growth of His Policy.* Berkeley: University of California Press, 1938.

JONES, ARNOLD HUGH MARTIN. *The Athens of Demosthenes.* Cambridge, England: Cambridge University Press, 1952.

MCCABE, DONALD F. *The Prose-Rhythm of Demosthenes.* New York: Arno, 1981.

PEARSON, LIONEL IGNACIUS. *The Art of Demosthenes.* Meisenheim am Glan: A. Hain, 1976.

EURIPIDES

BATES, WILLIAM NICKERSON. *Euripides, a Student of Human Nature.* New York: Russell & Russell, 1969.

BLAIKLOCK, E. M. *The Male Characters of Euripides. A Study in Realism.* Wellington: New Zealand University Press, 1952.

CONACHER, D. J. *Euripidean Drama. Myth, Theme, and Structure.* Toronto: University of Toronto Press, 1967.

GREENWOOD, LEONARD HUGH GRAHAM. *Aspects of Euripidean Tragedy.* Cambridge, England: Cambridge University Press, 1953.

GRUBE, GEORGE M. A. *The Drama of Euripides.* London: Methuen, 1973.

KLOTSCHE, ERNEST H. *The Supernatural in the Tragedies of Euripides.* Chicago: Ares, 1980.

NORWOOD, GILBERT. *Essays on Euripidean Drama*. Berkeley: University of California Press, 1954.

SALE, WILLIAM. *Existentialism and Euripides*. Berwick, Austria: Aureal, 1977.

SCODEL, RUTH. *The Trojan Trilogy of Euripides*. Gottingen: Vandenhoeck & Ruprecht, 1980.

SEGAL, ERICH W., comp. *Euripides: A Collection of Critical Essays*. Englewood Cliffs, New Jersey: Prentice-Hall, 1968.

VELLACOTT, PHILIP. *Ironic Drama: A Study of Euripides' Method and Meaning*. New York: Cambridge University Press, 1975.

WEBSTER, THOMAS B. L. *The Tragedies of Euripides*. London: Methuen, 1967.

WHITMAN, CEDRIC H. *Euripides and the Full Circle of Myth*. Cambridge, Massachusetts: Harvard University Press, 1974.

ZUNTZ, GUNTHER. *The Political Plays of Euripides*. Manchester: Manchester University Press, 1963.

GREEK HISTORY

AUSTIN, NORMAN, comp. *The Greek Historians: Herodotus, Thucydides, Polybius, Plutarch*. New York: Van Nostrand-Reinhold, 1969.

BENGTSON, HERMANN. *Introduction to Ancient History*. Berkeley: University of California Press, 1970.

_____. *The Greeks and the Persians from the Sixth to the Fourth Centuries*. London: Weidenfeld and Nicholson, 1969.

BICKERMAN, ELIAS JOSEPH. *Chronology of the Ancient World*. Ithaca, New York: Cornell University Press, 1980.

CALDWELL, WALLACE EVERETT. *The Ancient World*. New York: Farrar & Rinehart, 1937.

GLOVER, TERROT REAVELEY. *The Ancient World: A Beginning*. Baltimore: Penguin, 1966.

GODOLPHIN, FRANCIS RICHARD BORROUM, ed. *The Greek Historians*. New York: Random House, 1942.

HAMMOND, NICHOLAS G. L., ed. *Atlas of the Greek and Roman World in Antiquity*. Park Ridge, New Jersey: Noyes Press, 1981.

MELLERSH, H. E. L. *Chronology of the Ancient World, 10,000 B.C. to A.D. 799*. London: Barrie & Jenkins, 1976.

PARETI, LUIGI. *The Ancient World, 1200 B.C. to A.D. 500*. trans. Guy E. F. Chilver. New York: Harper & Row, 1965.

SINNIGEN, WILLIAM GURNEE. *Ancient History from Prehistoric Times to the Death of Justinian*. New York: Macmillan, 1981.

STARR, CHESTER. *A History of the Ancient World*. New York: Oxford University Press, 1983.

HERODOTUS

BENARDETE, SETH. *Herodotean Inquiries*. The Hague: Martinus Nijhoff, 1970.

DREWS, ROBERT. *The Greek Accounts of Eastern History*. Washington: Center for Hellenic Studies, 1973.

EVANS, J. A. S. *Herodotus*. Boston: Twayne, 1982.

FORNARA, CHARLES W. *Herodotus: An Interpretive Essay*. Oxford: Clarendon Press, 1971.

HART, JOHN. *Herodotus and Greek History*. New York: St. Martin's, 1982.

HUNTER, VIRGINIA J. *Past and Process in Herodotus and Thucydides*. Princeton: Princeton University Press, 1982.

SELECTED BIBLIOGRAPHY

SELECTED BIBLIOGRAPHY

IMMERWAHR, HENRY R. *Form and Thought in Herodotus.* Cleveland: Western Reserve University Press, 1966.

LINFORTH, IVAN MORTIMER. *Greek Gods and Foreign Gods in Herodotus.* New York: Johnson Reprints, 1971.

LISTER, RICHARD PERCIVAL. *The Travels of Herodotus.* New York: Gordon & Cremonesi, 1979.

SHEPHERD, WILLIAM, trans. *The Persian War.* New York: Cambridge University Press, 1982.

WATERS, KENNETH H. *Herodotus on Tyrants and Despots.* Wiesbaden: F. Steiner, 1971.

WELLS, JOSEPH. *Studies in Herodotus.* Freeport, New York: Books for Libraries Press, 1970.

WILSON, JOHN ALBERT. *Herodotus in Egypt.* Leiden: Nederlands Instituut voor het Nebije Oosten, 1970.

WOOD, HENRY. *The Histories of Herodotus. An Analysis of the Formal Structure.* The Hague: Mouton, 1972.

HESIOD

BURN, ANDREW ROBERT. *The World of Hesiod. A Study of the Greek Middle Ages c. 900-700 B.C.* New York: B. Blom, 1966.

EVELYN-WHITE, HUGH G., trans. *Hesiod, the Homeric Hymns, and Homerica.* Cambridge, Massachusetts: Harvard University Press, 1954.

FRAZER, R. M. *The Poems of Hesiod.* Norman, Oklahoma: University of Oklahoma Press, 1983.

JANKO, RICHARD. *Homer, Hesiod, and the Hymns. Diachronic Development in Epic Diction.* New York: Cambridge University Press, 1981.

LAWTON, WILLIAM CRANSTON. *The Successors of Homer*. New York: Cooper Square, 1969.

PEABODY, BERKLEY. *The Winged Word: A Study in the Technique of Ancient Greek Oral Composition as seen principally through Hesiod's* Works and Days. Albany: State University of New York Press, 1975.

PUCCI, PIETRO. *Hesiod and the Language of Poetry*. Baltimore: The Johns Hopkins University Press, 1977.

ROWE, C. J. *Essential Hesiod*. Bristol, England: Bristol Classical Press, 1978.

HOMER

ATCHITY, KENNETH JOHN. *Homer's* Iliad: *The Shield of Memory*, with a foreword by John Gardner. Carbondale: Southern Illinois University Press, 1978.

AUSTIN, NORMAN. *Archery at the Dark of the Moon. Poetic Problems in Homer's* Odyssey. Berkeley: University of California Press, 1975.

CAMPS, WILLIAM ANTHONY. *An Introduction to Homer*. New York: Oxford University Press, 1980.

CLARKE, HOWARD W. *Homer's Readers: A Historical Introduction to the* Iliad *and the* Odyssey. Newark, New Jersey: University of Delaware Press, 1981.

FENIK, BERNARD. *Studies in the* Odyssey. Wiesbaden: F. Steiner, 1974.

FERRUCCI, FRANCO. *The Poetics of Disguise. The Autobiography of the Work in Homer, Dante, and Shakespeare*. trans. Ann Dunnigan. Ithaca, New York: Cornell University Press, 1980.

FINLEY, JOHN HUSTON. *Homer's* Odyssey. Cambridge, Massachusetts: Harvard University Press, 1978.

JACKSON, W. T. H. *The Hero and the King: An Epic Theme.* Columbia University Press, 1982.

KESSELS, A. H. M. *Studies on the Dream in Greek Literature.* Utrecht: HES, 1978.

LUCE, JOHN VICTOR. *Homer and the Heroic Age.* London: Thames and Hudson, 1975.

MURRAY, GILBERT. *The Rise of the Greek Epic.* New York: Galaxy Books, 1962 (paperback).

POST, LEVI ARNOLD. *From Homer to Menander. Forces in Greek Poetic Fiction.* Berkeley: University of California Press, 1951.

SINCLAIR, T. A. *A History of Classical Greek Literature from Homer to Aristotle.* New York: Collier Books, 1962 (paperback).

SOWA, CORA ANGIER. *Traditional Themes and the Homeric Hymns.* Chicago: Bolchazy-Carducci, 1984.

STEINER, GEORGE, ed. *Homer: A Collection of Critical Essays.* Englewood Cliffs, New Jersey: Prentice-Hall, 1962.

STEWART, DOUGLAS J. *The Disguised Guest: Rank, Role, and Identity in the* Odyssey. Lewisburg, Pennsylvania: Bucknell University Press, 1976.

TAYLOR, CHARLES HENRY. *Essays on the* Odyssey. Bloomington: Indiana University Press, 1963.

TSAGARAKIS, ODYSSEUS. *Form and Content in Homer.* Wiesbaden: F. Steiner, 1982.

VIVANTE, PAOLO. *The Epithets in Homer. A Study in Poetic Values.* New Haven: Yale University Press, 1982.

_____. *The Homeric Imagination. A Study of Homer's Poetic Perception of Reality.* Bloomington: Indiana University Press, 1970.

WADE-GERY, H. T. *The Poet of the* Iliad. Cambridge: Cambridge University Press, 1952.

WILLOCK, MALCOLM W. *A Companion to the* Iliad, *Based on the Translation by Richmond Lattimore.* Chicago: University of Chicago Press, 1976.

LYSIAS

DOVER, KENNETH JAMES. *Lysias and the Corpus Lysiacum.* Berkeley: University of California Press, 1968.

SNELL, F. J., ed. *Epitaphios.* New York: Arno, 1979.

MENANDER

BAIN, D. M. *Menander.* Oak Park, Illinois: Bolchazy-Carducci, 1985.

GOLDBERG, SANDER M. *The Making of Menander's Comedy.* Berkeley, California: University of California Press, 1980.

GOMME, A. W., and F. H. SANDBACH. *Menander: A Commentary.* New York: Oxford University Press, 1973.

TURNER, E. G. *The Lost Beginning of Menander.* Wolfeboro, New Hampshire: Longwood Publishing Group, 1978.

WEBSTER, T. B. *The Birth of Modern Comedy of Manners.* Folcraft, Pennsylvania: Folcraft, 1959.

PINDAR

BURTON, REGINALD W. B. *Pindar's Pythian Odes. Essays in Interpretation.* Oxford: Oxford University Press, 1962.

CAREY, CHRISTOPHER. *A Commentary on Five Odes of Pindar.* New York: Arno, 1981.

CROTTY, KEVIN. *Song and Action. The Victory Odes of Pindar*. Baltimore, Maryland: The Johns Hopkins University Press, 1982.

GERBER, DOUGLAS E. *Pindar's* Olympian One. *A Commentary*. Toronto: University of Toronto Press, 1982.

HAMILTON, RICHARD. *Epinikion. General Form in the Odes of Pindar*. The Hague: Mouton, 1974.

KIRKWOOD, GORDON MACDONALD, ed. *Selections from Pindar*. Chico, California: Scholars Press, 1982.

PLATO

CLEGG, JERRY S. *The Structure of Plato's Philosophy*. Lewisburg, Pennsylvania: Bucknell University Press, 1977.

ERICKSON, KEITH. *Plato. True and Sophistic Rhetoric*. Amsterdam: Rodopi, 1979.

GRUBE, GEORGE MAXIMILIAN A. *Plato's Thought*. Indianapolis: Hackett, 1980.

GULLEY, NORMAN. *Plato's Theory of Knowledge*. London: Methuen, 1962.

HARE, RICHARD MERVYN. *Plato*. New York: Oxford University Press, 1982.

JORDAN, NEHEMIAH. *The Wisdom of Plato. An Attempt at an Outline*. Lanham, Maryland: University Press of America, 1981.

KEULS, EVA. *Plato and Greek Painting*. Leiden: Brill, 1978.

LODGE, RUPERT CLENDON. *The Philosophy of Plato*. London: Routledge & Paul, 1956.

_____. *Plato's Theory of Art*. London: Routledge & Paul, 1953.

_____. *Plato's Theory of Education*. New York: Harcourt, Brace, 1947.

_____. *Plato's Theory of Ethics*. London: Routledge & Paul, 1928.

MACKENZIE, MARY MARGARET. *Plato on Punishment*. Berkeley: University of California Press, 1981.

MOLINE, JON. *Plato's Theory of Understanding*. Madison: University of Wisconsin Press, 1981.

MORROW, GLENN RAYMOND. *Plato's Law of Slavery in its Relation to Greek Law*. New York: Arno, 1975.

MURDOCH, IRIS. *The Fire & the Sun*. Oxford: Clarendon Press, 1977.

RIST, JOHN M. *Eros and Psyche*. Toronto: University of Toronto Press, 1964.

ROBINSON, RICHARD. *Essays in Greek Philosophy*. Oxford: Clarendon Press, 1969.

ROBINSON, T. M. *Plato's Psychology*. Toronto: University of Toronto Press, 1970.

ROSS, WILLIAM DAVID. *Plato's Theory of Ideas*. Westport, Connecticut: Greenwood Press, 1976.

SKEMP, JOSEPH BRIGHT. *Plato*. Oxford: Clarendon Press, 1976.

VERSENYI, LASZLO. *Holiness and Justice. An Interpretation of Plato's* Euthyphro. Washington, D.C.: University Press of America, 1982.

WEST, THOMAS G. *Plato's* Apology of Socrates. *An Interpretation*. Ithaca, New York: Cornell University Press, 1979.

WHITE, F. C. *Plato's Theory of Particulars*. New York: Arno, 1981.

WOOZLEY, ANTHONY DOUGLAS. *Law and Obedience: The Arguments of Plato's* Crito. Chapel Hill: University of North Carolina Press, 1979.

SAPPHO and the LESBOS POETS

ALDINGTON, RICHARD. *Medallions in Clay*. New York: Knopf, 1921.

BARNSTONE, WILLIS, trans. *Greek Lyric Poetry*. New York: Bantam, 1962.

BOWRA, C. M. *Problems in Greek Poetry*. Oxford: Clarendon Press, 1953.

EDMONDS, JOHN MAXWELL, ed. and trans. *Lyra Graeca: Being the Remains of All the Greek Lyric Poets from Eumelus to Timotheus Excepting Pindar*. 3 vols. The Loeb Classical Library. Rev. ed. Cambridge, Massachusetts: Harvard University Press, 1952.

GOW, A. S. F. and DENYS LIONEL PAGE, eds. *The Greek Anthology: Hellenistic Epigrams*. 2 vols. Cambridge: Cambridge University Press, 1965.

LOBEL, EDGAR and DENYS PAGE, eds. *Poetarum Lesbiorum Fragmenta*. Oxford: Clarendon Press, 1955.

MACKAIL, JOHN WILLIAM. *Lectures on Greek Poetry*. London: Longmans, Green & Company, 1926.

PAGE, DENYS LIONEL. *Sappho and Alcaeus. An Introduction to the Study of Ancient Lesbian Poetry*. Oxford: Clarendon Press, 1955.

PATON, W. R., trans. *The Greek Anthology*. 5 vols. The Loeb Classical Library. Cambridge, Massachusetts: Harvard University Press, 1916–1918.

PRENTICE, WILLIAM K. "Sappho." *Classical Philology*, XIII (October, 1918), 347–360.

ROBINSON, DAVID M. *Sappho and Her Influence*. New York: Cooper Square, 1963.

SAPPHO. *Lyrics in the Original Greek with Translation*. trans. Willis Barnstone. New York: New York University Press, 1965.

_____. *The Poems and Translations.* ed. and trans. C. R. Haines. London: George Routledge & Sons, 1926.

SMYTH, HERBERT WEIR. *Greek Melic Poets.* New York: Biblo and Tannen, 1963.

WHARTON, HENRY THORNTON. *Memoir, Text, Selected Readings, and a Literal Translation.* 2nd edition. Chicago: A. C. McClurg, 1887.

SOCRATES

ALLEN, REGINALD E. *Socrates and Legal Obligation.* Minneapolis: University of Minnesota Press, 1980.

BECKMAN, JAMES. *The Religious Dimension of Socrates' Thought.* Waterloo, Ontario: Wilfrid Laurier University Press, 1979.

BEDELL, GARY. *Philosophizing with Socrates. An Introduction to the Study of Philosophy.* Lanham, Maryland: University Press of America, 1980.

BLUM, ALAN F. *Socrates. The Original and Its Images.* London: Routledge & K. Paul, 1978.

CLAUS, DAVID B. *Toward the Soul.* New Haven: Yale University Press, 1981.

DRAKE, HENRY L. *The People's Plato.* New York: Philosophical Library, 1958.

GULLEY, NORMAN. *The Philosophy of Socrates.* New York: St. Martin's, 1968.

KRAUT, RICHARD. *Socrates and the State.* Princeton: Princeton University Press, 1984.

SAUVAGE, MICHELINE. *Socrates and the Human Conscience.* trans. Patrick Hepburne-Scott. New York: Harper, 1961.

STRAUSS, LEO. *Socrates and Aristophanes.* Chicago: University of Chicago Press, 1980.

VLASTOS, GREGORY, comp. *The Philosophy of Socrates. A Collection of Critical Essays.* Garden City, New York: Anchor, 1971.

WOOD, ELLEN MEIKSIUS. *Class Ideology and Ancient Political Theory: Socrates, Plato, and Aristotle in Social Context.* New York: Oxford University Press, 1978.

SOPHOCLES

BURTON, REGINALD W. B. *The Chorus in Sophocles' Tragedies.* New York: Oxford University Press, 1980.

BUXTON, R. G. A. *Sophocles.* Oxford: Clarendon Press, 1984.

EARP, FRANK RUSSELL. *The Style of Sophocles.* New York: Russell & Russell, 1972.

ELSE, GERALD FRANK. *The Madness of Antigone.* Heidelberg: Winter, 1976.

KIRKWOOD, GORDON MACDONALD. *A Study of Sophoclean Drama.* Ithaca, New York: Cornell University Press, 1958.

LINFORTH, IVAN MORTIMER. *Religion and Drama in* Oedpius at Colonus. New York: Johnson Reprint, 1971.

MOORHOUSE, ALFRED C. *The Syntax of Sophocles.* Leiden: Brill, 1982.

O'BRIEN, MICHAEL JOHN, comp. *Twentieth Century Interpretations of* Oedipus Rex: *A Collection of Critical Essays.* Englewood Cliffs, New Jersey: Prentice-Hall, 1968.

SEALE, DAVID. *Vision and Stagecraft in Sophocles.* Chicago: University of Chicago Press, 1982.

SEGAL, CHARLES. *Tragedy and Civilization. An Interpretation of Sophocles.* Cambridge, Massachusetts: Harvard University Press, 1981.

WINNINGTON-INGRAM, REGINALD P. *Sophocles. An Interpretation.* New York: Cambridge University Press, 1980.

WOODARD, THOMAS MARION. *Sophocles: A Collection of Critical Essays.* Englewood Cliffs, New Jersey: Prentice-Hall, 1966.

THUCYDIDES

COCHRANE, CHARLES NORRIS. *Thucydides and the Science of History.* New York: Russell & Russell, 1965.

COGAN, MARC. *The Human Thing. The Speeches and Principles of Thucydides' History.* Chicago: University of Chicago Press, 1981.

CONNOR, WALTER ROBERT. *Thucydides.* Princeton: Princeton University Press, 1984.

EDMUNDS, LOWELL. *Chance and Intelligence.* Cambridge, Massachusetts: Harvard University Press, 1975.

GOMME, ARNOLD WYCOMPE. *Essays in Greek History and Literature.* Freeport, New York: Books for Libraries Press, 1967.

HUNTER, VIRGINIA. *Thucydides, the Artful Reporter.* Toronto: Hakkert, 1973.

WESTLAKE, HENRY DICKINSON. *Individuals in Thucydides.* London: Cambridge University Press, 1968.

WOODHEAD, ARTHUR GEOFFREY. *Thucydides on the Nature of Power.* Cambridge, Massachusetts: Harvard University Press, 1970.

XENOPHON

ANDERSON, J. K. *Xenophon.* Wolfeboro, New Hampshire: Longwood Publishing Group, 1974.

HIGGINS, W. E. *Xenophon the Athenian: The Problem of the Individual and the Society of the Polis*. Albany, New York: State University of New York Press, 1977.

HIRSCH, STEVEN W. *The Friendship of the Barbarians: Xenophon and the Persians*. Hanover, New Hampshire: University Press of New England, 1985.

JAMESON, MICHAEL. *The Greek Historians: Literature and History*. Saratoga, California: Anma Libri, 1985.

MOORE, JOHN M. *Aristotle and Xenophon on Democracy and Oligarchy*. Berkeley, California: University of California Press, 1975.

SCHMELING, GARETH L. *Xenophon of Ephesus*. Boston: G. K. Hall, 1980.

Ω

INDEX

Ω